INTERNATIONAL
PROPAGANDA
AND
COMMUNICATIONS

INTERNATIONAL PROPAGANDA AND COMMUNICATIONS

General Editor:

DR. CHRISTOPHER H. STERLING
Temple University

Editorial Advisory Board:

DR. MORRIS JANOWITZ
University of Chicago
DR. JOHN M. KITTROSS
Temple University
DR. BRUCE LANNES SMITH
Michigan State University

HOW WE
ADVERTISED AMERICA

By

GEORGE CREEL

ARNO PRESS
A New York Times Company
New York • 1972

Reprint Edition 1972 by Arno Press Inc.

Reprinted from a copy in The Newark Public
Library

International Propaganda and Communications
ISBN for complete set: 0-405-04740-1
See last pages of this volume for titles.

Manufactured in the United States of America

Library of Congress Cataloging in Publication Data

Creel, George, 1876-1953.
    How we advertised America.

    (International propaganda and communications)
    1. United States. Committee on Public Information.
2. European War, 1914-1918--Public opinion.
I. Title. II. Series.
D632.C7 1972   940.4'886'73   72-4664
ISBN 0-405-04745-2

HOW WE ADVERTISED
AMERICA

GEORGE CREEL, CHAIRMAN

NEWTON D. BAKER,
SECRETARY OF WAR

JOSEPHUS DANIELS,
SECRETARY OF THE NAVY

ROBERT L. LANSING,
SECRETARY OF STATE

HOW WE
ADVERTISED AMERICA

The First Telling of the Amazing Story
of the Committee on Public Information
that Carried the Gospel of Americanism to Every Corner of the Globe

By

GEORGE CREEL

Author of
"IRELAND'S FIGHT FOR FREEDOM"

HARPER & BROTHERS PUBLISHERS
NEW YORK AND LONDON

CONTENTS

		PAGE
DEDICATORY	. . . .	ix
FOREWORD	. . . .	xi

PART I—THE DOMESTIC SECTION

CHAP.

I.	THE "SECOND LINES"	3
II.	THE "CENSORSHIP" BUGBEAR	16
III.	THE "FOURTH OF JULY FAKE"	28
IV.	THE COMMITTEE'S "AIRCRAFT LIES"	45
V.	RELATIONS WITH CONGRESS	51
VI.	THE DIVISION OF NEWS	70
VII.	THE FOUR MINUTE MEN	84
VIII.	THE FIGHT FOR THE MIND OF MANKIND	99
IX.	THE BATTLE OF THE FILMS	117
X.	THE "BATTLE OF THE FENCES"	133
XI.	THE WAR EXPOSITIONS	142
XII.	THE SPEAKING DIVISION	148
XIII.	THE ADVERTISING DIVISION	156
XIV.	THE "AMERICANIZERS"	166
XV.	WORK AMONG THE FOREIGN-BORN	184
XVI.	A WONDERFUL FOURTH OF JULY	200
XVII.	THE "OFFICIAL BULLETIN"	208
XVIII.	DIVISION OF WOMEN'S WAR-WORK	212
XIX.	OTHER DIVISIONS	222
XX.	SHOWING AMERICA TO THE FOREIGN PRESS	227

PART II—THE FOREIGN SECTION

I.	THE FIGHT IN FOREIGN COUNTRIES	237
II.	AMERICA'S WORLD NEWS SERVICE	250
III.	THE FOREIGN MAIL SERVICE	261

CONTENTS

CHAP.   PAGE

IV.   FIGHTING WITH FILMS 273

V.   BREAKING THROUGH THE ENEMY CENSORSHIP 283

VI.   FRANCE, ENGLAND, AND ITALY 290

VII.   THE WORK IN MEXICO 303

VIII. THE WORK IN SWITZERLAND 317

IX.   THE WORK IN HOLLAND 327

X.   THE WORK IN SPAIN 336

XI.   THE WORK IN SCANDINAVIA 348

XII.   THE WORK IN THE ORIENT 358

XIII   THE WORK IN SOUTH AMERICA 365

XIV.   THE RUSSIAN CAMPAIGN 374

PART III—DEMOBILIZATION

I.   AFTER THE ARMISTICE 401

II.   "AMERICANIZING" MITTEL EUROPA 417

III.   CONFUSION AND NEGLECT 427

APPENDIX

I.   THE AMERICAN NEWSPAPER PUBLISHERS' ASSOCIATION   437

II.   "SAVAGERY" VS. SANITY 443

       PUBLICATIONS OF THE COMMITTEE ON PUBLIC INFORMA-
           TION IN THE UNITED STATES 455

       INDEX 461

ILLUSTRATIONS

GEORGE CREEL, CHAIRMAN; NEWTON D. BAKER, SECRETARY OF WAR; JOSEPHUS DANIELS, SECRETARY OF THE NAVY; ROBERT L. LANSING, SECRETARY OF STATE *Frontispiece*

MARLEN E. PEW, HARVEY J. O'HIGGINS, LEIGH REILLY, MAURICE F. LYONS . . . . *Facing p.* 70

CLAYTON D. LEE, WILLIAM H. INGERSOLL, WILLIAM McCORMICK BLAIR, E. T. GUNDLACH . . . . . " 84

J. J. PETTIJOHN, GUY STANTON FORD, ARTHUR BESTOR, SAMUEL G. HARDING . . . . " 100

F. DeSALES CASEY, CHARLES S. HART, CHARLES DANA GIBSON, L. E. RUBEL . . . . " 118

CHICAGO WAR EXPOSITION . . . . " 134

W. C. D'ARCY, HERBERT S. HOUSTON, L. B. JONES, W. H. JOHNS, THOMAS CUSACK, JESSE H. NEALE, O. C. HARN " 156

ALEXANDER KONTA, JOSEPHINE ROCHE, JULIUS KOETTGEN, ROBERT E. LEE, EDWIN BJORKMAN, DR. ANTONIO STELLA . . . . " 184

F. W. McREYNOLDS, L. AMES BROWN, CLARA SEARS TAYLOR, E. S. ROCHESTER . . . . " 208

CARL BYOIR, WILL IRWIN, HARRY N. RICKEY, EDGAR G. SISSON . . . . " 238

PAUL KENNADAY, ERNEST POOLE, W. S. ROGERS, PERRY ARNOLD . . . . " 250

LLEWELLYN THOMAS, JULES BRULATOUR, GUY CROSWELL SMITH, E. L. STARR, LT. JOHN TUERK, WILBUR H. HART . . . . " 274

JAMES F. KERNEY, ROBERT H. MURRAY, CHARLES E. MERRIAM, HENRY SUYDAM, PAUL PERRY . . . . . " 290

ERIC PALMER, GEORGE RIIS, H. H. SEVIER, VIRA B. WHITEHOUSE, FRANK J. MARION . . . . " 304

MALCOLM W. DAVIS, GRAHAM R. TAYLOR, ARTHUR BULLARD, READ LEWIS . . . . " 374

DEDICATORY

THE Committee on Public Information was wiped out of existence on June 30, 1919, by action of Congress. The work of the Committee had been discontinued months before, and only an orderly liquidation was in progress. It was this liquidation that Congress desired to interrupt and confuse. No one was left with power to rent a building, employ a clerk, transfer a bank balance, or to collect a dollar. This condition of chaos endured for weeks—for it was not until August 21st that the President found power to turn the records of the Committee over to the Council of National Defense—and it is only to-day that a final accounting to the people is able to be made.

At the time of the Committee's annihilation a complete report of its activities was on the presses in the Government Printing Office. This was included in the general slaughter, for not only was it the purpose of Congress to prevent any final audit, but also to keep the Committee from making a statement of achievement for the information of the public.

It was to defeat this purpose that this book has been written. It is not a compilation of incident and opinion, but a *record* and a *chronicle*. I have followed through the work of the organization from beginning to end, division by division, both as a matter of duty and as a partial discharge of my debt of gratitude to the men and women who worked with me.

DEDICATORY

It is to them and to Woodrow Wilson—great and inspired leader in the fight for the moral verdict of mankind —that this volume is dedicated.

THE AUTHOR.

NEW YORK, *May 1, 1920.*

A very special word of thanks is due to Mr. Maurice Lyons, secretary of the Committee from first to last, and to Mr. Harvey J. O'Higgins, associate chairman.

FOREWORD [1]

In view of the fact that the works which Mr. Creel has performed are supposed to have been performed under the guidance of, or, at least, in association with, the Committee on Public Information, consisting of the Secretary of State, the Secretary of the Navy, and the Secretary of War, I am afraid that if I were to indulge in extravagant eulogy of the wise and helpful things Mr. Creel has done it might be assumed that I was seeking to reserve for the remainder of the Committee some share of the praise. I feel sure, however, that if the Secretary of State were present he would assent, as the Secretary of the Navy, being present, I know does assent, to a statement of the attitude of the remaining members of that Committee toward Mr. Creel; the feeling is that while our names have been used as members of the Committee on Public Information, its labors have been the labors of Mr. Creel, and, for myself, at least, I can say that the helpfulness has been from him to me rather than in the reverse direction.

I remember a statement of Sir William Hamilton that there is nothing great in the world but man, and nothing great in man but mind. It is obviously too soon to begin to appraise either what this war means to mankind or what forces have correlated in the winning of the war, and yet our minds have been, I think, rather more occupied in observing the correlation of physical forces than

[1] Being the informal address of Mr. Newton D. Baker, Secretary of War, at a dinner given to Mr. Creel in Washington, November 29, 1918.

they have in observing the correlation of mental forces; and I have a feeling, a very strong feeling, that future historians, when they are farther removed from the events of to-day, will lay stress upon the latter, not neglecting, but at least less emphasizing, the former. When you are near the trenches the biggest thing in the world is the man in the trenches, and he is a very big thing in the world while the war is on. Our minds are fascinated by the presence of Americans in France. We see stretching over France the products of our mills and our factories; we see the boys we have taken from field and workshop and factory and office and school manufactured overnight into an altogether unsuspected stature of heroism and capacity for sacrifice in the field. We see the trained and veteran armies of the countries which have long maintained a great military policy caught up with by our own recruits, hastily trained; we see the ocean, filled with new and difficult perils, carrying larger numbers of American soldiers than have ever been transported in the history of mankind. Perhaps the greatest foreign army that ever crossed a sea in the history of the world prior to the present war was the Persian army of a million men, which bridged and crossed the Hellespont, and here the American army has sent two millions of men across the Atlantic. We see workshops and factories in America transferred from civilian occupations and learning new and difficult arts, accustoming their tools to the manufacture of war supplies, and we see American labor learning new skills, new mechanical inventions brought into quantity production among us.

So we think of the physical things accomplished because we are close to them and because they are visible to the senses. Our minds naturally dwell chiefly upon the physical things that have been done. There are many people in this room who have been in Europe since we entered this war, and nobody could possibly go to France, enter a port, and travel from any port of France to the front-line trenches without recognizing the energy and efficiency of his own nation; the strength and skill of his own fellow-countrymen; the inventive genius of America; the large capacity for industrial output of America stamped all over France.

These things form our imagination; it is our disposition to think of the war as a great conflict of physical forces in which the best mechanic won, and in which the nation that was strongest in material things, which had the largest accumulation of wealth and the greatest power of concentrating its industrial factors, was the victorious nation. Yet, as I said at the outset, I suspect the future historian will find under all these physical manifestations their mental cause, and will find that the thing which ultimately brought about the victory of the Allied forces on the western front was not wholly the strength of the arm of the soldier, not wholly the number of guns of the Allied nations; but it was rather the mental forces that were at work nerving those arms, and producing those guns, and producing in the civil populations and military populations alike of those countries that unconquerable determination that this war should have but one end, a righteous end.

The whole business of mobilizing the mind of the world so far as American participation in the war was concerned was in a sense the work of the Committee on Public Information. We had an alternative to face when we went into this war. The instant reaction of habit and tradition was to establish strict censorship, to allow to ooze out just such information as a few select persons might deem to be helpful, and to suppress all of the things which these persons deemed hurtful. This would have been the traditional thing to do. I think it was Mr. Creel's idea, and it was certainly a great contribution to the mobilization of the mental forces of America, to have, in lieu of a Committee on Censorship, a Committee on Public Information for the production and dissemination as widely as possible of the truth about America's participation in the war. Undoubtedly for the country to adopt the censorship plan would have been to say, "Now, we must all sit still and breathe cautiously lest we rock the boat." It was an inspiration to say, instead: "Now, this boat is just so many feet long, it is so many feet wide, it weighs just so much, and the sea is just so deep. If, after having all of these facts before you, you think rocking the boat will help the cause, *rock*." That is what the Committee on Public Information did, and it required a stroke of genius —perhaps not a stroke of genius, but something better than genius—to see that it required faith in democracy, it required faith in the fact; for it is a fact that our democratic institutions over here would enable us to deal with information safely; that, as Mr. Creel believed, if we received the facts we could be trusted.

Now the men who said that, and started out to give the American people all the facts there were, to see that the story was fully told, to dig it up out of hidden places and put it before the people, performed a very distinct service in the war, and, if I may say so, it seems to me a very great service to the future of our development, and in the application of the fruits of the victory which democracy has just won in the world. But it did not stop there. Of course, as the head of the War Department I am committed irrevocably, and no matter what my private opinions may be, to a belief on the much mooted question as to whether the pen is mightier than the sword. I am obliged to believe that the sword is mightier than the pen. But this war wasn't to be won by the sword alone. It was to be won by the pen as well as by the sword, and I am not speaking now of a purely military victory, because the

victory is simply a point in time. The Germans signed the
armistice and began to go pell-mell toward the Rhine;
they turned over a certain number of ships and railroad-
cars and big guns, etc., and if that were to end the war, the
end of it would be no end whatever. The question which
still remains as a part of winning the war is gathering up
the results of that war and extracting the real fruits. Of
course, we should all be happy over the military victory,
but the things in the victory that will make for our happiness and for the happiness of our children twenty years
from now, and our grandchildren forty years from now,
are the real winnings of the war; these are the things that
will count most both for our enduring happiness and the
profit of our children and grandchildren, the things that
will make most for the truth and the freedom and liberty
of mankind always; and these are the things that are to
be won out of this war, not by our way of fighting, but by
what we fought for, and what other people believe we
fought for.

So, it was of the greatest importance that America in
this war should be represented not merely as a strong man
fully armed, but as a strong man fully armed and believing
in the cause for which he was fighting. It was necessary
to have somebody who understood why we were at war,
and in saying that I speak not of a man who could com-
prehend merely the difficult international problems with
regard to it, but the spirit that made us go into this war,
and the things we were fighting for. Wars are sometimes
fought for land, sometimes for dynastic aspiration, and
sometimes for ideas and ideals. We were fighting for ideas
and ideals, and somebody who realized that, and knew it,
had to say it and keep on saying it until it was believed.
That was a part of the function of the Committee on
Public Information. Its body was in Washington, but
its hands reached out into the capitals of neutral countries

and elsewhere; its representatives were in constant communication by cable and telegraph and letter with the central place here in Washington where there were gathered together men of talent and genius and comprehension, and the inspiration of their appreciation of America had to go out from Washington to all of these outlying places. Sometimes it appeared in the newspapers of neutral capitals, and sometimes it dropped from balloons in written statements that were meant to convey to the enemy not the size of our army, not the dreadfulness of our means of conducting warfare, but the invincible power of our ideas.

So, when the military end came to this war, it was a composite result which was won undoubtedly in part by the superb heroism of the American soldiers and the veteran soldiers of the nations with whom we were associated. Nothing that is said about any other part of it ought to be permitted to take away from these splendid soldiers in their hour of triumph any part of the imperishable glory which they have brought to themselves and to the nation which they have served. But it was this unseen but persuasive and unending flood of ideas that aroused a correct apprehension of the true spirit and idealism of America in the war, and when the armistice was signed and peace came back into the world, it came, led by one hand by the military prowess of the great free peoples, and led by the other hand by the conquering idea of justice and freedom as expressed in America's idealism.

Now we are all facing the future rather than the past. We are thinking of what we are going to get out of this war, and nobody is counting it in gains which can be deposited in a bank; nobody is thinking of it in terms composed of subject peoples, but in terms of the return of law, the reign of justice, and the establishment of that complete morality in the relations of people which we have always observed as necessary in the relations of individuals.

FOREWORD

It is a great thing to have fought in this war. Every man who fought in this war, and every woman who fought in it, will for the rest of his or her life be telling those who gather round of the stirring things which took place during the years of the war. We shall be telling the new-comers on the stage of life, or those who were very young while the war was on, of the unselfishness of the sacrifices which were made, of the beauty of community co-operation, and of the great strength of a nation which is strengthened by high purposes. We shall be telling them all the rest of our lives, and I say *we* because we share with the soldiers who went to France the dignity and the glory of having fought as they fought, along a somewhat different front and with not quite the same peril; but we fought with the same spirit, we fought for the same cause, we fought with them, and when the night was dark in France, when the stars were not visible over the trenches and the noise of hostile artillery was menacing and fearful, when it was lonesome for the sentinel, the thing that sustained him there, the thing that made it possible for him to stay, was the unseen but almost palpable hand of his country resting on his shoulder. That country has kept true to its ideals and its cause, and these have been kept untarnished by the principles which were worked out in this country for a democratic nation; our ideals have been strengthened by their wide-spread dissemination throughout the world.

It would be impossible, if anybody wanted to do it, to pick out the particular persons to whom credit is due for these great things. Of course, it is very easy to know where the chief credit lies. Nobody could deny that the chief credit lies with the Chief Executive of this nation. As to all the rest, it is glory enough and credit enough to have been permitted to serve under his leadership, and in the cause of which he was the leader; but I want to close what I have to say by pointing out that the mobilization of America, superb as it was, was a mobilization not of men alone, nor of money, nor of industry or labor, but a mobilization of true appreciation of the rights of man. It was a democratic movement which made this great result possible, and in that mobilization of ideas the Committee on Public Information played a part of great distinction and value, and when I speak of the Committee on Public Information, of course, I speak largely of Mr. Creel. The land forces, for which I speak especially, recognize with gratitude the debt which they owe for making their victory possible, and also making it worth while.

Part I
THE DOMESTIC SECTION

HOW WE ADVERTISED AMERICA

I

A S Secretary Baker points out, the war was not fought
in France alone. Back of the firing-line, back of
armies and navies, back of the great supply-depots, another struggle waged with the same intensity and with
almost equal significance attaching to its victories and
defeats. It was the fight for the *minds* of men, for the
"conquest of their convictions," and the battle-line ran
through every home in every country.

It was in this recognition of Public Opinion as a major
force that the Great War differed most essentially from
all previous conflicts. The trial of strength was not only
between massed bodies of armed men, but between opposed ideals, and moral verdicts took on all the value of
military decisions. Other wars went no deeper than the
physical aspects, but German *Kultur* raised issues that had
to be fought out in the hearts and minds of people as well
as on the actual firing-line. The approval of the world
meant the steady flow of inspiration into the trenches;
it meant the strengthened resolve and the renewed determination of the civilian population that is a nation's
second line. The condemnation of the world meant the

3

destruction of morale and the surrender of that conviction of justice which is the very heart of courage.

The Committee on Public Information was called into existence to make this fight for the "verdict of mankind," the voice created to plead the justice of America's cause before the jury of Public Opinion. The fantastic legend that associated gags and muzzles with its work may be likened only to those trees which are evolved out of the air by Hindu magicians and which rise, grow, and flourish in gay disregard of such usual necessities as roots, sap, and sustenance. *In no degree was the Committee an agency of censorship, a machinery of concealment or repression. Its emphasis throughout was on the open and the positive. At no point did it seek or exercise authorities under those war laws that limited the freedom of speech and press.* In all things, from first to last, without halt or change, it was a plain publicity proposition, a vast enterprise in salesmanship, the world's greatest adventure in advertising.

Under the pressure of tremendous necessities an organization grew that not only reached deep into every American community, but that carried to every corner of the civilized globe the full message of America's idealism, unselfishness, and indomitable purpose. We fought prejudice, indifference, and disaffection at home and we fought ignorance and falsehood abroad. We strove for the maintenance of our own morale and the Allied morale by every process of stimulation; every possible expedient was employed to break through the barrage of lies that kept the people of the Central Powers in darkness and delusion; we sought the friendship and support of the neutral nations by continuous presentation of facts. We did not call it propaganda, for that word, in German hands, had come to be associated with deceit and corruption. Our effort was educational and informative throughout, for we had such confidence in our case as to feel that no other argument was needed than the simple, straightforward presentation of facts.

There was no part of the great war machinery that we did not touch, no medium of appeal that we did not employ. The printed word, the spoken word, the motion picture, the telegraph, the cable, the wireless, the poster, the sign-board—all these were used in our campaign to make our own people and all other peoples understand the causes that compelled America to take arms. All that was fine and ardent in the civilian population came at our call until more than one hundred and fifty thousand men and women were devoting highly specialized abilities to the work of the Committee, as faithful and devoted in their service as though they wore the khaki.

While America's summons was answered without question by the citizenship as a whole, it is to be remembered that during the three and a half years of our neutrality the land had been torn by a thousand divisive prejudices, stunned by the voices of anger and confusion, and muddled by the pull and haul of opposed interests. These were conditions that could not be permitted to endure. What we had to have was no mere surface unity, but a passionate belief in the justice of America's cause that should weld the people of the United States into one white-hot mass instinct with fraternity, devotion, courage, and deathless determination. The *war-will*, the will-to-win, of a democracy depends upon the degree to which each one of all the people of that democracy can concentrate and consecrate body and soul and spirit in the supreme effort of service and sacrifice. What had to be driven home was that all business was the nation's business, and every task a common task for a single purpose.

Starting with the initial conviction that the war was not the war of an administration, but the war of one hundred million people, and believing that public support was a matter of public understanding, we opened up the actiyities of government to the inspection of the citizenship. A voluntary censorship agreement safeguarded military information of obvious value to the enemy, but in all else the rights of the press were recognized and furthered. Trained men, at the center of effort in every one of the war-making branches of government, reported on progress and achievement, and in no other belligerent nation was there such absolute frankness with respect to every detail of the national war endeavor.

As swiftly as might be, there were put into pamphlet form America's reasons for entering the war, the meaning of America, the nature of our free institutions, our war aims, likewise analyses of the Prussian system, the purposes of the imperial German government, and full exposure of the enemy's misrepresentations, aggressions, and barbarities. Written by the country's foremost publicists, scholars, and historians, and distinguished for their conciseness, accuracy, and simplicity, these pamphlets blew as a great wind against the clouds of confusion and misrepresentation. Money could not have purchased the volunteer aid that was given freely, the various universities lending their best men and the National Board of Historical Service placing its three thousand members at the complete disposal of the Committee. Some thirty-odd booklets, covering every phase of America's ideals, purposes, and aims, were printed in many languages other than English. Seventy-five millions reached the people of America, and other millions went to every corner of the world, carrying our defense and our attack.

The importance of the spoken word was not underestimated. A speaking division toured great groups like the Blue Devils, Pershing's Veterans, and the Belgians, arranged mass-meetings in the communities, conducted forty-five war conferences from coast to coast, co-ordinated the entire speaking activities of the nation, and assured consideration to the crossroads hamlet as well as to the city.

The Four Minute Men, an organization that will live in history by reason of its originality and effectiveness, commanded the volunteer services of 75,000 speakers, operating in 5,200 communities, and making a total of 755,190 speeches, every one having the carry of shrapnel.

With the aid of a volunteer staff of several hundred translators, the Committee kept in direct touch with the foreign-language press, supplying selected articles designed to combat ignorance and disaffection. It organized and directed twenty-three societies and leagues designed to appeal to certain classes and particular foreign-language groups, each body carrying a specific message of unity and enthusiasm to its section of America's adopted peoples.

It planned war exhibits for the state fairs of the United States, also a great series of interallied war expositions that brought home to our millions the exact nature of the struggle that was being waged in France. In Chicago alone two million people attended in two weeks, and in nineteen cities the receipts aggregated $1,432,261.36.

The Committee mobilized the advertising forces of the country—press, periodical, car, and outdoor—for the patriotic campaign that gave millions of dollars' worth of free space to the national service.

It assembled the artists of America on a volunteer basis for the production of posters, window-cards, and similar material of pictorial publicity for the use of various government departments and patriotic societies. A total of 1,438 drawings was used.

It issued an official daily newspaper, serving every department of government, with a circulation of one hundred thousand copies a day. For official use only, its value was such that private citizens ignored the supposedly prohibitive subscription price, subscribing to the amount of $77,622.58.

It organized a bureau of information for all persons who sought direction in volunteer war-work, in acquiring knowledge of any administrative activities, or in approaching business dealings with the government. In the ten months of its existence it gave answers to eighty-six thousand requests for specific information.

It gathered together the leading novelists, essayists, and publicists of the land, and these men and women, without payment, worked faithfully in the production of brilliant, comprehensive articles that went to the press as syndicate features.

One division paid particular attention to the rural press and the plate-matter service. Others looked after the specialized needs of the labor press, the religious press, and the periodical press. The Division of Women's War Work prepared and issued the information of peculiar interest to the women of the United States, also aiding in the task of organizing and directing.

Through the medium of the motion picture, America's war progress, as well as the meanings and purposes of democracy, were carried to every community in the United States and to every corner of the world. "Pershing's Crusaders," "America's Answer," and "Under Four Flags" were types of feature films by which we drove home America's resources and determinations, while other pictures, showing our social and industrial life, made our free institutions vivid to foreign peoples. From the domestic showings alone, under a fair plan of distribution, the sum of $878,215 was gained, which went to support the cost of the campaigns in foreign countries where the exhibitions were necessarily free.

Another division prepared and distributed still photographs and stereopticon slides to the press and public.

8

Over two hundred thousand of the latter were issued at cost. This division also conceived the idea of the "permit system," that opened up our military and naval activities to civilian camera men, and operated it successfully. It handled, also, the voluntary censorship of still and motion pictures in order that there might be no disclosure of information valuable to the enemy. The number of pictures reviewed averaged seven hundred a day.

Turning away from the United States to the world beyond our borders, a triple task confronted us. First, there were the peoples of the Allied nations that had to be fired by the magnitude of the American effort and the certainty of speedy and effective aid, in order to relieve the war-weariness of the civilian population and also to fan the enthusiasm of the firing-line to new flame. Second, we had to carry the truth to the neutral nations, poisoned by German lies; and third, we had to get the ideals of America, the determination of America, and the invincibility of America into the Central Powers.

Unlike other countries, the United States had no subsidized press service with which to meet the emergency. As a matter of bitter fact, we had few direct news contacts of our own with the outside world, owing to a scheme of contracts that turned the foreign distribution of American news over to European agencies. The volume of information that went out from our shores was small, and, what was worse, it was concerned only with the violent and unusual in our national life. It was news of strikes and lynchings, riots, murder cases, graft prosecutions, sensational divorces, the bizarre extravagance of "sudden millionaires." Naturally enough, we were looked upon as a race of dollar-mad materialists, a land of cruel monopolists, our real rulers the corporations and our democracy a "fake."

Looking about for some way in which to remedy this

9

evil situation, we saw the government wireless lying comparatively idle, and through the close and generous cooperation of the navy we worked out a news machinery that soon began to pour a steady stream of American information into international channels of communication. Opening an office in every capital of the world outside the Central Powers, a daily service went out from Tuckerton to the Eiffel Tower for use in France and then for relay to our representatives in Berne, Rome, Madrid, and Lisbon. From Tuckerton the service flashed to England, and from England there was relay to Holland, the Scandinavian countries, and Russia. We went into Mexico by cable and land wires; from Darien we sent a service in Spanish to Central and South-American countries for distribution by our representatives; the Orient was served by telegraph from New York to San Diego, and by wireless leaps to Cavite and Shanghai. From Shanghai the news went to Tokio and Peking, and from Peking on to Vladivostok for Siberia. Australia, India, Egypt, and the Balkans were also reached, completing the world chain.

For the first time in history the speeches of a national executive were given universal circulation. The official addresses of President Wilson, setting forth the position of America, were put on the wireless always at the very moment of their delivery, and within twenty-four hours were in every language in every country in the world. Carried in the newspapers initially, they were also printed by the Committee's agents on native presses and circulated by the millions. The swift rush of our war progress, the tremendous resources of the United States, the Acts of Congress, our official deeds and utterances, the laws that showed our devotion to justice, instances of our enthusiasm and unity—all were put on the wireless for the information of the world, Teheran and Tokio getting them as completely as Paris or Rome or London or Madrid.

Through the press of Switzerland, Denmark, and Holland we filtered an enormous amount of truth to the German people, and from our headquarters in Paris went out a direct attack upon Hun censorship. Mortar-guns, loaded with "paper bullets," and airplanes, carrying pamphlet matter, bombarded the German front, and at the time of the armistice balloons with a cruising radius of five hundred miles were ready to reach far into the Central Powers with America's message.

This daily news service by wire and radio was supplemented by a mail service of special articles and illustrations that went into foreign newspapers and magazines and technical journals and periodicals of special appeal. We aimed to give in this way a true picture of the American democracy, not only in its war activities, but also in its devotion to the interests of peace. There were, too, series of illustrated articles on our education, our trade and industry, our finance, our labor conditions, our religions, our work in medicine, our agriculture, our women's work, our government, and our ideals.

Reading-rooms were opened in foreign countries and furnished with American books, periodicals, and newspapers. Schools and public libraries were similarly supplied. Photographs were sent for display on easels in shop windows abroad. Window-hangers and news-display sheets went out in English, French, Italian, Swedish, Portuguese, Spanish, Danish, Norwegian, and Dutch; and display-sheets went to Russia, China, Japan, Korea, parts of India and the Orient, to be supplemented with printed reading-matter by the Committee's agents there.

To our representatives in foreign capitals went, also, the feature films that showed our military effort—cantonments, shipyards, training - stations, war - ships, and marching thousands—together with other motion pictures expressing our social and industrial progress, all to be retitled in the language of the land, and shown either in theaters, public squares, or open fields. Likewise we supplied pamphlets for translation and distribution, and sent speakers, selected in the United States from among our foreign-born, to lecture in the universities and schools, or else to go about among the farmers, to the labor unions, to the merchants, etc.

Every conceivable means was used to reach the foreign mind with America's message, and in addition to our direct approach we hit upon the idea of inviting the foremost newspaper men of other nations to come to the United States to see with their own eyes, to hear with their own ears, in order that they might report truly to their people as to American unity, resolve, and invincibility. The visits of the editors of Mexico, Italy, Switzerland, Denmark, Sweden, and Norway were remarkable in their effect upon these countries, and no less successful were the trips made to the American front in France under our guidance by the newspaper men of Holland and Spain.

Before this flood of publicity the German misrepresentations were swept away in Switzerland, the Scandinavian countries, Italy, Spain, the Far East, Mexico, and Central and South America. From being the most misunderstood nation, America became the most popular. A world that was either inimical, contemptuous, or indifferent was changed into a world of friends and well-wishers. Our policies, America's unselfish aims in the war, the services by which these policies were explained and these aims supported, and the flood of news items and articles about our normal life and our commonplace activities— these combined to give a true picture of the United States to foreign eyes. It is a picture that will be of incalculable value in our future dealings with the world, political and commercial. It was a bit of press-agenting that money could not buy, done out of patriotism by men and women whose services no money could have bought.

In no other belligerent nation was there any such degree of centralization as marked our duties. In England and France, for instance, five to ten organizations were intrusted with the tasks that the Committee discharged in the United States. And in one country, in one year, many of the warring nations spent more money than the total expenditure of the Committee on Public Information during the eighteen months of its existence in its varied activities that reached to every community in America and to every corner of the civilized world. From the President's fund we received $5,600,000, and Congress granted us an appropriation of $1,250,000, a total working capital of $6,850,000. From our films, war expositions, and minor sources we earned $2,825,670.23, and at the end were able to return $2,937,447 to the Treasury. Deduct this amount from the original appropriations, and it is seen that the Committee on Public Information cost the taxpayers of the United States just $4,912,553! These figures might well be put in bronze to stand as an enduring monument to the sacrifice and devotion of the one hundred and fifty thousand men and women who were responsible for the results. A world-fight for the verdict of mankind—a fight that was won against terrific odds— and all for less than five millions—less than half what Germany spent in Spain alone!

It is the pride of the Committee, as it should be the pride of America, that every activity was at all times open to the sun. No dollar was ever sent on a furtive errand, no paper subsidized, no official bought. From a thousand sources we were told of the wonders of German propaganda, but our original determinations never altered. Always did we try to find out what the Germans were doing and then we *did not do it.*

13

There is pride, also, in the record of stainless patriotism and unspotted Americanism. In June, 1918, after one year of operation—a year clamorous with ugly attack—the Committee submitted itself to the searching examination of the House Committee on Appropriations. Every charge of partizanship, dishonesty, inaccuracy, and inefficiency was investigated, the expenditure of every dollar scrutinized, and the Congressmen even went back as far as 1912 to study my writings and my political thought. At the end of the inquiry the appropriation was voted unanimously, and on the floor of the House the Republican members supported the recommendation as strongly as did the Democrats. Mr. Gillett of Massachusetts, then acting leader of the Republican minority, and now Speaker, made this declaration in the course of the debate:

But after examining Mr. Creel and the other members of his bureau I came to the conclusion that as far as any evidence that we could discover it had not been conducted in a partizan spirit.

Mr. Mondel of Wyoming, after expressing his disapproval of Initiative and Referendum editorials written by me in 1912, spoke as follows:

Having said this much about Mr. Creel and his past utterances, I now want to say that I believe Mr. Creel has endeavored to patriotically do his duty at the head of this bureau. I am of the opinion that, whatever his opinions may have been or may be now, so far as his activities in connection with this work are concerned, they have been, in the main, judicious, and that the work has been carried on for the most part in a businesslike, thoroughgoing, effective, and patriotic way. Mr. Creel has called to his assistance and placed in positions of responsibility men of a variety of political views, some of them Republicans of recognized standing. I do not believe that Mr. Creel has endeavored to influence their activities and I do not believe there have been any activities of the bureau consciously and

14

intentionally partizan. A great work has been done. A great work has been done by the Four Minute Men, forty thousand of them speaking continuously to audiences, ready-made, all over the country. A great work has been done and will be done through the medium of the picture-film. A great work has been done through the medium of the publications of the bureau, which I believe can be commended and approved by every good citizen. Much remains to be done, and I believe the committee has not granted any too much money for this work.

II

THE "CENSORSHIP" BUGBEAR

THE initial disadvantages and persistent misunderstandings that did so much to cloud public estimation of the Committee had their origin in the almost instant antagonism of the metropolitan press. At the time of my appointment a censorship bill was before Congress, and the newspapers, choosing to ignore the broad sweep of the Committee's functions, proceeded upon the exclusive assumption that I was to be "the censor." As a result of press attack and Senate discussion, the idea became general and fixed that the Committee was a machinery of secrecy and repression organized solely to crush free speech and a free press.

As a matter of fact, I was strongly opposed to the censorship bill, and delayed acceptance of office until the President had considered approvingly the written statement of my views on the subject. It was not that I denied the need of some sort of censorship, but deep in my heart was the feeling that the desired results could be obtained without paying the price that a formal law would have demanded. Aside from the physical difficulties of enforcement, the enormous cost, and the overwhelming irritation involved, I had the conviction that our hope must lie in the aroused patriotism of the newspaper men of America.

With the nation in arms, the need was not so much to keep the press from doing the hurtful things as to get it to do the helpful things. It was not servants we wanted, but associates. Better far to have the desired compulsions proceed from within than to apply them from without. Also, for the first time in our history, soldiers of the United States were sailing to fight in a foreign land, leaving families three thousand miles behind them. Nothing was more important than that there should be the least possible impairment of the people's confidence in the printed information presented to them. Suspicious enough by reason of natural anxieties, a censorship law would have turned every waiting heart over to the fear that news was being either strangled or minimized.

Aside from these considerations, there was the freedom of the press to bear in mind. No other right guaranteed by democracy has been more abused, but even these abuses are preferable to the deadening evil of autocratic control. In addition, it is the inevitable tendency of such legislation to operate solely against the weak and the powerless, and, as I pointed out, the European experience was thick with instances of failure to proceed against great dailies for bold infraction.

Censorship laws, too, even though they protest that the protection of military secrets is their one original object, have a way of slipping over into the field of opinion, for arbitrary power grows by what it feeds on. "Information of value to the enemy" is an elastic phrase and, when occasion requires, can be stretched to cover the whole field of independent discussion. Nothing, it seemed to me, was more dangerous, for people did not need less criticism in time of war, but more. Incompetence and corruption, bad enough in peace, took on an added menace when the nation was in arms. One had a right to hope that the criticism would be honest, just, and constructive, but even a blackguard's voice was preferable to the dead silence of an iron suppression.

17

My proposition, in lieu of the proposed law, was a voluntary agreement that would make every paper in the land its own censor, putting it up to the patriotism and common sense of the individual editor to protect purely military information of tangible value to the enemy. The plan was approved and, without further thought of the pending bill, we proceeded to prepare a statement to the press of America that would make clear the necessities of the war-machine even while removing doubts and distrusts. The specific requests of the army and the navy were comparatively few, and were concerned only with the movements of troops, the arrival and departure of ships, location of the fleet, and similar matters obviously secret in their nature. As illustrative of the whole tone of the discussion that accompanied the requests, these paragraphs are cited:

The European press bureaus have also attempted to keep objectionable news from their own people. This must be clearly differentiated from the problem of keeping dangerous news from the enemy. It will be necessary at times to keep information from our own people in order to keep it from the enemy, but most of the belligerent countries have gone much farther. In one of the confidential documents submitted to us there is, under Censorship Regulations, a long section with the heading, "News likely to cause anxiety or distress." Among the things forbidden under this section are the publication of "reports concerning outbreaks of epidemics in training-camps," "newspaper articles tending to raise unduly the hopes of the people as to the success" of anticipated military movements. This sort of suppression has obviously nothing to do with the keeping of objectionable news from the enemy.

The motive for the establishment of this internal censorship is not merely fear of petty criticism, but distrust of democratic common sense. The officials fear that the people will be stampeded by false news and sensational scare stories. The danger feared is real, but the experience of Europe indicates that censorship regulations do not solve the problem. A printed story is tangible even if false. It can be denied. Its falsity can be proven. It is not nearly so dangerous as a false rumor.

The atmosphere created by common knowledge that news is being suppressed is an ideal "culture" for the propaganda of the bacteria of enemy rumors. This state of mind was the thing which most impressed Americans visiting belligerent countries. Insane and dangerous rumors, some of obvious enemy origin, were readily believed, and they spread with amazing rapidity. This is a greater danger than printing scare stories. No one knows who starts a rumor, but there is a responsible editor behind every printed word. But the greatest objection to censoring of the news against the home population is that it has always tended to create the abuse of shielding from public criticism the dishonesty or incompetency of high officials. While it certainly has never been the policy of any of the European press bureaus to accomplish this result, the internal censorship has generally worked out this way. And there are several well-established instances where the immense power of the censor has fallen into the control of intriguing cliques. Nominally striving to protect the public from pernicious ideas, they have used the censorship to protect themselves from legitimate criticism.

A proof of the statement was sent to every member of the press gallery, and after sufficient time for proper study a meeting was called at which Mr. Arthur Bullard, Mr. Edgar G. Sisson, and I presented ourselves for questioning and full examination. We explained that as the agreement was to be both public and voluntary, their assent must not be qualified by any doubt, and that we stood ready to make any proper changes, either in phraseology or principle. The temper of the gathering, hostile at first, grew more friendly as understandings were reached, and when we left it seemed a certainty that the plan would be approved. Unfortunately, however, the papers of the following morning contained a letter from the President in which he entered denial of the report that he had withdrawn his support from the proposed censorship law. This was the position of the military authorities, and as the

President had agreed to their suggestions in the beginning, he felt, without doubt, that his pledge of approval could not be canceled while the various generals and admirals were still unchanged in their insistence that they must have the protection afforded by an explicit statute.

Even though we knew the utter hopelessness of it, we went ahead with our plans and issued the statement to the press exactly as presented to the Washington correspondents. What followed quickly was another act in the serio-tragic drama of misunderstanding. The Secretaries of State, War, and the Navy had each been asked to give his views, and those that came from the office of Mr. Lansing read as follows:

The Department of State considers it dangerous and of service to the enemy to discuss differences of opinion between the Allies and difficulties with neutral countries.

The protection of information belonging to friendly countries is most important. Submarine-warfare news is a case in point. England permits this government to have full information, but as it is England's policy not to publish details, this government must support that policy.

Speculation about possible peace is another topic which may possess elements of danger, as peace reports may be of enemy origin put out to weaken the combination against Germany.

Generally speaking, articles likely to prove offensive to any of the Allies or to neutrals would be undesirable.

Convinced that a trick had been attempted and eager to find something to sustain their suspicions, the papers seized upon Mr. Lansing's ideas and held them up to heaven in witness of the Administration's dark plot. Not one took into account that the whole proposal rested upon voluntary agreement entirely, not upon law, and that the suggestions of the Department of State were advisory only and without larger power to bind than that allowed by the individual editor. Equally did every paper ignore the fact that the statement itself, in the outline of fundamental principles, contained these explicit guaranties:

Nearly all the European belligerents have also tried to prevent the publication of news likely to offend their allies or create friction between them. The Committee is of the opinion that the more full the interally discussion of their mutual problems the better. Matters of high strategy, and so forth, will of course have to be kept secret by the war council, but the more the people of the Allied countries get acquainted with one another through their newspapers the better. If any case arises where one of our papers uses insulting or objectionable language against our comrades in arms it had best be dealt with individually. But so far as possible this Committee will maintain the rule of free discussion in such matters.

The clamor refused to be stilled, however, and Mr. Hearst and the Republican Senators reached the stage of hysteria in their passionate defense of the "freedom of the press," that "guardian of liberty," that "palladium," etc. The bill, brought again into consideration, was defeated decisively and finally. And with this irritation out of the way, we had hope of a return to common sense and so, without more ado, we issued the following card:

WHAT THE GOVERNMENT ASKS OF THE PRESS

The desires of the government with respect to the concealment from the enemy of military policies, plans, and movements are set forth in the following specific requests. They go to the press of the United States directly from the Secretary of War and the Secretary of the Navy and represent the thought and advice of their technical advisers. They do not apply to news despatches censored by military authority with the expeditionary forces or in those cases where the government itself, in the form of official statements, may find it necessary or expedient to make public information covered by these requests.

For the protection of our military and naval forces and of

3   21

merchant shipping it is requested that secrecy be observed in all matters of—

1. Advance information of the routes and schedules of troop movements. (See Par. 5.)

2. Information tending to disclose the number of troops in the expeditionary forces abroad.

3. Information calculated to disclose the location of the permanent base or bases abroad.

4. Information that would disclose the location of American units or the eventual position of the American forces at the front.

5. Information tending to disclose an eventual or actual port of embarkation; or information of the movement of military forces toward seaports or of the assembling of military forces at seaports from which inference might be drawn of any intention to embark them for service abroad; and information of the assembling of transports or convoys; and information of the embarkation itself.

6. Information of the arrival at any European port of American war-vessels, transports, or any portion of any expeditionary force, combatant or non-combatant.

7. Information of the time of departure of merchant ships from American or European ports, or information of the ports from which they sailed, or information of their cargoes.

8. Information indicating the port of arrival of incoming ships from European ports or after their arrival indicating, or hinting at, the port at which the ship arrived.

9. Information as to convoys and as to the sighting of friendly or enemy ships, whether naval or merchant.

10. Information of the locality, number, or identity of vessels belonging to our own navy or to the navies of any country at war with Germany.

11. Information of the coast or anti-aircraft defenses of the United States. Any information of their very existence, as well as the number, nature, or position of their guns, is dangerous.

12. Information of the laying of mines or mine-fields or of any harbor defenses.

13. Information of the aircraft and appurtenances used at government aviation-schools for experimental tests under military authority, and information of contracts and production of air material, and information tending to disclose the numbers and

organization of the air division, excepting when authorized by the Committee on Public Information.

14. Information of all government devices and experiments in war material, excepting when authorized by the Committee on Public Information.

15. Information of secret notices issued to mariners or other confidential instructions issued by the navy or the Department of Commerce relating to lights, lightships, buoys, or other guides to navigation.

16. Information as to the number, size, character, or location of ships of the navy ordered laid down at any port or shipyard, or in actual process of construction; or information that they are launched or in commission.

17. Information of the train or boat schedules of traveling official missions in transit through the United States.

18. Information of the transportation of munitions or of war material.

Photographs.—Photographs conveying the information specified above should not be published.

These requests to the press are without larger authority than the necessities of the war-making branches. Their enforcement is a matter for the press itself. To the overwhelming proportion of newspapers who have given unselfish, patriotic adherence to the voluntary agreement the government extends its gratitude and high appreciation.

COMMITTEE ON PUBLIC INFORMATION,
By GEORGE CREEL, *Chairman.*

Will any American deny that these requests proceeded properly and inevitably from the necessities of war, and that each one had its base in common sense? Do they suggest any attempt on the part of the government to curb, influence, or confine the right of criticism? Even to-day, when the war is a thing of the past, can it be said that the card contained a word or a phrase to which any decent American could take objection? Newspaper men, it must be remembered, were holding peace-time jobs while others sacrificed or fought. Should it not have been their glad duty to aid enthusiastically in the provision of a veil of secrecy that meant larger safety for American ships and troops and larger chances for American military success?

Our European comrades in arms viewed the experiment with amazement, not unmixed with anxiety, for in every other belligerent country censorship laws established iron rules, rigid suppressions, and drastic prohibitions carrying severe penalties. Yet the American idea *worked*. And it worked *better* than any European law. Troop-trains moved, transports sailed, ships arrived and departed, inventions were protected, and military plans advanced, all behind a wall of concealment built upon the honor of the press and the faith of the individual editor. Yet while the thing itself was done there was no joy and pride in the doing. Never at any time was it possible to persuade the whole body of Washington correspondents to think of the voluntary censorship in terms of human life and national hopes. A splendid, helpful minority caught the idea and held to it, but the majority gave themselves over to exasperation and antagonism, rebelling continuously against even the appearance of restraint. Partizanship, as a matter of course, played a larger part in this attitude, but a great deal of it proceeded from what the French call "professional deformation." Long training had developed the conviction that nothing in the world was as important as a "story," and not even the grim fact of war could remove this obsession.

In face of the printed card, with its simple requests unsupported by law, the press persisted in spreading the belief that I *was* a censor, and with mingled moans and protests each paper did its best to make the people believe that the voluntary censorship was *not* voluntary, and that the uncompelled thing the press was doing was not really uncompelled at all.

When one paper violated the agreement, as many did in the beginning, all the others were instant in their clamor that the Committee should straightway inflict some sort of "punishment." This was absurd, for we had no authority, and they knew that we had none, yet when we made this obvious answer, a general cry would arise that the "whole business should be thrown over." Never at any time did it occur to the press to provide its own discipline for the punishment of dishonor.

All through the first few months it was a steady whine and nag and threat. Every little triviality was magnified into an importance, and the manufacture of mole-hills into mountains was the favorite occupation. The following letter, written on July 12, 1917, to the editor of a great metropolitan daily may serve to give some idea of the general attack:

Your signed article on censorship, "What We, and You, Are Up Against," is written so fairly, and in such evident honesty of purpose, that I feel sure you will be glad to have me inform you with respect to its various inaccuracies.

1. Never at any time did this Committee ask suppression of the name of the monitor *Amphitrite* that rammed the steamer *Manchuria*. It is the policy of the navy to give instant and complete publicity to all accidents and disasters, and a full report of the ramming was sent out at once. Your own correspondent argued that the name of the *Amphitrite* should not be used, and if you did not get the information it was because he did not send it. Even so, you had the name in the Associated Press despatches with full permission to use it.

2. With regard to the closing of the port of New York, this was done by order of the port commandant. The Navy Department was not informed officially, and when queried by the press asked that the news be withheld until an explanation could be gained from the New York authorities. This was at 11 A.M. At one o'clock this Committee gave out a complete statement as to the closing and reopening, and all the afternoon papers, in their later editions, carried the story. No request of any kind was made upon the morning papers.

3. You state that your paper applied to the Committee for permission to print that the Root Mission was passing through

Chicago on its way to Russia, and that it was given. Your Washington correspondent cannot tell us the name of the man that answered the telephone, nor have I been able to discover it myself. I do not doubt for a minute that the call was made, but the fact remains that it was not until a full week after the Root incident that this Committee commenced its day and night reference service. At the time we were about ten days old and trying to get offices.

4. The facts regarding the landing of the first contingent of the Pershing expedition are few and simple. The War Department had requested that no announcement of any kind be made until the arrival in port of the last troop-ship. The Associated Press released the news from its New York office. This was done without the consent or knowledge of this Committee or of the War Department.

Our first intimation was a telephone-call from the United Press, stating the action of the Associated Press, and informing us that the United Press felt itself released from its word, and was sending the news out over its own wires. I told the United Press manager that the War Department still insisted upon secrecy, and he straightway issued a bulletin asking a "kill." I called up the Associated Press at once, and was informed that the story had been released from the New York office an hour before, that it was "on the street," and that a "kill" was impossible. I then telephoned the United Press that it was at liberty to disregard my request for the "kill." I have no apology whatever to make for this honest attempt to protect good faith.

5. With regard to Secretary Daniels's statement of encounter with submarines, any doubt you may have had as of its accuracy should have been dispelled by a careful reading of your own paper. In the same issue that carried your article on censorship there appeared a front-page story that told of two separate attacks by submarines, making the claim that *two* U-boats were sunk. If you should be worried again as to the truth of Secretary Daniels's statement, I would urge you to read your own vivid, convincing narrative.

So much, then, for what you term "hodge-podge official handling of information." In view of my explanations, will you still insist that we are to blame for the "hodge-podge"? But if all that you allege were true, if we *had* been guilty of the blunders that you charge, what of it?

THE "CENSORSHIP" BUGBEAR

The secrecies sought to be obtained by the War and Navy Departments have concern with the lives of America's youth. Irritation and impatience are the worst that can possibly befall you and your readers, but death may be the fate of the soldiers and sailors that are called upon to run the gantlet of submarines. When men are going forth to fight and die, surely it is not a time for those who remain at home in ease and safety to wax angry over things that, even if true, are essentially trivial.

Very sincerely,

[Signed] GEORGE CREEL.

This voluntary agreement, having no force in law, and made possible only by patience, infinite labor, and the pressure of conscience upon the individual, was the Committee on Public Information's one and only connection with censorship of any kind. At no time did the Committee exercise or seek authorities under the war measures that limited the peace-time freedom of individuals or professions. Not only did we hold aloof from the workings of the Espionage law, operated by the Postmaster-General and the Attorney-General, but it was even the case that we incurred angers and enmities by incessant attempt to soften the rigors of the measure.

III

ASIDE from the regulation "censorship" cry, the thing
that worked principally to the prejudice of the Committee on Public Information was the charge that I "elaborated" a "cryptic" cable sent by Admiral Gleaves, and
gave to the country an utterly false account of submarine
attack upon our first transports. Although disproved
fully, the falsehood persisted to our hurt and discredit,
and even to this day there are people honestly of the
opinion that the initial troop-ships had a "safe and uneventful voyage." Of the many lies leveled against the
Committee during its existence, I think I minded this lie
the most, for not only was it peculiarly indecent in its
groundlessness, but its contemptible course carried far
beyond me and struck down a people's pride in their navy
at the exact moment when that pride was a war necessity.
For the first time in history American soldiers were being
sent to fight on foreign soil, traveling ocean lanes thick
with U-boats, and the period of suspense was our "zero
hour." The news of safe arrival, of dangers met and conquered, was a clarion to the courage of the nation, yet this
helpful enthusiasm was changed into a sneer for no greater
reason than that a press association might have a "story"
and that partizan Senators might take a fling at the Administration. Here are the facts:

The first transports, leaving in June, sailed in four separated groups to minimize the danger of submarine attack. We had no cable censorship at the time, and out of fear of enemy communication, the press was asked to make no announcement of departure or arrival until the last of the four groups reached St. Nazaire. On June 27th, however, through some blunder in France, the Associated Press received a despatch announcing the arrival of the first group, and without reference to the War Department or to the Committee it put the news upon its wires from its New York office. By way of contribution to the general confusion, various correspondents attempted to prove that I had given the Associated Press authorization for the release, and printed the falsehood that the Secretary of War had "broken" relations with the Committee in consequence.

At the very time of the premature announcement we knew that the other three groups were either in or near the danger zone. Adding to the anxiety occasioned, a cable came from Admiral Gleaves in command of the transports, telling of attacks by submarines, their repulse, and the certain sinking of one U-boat. Even without this news the tension was extreme and there was not a heart in any department in Washington that did not wait in sick impatience.

Late in the afternoon of July 3d the navy received the flash that announced the safe arrival of the last group, and the correspondents were told on the instant. As the word traveled a great happiness took possession of every one. When I entered the office of Secretary Daniels in response to a summons, tears were in his eyes, and his first words were, "What a Fourth-of-July present for the people!"

As a matter of course, the press clamored for the details of the submarine attack and I urged the verbatim release of the cable received from Admiral Gleaves. The high admirals flatly refused permission, informing me that it was the immemorial policy of the navy, in time of war, not to employ the language of a message coming in code, as it would acquaint the enemy with the cipher. Moreover, the Gleaves cable gave the names of the ships, set down latitude and longitude, and furnished other information of equal value to the enemy.

Because of these considerations, it was then determined to issue the information in the form of a statement to the people from the Secretary of the Navy. Out of his relief, his pride and joy, Mr. Daniels gave me his ideas as to the subject-matter, naval experts checking from the Gleaves cable, and the statement was written then and there. With every correspondent in Washington panting for the release, and with wires cleared for the sending, there was not time for word-picking and word-shading, even had the emotions of the moment not precluded all thought of "style" and meticulous phrasing. Every care was taken to set down the *facts*, but the spirit of thanksgiving that flooded every heart insensibly took charge of phraseology. This was the statement that went to the press within one hour from the time of the original announcement:

PRESS STATEMENT

[From the Committee on Public Information. For immediate release.]

July 3, 1917.

The Navy Department at five o'clock this afternoon received word of the safe arrival at a French port of the last contingent of General Pershing's expeditionary force. Announcement was made instantly, and at the same time the information was re- leased that the transports were twice attacked by submarines on the way across.

No ship was hit, not an American life was lost, and while the navy gunners report the sinking of one submarine only, there is reason to believe that others were destroyed in the first night attack.

THE "FOURTH OF JULY FAKE"

OFFICIAL STATEMENT OF SECRETARY DANIELS

It is with the joy of a great relief that I announce to the people of the United States the safe arrival in France of every fighting-man and every fighting-ship.

Now that the last vessel has reached port it is safe to disclose the dangers that were encountered and to tell the complete story of peril and courage.

The transports bearing our troops were twice attacked by German submarines on the way across. On both occasions the U-boats were beaten off with every appearance of loss. One certainly was sunk, and there is reason to believe that the accurate fire of our gunners sent others to the bottom.

For purposes of convenience, the expedition was divided into contingents, each contingent including troop-ships and a naval escort designed to keep off such German raiders as might be met.

An ocean rendezvous had also been arranged with the American destroyers now operating in European waters, in order that the passage of the danger zone might be attended by every possible protection.

The first attack took place at 10.30 on the night of June 22d. What gives it peculiar and disturbing significance is that our ships were set upon at a point well this side of the rendezvous, and in that part of the Atlantic presumably free from submarines.

The attack was made in force, although the night made impossible any exact count of the U-boats gathered for what they deemed a slaughter.

The high-seas convoy, circling with their search-lights, answered with heavy gun-fire, and its accuracy stands proved by the fact that the torpedo discharge became increasingly scattered and inaccurate. It is not known how many torpedoes were launched, but five were counted as they sped by bow and stern.

A second attack was launched a few days later against another contingent. The point of assault was beyond the rendezvous and our destroyers were sailing as a screen between the transports and all harm. The results of the battle were in favor of American gunnery.

Not alone did the destroyers hold the U-boats at a safe distance, but their speed also resulted in the sinking of one submarine at least. Grenades were used in firing, a depth-charge explosive timed to go off at a certain distance under water. In one instance oil and wreckage covered the surface of the sea after a shot from a destroyer at a periscope, and the reports make claim of sinking.

Protected by our high-seas convoy, by our destroyers, and by French war-vessels, the contingent proceeded and joined the others in a French port.

The whole nation will rejoice that so great a peril is past for the vanguard of the men who will fight our battles in France. No more thrilling Fourth-of-July celebration could have been arranged than this glad news that lifts the shadow of dread from the heart of America.

A wave of joyful enthusiasm swept the nation. Every newspaper in the land carried the statement in full, and not even the partizan press, always so eager to criticize, had a word to say about "bombast" or "flamboyancy." For the moment, at least, the meannesses of prejudice were subordinated to the exaltations of patriotism.

Three days later Mr. Melville Stone, of the Associated Press, received a despatch from his London correspondent stating that officers at the American flotilla base in English waters had declared that the transports were *not* attacked by submarines at all, and that it was more than likely that the supposed U-boats were merely floating spars or blackfish. Mr. Stone telephoned the Secretary of the Navy from New York and Mr. Daniels gained the impression that a representative of the Associated Press would call upon him with the despatch before its release. When the Washington correspondent came, however, the Secretary was astounded to learn that the London cable had already been put on the wires and that the visit had no greater purpose than to find out "if he had anything to say." Mr. Daniels pointed out that the despatch was absolutely anonymous in that it did not give the name of a single American officer responsible for the slander, and declared his sense of outrage that the comment of unknown persons, far from the scene of the incident, should be matched against the report of an admiral of the navy. As a result the Associated Press sent out a "kill," but with such a start the story could not be caught.

The partizan press leaped forward instantly in eager acceptance of the truth of the anonymous cable, and even friendly papers, unwilling to lose a "good story," joined in the hue and cry. The Secretary of the Navy was besieged by correspondents demanding the original cable from Admiral Gleaves, and when he refused for the very same reasons that had prevented publication in the beginning, a great shout arose that the whole occurrence had been nothing more than a "Fourth of July hoax." Then, and only then, did every solemn editorial ass discover that the statement was "lurid" and "bombastic."

A reporter of *The Tribune* called at my office the following afternoon on some personal matter, and while we were discussing it several other correspondents came into the room. The submarine controversy came up, and I told them, naturally enough, that I had no comments to make whatsoever, as any statement must properly come from the Secretary of the Navy. In the course of what I conceived to be personal conversation I tried to explain the point of view of the admirals, citing the importance of the navy code, the value to the enemy of the information as to longitude and latitude, and remarked also that a navy cable would have small news value, anyway, inasmuch as its technical wording made it cryptic to civilians.

One of the men then sneered something about "elaboration," and I answered that the veriest fool could see that the release did not purport to be the Gleaves cable, but was openly and frankly a statement of the Secretary of the Navy based upon the facts contained in the cable. I should have been conscious of the possibility of distortion, but aside from the fact that I did not consider it an inter-

33

view, the savage contempt that filled my heart left little room for other considerations. The men standing before me, every one husky, healthy, and within the military age, were holding down their peace-time jobs, while others sailed across the sea to offer their lives on the altar of American ideals. Surely the least that they could do was to think in terms of helpfulness, yet there they were, fairly quivering with eagerness to attack, to decry, and to defame.

The two words, "cryptic" and "elaboration," were fatal. Although only the three or four reporters saw me, virtually every paper carried a story the following day in which I was actually quoted as having admitted that the Gleaves cable was "cryptic" and that I "elaborated" it in the sense of supplying facts and details out of my own fancy. Senator Penrose, an ancient enemy, rose joyfully to take advantage of the opportunity for a display of scurvy partizanship. His resolution not only called for an investigation of the "Fourth of July fake," but for an inquiry into every act and activity of the Committee. Reed, Watson, Johnson, and other Senators with old angers to satisfy, joined in the attack and the press came in as chorus.

What gave a touch of malignancy to the whole affair was that reports fully corroborating Secretary Daniels's statement were regularly pouring in from independent sources. As early as July 7th *The New York Times* carried an account of the attack on the transports, written by its Paris correspondent. *The New York World* a few days later printed an interview with "the captain of an American ship" telling of the encounters and quoting him to the effect that "almost every vessel in the convoy was fired at by the U-boats, but American gunners proved too quick for the Germans." The correspondent of *The Philadelphia Public Ledger* cabled a graphic story of submarine attack, claiming the destruction of one U-boat, and in a score of metropolitan dailies appeared interviews with sailors, hospital apprentices, officers, etc., all thrilling in their description of the sea battle. On July 20th *The New York Tribune*, a paper most horrified by our "fake," published a letter received from a private in France in which these statements were made:

The Dutch must have known we were coming, because they took their first crack at night, before the destroyers joined up with the fleet. It was about eleven o'clock and dark, but there was some phosphorus in the water and it was easy to see the bubbles from the torpedoes. The "subs" took two shots at one transport. They didn't miss her much. The "subs" got busy and shot at five other boats. They missed them all, but it was close squeaking all right. It was sort of bad that night because the destroyers didn't meet up with the fleet until the morning. They put a smoke screen around the transports and went out after the "subs." One of our ships got one spotted close and nailed her after she dodged. That was pretty neat. She nailed her 'way down under the water. We got the "sub" all right. There was more than oil came up.

Most delightful contribution of all was this report that the Associated Press itself sent out:

HALIFAX, N. S., *July 25th.*—British sailors arriving here to-day, who claim to have been among crews of vessels in the vicinity of the transports which conveyed the first American troops to France, say they were credibly informed that German submarines made a concentrated attack and were beaten off, with a loss of six U-boats, only one submarine escaping.

The sailors said they were within three miles of the transports and witnessed heavy and continuous fire. The men were on three former Dutch vessels which had been taken over by the British government and were on their way to Europe.

The very papers, however, that carried sensational and even lurid accounts of the battle in their news columns at the very same time thundered editorially against the "Fourth of July hoax" and gravely condemned me for what they were pleased to term my "flamboyancies."

All the while we were awaiting the return of Admiral Gleaves in order to receive the full report that it was his duty to file with the Commander-in-Chief of the fleet. In the mean time, just as the newspaper attack was abating, Senator Penrose called up his resolution and for a day the Chamber rang to a bitter debate. In his most brazen manner, Penrose declared that the American public had been "regaled on the Fourth of July with the bombastic account of a battle which never occurred, and relating to a squadron which crossed the ocean in placid seas and arrived on the other side without an important event."

Senator Swanson of Virginia openly charged dishonest purpose. Senator Penrose, he said, had been informed by the Navy Department that every one of the documents in the case was at his disposal, including the original cable from Admiral Gleaves, and his flat refusal to avail himself of the offers proved that he had no interest in facts. Senator James of Kentucky talked plainly of "copperheadism" and coined a new word when he substituted "Penrosing" for "sniping." Nothing came of the resolution because it was never meant that anything should come of it. Having hurled his insults and launched his charges, nothing was farther from the Penrose mind than that there should be any hearing at which his assertions might be answered.

At last, however, after what seemed an interminable delay, the report of Admiral Gleaves came to hand, and not only did it bear out the original statement in every degree, but *went beyond it*. I submit a verbatim copy of the document:

THE "FOURTH OF JULY FAKE"

REPORT OF ADMIRAL GLEAVES

DESTROYER FORCE,
ATLANTIC FLEET, FLAGSHIP,
———, *France, July 12, 1917.*

From: Commander, Destroyer Force.
To: Commander-in-Chief, Atlantic Fleet.
Subject: Attacks on convoy by submarines on the nights of June 22d, June 26th, and June 28th, 1917.

1. About 10.15 P.M., June 22d, the first group of the expeditionary force of which the flagship was the leader, encountered the enemy's submarine in latitude ———., longitude ——— W.

2. At the time it was extremely dark, the sea unusually phosphorescent; a fresh breeze was blowing from the northwest which broke the sea into whitecaps. The condition was ideal for a submarine attack.

3. (Paragraph 3 gives the formation and names of the vessels, together with the speed they were making and method of proceeding; nothing else. It is therefore omitted for obvious reasons.)

4. Shortly before the attack the helm of the flagship had jammed, and the ship took a rank sheer to starboard; the whistle was blown to indicate this sheer. In a few minutes the ship was brought back to the course. At this time the officer of the deck and others on the bridge saw a white streak about 50 yards ahead of the ship, crossing from starboard to port, at right angles to our course. The ship was immediately run off 90° to starboard at full speed. I was asleep in the chart-house at the time. I heard the officer of the deck say, "Report to the admiral a torpedo has just crossed our bow." General alarm was sounded, torpedo crews being already at their guns. When I reached the bridge the *A* and one of the transports astern had opened fire, the former's shell fitted with tracers. Other vessels of the convoy turned to the right and left, in accordance with instructions. *B* crossed our bow at full speed and turned toward the left column in the direction of the firing.

5. At first it was thought on board the flagship that the wake was that of a torpedo, but from subsequent reports from other ships and in the opinion of Lieut. X, who was on the bridge, it was probably the wake of the submarine boat itself. Two torpedoes passed close to the *A* from *port to starboard*, one about

30 yards ahead of the ship and the other under her stern, as the ship was turning to the northward. Capt. Y reports the incident thus:

"Steaming in formation on zigzag courses, with base course 75° p. s. c., standard speed. At 10.25 sighted wake of a torpedo directly across our bow about 30 yards ahead of the ship. Changed course 90° to left and went to torpedo-defense stations. Fired two 1-pounder shots and one 5-inch shot from port battery in alarm in addition to six blasts from siren. Passed through two wakes, one being that from the U. S. S. C. in turning to northward, the other believed to have been from the passing submarine. A second torpedo wake was reported at about 10.35 from after lookouts. After steaming in various courses at full speed, resumed course 89° p. s. c. at 11.10 for rendezvous. At 12 set course 56° p. s. c. ——."

6. The torpedo fired at the *D* passed from *starboard to port*, about 40 yards ahead of the ship, leaving a distinct wake which was visible for about four or five hundred yards. Col. Z, United States Army, was on the starboard wing of the bridge of the *D* at the time and states: "I first saw a white streak in the water just off the starboard bow, which moved rapidly across the bow very close aboard. When I first saw it, it looked like one very wide wake and similar to the wake of a ship, but after crossing the bow and when in line with it there appeared two distinct and separate wakes, with a streak of blue water between. In my opinion they were the wakes of two torpedoes."

7. The submarine, which was sighted by the flagship, was seen by the *B* and passed under that ship. The *B* went to quarters. When the alarm was sounded in the *B*, Lieut. W was roused out of his sleep, and went to his station and found unmistakable evidence of the presence of a submarine. He had been there only a few seconds when the radio operator reported, "Submarine very close to us." As the submarine passed the *B* and the flagship's bow and disappeared close aboard on our port bow, between the columns, it was followed by the *B*, which ran down between the columns, and when the latter resumed her station she reported that there were strong indications of the presence of two submarines astern, which were growing fainter. The *B* was then sent to guard the rear of the convoy.

8. When I was in Paris I was shown by the United States naval attaché a confidential official bulletin of information

issued by the General Staff, dated July 6th, which contained the following:

"Punta Delgada, Azores, was bombarded at 9 A.M., July 4th. This is undoubtedly the submarine which attacked the *E* on June 25th, 400 miles north of the Azores, and sank the *F* and *G* on the 29th of June, 100 miles from Terceira (Azores). This submarine was ordered to watch in the vicinity of the Azores at such a distance as it was supposed the enemy American convoy would pass from the Azores."

9. It appears from the French report just quoted above, and from the location of the attack, that enemy submarines had been notified of our approach and were probably scouting across our route. It is possible that they may have trailed us all day on June 22d, as our speed was well within their limits of surface speed, and they could have easily trailed our smoke under the weather conditions without being seen; their failure to score hits was probably due to the attack being precipitated by the fortuitous circumstances of the flagship's helm jamming and the sounding of her whistle, leading enemy to suppose he had been discovered.

10. The *H*, leading the second group, encountered two submarines, the first about 11.50 A.M., June 26, 1917, in latitude —— N., longitude —— W., about a hundred miles off the coast of France, and the second two hours later. The *I* investigated the wake of the first without further discovery. The *J* sighted the bow wave of the second at a distance of 1,500 yards and headed for it at a speed of 25 knots. The gun-pointers at the forward gun saw the periscope several times for several seconds, but it disappeared each time before they could get on, due to the zigzagging of the ship. The *J* passed about 25 yards ahead of a mass of bubbles which were coming up from the wake and let go a depth charge just ahead. Several pieces of timber, quantities of oil, bubbles, and debris came to the surface. Nothing more was seen of the submarine. The attacks on the second group occurred about 800 miles to the eastward of where the attacks had been made on the first group.

11. The voyage of the third group was uneventful.

12. In the forenoon of June 28th, when in latitude —— N., longitude —— W., the *K* opened fire on an object about 300 yards distant which he thought was a submarine. The commander of the group, however, did not concur in this opinion,

but the reports subsequently received from the commanding officer of the *K* and Lieut. V are too circumstantial to permit the incident from being ignored. The commanding officer states:

"(*b*) The only unusual incident of the trip worth mentioning was on the 28th day of June, about 10.05 A.M., the lookouts reported something right ahead of the *K*. (I had the bridge at the time.) When I looked I saw what appeared to be a very small object on the water's surface, about a foot or two high, which left a small wake; on looking closer and with the aid of binoculars I could make out a shape under the water about 250 to 300 yards ahead and which was too large to be a blackfish, lying in a position about 15 degrees diagonally across the *K's* course.

"(*b-1*) I ordered the port-bow gun to open fire on the spot in the water and sounded warning siren for convoy. When judging that ship had arrived above the spot first seen I ordered right rudder in order to leave the submarine astern.

"(*b-2*) A minute or two later the port after gun's crew reported sighting a submarine on port quarter and opened fire at the same time. The lookouts from the top also reported seeing the submarine under the water's surface and about where the shots were landing.

"(*b-3*) The ship kept zigzagging and firing from after guns every time something was sighted.

"(*b-4*) Lieut. V, United States Navy, was in personal charge of the firing and reports that he saw, with all the gun crews and lookouts aft, the submarine fire two torpedoes toward the direction of the convoy, which sheered off from base course to right 90° when alarm was sounded.

"(*b-5*) All the officers and men aft had observed the torpedoes traveling through the water and cheered loudly when they saw a torpedo miss a transport. They are not certain, though, which one it was, as the ships were not in line then and more or less scattered.

"(*b-6*) The gunnery officer and all the men, who were aft at the firing, are certain that they saw the submarine and the torpedoes fired by same.

"(*b-7*) A separate report of Lieut. V, United States Navy, the gunnery officer, is herewith appended.

"(*b-8*) The *K* kept zigzagging until it was considered that danger was past, and in due time joined the escorts and convoy, formed column astern.

"(*b-9*) Report by signal was made to group commander of sighting submarines and torpedoes."

13. (Paragraph 13 deals exclusively with a recommendation as to the best methods to be employed in the future for the purpose of saving life. It is plain this ought not to be made public.)

14. Copies of reports of commanding officer's flagship, A, D, and H, are inclosed; also copy of report of Lieut. V, of the *K*.

ALBERT GLEAVES.

Here at last was the ultimate word, the complete story, the conclusive proof. The Secretary of the Navy had not lied, the first joy and enthusiasms of the people were not unjustified. Even though a month of lying had worked grave injury to American morale, it seemed a certainty that the publication of the report would remedy the evil in great degree. What happened? The Senate ignored the report, and the press, almost without exception, chopped it to pieces and printed it, obscurely, as the "last chapter in an unfortunate incident."

I had no intention of letting the matter rest, however, and under my insistence a request was made upon Admiral Sims to investigate the sending of the Associated Press despatch that started the whole train of calumny. In due time the following report was received:

3 August, 1917.

From: Commander J. R. P. Pringle, U. S. Navy.

To: Commander, U. S. Naval Forces Operating in European Waters.

Subject: Cablegram—OpNav. 49.

1. Upon receipt and after consideration of the above-mentioned cable forwarded from your office in London, I decided that the matter was one which would have to be brought to the attention of the Commander-in-Chief, Queenstown, since the sending of the despatch referred to in OpNav. 49 had not been authorized

by me and, as a consequence, if authorized at all, could only have been authorized by competent British authority.

2. I accordingly requested an interview with the Commander-in-Chief and also permission to bring with me Mr. Frank America, the Associated Press Correspondent at Queenstown. At 10.30 A.M. to-day I went, in company with Mr. America, to the Commander-in-Chief's office and found Lieutenant-Commander Olebar, R. N., the British Naval Censor for Queenstown also there.

3. The Commander-in-Chief read the cablegram (OpNav. 49) and then interrogated Mr. America, who stated in substance as follows: That he had received a wire from the London office of the Associated Press stating that certain information had been given out by the Secretary of the Navy, and asking if there was a Queenstown end to the story. That he had received shortly afterward a second wire from the same source telling him that a "follow up" story was desired. That he got into communication with Commander Pringle and asked permission to write a "follow up" story. That Commander Pringle refused to allow him to do so as the Censorship Regulations would not permit of its being done, and that Commander Pringle refused to enter into any further discussion of the subject. That he sent to the London office of the Associated Press a wire intended for the private information of his superiors in that office and not intended for publication, and that since the wire was "private" he did not consider it necessary to submit it to censorship by either the British authorities or myself, and accordingly did not submit it. That the information contained in this wire was substantially as given in OpNav. 49, and represented his general impression formed as the result of casual conversations held with a couple of officers and some men. That he did not know any one of the officers or men, but had met them on the pier, in the streets, or at the hotel.

4. About July 5th or 6th, Mr. America came on board the *Melville* to see me and showed me a wire which he had received from his London office which stated in substance that the Navy Department denied the statements contained in his (Mr. America's) wire, and, further, that the statement given out by the Secretary of the Navy was based upon official reports made by Rear-Admiral Gleaves. This was the first intimation that I had of Mr. America's having sent his wire, and, as Mr. America

seemed to wish to renew his efforts to get me to discuss the subject, I sent for the Executive Officer of the *Melville*, Lieut.-Commander Arwine, and, in his presence, informed Mr. America that I had declined to permit him to send any communication on the subject in question; that it would be entirely improper for me to discuss statements which had been issued by the Secretary of the Navy, and that, once again, I declined to do so.

5. In accordance with your verbal instructions, I had an interview with Mr. America shortly after your departure from Queenstown and informed him that he should come to me for information; that I would always give him such items as it was possible to give without violating the Censorship Rules, and that what news he got from me would be accurate. It was, therefore, entirely proper for him to have come to me for permission to write the "follow up" story requested.

6. The above is a recital of the facts in the case so far as I am able to ascertain them.

7. As a matter of opinion, it appears to me that, so far as the publication of his despatch is concerned, Mr. America is more sinned against than sinning, if the ordinary procedure regarding the publication of despatches received by the Central Office from correspondents is as stated by him. He felt that his despatch would not be published, and it seems to me that, if he was justified in his belief, his superiors in London have put him in a very embarrassing position.

8. With regard to any criticism either express or implied of statements given to the press by the Secretary of the Navy, I doubt very much whether any of the persons from whom Mr. America got his information were aware of the fact that the Secretary had given out a statement. There is a general tendency among officers and men of the Force to attribute many cases of supposed torpedo attack to the sighting of blackfish or porpoise, while spars are sometimes mistaken for periscopes, and any statements made are much more likely to have been intended to express a belief that the reports were exaggerated at the source than to express anything else.

J. R. P. PRINGLE.

Forwarded, approved.

WM. S. SIMS.

What a record!

The word of an admiral of the navy, the authorized statement of the Secretary of the Navy, set aside and publicly shamed on the authority of men "met on the docks, at the hotels, and in the street," and whose names were not even known to the correspondent!

The message sent as *private*—meaning that it was not intended for publication—thereby evading the censorship!

IV

THE COMMITTEE'S "AIRCRAFT LIES"

THE only other charges of inaccuracy against the Committee were based upon announcements with respect to the progress of the aircraft program. On February 21, 1918, we released a statement from the Secretary of War in which this assertion was made: "The first American-built battle-'planes are to-day *en route* to the front in France. This first shipment, though in itself not large, marks the final overcoming of many difficulties met in building up this new and intricate industry."

Almost immediately it developed that *one* 'plane only had been delivered for shipment to the American Expeditionary Forces, and that even this single machine was not yet on the water. Straightway the storm broke and the press vied with the Senate in denunciation of the Committee for its "brazen attempt to deceive the public." Utterly ignoring the report of Admiral Gleaves, the attack upon the Fourth-of-July statement was revived in order to give keener point to my own personal disregard for truth.

A sure defense was at hand had we cared to use it. The information as to the shipment of battle-'planes did not originate in the Committee, but came directly from Col. Edward A. Deeds, the officer in virtual charge of aircraft production at the time. More than that, Secretary Baker himself had formally authorized its issuance, accepting responsibility for its accuracy. The original copy

45

was in our possession, carrying the initialed approval of these officials and containing certain corrections in Colonel Deeds's handwriting. All that was necessary to establish the Committee's complete innocence was to produce this sheet.

As a matter of course, we did not take advantage of our position. The Secretary of War stood at the head of the armed forces of America, while upon the shoulders of Colonel Deeds, in large measure, rested the burden of the great aircraft program. Public confidence in them was more important than public confidence in the Committee, and if, by accepting the rôle of scapegoat, we were able to guard executives from the delays of harassment, it seemed a service. We made no defense, therefore, permitting press and partizans to continue in the assumption that the Committee was primarily responsible.

The facts in the case did not come out until October 25th, when Judge Charles E. Hughes reported the results of his investigation into the whole conduct of aircraft production. We were absolved from all responsibility, and one of the two counts returned against Colonel Deeds was that he had given "to the representatives of the Committee on Public Information a false and misleading statement with respect to the progress of aircraft production for the purpose of publication with the authority of the Secretary of War." Not a paper, nor yet a Senator, took sufficient cognizance of this vindication to withdraw their charges against the Committee, and, after a cautious interval, even commenced to repeat them.

I would not have it believed, however, that we sought, by our course, to conceal dishonesty or to protect bad faith. I had then, as I have to-day, the fullest confidence in Colonel Deeds's honor and high purpose, and his fault, if it can be called that, was an amazing enthusiasm that persisted in discounting the possibilities of delay. At the time he gave the statement, machines *had* been shipped from the factory bound for France: what happened was that they were suddenly diverted to Gerstner Field to undergo further radiator tests. Out of his certainty that quantity production was achieved at last, and in his eagerness to relieve the impatiences and anxieties of the public, Colonel Deeds simply failed to make sure that the machines were safely in the hold of a ship before making his announcement.

At about the same time, Colonel Deeds also gave four photographs to the Division of Still Pictures, a branch of the Committee that tried to meet the demands of the press for photographs taken by the Signal Corps in France and in those factories in the United States where private camera-men were not allowed. The pictures showed airplane bodies and engines, and under the thrall of Colonel Deeds's enthusiasm one of the young assistants in the division put captions on them that were admittedly flamboyant and overcolored.

This fault was freely admitted by us, and the four pictures were withdrawn. The services of the caption-writer were dispensed with, and orders given that all future pictures should be released with no more descriptive matter than the bare titles supplied by the Signal Corps. A Senate committee, however, continued to attack us because we had not attached to the pictures some such legend as this: "Do not be deceived, good people. These engines and bodies that you see before you are *not* battle-'planes."

The next explosion in connection with airplane photographs occurred in the following July. It is interesting as showing how painstaking hands can fashion a lie out of whole cloth. On the floor of the Senate one day, Reed of Missouri made the charge that the Committee on Public Information had issued a statement to the effect that

47

Secretary Baker, while in France, had seen "one thousand
American airplanes in the air." Also that the Committee,
in order to support this false claim, had issued photographs
of "penguins," a training-'plane that rises only a few feet
from the ground. Further, on the word of one Woodhouse,
editor of a flying-paper, Reed charged that the Committee
had deliberately attempted to make it appear that these
"penguins" were battle-'planes.

Our investigation instantly proved the utter falsity of
the whole rigmarole. The statement about Secretary Baker
and the one thousand American airplanes was not a product of the Committee at all, but merely a story in
the Paris *Herald*. As for Woodhouse, his explanation as
to the manner in which we practised deception was followed
by this naïve remark, "I am taking this for granted and
have nothing to base it on."

Utterly without faith in Reed, but in order that the record
should be kept clear, I sent him this letter, together with
a bundle of photographs:

July 17, 1918.

HON. JAMES A. REID,
    United States Senate,
        Washington, D. C.

DEAR SIR:

In *The New York Times* of July 13th, under the heading,
"Says Creel Misled Public; Reed on Assertion that Baker Saw
1,000 American 'Planes in France," there appeared an article
that commenced as follows:

"Senator Reed read to the Senate to-day parts of the
testimony of Henry Woodhouse of the Aero Club of America
before the Senate Aircraft sub-committee to prove that
pictures and statements sent out by the Committee on
Public Information to prove that Secretary of War Baker,
on his trip to France, saw 1,000 American airplanes in the
air, were false and misleading."

I am sure that you will be glad to know that the Woodhouse
charges and inferences are without the slightest foundation in

truth. Never at any time did this Committee, or any other department of government, issue any statement to the effect that Mr. Baker "saw 1,000 American airplanes in France." It may be, as alleged, that the Paris *Herald* printed the statement, but, if so, it came through no official source and had no official sanction.

I send you herewith copies of all aircraft photographs sent to us from France, together with the captions, submitting them as a complete answer to the charge that we issued pictures of non-flying machines in an attempt to make the people believe that they were fighting-'planes. As you can see for yourself, the majority of the pictures show machines high in the air, and in all cases of ground-machines the caption is explicit.

These photographs were made by the Signal Corps operators in France, the captions were written by Signal Corps officials in France, and our release of them in this country is a purely mechanical function.

These photographs come to us as part of regular deliveries from the Signal Corps in which the entire activities of the American Expeditionary Force are covered by the camera. No one branch of the service is put before another, and the inference that the Signal Corps in France is lending itself to a campaign of deceit is as untrue as it is unjust.

Very truly,
[Signed]   GEORGE CREEL,
Chairman.

As a matter of course, Reed paid no attention to the letter. Having gained circulation for his falsehoods, thereby gratifying his hatred of me and his antagonism to the Administration, his interest ended. Nothing is so keen a commentary upon the honesty of this whole inimical Senate group as the fact that not once was I called before a committee, either for explanation or defense.

To sum up then, the entire attack upon the credibility of the Committee on Public Information centered in these four charges:

(1) Falsely informing the people that the first transports were attacked by submarines.

(2) Issuing a false statement as to the shipment of airplanes to France.

(3) Issuing four photographs of airplane production designed to make the people believe that battle-'planes were being produced.

(4) Releasing a false statement that Secretary Baker saw one thousand airplanes in France, and supporting the lie by releasing pictures of ground-machines.

The answer to the first is found in the report of Admiral Gleaves; the answer to the second in the report of Judge Hughes; the answer to the third is the misguided enthusiasm of a young subordinate, and the answer to the fourth is contained in the letter to Senator Reed.

Consider for a moment! More than six thousand separate and distinct news releases, each one dealing with an importance; some half-hundred separate and distinct pamphlets, brimmed with detail; seventy-five thousand Four Minute Men speaking nightly; other hundreds delivering more extended addresses regularly; thousands of advertisements; countless motion and still pictures, posters and painted signs; war expositions; intimate contacts with twenty-three foreign-language groups; the *Official Bulletin*, appearing daily for two years; and in every capital of the world, outside the Central Powers, offices and representatives, served by daily cable and mail services rich in possibilities for mistake.

All done by an organization forced to function from the moment of its creation, working at all times under extremest pressure, handicapped by insufficient funds and harassed by partizanship.

And only the four charges!

The record stands unparalleled for honesty, accuracy, and high purpose, and in itself is an enduring testimonial to the sincerities of the thousands of men and women who made possible the accomplishments of the Committee.

V

SINCE the discussion of falsehood and slander has been commenced, it may be well to exhaust the subject before proceeding with the detailed story of the Committee and its activities. Let me make the statement, therefore, calmly and carefully, that domestic disloyalty, the hostility of neutrals, and the lies of the German propagandists, all combined, were not half so hard to combat as the persistent malignance of a partizan group in the Congress of the United States. From the very day of its creation to the day of its assassination, the Committee was compelled to endure an incessant fire from behind, working at all times under this handicap of a blind malice that had all the effect of treachery.

Our case, however, was neither isolated nor peculiar. Of all the war-work executives in Washington, Republicans and Democrats alike, it is safe to say that there was not one who did not go to bed at night with the prayer that he might wake in the morning to find Congress only the horrible imagining of uneasy slumber. It was not that any one resented criticism or inquiry or feared investigation. As a matter of fact, every man of them begged criticism, invited inquiry, and hoped with all his heart for a real investigation that would put an end to slanderous rumors. But Congress refused to do any of these things, confining itself entirely and enthusiastically to the business of attack.

Washington heard many absurdities, but most absurd of all was the frequent bleat that the trouble was due to "misunderstanding," and that the quick and easy remedy was to "establish closer relations with Congress—win their friendship and support by explanation." One might as well have babbled about establishing "closer relations" with a water-moccasin. Men like Penrose, Sherman, Watson, New, Johnson, and Longworth had no interest in "better understanding." *Bushwhacking was their business.* And while the Committee on Public Information was a favorite target, no war organization escaped their fire. Bernard Baruch and his associates on the War Industries Board were accused of using their positions to get inside information for Stock Exchange deals. John D. Ryan was held up to shame as a man who spent aircraft funds to enlarge his personal profits; Clarence Woolley was charged with manipulating the War Trade Board for the benefit of the American Radiator Company; Julius Rosenwald was regularly dragged in mud; Vance McCormick was branded as a rascal who made thousands out of our dealings with Russia; Col. E. A. Deeds was continually accused of secret corruptions, etc. To be sure, many of these men were Republicans, but that did not matter. They were part of the war-machine, and, since this machine was operating under the direction of a Democratic President, it had to be discredited.

There was no way in which effective reply could be made. Under the provisions of our Constitution a member of Congress cannot be held to account for any utterance on the floor of the Senate or House. It is the one place in the whole United States in which a mouth is above the law, and in which there is not only free speech, but immunity for speech. The heavens may fall, the earth be consumed, but the right of a Congressman to lie and defame remains inviolate. Even were this constitutional protection lacking, conditions would be about the same. It is Congress that makes the appropriations with which to carry on the business of government—the iron hand that holds the purse-strings. If denial of a Congressman's charge does manage to escape contempt proceedings, there is still his power to curtail or to deny requested funds.

Strangely enough, however, Congress is not a body without its strong, honest men. Fully 50 per cent. of the membership of the House and Senate are above the average in ability and conscientious purpose. The trouble is that these men seldom figure in public print. And they do not figure because the press has no interest in them. There are to-day, and have always been, two kinds of news: one is concerned with the fundamental significances of life and is educational, vital, and interpretative, the other deals entirely with the satisfaction of curiosity and dies with the day that witnesses the events which it chronicles. One is truth; the other is tattle. It is this second definition that is accepted by the press, and as a consequence the Congressman who gets into print is not the worker, but the blatherskite; not the man concerned with service, but the man concerned with sensationalism. It is this condition that puts a premium on blackguardism and places public servants at the mercy of reckless attack.

Of all the assaults made upon the Committee by Senators and Representatives, not one was ever prefaced by any attempt at investigation, not one was ever followed through, and not once was I ever allowed to appear before a committee to make answer to specific accusations. Throughout the Fourth-of-July furor and the aircraft mess I was not seen by a single Congressman or allowed to state the facts in the case at any hearing. Charges of partizanship, dishonesty, and disloyalty were hurled regularly at the Committee, and when I asked to be heard I was told, invariably, that "the incident was closed."

As an instance of procedure, a Representative from Massachusetts named Treadway emerged from obscurity one day by charging that the soldiers of the American Expeditionary Force were not able to get letters because the "Creel Committee filled the mails to France with tons of pamphlets." Others joined in the attack and the result was a resolution calling upon the Postmaster-General to report the amount of matter sent to the American soldiers abroad by the Committee on Public Information. Mr. Burleson, naturally enough, was not able to find any records on the subject, inasmuch as *the Committee had never sent a single pamphlet of any kind to any member of the American Expeditionary Force.* In order to make assurance doubly sure, he asked me for specific information, and in my letter of reply I finished by saying that Mr. Treadway had made "an assertion the absolute baselessness of which could have been ascertained by telephone inquiry."

Because of this paragraph the House declined to receive the report. At a time when the war hung in the balance virtually a day was wasted on this absurd debate and then the report was referred to a special committee to decide whether or not I should be brought before the bar of the House on a contempt charge. To the very last, Mr. Treadway insisted that he could "produce evidence in this House that there have been placed in the hands of the soldiers abroad tons of the Creel reports." There the matter dropped. The special committee never reported, Mr. Treadway never produced any such evidence, nor was I given the chance to face him.

Representative Fordney, a perfect type of a partizan, rose in the House one day and made the flat charge that I was issuing pamphlets in support of Free Trade and other Democratic heresies. The one specific instance he cited was a pamphlet by a writer named Burt Etheridge Barlow.

The attack was vicious, and after it had continued for quite a while another Congressman managed to obtain a copy of the pamphlet and this dialogue ensued:

MR. GANDY. I just wanted to know if the gentleman meant to leave the inference by the statement he made that the publication he referred to, which I have in my hand, was a government document?

MR. FORDNEY. I think so.

MR. GANDY. Will the gentleman look at it.

MR. FORDNEY. I think it was sent out by George Creel. There is a slip pasted on the first page, headed, "Committee on Public Information, George Creel, chairman"; and I think undoubtedly George Creel induced Burt Etheridge Barlow to write the article.

MR. GANDY. If the gentleman will look at that statement he will find that it is simply a statement by Mr. Creel that that publication has passed the military censor. It is not a government publication and does not purport to be a government document, and it is not sent out by the Committee on Public Information.

MR. FORDNEY. You cannot make me believe that George Creel can send that out broadcast without it costing the government some money.

I wrote a letter to Mr. Fordney at once stating that not only had the Committee never sent out one single copy of the pamphlet, but was without other knowledge of its existence than the mechanical act of returning it to the author after his submission of it to the Division of Military Intelligence out of an over-scrupulous desire not to print anything that might reveal military information. Mr. Fordney refused to retract his falsehoods and continued them at every opportunity.

Another Congressman, Knutson of Minnesota, charged that the pamphlets issued by the Committee were Democratic doctrines from cover to cover. These pamphlets, prepared by American historians of the highest standing, were not only going into every home in the United States, but were being circulated by the hundreds of thousands in neutral countries. A work of fundamental importance, yet this petty malignant did not scruple to attempt its discredit and destruction. And they shoot a soldier for a passive act like sleeping at his post!

Our motion-picture activities were a constant source of attack. Any "movie" man angered by our refusal to give him special privileges for money-making could slip up to Congress in full confidence that his lies would be shouted from the floor. The usual procedure was the making of the charge, the introduction of a resolution, and then futile efforts on my part to get a hearing. Once when I had secured permission to testify before the House Committee on Military Affairs, the chairman immediately gave out a statement that I had "refused to appear," and when I duly presented myself the committee declined to hear me on the usual "closed incident" grounds. This method permitted free circulation of lies even while it denied me the right of answer.

A chief offense of the Committee was its attitude in regard to "atrocity stories." From the very first we held that unprovable accounts of "horrors" were bound to result in undesirable reactions, for if the Germans could manage to refute one single charge, they would straightway use it to discredit our entire indictment. This view was shared by the War Department, and once on the authority of General Pershing, and a second time by direction of General March, we issued denials of gross exaggeration. Senator Poindexter, who made up in voice what he otherwise lacked, was the "atrocity expert of Congress," and because of these denials he charged the Committee with the circulation of German propaganda and devoted much of his time to a direct attempt to discredit our work. We sent him two of our pamphlets, *German War Practices* and *German Treatment of Conquered Territory*, perhaps the most terrible indictment ever framed against a nation, and explained to him that these established facts were preferable to baseless rumors, but it changed his malice in no degree.

In the Senate, however, most of my trouble came from enmities of long standing. The persistent attacks of Johnson of California and Reed of Missouri were in no sense due to what the Committee did or did not do, but were absolutely and entirely personal. Back in 1913 I wrote an article for *Everybody's Magazine* in which I tried to give a fair and dispassionate study of Johnson as a presidential candidate. It was not a flattering estimate and the abnormal vanity of the man never forgave it. The Johnson wattles swelled and reddened to a state of chronic inflammation as far as I was concerned, and my assumption of public office gave him the chance for which he had been waiting. As for Reed, I had known the fellow from the start of his career, and during the ten years in which I lived and wrote in Kansas City there was not a week in which I did not try to hold him up to the contempt and ridicule that were deserved by his character and abilities.

Another ancient foe was "Jim" Watson of Indiana. At various times in my writings I had voiced the opinion that the "Mulhall exposures" should have retired Watson from public life. His anger, coupled with malignant partizanship, made him at all times an unscrupulous enemy. Reed and Johnson contented themselves with daily abuse, but Watson was more thorough. One of his dignified activities was to send to Denver for a thorough investigation of my "past." Unfortunately, however, his agents in Colorado were not able to develop anything that shamed my character or general reputation, and were forced to rely entirely upon editorials that I had written in *The Rocky Mountain News* between 1912 and 1914. At that time I was supporting certain initiated measures that gave us the right to recall officials, including judges, and the phraseology in many cases reflected the heat of a bitter campaign.

In the midst of an important debate Senator Watson wasted hours of time by reading these editorials, written seven years before, and, what was worse, he did not scruple to separate passages from the context in order to produce false impressions. For instance, he recited certain charges in which I was made to appear as having alleged a diabolical conspiracy between the Supreme Court, President Taft, and the Vatican in order to sway and deliver the Catholic vote. As a matter of fact, the charges were not made by me, but by others, and I recited them merely in order to disapprove them. What he did, maliciously and dishonestly, was to put the charges in my mouth, carefully omitting the disproof.

Senator Sherman of Illinois charged on the floor that I had given a monopoly of war films to one moving-picture concern, and others accused me repeatedly of having turned over valuable motion-picture rights to Hearst. I spent two days trying to get before some committee to answer these plain, downright lies, but failed absolutely in the attempt. This, however, was about the only specific attack that ever came from Senator Sherman. As a rule, he confined himself to billingsgate directed against me personally, devoting whole days to speeches in which he characterized me as a "toad-eater," a swollen "rake hell," and other gentlemanly epithets. As a matter of fact, Sherman always aroused pity in me rather than anger. We were in the middle of a great war, with civilization hanging in the balance, and here was the Senator from a great state without ability to make any other contribution to the national service than dreary maunderings.

In open debate, Senator Penrose made the specific

charge that the Committee on Public Information, after establishing certain rules of censorship, "shocked and surprised the censorship authorities" by its own violations of the rules. He cited the case of a despatch filed by the manager of the Central News in New York which was stopped by the censors until they learned that the information came from the Committee. Of his own volition, Mr. Edward Rascovar, president of the Central News, wrote a letter to *The New York Times* in which he said that "no such story was ever filed," and Captain Todd, head of the Naval Censorship, also branded the Penrose charge as absolute fiction. Penrose kept insisting that he "had the proof," but we were never able to make him produce it.

Senator Lodge, in the course of a tirade, made this statement: "The question before us is that of Mr. Creel, a man to whom Congress refused to give power. The office he holds is created under the one-hundred-million-dollar fund given to the President for the general defense of the country. Mr. Creel, apparently, is part of the general defense of the country, and the little government publication which he is publishing, and the scores of people whom I am told he has employed to do what might be done by a stenographer and a couple of clerks, are being paid for out of that fund."

Either he was premeditatedly untruthful or else incredibly ignorant, for at the time the Committee's foreign activities were well known, its pamphlets were in circulation by the millions, the Four Minute Men were already famous, our motion pictures filled the theaters, and every Washington correspondent was receiving the official news from our office. I was always inclined to give Senator Lodge the benefit of the doubt, crediting him with ignorance rather than dishonesty. As some one once said, the Lodge mind was like the soil of New England—highly cultivated, but naturally sterile. An exceedingly dull man and a very vain one—deadly combination—his vanity fosters his ignorance by persistent refusal to confess it. More than any other Senator he has the conviction of omniscience, and his solemn expression and conservative whiskers persuade many people to accept him at his own valuation.

This "sniping" kept up steadily throughout the first year of the Committee's existence, each day bringing new charges and fresh abuse. Congressmen refused to see me and I could not get an opportunity to see Congress. We made attempt after attempt to establish a basis of understanding, if not friendship, for it was not only that the continual sharpshooting interfered with the workers, but it hurt the work itself. In virtually every foreign country we were preaching the gospel of an honest, idealistic America, and the task was difficult enough without having German propagandists quoting American Senators to the effect that the Committee on Public Information was a "pack of liars." And then in May, 1918, there came the explosion that brought things to a climax.

After a speech at the Church of the Ascension in New York, I yielded to the custom of Doctor Grant's forum and submitted to questions. The majority of the audience were "radicals," out of sympathy with the war, and their rapid-fire interrogations had the spat of bullets. At the end of an hour, when the questions were getting fewer and weaker, and when fatigue had robbed me of mental quickness, some fool asked what I thought about the "heart of Congress." A titter swept the crowd, and because the absurdity was so plain, I made the quick and thoughtless answer that "I had not been slumming for years." The moment the words left my mouth I could have bitten my tongue out, but I did not dare to give the incident point by attempting any withdrawal. It was one of those arrant, incredible stupidities for which there is no excuse. I suppose that the mention of Congress evoked instant thought of Reed, Penrose, Watson, Longworth, and others of their kind, and that the retort slipped out before my tired mind could call a halt.

As a matter of course, the morning papers ignored the carefully prepared speech of an hour, and made no comment upon the second hour of serious questioning, but put entire emphasis upon the "slumming" remark. My enemies in the House and Senate rallied with a cry of joy, and the dictionary was brought into play to prove that I had accused Congressmen of being "poor, dirty, degraded, and often vicious." The hatreds and accusations of the whole past year were resurrected, the inevitable Treadway introduced a resolution to institute contempt proceedings and the clamor rose high above the noise of the war itself. My one decent, honorable course was an open apology, for nothing had been farther from my thought than insult or defiance. My soul ached to make the flat statement that I was not referring to Congress as a whole, but had only Reed, Penrose, Watson, *et al.*, in mind. I swallowed the impulse, however, and wrote as follows to Mr. Edward W. Pou, chairman of the House Rules Committee:

May 17, 1918.

My DEAR MR. POU:

While the Rules Committee has not yet indicated any course of action with respect to the resolution of Mr. Treadway, I cannot permit myself to remain under the imputation of having passed public and insulting criticism upon the Congress of the United States.

My estimate of your honorable body is expressed in the pamphlet issued by the Committee on Public Information in October, 1917, under the title, *First Session of the War Congress*. So remarkable did the record of achievement appear to me that I had it summarized for general distribution, and in the signed preface I tried to bear testimony to the courage and patriotism of the men behind the record.

61

Even were it not the case that I am so committed by the frank and uncompelled expression of an honest conviction, I beg you to believe that I am not so lost to the proprieties as to indulge in attack upon the legislative branch while I myself am in the service of the government.

At a time like this I would take shame to myself if I attempted to weaken in any degree the public confidence in any public body, much less the great legislative body of our nation.

At the Church of the Ascension, I had spoken for an hour, and for more than an hour answered questions bearing upon every phase of public misunderstanding. The question under discussion seemed so utterly silly, and its silliness was so well understood by the audience, that I made a quick and thoughtless answer that lent itself to exaggeration and distortion. I admit the indiscretion and regret it deeply.

I have given my thought so wholly to the service of this war that I have, perhaps, been careless in the matter of guarding every word of my utterances against the possibility of misconstruction. But I have the feeling that sincere men see down to the heart of intent and will appreciate my desire at all times to avoid anything that might create the dissension and confusion so dangerous to our necessary unity.

Please let me take this opportunity to assure you of my willingness at all times to co-ordinate the work of the Committee with the wish and thought of Congress. What we have done and are doing is always open to the inspection of the individual member or committee, and I cannot but feel that our task here would be wisely strengthened by more intimate contact and co-operation.

The fair-minded members of Congress accepted the apology in the spirit in which it was written, but those who hated me refused to be placated, and conceived an attack that had every promise of success. At the outset of the war the President had been voted the sum of fifty million dollars to be used for the National Security and Defense, a mobile body of money designed to meet emergencies and for the support of organizations whose necessities were too immediate to wait on red tape. The Committee on Public Information operated from this fund, and here was the spot at which the opposition struck. Word went to the President that he must discharge me if he expected to have the appropriation renewed on June 30th.

It was a blow that menaced the proper prosecution of the war, and as a matter of course there was but one thing for me to do. I saw the President at once and offered my resignation. He refused to accept it, generously insisting that one indiscretion was not heavy enough to weigh against a year of effective service. It was also the case, he pointed out, that the Committee was so peculiarly my own creation that its manifold and important activities would suffer hurt if transferred to other hands. Moreover, he was of the opinion that my "manly letter" met the situation, and that the unfortunate incident would soon be closed.

While deeply grateful, the position in which I found myself was unendurable. It was a certainty that the President would be attacked for keeping me, and while I had no doubt of his ability to win out on the issue, the fight constituted another burden that no one had the right to impose. What I suggested was this—that he should cut me loose from his fund as far as the domestic work of the Committee was concerned, letting me go to Congress with my own request for an appropriation for the Committee. This, I urged, would give me the long-sought opportunity to make full and official report on the work, meeting accusers and accusations squarely and in the open. If I failed I would have had my day in court, while if I succeeded there would be an end to the cry that the President was "defying Congress" by his maintenance of the Committee.

I carried my point, filed my request for an appropriation, and on June 11th presented myself before the House Committee on Appropriations to justify my official existence.

Among those who faced me I did not find a friend. Mr. Sherley and Mr. Byrnes, the two Democrats, were of another school of political thought, while of the Republicans, Mr. Gillett and Mr. Mondell had only horror for my economic beliefs. As for "Uncle Joe" Cannon, he was on record with the statement that I "ought to be taken by the nape of the neck and the slack of the pants and thrown into space."

All Washington had its eyes on the hearing, and gossip had but one verdict. The Committee "was going to be exposed as a worthless, partizan body," not a dollar would be granted, nor would continued existence be allowed. For three days, eight hours a day, the Committee's activities and personnel were subjected to the most searching examination, and while the general attitude was critical to the point of hostility, they gave me a "square deal" every step of the way. Division by division, man by man, dollar by dollar, we offered the Committee for scrutiny, and when this inspection was finished, I insisted that every charge of partizanship, inaccuracy, and dishonesty should be taken up. One by one we nailed the lies that had bedeviled the Committee, laying down our proof, submitting to cross-examination, and inviting contradiction of our facts. The Fourth-of-July story, the aircraft publicity, the political affiliations of executives, my speeches, every published criticism and attack—all were considered in turn, and at the end there was a verdict in our favor with not even "Uncle Joe" raising his voice in dissent.

The one question remaining was as to my "temperamental qualifications." The editorials that I wrote in Colorado in 1912 and 1913 in support of the Initiative and Referendum, the right of the people to recall elected officials, etc., were read at length, and on the following morning the press carried the statement that I had "recanted." While it is true that I regretted certain phrases, I recanted no belief, but asserted my continuing faith in these words:

MR. CREEL. I want to say that every single thing in which I have believed and every single thing for which I have fought— and this is without exception—is to-day law, either in federal statutes, state statutes, or in municipal charters. There is not a single advocacy of mine that has not been approved by American majorities. My crime is that I fought for these things before they became fashionable. I think it is significant also that it has never once been charged that I have intruded a single pre-war enthusiasm into the discharge of my duties here; that no allegation has been made that I have allowed the specific reforms in which I believed before the war to influence me or even to appear in my work since our declaration of war. They go back ten years to things I wrote, but avoid carefully any investigation of my activities since April 6, 1917.

THE CHAIRMAN. Aside from the character of the editorials themselves, the charges that have been brought, in large measure, are that they show the viewpoint, touching the Presidency, touching the Constitution, touching the Supreme Court, and touching the Congress, of one who believed that these various institutions were of such a character as to prevent the man holding such views from being now the advocate of this government and of democracy in its warfare against autocratic government. That is the essence, is the gravamen of the charge, as I understand it.

MR. CREEL. Never at any time have I urged any instrument of change except the ballot; it is true that I have urged constitutional changes, nor do I feel that this was sacrilege. I think it is one of the greatest documents ever written, but times change, new needs arise, and I hold it well within the rights of citizens to alter and advance. Never at any time have I preached any doctrine of revolution, only the propriety of change. I have always held steadfastly, and to-day more so than ever, to the belief that this is the greatest government in the history of the world; that its institutions represent all that is best in human thought and all that is best in human endeavor. My animating impulse has been the belief in larger civic intelligence and enthusiasm; my effort to get citizenship, the electorate, to take a more active interest in governmental affairs—to vote honestly and solemnly almost. As a consequence, I have urged all those things that would more closely identify people with government, seeking to intensify interest in public business and public affairs. I do not believe there is a man in the United States who has a firmer belief in our form of government and in our institutions than myself, and if I made attacks upon them it was because I felt there were certain things which were the proper subjects of change.

Mr. MONDELL. You realize, I assume, that the German propagandists could make very effective use now of these utterances of the gentleman who, at the present time, is at the head of the publicity of the government and is leading the propaganda to express and prove the splendor and justice of our institutions?

Mr. CREEL. I feel that if the gentleman who introduced these editorials into the *Record* had troubled to make some investigation of my present work, instead of going clear out of Colorado to find out what I wrote seven years ago, probably the German propagandists would not have any chance for exploitation, Mr. Mondell.

At the close, character witnesses" were put on the stand, as it were, in an effort to develop my "temperamental" fitness or unfitness. Mr. Blair and Mr. Byoir, business men and Republicans, were asked as to my executive abilities, and Professor Ford, as a Republican and as one holding the sane and conservative post of dean of the University of Minnesota, was told to give his frank opinion of me. The statement of Professor Ford contains points that lift it above the personal:

Mr. FORD. I never saw Mr. Creel until I came down to Washington in response to a telegram from him. It was through no personal connection of any kind, so that my view of him has been to that extent simply that of a man dispassionately watching him. He was directing what seemed to me to be one of the most important functions that had been created as a result of war activities. I feel that I can say now that it seems to me that Mr. Creel has really succeeded in this work. Apparently he lacked all of the qualifications that most of us would have put together as making up the ideal man to do this job. He succeeded because he lacked most of the qualities and all of the experience that an average wiseacre would have said were essential to success. If anybody had asked me to sit down and say what kind of man should be put in such a position, I should have said, "This man must have certain ideas about administration and organization; he must have worked in organizations; and he must be a man who sits down and thinks out plans and then has the plan of an organization all charted out with which to execute his plans." I should have said that he must be a man who would be able to drive those other men in the organization as the usual so-called executive type drive other men.

This war has put most such standards of judging men entirely out of business. What Mr. Creel really was—I saw it at once—was an educator running what might be called a war Chautauqua. Now, for the purpose of doing that, the man who has fixed ideas, and who has had an experience that makes him discard everything except certain "safe and sane" things, would have followed his own rule-of-thumb methods, and would never have exhibited the ideals and encouraged the development of the things that have gone on here. The "safe and sane" type could have kept himself out of the press and free from criticism, but the Committee would have early made its appearance in the obituary column. The thing wanted in this work was not any definable administrative experience or any set of fixed ideas about organization. What you want are two things: You want a man with the right spirit, and that spirit can be covered in just one word, and that is "service." The second thing is that you want a man who is open-minded and responsive and quick to accept suggestions and see possibilities beyond the vision of the man who makes them. I think that Mr. Creel possesses pre-eminently these two essential things.

That is the reason why this Committee has grown so flexible, has met situations that none of us foresaw, and has done a work so big that none of us could ever conceive for a moment it was within the range of possibilities in twelve months. The Committee has done big things and worked effectively. Mr. Creel took things that the normal routine mind would have discarded. I know what my reaction was when a man came from Chicago to suggest to us that we take the Four Minute Men. I hesitated, but Mr. Creel said, go ahead. Nothing like that had ever been done. It was a perilous experiment in many ways to organize men all over the country to speak for the government with something like the authority of the government. They had never had such responsibility and one could easily imagine indiscretions that would keep us in hot water. Mr. Creel took it as a form of service to meet something that had never occurred before, and he was right, and the thing has worked out well.

A man who had worked in the government in the ordinary way would have said at once, "The government cannot go into the motion-picture business." But here was a man who saw what others had not seen clearly enough in the past, that such a thing has infinite possibilities for good if it is organized in the right way, and that you can teach through the eyes and through these pictures what neither the printed nor spoken word can teach. He caught the idea and he pushed it; and its possibilities as an instrument in patriotic education are evident. I could go from point to point, but I want to emphasize this fact, that he has constantly kept before his mind the idea of service and just doing the job and thinking of everything simply in relation to the great task. Notwithstanding the extraordinary situation which confronted him in an office which brought endless strain and ceaseless labor, he has made decisions that were right in the long run and which have been extraordinarily fruitful in results. He has made them quickly, made them advisedly, and he has done the work of a real executive. We have had a sense of responsibility, but everything we have done has been under his supervision. It may be said that this Committee, in its spirit of service, in its willingness to get behind any good thing and claim no vainglorious credit, has really shown the spirit of service that has animated the chairman. All of us had this spirit, of course, or we would not have gone into the work and stuck to it through misrepresentation and misunderstanding; but that spirit of service would not have been dominant in the Committee on Public Information except under a man who clearly was above self-seeking and pettiness.

When it was all over I had the feeling that the Committee had won respect and approval. Developments bore me out, for, while cuts were made, *an appropriation of*

$1,250,000 was voted. The committee members were unanimous in allowing it, and, as I have stated in a previous chapter, Republicans and Democrats were equally generous on the floor of the House, reporting that the work was important and that it had been discharged competently and patriotically.

All of us had the hope that this would end our troubles, but the respite was brief. The press generally ignored the hearing, and after a lapse of time sufficient to dull memory the same old lies were brought forth again and put through their spavined paces.

6

VI

LOOKING back, it seems a miracle that the original purpose of the Committee's existence should have survived the terrific strain of creation. Everything with which we had to do was new and foreign to the democratic process. There were no standards to measure by, no trails to follow, and, as if these were not difficulties enough, the necessities of the hour commanded instant action. Even before any allotment of funds, before an organization could be gathered or quarters secured, the Committee was forced into urgent duties and decisions.

We found temporary lodgment in the navy library, a shadowy, shelf-filled room peopled by quiet, retiring gentlewomen, who shuddered in corners while noisy mobs invaded their sanctuary. Every day saw and heard its hundreds of callers—eager patriots, duty-dodgers, job-hunters, cranks, inventors, Congressmen with constituents to place—buzzing like a locust swarm and devouring time with much the same rapacity.

Arthur Bullard and Ernest Poole, quitting their literary work at the first call to arms, came to my aid, and were followed by Edgar G. Sisson, who resigned his post as editor of *The Cosmopolitan* that he might serve. When I think of their unselfish drudgeries, their contributions from loyal hearts and driving minds, I find fault with every phrase designed to convey appreciation. Bullard,

MARLEN E. PEW

HARVEY J. O'HIGGINS

LEIGH REILLY

MAURICE F. LYONS

with his first-hand knowledge of countries and peoples and his even more intimate study of the Allied effort to capture public opinion; Poole, with his clear, democratic vision; and Sisson, with his tireless energy and rare executive genius—shot light through the general confusion, and, in spite of every hopelessness, purposes commenced to take form.

The voluntary censorship, driven through in the best fashion that conditions permitted, was companioned by the creation of machinery for the collection and issuance of the official news of government. Out of that early chaos also came the *Official Bulletin*, the Four Minute Men, the mobilization of the artists and the novelists, and various other ideas that had a later fruitage.

For shelter we managed finally to rent quarters at 10 Jackson Place, an old dwelling-house once the home of either Daniel Webster or John C. Calhoun, tradition dividing sharply in the matter. What we should have done was to have commandeered an apartment-house at the very start, but as a result of incessant attack economy obsessed me, an obsession, by the way, that remained to hamper and delay. The house next door was not leased until we had men and women working in basement cubbyholes and attic cells, and a third dwelling was taken over only when kitchens and hallways were filled to overflowing.

The Division of News, fitting the voluntary censorship as skin fits the hand, was equally fundamental as far as the purpose of the Committee was concerned. With the press depended upon to protect military information of tangible benefit to the enemy, it became an obligation to meet the legitimate demand for all war news that contained no military secrets. It was not a duty, however, that could be left safely to the peace-time practice of the press with its uninterrupted daily swing of reporters through the various departments, the buttonholing of clerks, and the haphazard business of permitting minor officials to make unchecked and unauthorized statements. Nor was there room for the "scoop," since war news could not be looked upon in any other light than common property calling for common issuance.

There were also dangers from the other side. Admirals and generals had been reared in a school of iron silence, and as a result of their training looked upon the war-machinery as something that had to be hidden under lock and key. To the average military mind everything connected with war was a "secret," and the press itself had no rights that needed to be respected. Even in the few cases where officials appreciated the value of publicity there was an utter lack of the "news sense," with the result that trivialities were brought forward and real importances buried.

What was needed, and what we installed, was official machinery for the preparation and release of all news bearing upon America's war effort—not opinion nor conjecture, but *facts*—a running record of each day's progress in order that the fathers and mothers of the United States might gain a certain sense of partnership. Newspaper men of standing and ability were sworn into the government service and placed at the very heart of endeavor in the War and Navy departments, in the War Trade Board, the War Industries Board, the Department of Justice, and the Department of Labor. It was their job to take dead-wood out of the channels of information, permitting a free and continuous flow.

A more delicate and difficult task could not have been conceived, for both the press and the officials viewed the arrangement with distrust, if not hostility. On the side of government there was the deep conviction that necessary concealments were being violated, and even when this antagonism was overcome there developed the assumption that only "favorable news" should be given out for publication. It was our insistence that the bad should be told with the good, failures admitted along with the announcements of success, and that the representatives of the Committee should have the unquestioned right to exercise their news sense and to check up every statement in the interest of absolute accuracy. Owing to the unswerving support of Secretary Baker and Secretary Daniels, we carried our contentions, and after much preliminary creaking the machine commenced to function with smoothness and certainty.

On the part of the press there was the fear, and a very natural one, that the new order of things meant "press-agenting" on a huge scale. This fear could not be argued away, but had to be met by actual demonstration of its groundlessness. Our job, therefore, was to present the facts without the slightest trace of color or bias, either in the selection of news or the manner in which it was presented. Thus, in practice, the Division of News set forth in exactly the same colorless style the remarkable success of the Browning guns, on the one hand, and on the other the existence of bad health conditions in three or four of the cantonments. In time the correspondents realized that we were running a government news bureau, not a press agency, and their support became cordial and sincere.

The Division of News kept open the whole twenty-four hours. Every "story," on the moment of its completion, was mimeographed and "put on the table" in the press-room where the news associations kept regular men, and to which the correspondents came regularly. These "stories" were "live news," meant for the telegraph-wire, and the method employed assured speedy, authoritative, and equitable distribution of the decisions, activities and intentions of the government in its war-making branches.

Not only this, but the Division of News was the one central information bureau. Before its creation Washington correspondents, running down a "story" or tracking a rumor, were compelled to visit innumerable offices, working delay to overburdened officials, or else telephoning endlessly, even dragging department heads out of their beds at ungodly hours. Our desk men, in touch with every happening at every hour of the day and night, were able to confirm or deny, so that one visit or one telephone-call met the need of the correspondent, saving his time and likewise the time of officials.

No attempt was made, however, to prevent independent news-gathering or to interfere with individual contacts. It was our insistence and arrangement that correspondents should have daily interviews with all executive heads, and in every case where a correspondent, feature-writer, or magazine-writer had an idea for a "story" either we supplied him with the facts, information, and statistics desired or else cleared the way for him to get his material first hand.

When we found that the rural press was experiencing a sense of neglect, in that it had neither wire service nor Washington correspondents, we secured the services of a capable "country editor" from the state of Washington, and had him prepare a weekly digest of the official war news that went to the country weeklies in galley form. Country dailies also asked to be put on this list, which grew to more than twelve thousand. At any intimation that this matter was not desired the paper was removed from the mailing-list, and by this and other checking we were able to keep a more or less careful watch on the extent to which the service was used. It ran as high as six thousand columns a week.

The Division of News also operated the voluntary censorship, advising and interpreting the government's requests for secrecy in the matter of purely military information. Each Washington correspondent, likewise every newspaper office in the United States, had the card that bore these requests; nevertheless, there were hundreds of inquiries daily as to "what the government wanted" or did not want. The men on the reference-desk either insisted that the news item in point was fully covered by the card or advised that there was no objection to publication. In all cases of doubt, decision was referred to Gen. Frank McIntyre, acting for the War Department, or to the navy representative, who rendered the official ruling. In no instance, however, was any direct order laid upon the press. It was up to each correspondent to comply with the wishes of the government or to reject them, the decision being left entirely to his common sense and patriotism. The Committee itself was at all times careful to avoid any appearance of censorship, refusing to assume authorities and holding fast to the safe rôle of adviser and interpreter.

There can be no question as to the value of the Division of News to the government itself. Through its news-gathering machinery it gave to the people a daily chronicle of the war effort so frank, complete, and accurate that in time it developed a public confidence that stood like iron against the assaults of rumor and the hysteria of whispered alarm.

Nor can there be any question as to the value of the division to the press. It saved the newspapers thousands of dollars in time and in men by the daily delivery and equitable distribution of the official war news, and was equally quick to assist in the handling of larger problems. In the case of the casualty lists, for instance, ordinary procedure would have compelled the three press associations, and such papers as maintained independent services, to make separate copies for separate distribution over the telegraph-wires. This duty was assumed by the Division of News, and a plan was worked out by which the Committee printed the lists and mailed them to newspapers with a five-day release date. By this method the press was saved the time and money and the overburdened wires out of Washington were relieved of a crushing burden. The system meant no delay in the notification of relatives, who received word by telegram from the Adjutant-General's office several days in advance of publication in the newspapers.

As a matter of fact, the Division of News stood at all times as the servant and champion of the newspapers, making daily and vigorous fight against unnecessary secrecies. By way of illustration, it was the original decision that correspondents should not be permitted to accompany General Pershing and the first troops that went to France. The Committee insisted that such a course would arouse just and wide-spread indignation, and by dint of unanswerable argument we won a ruling from Secretary Baker that recognized the right of the press to adequate representation. Commencing with the men selected by the news associations, the number was increased carefully and intelligently until twenty-three accredited correspondents were at headquarters in France. At this point General Pershing put his foot down hard, cabling that there were twice as many correspondents with the small American force as with the great armies of England and France, a fact that was commencing to cause laughter and ridicule.

All of which was true, but it was equally true that neither England nor France was sending soldiers three thousand miles from home, nor was it taken into consideration that the United States had ten times as many papers as the French or the English. The order held, but the Committee refused to admit defeat and devised a scheme of "war-zone visits." Our Paris office, working in conjunction with the American, French, and English authorities, gained permission to conduct correspondents to the various fronts on inspection tours. This done, the Washington office made itself reponsible for passports and letters of introduction, with the result that no responsible, duly accredited American newspaper man was denied the right to see and study the American effort in France.

The Grand Fleet was another case in point. We were willing to admit that there should be secrecy as to the number and whereabouts of our war-ships, but we saw only absurdity in the attempt to hide the fact that there really *was* a fleet and that it *was* ready to fight. One of the most popular pre-war lies was the "demoralization of the navy." What finer message to carry to the people than the might of "the gray, mailed fist"? Secretary Daniels and Admiral Mayo saw the force of the argument, and the Committee was permitted to send party after party of correspondents and writers to Yorktown, where the war-ships of the United States lay at anchor in the early days of the war. Not one word was ever printed as to location or number, but the daily and periodical press was filled with columns that told America of our naval invincibility. The two articles by Mary Roberts Rinehart, published in *The Saturday Evening Post*, were worth a host of recruiting officers, for they told the people that the first line of defense was worthy of full confidence and complete reliance.

The same system was followed with respect to cantonments, shipyards, and munition-factories, and as a result a flood of positive news crowded out the negative and destructive. Another thing that aided materially in the stabilization of public opinion was the open pledge of the army and the navy that all accidents, disasters, and casualties would be given instant announcement. *It was a pledge that was kept.*

The Committee, while safeguarding the interests of the

government and upholding the rights of the press, felt that its true responsibility was to the people of the United States. As a consequence of this belief, which put us between the press and the government as an independent, impartial force, the Committee met with almost constant attack from either one side or the other. When we supported the contentions of the correspondents, the admirals and generals declared that we wanted "to run the war in the interest of the newspapers," and when we accepted censorship rulings as sound and reasonable, the press talked wildly of gags and muzzles. Sometimes it was the case that both sides joined in attack, forgetting differences in the joy of a common irritation.

For instance, in March, 1918, in the absence of Secretary Baker, and without previous warning or consultation, the War Department curtly informed us that thereafter all casualty lists must be issued to the press without the home address or the name of the next of kin. The form that we had been following was as follows:

Wounded: Private John Jones. S. J. Jones (father)
2 Yale Street, Brooklyn, N. Y.

The new War Department order prescribed this form:

Wounded: Private John Jones.

We realized at once that the thousands of identical names in the United States made it certain that the new form would work anxiety and suffering to countless homes. Merely to announce that John Jones or Patrick Kelly was killed or wounded meant that the parents, relatives, and friends of the innumerable John Joneses and Patrick Kellys would be given over to every fear and grief, since there was nothing to indicate exact identity.

We took up the matter with Assistant-Secretary Crowell

at once, and asked the reason for the sudden and astonishing change in plans. Boiled down, this was the explanation given: The German spies, reading the printed casualty lists, would proceed at once to the home and there, under some pretense, worm out of the family the unit to which the soldier belonged. Then the spy would transmit the information to Berlin and Berlin would then send it to the front, thus acquainting the German generals with the character of the American troops that faced them.

As we pointed out, why should the Germans adopt this tedious, roundabout method when a trench raid would give them the same information in a night? And even if we granted the absurd contention that there were enough German spies in America to visit homes in every city, how would they convey their information to Germany? Assistant-Secretary Crowell ended the discussion by the brusk declaration that the military authorities were in possession of conclusive proof that Berlin received American news within twenty-four hours of its publication. Unable to secure any modification of the order, and deeply convinced that it was as stupid as it was cruel, the Committee refused to issue casualty lists in the new form.

For a full year the press had thundered at the Committee as an "agency of repression," yet now, when we were standing for a sane and proper publicity, the papers described a virtuous roundabout, and attacked the Committee for its "impudent presumption" in daring to question the War Department's efforts to safeguard the military secrets of America.

The Committee stood by its position, and I deemed the matter of sufficient gravity to carry it to the President himself. I cited hundreds of cases of families needlessly torn by anguish and told of the avalanche of telephone-calls and telegrams from all parts of the country. In addition to this I insisted that the War Department should produce its proof that German spies in this country were in communication regularly with Berlin. Grudgingly enough, the alleged proof was brought forward and was seen to be the desired publication in German papers of news of American effort designed to weaken German morale by steady hammering on the inevitability of German defeat from the growing American force—news that the Committee itself had sent to Holland and which our representative in The Hague had managed to slip into Germany past the censorship.

In five minutes the whole Crowell contention was shown to be the last word in absurdity, and the President ordered a return to the former method that gave the home address and the next of kin

Such conditions inevitably made the Division of News a storm-center, and the fact that it rode the waves to success is in itself the best commentary upon the devotions and abilities of the men who were called upon to direct this most important department of the Committee's endeavor.

It was Mr. Sisson who gave form and purpose to the division, organizing the machinery to operate the voluntary censorship, as well as gathering and training the organization for news collection and distribution. Passing time compelled many changes, but they were in detail only, for Mr. Sisson built on the solid rock of common sense, justice, efficiency, and impartiality. L. Ames Brown, the Washington writer and newspaper man, was the first director of the division, and, when transferred to inaugurate a new line of work, was succeeded by Mr. J. W. McConaghy, who left his position in the New York newspaper field to serve with us. He brought energy and ideas, and during his régime the scope of the work was broadened materially. Mr. McConaghy, drafted by the Foreign Section to make a survey of the Central-American countries, was succeeded by Mr. Leigh Reilly, formerly managing editor of The

Chicago Record-Herald, a man of rich experience and highest standing in the newspaper profession. He bore the great burden of the summer and autumn of 1918, and the credit for efficiency in the period of supreme stress is his.

As far as the work itself was concerned, the two most important tasks were in connection with the army and the navy, for these afforded not only the bulk of the news, but it was the news that dealt with the importances of life and death. With respect to the navy, we were fortunate at the very outset in securing the services of John Wilbur Jenkins, dean of the Baltimore newspaper fraternity, for in his indefatigable little body he coupled an invincible placidity with amazing steadfastness. Storms might break upon him and every wind of confusion roar about him, but when the sun came out again it was invariably the case that John Wilbur was to be seen plugging along at his original task, serene and unchanged. He won the respect of every naval official, and this relationship was no small factor in promoting the success of a working arrangement bound up with so many prejudices and decisions.

It was Secretary Daniels himself, however, who made the Committee's contacts with the navy as effective as they were pleasant, for, more than any other high official in Washington, save the President, he had common sense and abiding faith in straightforward truth-telling. He wanted the people to *know,* and in every dispute his decision was always on the side of openness. Admiral Benson early caught the spirit of the Committee's endeavor, and gave it confidence and undeviating support. Admiral Earle, Admiral Taylor, and Admiral Palmer were also our honored helpers.

The War Department was no such easy problem. Infinitely more huge and complex than the navy, it bubbled new activities each day, all far-reaching, and each one a mass of delicate detail. First we "tried out" Heywood

Brown, of *The New York Tribune*, but he returned to his paper in a short while, and we then reached forth and plucked Wallace Irwin away from his prose and poetry. While his bodily strength lasted the brilliance of his work was equaled only by his personal popularity, but he didn't last long enough. There was no question as to the drudgery of the position, but what really brought about his collapse was worry. Strangely enough for a poet and novelist, Wallace had an ingrowing conscience, and after working eighteen hours a day he spent the remaining six fretting over sins of omission. As a consequence, he took to his bed one fine day, and an indignant wife transported him to New York "beyond our clutches."

At that time Marlen Pew was running *The Editor and Publisher*, and before that was one of the "star men" of the Newspaper Enterprise Association. Of all the field, he looked the best, and there was never occasion to regret the choice. Every inch a progressive, with an insistent belief in the right of the people to have the facts, he had the courage of his very intense convictions, and he finished his service with the proud record of never having lost a battle with red tape or mossbackism. He created a machinery that functioned with almost automatic precision, even winning the reluctant admiration of the Washington correspondents to such a degree that they asked its continuance when the Committee abandoned the work after the armistice. Mr. Arthur Crawford, formerly of *The Chicago Herald*, looked after the Quartermaster's Department; Mr. Edwin Newdick, who came to us from *The Christian Science Monitor*, worked with the Surgeon-General; Mr. Carl H. Butman covered the Aircraft Board; and other representatives in other divisions of the War Department were Mr. Livy Richards of Boston and Mr. John Calvin Mellet, formerly with the International News Service.

Other branches of the government were no less well served by newspaper men of the same high character and proved ability. Mr. Archibald Mattingly, Mr. Charles P. Sweeney, Mr. Garrard Harris, and Mr. E. H. Hitchcock measured up to every demand of their difficult positions, contributing materially to the achievement of the division.

Mr. Kenneth Durant and Mr. Charles Willoughby, dividing the duties of the reference-desk, had difficult positions, for it was was to them that inquiries came. Hour in and hour out, they answered them with ability, patience, fairness, and never-failing tact.

Even to-day, when I review the work of the Division of News in critical dispassion, I thrill to the sheer wonder of the achievement. Here was a brand-new organization, called to do a brand-new thing, assembled under highest pressure and driven at top speed at all times, and yet its record for accuracy is without parallel in the annals of news-gathering. During the eighteen months of existence it cleared *all of the official war news of government*, issuing more than six thousand releases. Every one of these releases ran the gantlet of incessant and hostile scrutiny, yet only *three* were ever subjected to direct attack on the score of inaccuracy.[1] In two of these cases the Committee was justified by investigation, while the fault in the third instance was that of a high official whose word could not be questioned.

[1] See Chapters 3 and 4.

VII

THERE was nothing more time-wasting than the flood of people that poured into Washington during the war, each burdened with some wonderful suggestion that could be imparted only to an executive head. Even so, all of them had to be seen, for not only was it their right as citizens, but it was equally the case that the idea might have real value. Many of our best suggestions came from the most unlikely sources.

In the very first hours of the Committee, when we were still penned in the navy library, fighting for breath, a handsome, rosy-cheeked youth burst through the crowd and caught my lapel in a death-grip. His name was Donald Ryerson. He confessed to Chicago as his home, and the plan that he presented was the organization of volunteer speakers for the purpose of making patriotic talks in motion-picture theaters. He had tried out the scheme in Chicago, and the success of the venture had catapulted him on the train to Washington and to me.

Being driven to the breaking-point has certain compensations, after all. It forces one to think quickly and confines thought largely to the positive values of a suggestion rather than future difficulties. Had I had the time to weigh the proposition from every angle, it may be that I would have decided against it, for it was delicate and dangerous business to turn loose on the country an army of

CLAYTON D. LEE

WILLIAM H. INGERSOLL

WILLIAM McCORMICK BLAIR

E. T. GUNDLACH

speakers impossible of exact control and yet vested in large degree with the authority of the government. In ten minutes we had decided upon a national organization to be called the "Four Minute Men," and Mr. Ryerson rushed out with my appointment as its director.

When the armistice brought activities to a conclusion the Four Minute Men numbered 75,000 speakers, more than 7,555,190 speeches had been made, and a fair estimate of audiences makes it certain that a total of 134,454,514 people had been addressed. Notwithstanding the nature of the work, the infinite chances for blunder and bungle, this unique and effective agency functioned from first to last with only one voice ever raised to attack its faith and efficiency. As this voice was that of Senator Sherman of Illinois, this attack is justly to be set down as part of the general praise.

The form of presentation decided upon was a glass slide to be thrown on the theater-curtain, and worded as follows:

4 MINUTE MEN 4
(Copyright, 1917. Trade-mark.)

. . . .
(Insert name of speaker)

will speak four minutes on a subject
of national importance. He speaks
under the authority of

THE COMMITTEE ON PUBLIC INFORMATION
GEORGE CREEL, CHAIRMAN
WASHINGTON, D. C.

A more difficult decision was as to the preparation of the matter to be sent out to speakers. We did not want stereotyped oratory, and yet it was imperative to guard against the dangers of unrestraint. It was finally agreed that regular bulletins should be issued, each containing a budget of material covering every phase of the question to be discussed, and also including two or three illustrative four-minute speeches. Mr. Waldo P. Warren of Chicago was chosen to write the first bulletin, and when he was called away his duties fell upon E. T. Gundlach, also of Chicago, the patriotic head of an advertising agency. These bulletins, however, prepared in close and continued consultation with the proper officials of each government department responsible for them, were also gone over carefully by Professor Ford and his scholars.

The idea, from the very first, had the sweep of a prairie fire. Speakers volunteered by the thousand in every state, the owners of the motion-picture houses, after a first natural hesitancy, gave exclusive privileges to the organization, and the various government departments fairly clamored for the services of the Four Minute Men. The following list of bulletins will show the wide range of topics:

Topic	Period
Universal Service by Selective Draft.	May 12–21, 1917
First Liberty Loan.	May 22–June 15, 1917
Red Cross.	June 18–25, 1917
Organization.	
Food Conservation.	July 1–14, 1917
Why We Are Fighting.	July 23–Aug. 5, 1917
The Nation in Arms.	Aug. 6–26, 1917
The Importance of Speed.	Aug. 19–26, 1917
What Our Enemy Really Is.	Aug. 27–Sept. 23, 1917
Unmasking German Propaganda.	Aug. 27–Sept. 23, 1917 (supplementary topic)
Onward to Victory.	Sept. 24–Oct. 27, 1917
Second Liberty Loan.	Oct. 8–28, 1917
Food Pledge.	Oct. 29–Nov. 4, 1917
Maintaining Morals and Morale.	Nov. 12–25, 1917
Carrying the Message.	Nov. 26–Dec. 22, 1917
War Savings Stamps.	Jan. 2–19, 1918
The Shipbuilder.	Jan 28–Feb. 9, 1918

THE FOUR MINUTE MEN

Topic	Period
Eyes for the Navy	Feb. 11–16, 1918
The Danger to Democracy	Feb. 18–Mar. 10, 1918
Lincoln's Gettysburg Address	Feb. 12, 1918
The Income Tax	Mar. 11–16, 1918
Farm and Garden	Mar. 25–30, 1918
President Wilson's Letter to Theaters	Mar. 31–Apr. 5, 1918
Third Liberty Loan	Apr. 6–May 4, 1918
Organization	(Republished Apr. 23, 1918)
Second Red Cross Campaign	May 13–25, 1918
Danger to America	May 27–June 12, 1918
Second War Savings Campaign	June 24–28, 1918
The Meaning of America	June 29–July 27, 1918
Mobilizing America's Man Power	July 29–Aug. 17, 1918
Where Did You Get Your Facts?	Aug. 26–Sept. 7, 1918
Certificates to Theater Members	Sept. 9–14, 1918
Register	Sept. 5–12, 1918
Four Minute Singing	For general use
Fourth Liberty Loan	Sept. 28–Oct. 19, 1918
Food Program for 1919	Changed to Dec. 1–7; finally canceled
Fire Prevention	Oct. 27–Nov. 2, 1918
United War Work Campaign	Nov. 3–18, 1918
Red Cross Home Service	Dec. 7, 1918
What Have We Won?	Dec. 8–14, 1918
Red Cross Christmas Roll Call	Dec. 15–23, 1918
A Tribute to the Allies	Dec. 24, 1918

Almost from the first the organization had the projectile force of a French "75," and it was increasingly the case that government department heads turned to the Four Minute Men when they wished to arouse the nation swiftly and effectively. At a time when the Third Liberty Loan was lagging, President Wilson bought a fifty-dollar bond and challenged the men and women of the nation to "match" it. The Treasury Department asked the Committee to broadcast the message, and paid for the telegrams that went out to the state and county chairmen. Within a few days fifty thousand Four Minute Men were delivering the challenge to the people of every community in the United States, and the loan took a leap that carried it over the top. General Crowder followed the same plan in his registration campaign, putting up the money for the telegrams that went to the state and county chairmen, and, like Secretary McAdoo, he obtained the same swift service and instant results.

In June Mr. Ryerson left the Committee to take his commission in the navy. The soul of honor and loyalty and patriotism, and a dynamo of intelligent energy, the only thing that lessened the blow of his departure was that William McCormick Blair of Chicago, one of the originators of the idea, volunteered to build up a nation-wide organization. There was nothing easy about the task, for it demanded drudgery as well as vision, patience as well as drive, and high ability as well as patriotism. That Mr. Blair met these demands stands proved by the success of the Four Minute Men. No one ever saw him weary or discouraged, and his indomitable enthusiasm was at all times a source of inspiration to the Committee as a whole.

The first plan of an organization was the appointment of chairmen according to Federal Reserve districts, but this soon changed to organization by states, by counties, by cities, and even down to wards and townships. In every state the interest of the governor was enlisted, likewise the close co-operation of the State Council of Defense. Mr. Blair called to his side to serve on a National Advisory Council such men as William H. Ingersoll of "Ingersoll watch" fame, Prof. S. H. Clark of the University of Chicago, Samuel Hopkins Adams, the author, and "Mac" Martin of Minneapolis, and the work went forward until it reached from coast to coast. Philip L. Dodge volunteered to organize the New England States, Curtiss Nicholson went through the South, and Bertram G. Nelson, professor of public speaking at the University of Chicago, journeyed from city to city, gathering the Four Minute Men in each locality for instruction in the art of "putting talks across." These men, together with Mr. Gundlach and Mr. Thomas J. Meek, also served as associate directors.

The speakers in every case received their authority and appointment from the chairmen of the local branches of the organization, who, in turn, were appointed through the state chairman or direct from headquarters at Washington. Each local chairman was registered at once in Washington.

The original method of organizing a local branch was as follows: The written indorsement of three prominent citizens—bankers, professional or business men—written on their own stationery in a prescribed official form, was required for the nomination of a local chairman. These indorsements were forwarded to headquarters in Washington, together with the proper form of application for authority to form a local branch, with the privilege of representing the government, in which application the number of speakers available was stated, in order that material might be forwarded promptly in case the application was approved.

There was pathos as well as humor in many of the incidental happenings. Men of the most unlikely sort had the deep conviction that they were William J. Bryans, and when rejected by local organizations many of them traveled clear to Washington for the purpose of delivering a four-minute speech to *me* in order that I might see for myself the full extent of the injustice to which they had been subjected. Constant changes had to be made in the interests of improvement, and every elimination held its due portion of hurt. Through an effective system of inspection, Mr. Blair managed to keep in touch with each community, and the ax fell heavily whenever a speaker failed to hold his audiences, or injected the note of partizanship, or else proved himself lacking in restraint or good manners.

As the organization grew, there came increasing pressure to widen the scope of activities. Compelled to pinch pennies and harassed at all times by lack of adequate funds, we resisted expansion instead of encouraging it, but it was not long until the new demands "ran over us," as it were, giving us the choice between growth or disintegration. Even so, each new step was considered carefully, and subjected to every possible restraint and supervision.

National arrangements were made to have Four Minute Men appear at the meetings of lodges, fraternal organizations, and labor unions, and this work progressed swiftly. In most cases these speakers were selected from the membership of the organizations to whom they spoke.

Under the authority of state lecturers of granges, four-minute messages, based upon the official bulletins, were given also at all meetings of the granges in many states. The work was next extended to reach the lumber-camps of the country, some five hundred organizations being formed in such communities. Indian reservations were also taken in, and furnished some of the largest and most enthusiastic audiences.

The New York branch organized a church department to present four-minute speeches in churches, synagogues, and Sunday-schools. The idea spread from city to city, from state to state, and proved of particular value in rural communities. Some of the states, acting under authority from headquarters, organized women's divisions to bring the messages of the government to audiences at matinée performances in the motion-picture theaters, and to the members of women's clubs and other similar organizations.

College Four Minute Men were organized, under instructors acting as chairmen, to study the regular Four

Minute Men bulletins, and practise speaking upon the subjects thereof, each student being required to deliver at least one four-minute speech to the student body during the semester, in addition to securing satisfactory credits, in order to qualify as a Four Minute Man. This work was organized in 153 colleges.

At the request of the War Department, bulletins similar to those published for the use of the Four Minute Men were produced by national headquarters, to be used by company commanders in many cantonments throughout the country in preparing short talks to their men on the causes and issues of the war. The following campaigns of the kind were conducted to the complete satisfaction of the War Department, as expressed in its official report on the subject:

1. Why We Are Fighting.   January 2, 1918.
2. Insurance for Soldiers and Sailors.   February 1, 1918.
3. Back of the Trenches.   April 6, 1918.

As a matter of fact, we went far beyond the request and furnished hundreds of officers with the regular Four Minute Men bulletins as well as with the Committee's pamphlets. All were expected to make "morale talks" to their men, yet nothing was done to aid them, and the publications of the Committee were their one hope.

The Junior Four Minute Men was an expansion that proved to be almost as important as the original idea, for the youngsters of the country rallied with a whoop, and, what was more to the point, gave results as well as enthusiasm. Like so many other activities of the Committee, the Junior movement was more accidental than planned. At the request of the state of Minnesota the Washington office prepared a special War Savings Stamps bulletin. Results were so instant and remarkable that the idea had to be carried to other states, more than a million and a half copies of the bulletin being distributed to school-children during the campaign. Out of it all came the Junior Four Minute Men as a vital and integral part of the Committee on Public Information.

It was our cautious fear, at first, that regular school-work might be interrupted, but it soon developed that the idea had real educational value, helping teachers in their task instead of hindering. The general plan was for the teacher to explain the subject, using the bulletin as a text-book, and the children then wrote their speeches and submitted them to the teacher or principal. The best were selected and delivered as speeches or were read. In a few cases extemporaneous talks were given.

Details of the contests were left largely to the discretion of the teachers. In small schools there was generally one contest for the whole school. In schools of more than five or six classes it was usual to have separate contests for the higher and lower classes, and sometimes for each grade. There were many different ways of conducting these contests. Sometimes they were considered as a regular part of the school-work and were held in the class-room with no outsiders present, but more often they were made special events, the entire school, together with parents and other visitors, being present. Both boys and girls were eligible and the winners were given an official certificate from the government, commissioning them as four-minute speakers upon the specified topic of the contest.

Following the War Savings Stamps contest came the Third Liberty Loan contest of April 6 to May 4, 1917. A million copies of this bulletin were published and were sent directly to the schools from the stencils of the United States Bureau of Education in Washington. About two hundred thousand schools in all parts of the country were reached in this way. The same plan of distribution was used for the Junior Fourth Liberty Loan contest, and for the Junior Red Cross Christmas roll-call, and these two bulletins were published in connection with the School Service bulletin, which was then going out from the Committee twice monthly to all schools on this list.

Another innovation, forced by a general demand, was the addition of four-minute singing to the work. People seemed to want to exercise their voices in moments of patriotism, so a bulletin of specially selected songs was prepared and issued. The various chairmen appointed song-leaders, to take charge of motion-picture-theater audiences, and the venture was a success from the first.

In the summer of 1918 Mr. Blair resigned to enter an officers' training-camp, but again the Committee was fortunate in having a successor at hand. Mr. William H. Ingersoll, a member of the Advisory Council since 1917, put his own business to one side entirely, and poured the full flood of his splendid energy into the task laid down by Mr. Blair. To the three leaders—Ryerson, Blair, and Ingersoll—must go all credit for the remarkable record of accomplishment.

To summarize: Exact reports, covering approximately one-half of the full activities of the organization, give a total of 505,190 four-minute speeches made to audiences totaling 202,454,514 people. This total does not cover the six campaigns from October 27, 1918, to the closing date of December 24th, nor does it include the first campaigns from May 22 to October 27, 1917. At a very reasonable estimate, these first campaigns added 40,000,000 to the total audience reached and not less than 70,000 to the number of speeches delivered, while the final six campaigns added certainly not less than 72,000,000 to the total audience and 180,000 to the number of speeches. Adding these conservative estimates to the above incomplete reports, the following results are shown:

Number of speeches given.................... 755,190
Total audience......................... .. 314,454,514

A very reasonable allowance for the considerable number of communities from which incomplete or no reports were received justifies an estimate of final totals of a million speeches heard by 400,000,000 individuals during the eighteen months' life of the organization—an average of about 28,000 speeches, reaching more than 11,000,000 people, during each of the 36 distinct campaigns covered by the 46 bulletins.

And let it be borne in mind that these were no haphazard talks by nondescripts, but the careful, studied, and re-hearsed efforts of the *best* men in each community, each speech aimed as a rifle is aimed, and driving to its mark with the precision of a bullet. History should, and will, pay high tribute to the Four Minute Men, an organization unique in world annals, and as effective in the battle at home as was the onward rush of Pershing's heroes at St. Mihiel.

It was, and is to-day, our proud claim that no other war organization, with the exception of the Food Commission, paid such large returns on a small investment as the Com-mittee on Public Information. The policy of almost nig-gardly economy, forced upon us by the enmity of Congress, compelled us to beg running expenses from individuals, as well as the gift of time and specialized ability. Men and women, coming to us with their offers of volunteer effort, were not only drained of their energy, but were actually induced to go into their pockets for cash contributions to carry on the work. This was true of many divisions, but it was peculiarly true in the case of the Four Minute Men. Here, for instance, are the amounts expended from presi-dential and Congressional appropriations:

THE FOUR MINUTE MEN

	June, 1917–June, 1918	July–Dec., 1918	Totals
Salaries	$24,033 04	$18,711 96	$42,745 00
Printing	29,107 06	7,344 82	36,451 88
Slides	7,300 08	....	7,300 68
Traveling	4,942 09	1,000 00	5,942 09
General	5,856 90	3,258 55	9,115 45
Total	$71,239 77	$30,315 33	$101,555 10

What a showing! A national organization covering the country like a blanket with a maximum membership of 75,000, working day in and day out, and conducted for a year and a half at an expense of scarcely more than $100,-000. Each state director and each local chairman had to maintain his own office, as the Committee allowed nothing for such expenses. Each speaker gave not only his time, but had to foot his own bills, no matter what the amount. These contributions, figured below, have been recorded exactly wherever possible, and in other cases have been estimated very carefully from accurate data.

Actual expenses of state director's offices.......... $ 177,090
Expenses of local chairmen's offices; estimated at $10 monthly for the known average number of chairmen (4,422 averaged over the entire eighteen months' period)..................................... 795,960
Expenses of individual speakers, averaging ten speakers to the chairman and allowing for each speaker $2 monthly for all traveling and incidental expenses. 1,591,920

Total of contributed expenses........... ..... $2,564,970

Thus it may be seen that the established amounts expended from voluntary contributions were more than twenty-five times the expenditures from the official appropriations.

These figures, however, are only part of the story. It is, of course, impossible to set an adequate monetary valuation upon services contributed so generously and so patriotically as were those of all the Four Minute Men, the motion-picture theaters, newspapers, churches, granges, lodges, labor unions, and other agencies which furthered the work. It is possible, however, and eminently proper to put into some concrete and tangible form the material value of this work in relation to the actual cost thereof to the government.

It would not be reasonable to set a lower valuation than four dollars on the delivery of a four-minute speech, requiring the most painstaking and exact preparation and unusual skill in condensation and forcefulness of delivery.

Not with any suggestion of undervaluing the inestimable co-operation of the theaters and other places in which speeches were delivered, but rather with a view to the most thorough conservatism, we will estimate a "rental value" for the delivery of each speech at one half the speakers' rate.

In addition to the messages brought to the people by means of the spoken word, the Four Minute Men secured for the government publicity worth at least three-quarters of a million dollars. Articles containing the pith of each bulletin were sent out from headquarters and released through local chairmen and publicity managers in thousands of communities for use in the local papers.

The average number of press clippings received at headquarters from a single clipping bureau, covering only the larger newspapers of the country, was 873 a month, or more than 15,000 during the eighteen months' life of the organization. These clippings averaged certainly not less than 60 lines each, totaling 900,000 lines, which at a low rate for this type of publicity, if purchased, would have cost $225,000.

Hundreds of newspapers mailed to headquarters from the smaller towns indicate that much larger space was consistently devoted to the government message in these places, while during the ban on public meetings, due to the influenza epidemic, newspapers in all parts of the country devoted sufficient space to carry daily four-minute messages prepared for them by members of the organization. It is extremely conservative to estimate the total value of all this publicity at $750,000.

A summary of all these items gives the following figures:

Contributed expenditures......................	$2,564,970
One million speeches at $4 each..................	4,000,000
"Rent" of theaters, etc., to deliver above..........	2,000,000
Speeches (331) of traveling speakers..............	8,275
Publicity contributed by press...................	750,000
Grand total...............................	$9,313,245

All this on a government investment of $101,555.10.

No less an official than the President of the United States returned the thanks of the government to the Four Minute Men, and who shall say that the following tribute, impelled by sincere conviction, was not deserved:

THE WHITE HOUSE,
WASHINGTON, *November 29, 1918.*

To all the Four Minute Men of the Committee on Public Information:

I have read with real interest the report of your activities, and I wish to express my sincere appreciation of the value to the government of your effective and inspiring efforts. It is a remarkable record of patriotic accomplishment that an organization of 75,000 speakers should have carried on so extensive a work at a cost to the government of little more than $100,000 for the eighteen months' period—less than $1 yearly on an individual basis. Each member of your organization, in receiving honorable discharge from the service, may justly feel a glow of proper pride in the part that he has played in holding fast the inner lines. May I say that I, personally, have always taken the deepest and most sympathetic interest in your work, and have noted, from time to time, the excellent results you have procured for the various departments of the government. Now that this work has come to its conclusion and the name of the Four Minute Men (which I venture to hope will not be used henceforth by any similar organization) has become a part of the history of the Great War, I would not willingly omit my heartfelt testimony to its great value to the country, and indeed to civilization as a whole, during our period of national trial and triumph. I shall always keep in memory the patriotic co-operation and assistance accorded me throughout this period and shall remain deeply and sincerely grateful to all who, like yourselves, have aided so nobly in the achievement of our aims.

Cordially and sincerely yours,

WOODROW WILSON.

VIII

THE FIGHT FOR THE MIND OF MANKIND

DURING the Congressional hearing on our budget, which resolved itself into a searching inquiry into the work of the Committee, one of the Representatives asked if I did not think that the spectacle of American boys sailing for France was sufficient in itself to rouse the people of America. I answered that this very fact of departure for military service in a foreign land made it more imperative than ever that there should be a fundamental understanding of the causes of the war and of the absolute justice of America's position. A wave of national feeling might carry us into the war and national passions and hatred might whip us on, but froth and dregs would be the only ultimate result. Such methods might carry a mob a city block to tear something down, but they would not bear a self-determining democracy along the road of travail and uttermost sacrifice for great ideals. Could we count on a national understanding of such ideals? Could we be sure that a hundred million—the fathers, the mothers, the children of America, alien born and native alike—understood well enough so that they would support one loan after another, would bear new burdens of taxation and send wave after wave of America's young manhood to die in Flanders fields?

That the nation felt dimly that great issues were at stake was clear, but was it gripped by a conviction that those issues and their proper solutions were bound up with the permanent safety of America here and now and for-ever? It would have been blindness to assume such an understanding. Throughout our two and a half years of neutrality there had waged a daily battle of controversy, with press and public men alike divided. Some labored to range us at once on the side of the Allies, and another vigorous group, skilfully organized and cleverly directed, strenuously defended the Imperial German government. Public opinion was without shape and force. The country was in a state of mind in which it accepted the war and said, "The President has been patient; we are behind him; we are patriotic; and we fear a great danger." But the life-and-death character of the struggle was not under-stood. We felt that it had to be brought home to them as a matter of definite intellectual conviction. We wanted to reach the people through their minds, rather than through their emotions, for hate has its undesirable re-actions. We wanted to do it, not by over-emphasis of historical appeal, but by unanswerable arguments that would make every man and woman know that the war was a war of self-defense that had to be waged if free institu-tions were not to perish.

How? There was no precedent to guide us; the ground was unbroken. The various belligerents had issued White Books, Yellow Books, and Blue Books, made up almost entirely of state papers. The publication of diplomatic documents covering our relations with Germany seemed, therefore, the eminently respectable, safe, and accepted thing to do. With the co-operation of the State Depart-ment, we began the project, Arthur Bullard being assigned to the task of selecting the documents. The farther we went the more it seemed clear that we would be firing very heavy ammunition, with the chance of a large per-centage of such bulky volumes being "duds."

J. J. PETTIJOHN

GUY STANTON FORD

ARTHUR BESTOR

SAMUEL G. HARDING

THE FIGHT FOR THE MIND OF MANKIND

Big books were not what we wanted, and long, tedious state papers were not what we needed. Abruptly abandoning the original idea that dealt with archives and formal documents, we decided to go in for "popular pamphleteering." What faced us, therefore, was the problem of proceeding systematically with the work, of doing it with accuracy, with thorough scholarship, and with a full sense that what we put out would have the authority and responsibility of a government publication. Bullard was needed in the Foreign Section, so what we had to look for was a university man, the practised historian, the writer skilled in investigation, one who knew America and Europe equally well. It was at this moment that there came into my hands a pamphlet containing a patriotic address given out in Minnesota by one Guy Stanton Ford. I have rarely read anything that made a more instant impression, for it had beauty without sacrifice of force, simplicity, remarkable sequence, and obvious knowledge of every detail of America's spiritual progress. I made inquiries at once and found that Ford was head of the History Department of the University of Minnesota and Dean of the Graduate School, and before that a professor of Modern European History at the University of Illinois after five years as an instructor at Yale. I wired him that he was "drafted" and to report immediately. Here again the value of quick decision was proved, for I would have wasted months in search without finding any one so admirably fitted by temperament and training for the important position to which Professor Ford was called.

We were now prepared to initiate our first publication. Here we had a great advantage over similar organizations in England or other countries that had been drawn into the war. That advantage lay in the clear and moving address of President Wilson on April 2, 1917, before the Congress. A group of men at the University of Minnesota, headed by Prof. W. S. Davis of the Department of History, set to work under Dean Ford's direction on the annotation of that message, with the essential facts swept together in the broad compass of the President's eloquent presentation. The work was quickly and skilfully done and happily gaged for easy comprehension and thorough conviction. What should we do as to printing and distribution? We studied the newspaper directories and estimated that we could reach the press of the country with an edition of twenty thousand. Then we would see—and we did see. The press seized it and the consequent publicity overwhelmed us. The first day's mail was delivered to Professor Ford and his one clerk in a peach-basket. The next day there were two bushels of letters asking for copies. They came from all ranks and kinds of people; from boys going to the Officers' Reserve Training Camps, from fathers and mothers whose sons were going into service from farms and shops, banks and schools. One city superintendent wired for fifteen thousand so that it might go into every home in a community largely of foreign-born. As long as the war lasted the demand for the annotated war address of the President kept steadily up and the final figures at the end of our work were two and a half millions of this pamphlet alone.

When, with the aid of the Government Printing Office, we had dug ourselves out of this rush, we turned at once to the masterly introduction that Arthur Bullard had written to the proposed White Book. It was just the exposition of America's cause that was needed. It dealt with the two great American traditions, the Monroe Doctrine and the Freedom of the Seas. It explained the American effort to substitute arbitration for bloodshed; it followed the purposes and hopes of our neutrality from beginning to end, analyzed every note in the diplomatic exchange that marked our effort to keep the peace, and chronicled faithfully the bad faith of the Imperial German government, its intrigue in the United States, the course of the submarine warfare—in fact, it was a simple, straightforward story based upon the facts and ideals of America.

In authoritative judgment it stands to-day as the most moderate, reasoned, and permanent pamphlet put out by any government engaged in the war. And the way it was prepared was a cheering demonstration of citizens of a democracy doing its own defending and defining of its ideals. Bullard had the laboring oar, and the body of this anonymous pamphlet bears the imprint of his facile pen and clear brain. Sisson and Ford and I reviewed it after Ernest Poole had cast it into a popular form. Professors Shotwell of Columbia and Becker of Cornell, who were in Washington on the National Board for Historical Service, shaped up certain points more sharply and judiciously. Then Secretary Lansing and, ultimately, President Wilson himself went over it and approved. It went forth under the title, *How the War Came to America*, the first of a proud series—the Red, White, and Blue books. We printed fifty thousand, but this time we were better prepared for the public demand that ultimately carried the circulation to six and a quarter millions in English and in translations. Some of the great dailies issued it as a Sunday supplement, and others in every part of the country ran it serially. It was one pamphlet we could never let go out of print.

With these two pamphlets fairly swamping the Government Printing Office, we felt more clearly than ever that we were right in judging the need of the country for information clearly put with a sound scholarship behind every statement. Three series of pamphlets were ultimately decided on—the Red, White, and Blue books, the War Information series, and the Loyalty leaflets. It was further decided that we would develop our own machinery for printing and distribution, as the Government Printing Office was overburdened and unable to keep pace with our demands. Our own frank and envelopes were more certain of securing attention than the too familiar Congressional frank, which many members willingly put at our disposal.

I can only indicate the method pursued in issuing the several series. When the pamphlet was decided upon in conferences, the next question was the proper man, or men, to handle its preparation, and these men were then telegraphed a request to come to Washington. In no instance was there a refusal to serve, and not only is it my privilege to pay a high tribute to the devotion of individuals, but also to the patriotism of the universities, who loaned members of their faculties generously and wholeheartedly. The writers were given only one simple direction, and that was to do their work so that they would not be ashamed of it twenty years later. When the pamphlet was finished it was submitted to a general examination and then referred to the various divisions of government for checking, and it is my pride to be able to say that in all the mass of matter issued by Professor Ford's division, dealing with thousands of facts, only one public charge of misstatement was ever voiced and this was followed by an apology.

In the various series we set before ourselves three main aims: The first was to make America's own purposes and ideals clear both to ourselves and to the world, whether ally or enemy. The sane execution of this purpose, involving a presentation of what this great experiment in democracy meant to its own people and to all forward-looking peoples, had greater implications than the war needs of the moment. Through war the menace of autocracy made us conscious that here in the Western World we were following ideals that made us one with other great peoples and that separated us from the four in Middle Europe by a wide gulf. What we had accepted as unchallenged had to be redefined as well for the Brahmin of the Back Bay as for the Bolshevist of the Ghetto. When I think of the many voices that were heard before the war and are still heard, interpreting America from a class or sectional or selfish standpoint, I am not sure that, if the war had to come, it did not come at the right time for the preservation and reinterpretation of American ideals. A few years earlier would have found us still too absorbed in the problems of a frontier nation, too provincial to have responded unitedly to the world's cry of distress, too confident that the Atlantic was a barrier and not a hand. A decade or two later it might have found us unconsciously stratified in our own social organization and thinking, the prison-walks of class consciousness shutting out the visions of our nation's youth, with something too much gone of that abounding faith in ourselves and our institutions that had been our heritage from the eighteenth century, preserved by the pioneers and nation-builders of the fading Western frontiers.

Coming when it did, it found us ready to respond with the self-abandon of youth to great visions, and to direct our policies and weigh our actions with the ripened wisdom of maturity. President Wilson and his ultimate place in American history may now be a subject of debate, but there is one service that rises above the issues of war and partizanship, and that is that, in this transition period, of which the war made us conscious, he spoke the language of the New American instinct with the spirit of all our past history and traditions.

In this first series on our aims and purposes may be listed, *How the War Came to America, The Battle Line of Democracy, War Labor and Peace, Some Recent Addresses of the President*, all in the Red, White, and Blue series. In the War Information series, the *War Message and Facts Behind It, The Nation in Arms* (two addresses by Secretaries Lane and Baker); *The Great War: From Spectator to Participant*, by Prof. A. C. McLaughlin of Chicago; *American Loyalty by American Citizens of German Descent*, *Lieber and Schurz*, and *American Interest in Popular Government Abroad*, both by Prof. Evarts B. Greene of the University of Illinois; *American and Allied Ideals*, by Prof. Stuart P. Sherman of the University of Illinois; *The War for Peace*, compiled by Arthur D. Coll, secretary of the American Peace Society; and *America's War Aims and Peace Terms*, by Prof. Carl Becker of Cornell University. In the Loyalty leaflets could be counted Judge Buffington's *Friendly Words to Foreign Born; Labor and the War*, by Prof. John R. Commons of Wisconsin; and *Plain Issues of the War*, by Elihu Root.

Almost equally important from the standpoint of the unremitting prosecution of the war to a decisive finish was a thorough presentation of the aims, methods, and ideals of the dynastic and feudal government of Germany. Upon no pamphlets did we lavish so much care and scholarship as this series, and the pamphlets, as a group, proceeded logically and remorselessly to tear the mask of civilization and modernity from the medievally minded, medievally organized Prussian militaristic state that was dominating Germany and Central Europe and threatening the world. Disregarding the order of publication, which was by no means accidental, this group was divided as follows: In the Red, White, and Blue series, *The President's Flag Day Address with Evidence of German Plans* and *Conquest and Kultur*, both prepared by Profs. Wallace Notestein and E. E. Stoll of the University of Minnesota; *German War Practices* and *German Treatment of Conquered Territory*, both by Profs. D. C. Munroe of Princeton, G. C. Sellery of Wisconsin, and A. C. Krey of Minnesota; *German Plots and Intrigues*, by Profs. E. C. Sperry of Syracuse and W. M. West, the historian. In the War In-

THE FIGHT FOR THE MIND OF MANKIND

formation series, *The German Government of Germany*, by Prof. C. D. Hazen of Columbia; *The War of Self-defense*, by Secretaries Lansing and Louis F. Post; *The German War Code*, by G. W. Scott (formerly of Columbia) and Prof. J. W. Garner of Illinois; *German Militarism*, by Charles Altschul; *Why America Fights Germany*, by Prof. J. P. Tatlock of Leland Stanford University; and *The German Bolshevik Conspiracy*, by Edgar Sisson, our representative in Russia. In the Loyalty leaflets, *The Prussian System*, by Frederic C. Walcott of the Food Administration, was an admirable thumb-nail sketch in this series.

Taken together, these pamphlets make the most sober and terrific indictment ever drawn by one government of the political and military system of another government. It was a serious business to draw it; it was a highly important thing not only that it should sway the opinion of the moment, but that it should stand in the court of all time. To tamper with the opinion of an essentially fair-minded nation in any crisis is the ready device of charlatans and demagogues, and neither they nor their works have ever survived that moment when Truth dispels the mists of momentary and misguided passion. Fortunately, the Germans had made their own record, and from that there was and can be no appeal. We could and did give them their own day in court; let them reveal their own purposes, describe their own methods, glorify their own guilt, and it is their rulers and leaders that have been swept into oblivion.

When I recall the mad swirl of the Washington days, the pressure we were under to do this or to do that, to publish or republish this address or that pamphlet, to indorse some movement or idea, I am cheerful and a bit amazed at our success in avoiding pitfalls. For this we may never receive credit, least of all from the perfervid patriots who would have smeared with blood every page we published, or disfigured it by the distorted fancy they were willing to accept for fact. Insistent people who know how to save the country always throng to Washington even in peace-times, and in war-times we sometimes had to stand on tiptoe to see over their heads the great, grim, honest, unselfish nation behind them. And it was to the heart and mind of that nation that we directed our appeals—and their response was our reward.

The third group of pamphlets has as a purpose the giving in convenient form of information which would help in a constructive way in the daily tasks of a nation at war. *The National Service Handbook*, edited by Dr. J. J. Coss and James Gutmann of Columbia University, published in the summer of 1917, was just such a compendium about war-work and war organizations and served as a helpful guide to the thousands who could not enter the ranks and yet wanted to serve in some capacity, no matter how humble. *The War Cyclopedia*, published afterward, not only brought such information up to date, but made available, in compact form, all the information on war topics and policies that any speaker or writer might want at hand. Professors Paxson of Wisconsin, Corwin of Princeton, and Harding of Indiana, with the aid of scores of scholars throughout the land, did a permanently worth-while piece of work under great stress for time and space. Together with the syllabus, we published *The Study of the Great War*, by Professor Harding, which became a text-book in schools, colleges, and cantonments. Our last pamphlet, in distribution when the armistice came, had moved us forward into new ground by summarizing our peace terms and the chief expressions of American and Allied statesmen on the League of Nations. Our one disappointment was that the second edition of *The War Cyclopedia*, then in the press, never appeared. Perhaps an explanation of delay is due to individuals and organizations, particularly to the several hundred colleges that planned to use it as a text-book for the Student Army Training Corps. From July 1, 1918, we carried forward our domestic work on a limited Congressional appropriation. Foreseeing difficulties, we had asked that receipts from those publications on which a nominal cost price had been set might come into our receipts for further use and later accounting. The usual precedents had been followed, however, and all receipts, except from the film division, went into the Treasury, and nothing but another Act of Congress could make them available to our use. The net result was that the more successful we were, and the greater the demand for our publications, even though we charged for some, the more quickly we exhausted our fixed appropriation and brought our activities to an end.

Each pamphlet has its own story from the first suggestion through its execution by the best qualified scholar. For many of them I must refer to the plain but significant table in the appendix, and simply renew an expression of my own personal sense of obligation to Guy Stanton Ford and the distinguished leaders of thought who served with him. The figures will tell something of their usefulness, but not all. These pamphlets became an arsenal from which speakers and newspapers drew whole batteries of speeches and editorials and special articles. They helped fill out many pages of privately published patriotic collections and have even found their place in widely used text-books in history and civics. Many a good and misinformed citizen, who had an unformed but vivid impression that the "Creel Committee" was some iniquity of the devil, took with his breakfast a daily diet of our material from the same journal that had given him this impression, met us again at lunch when his children came home with what the teacher had given them from material we prepared, heard us again through *our* Four Minute Men organization when he went to the "movies," where our films might be part of the program, and rose to local prominence by the speeches he drew from the pamphlets of that *other* useful organization, the Committee on Public Information. Like the truant boy who ran away from the schoolmaster, Hugh Toil, he found us, recognized and unrecognized, at every turn of the road.

This material went out almost exclusively by request, either from individuals or responsible organizations, such as defense councils or the Loyalty Legion in Wisconsin. Even Congressmen, after the first few months, were furnished not with the pamphlets, but with return postal-cards on which was printed a list of our publications, any two of which could be checked as desired by his constituents. This arrangement was a means of conserving our limited resources and gave us a distribution to real readers.

In only one case did we vary from this program of distribution, and that was when we put in the hands of the trusty Boy Scouts several million copies of the President's Flag Day address with annotations on the German plans. The boys delivered it directly to householders and were to secure their promise to read it and pass it on. The boys did their work faithfully, but reported that they partly failed because they could not get the promise to pass on the pamphlet to some other reader!

The States Section of the National Defense Council was especially active in bringing our material to the attention of state and county defense organizations. Newspapers in all parts of the country willingly carried descriptive lists without charge, and the information syndicate headed by Frederick Haskins in Washington gave us publicity on the front page of many great dailies.

Even more important, in the early days when Professor Ford was first preparing pamphlets, was the support and aid given by the National Board for Historical Service,

through which the historians of the country organized perhaps more effectively than any similar group of scholars.
It was of great value to this division throughout the war
to have available the judgment and ripe scholarship of
men like Shotwell of Columbia, Greene of Illinois, Jameson
of *The American Historical Review*, Munro of Princeton,
Leland, secretary of the American Historical Association,
A. C. Coolidge and F. J. Turner of Harvard, Schafer of
Oregon, Johnson of Teachers College, Lingelbach of Pennsylvania, Hull of Cornell, Dodd of Chicago, Fish of Wisconsin, Hunt of the Library of Congress, Hazen of Columbia, Connor of North Carolina, Victor Clark of the
Carnegie Institution, Notestein of Minnesota, and S. B.
Harding of Indiana. The last named joined our staff in November, 1917, and remained throughout the war as an
able assistant to Professor Ford in all the multitudinous
work of checking and editing the pamphlets.

Our efforts were supported and supplemented by so
many organizations that it is difficult to single out many.
Excellent series of pamphlets were put out by the universities of Chicago, Wisconsin, North Carolina, Illinois, and
Columbia. Publishing-houses gave precedence to patriotic
books without thought of profit and offered us all their
material at the cost of printing.

Our last and perhaps our most unique and effective publication was *The National School Service*, a sixteen-page
semi-monthly periodical going free of charge to every
public-school teacher in the United States—about 600,-
000 in all. We foresaw a time when, perhaps, if the
war with its burdens and losses continued, the national
morale would need the support of a message that went
without fail into every home. For this purpose there was
no other agency so effective, so sure, as the public schools
with their twenty millions of pupils. Furthermore, so many
governmental and national organizations were flooding the

schools, as they had flooded the press, with their material that there was danger of confusion, conflict, and ineffectiveness. Could not the story of the war, of America's effort and ideals, of the work of the Red Cross, the Food Administration, the Liberty Loan, the War Savings Stamps, Public Health, School Gardens, and a score of other activities be brought together as a national unified program and treated in a way that would make it presentable in the schoolroom and effective in the homes? It was worth the effort, cost what it might in time and money. With the support of the National Educational Association, we engaged the co-operation of all the departments in Washington and launched the first publication in which the national government of the United States had ever attempted to reach every public school and home in the land. W. C. Bagley of Teachers College was enlisted as editor-in-chief, and J. W. Searson of Kansas Agricultural College as managing editor, and a staff of specialists prepared all the material so that it could be presented effectively in every kind of school from the primary to the high-school. Special editions were arranged for the Red Cross, War Savings, etc. Junior Four Minute Men contests were organized and supported with material through special supplements prepared by the staff and the Division of Four Minute Men. I shall always treasure the memory of the gratitude with which the underpaid and overworked school-teachers received National School Service; most of all, the letters that came from isolated rural teachers in out-of-the-way valleys and on the far reaches of the prairies. The national government had reached out and placed a hand on their shoulder to encourage them and to ask for their aid and support. They saw a new vision and a new, vitalizing mission. At the end, we were moved by the protests against discontinuing National School Service to present the matter to the

President, who promptly made available enough funds to continue it to the end of the year under the Department of the Interior with the same efficient staff of editors.

A number of the principal pamphlets were put into other languages—German, Italian, the Scandinavian tongues, Spanish, Portuguese, Bohemian, Polish, Yiddish, etc.— and given careful distribution through the clubs and churches of the foreign-language groups in America, while the translations themselves were sent to the various countries to be printed on daily presses and circulated by our representatives.

It is perfectly evident that we had to exercise care in making these translations, especially the German versions. We had in mind here not only our German-reading public, but the Germans of the Empire. We hoped to make them our readers if not in war-times, at least ultimately, when they might really seek to understand the voice of a world that had united against them. No awkward phrase or American colloquial German could be allowed to excite ridicule and rob our case of its full effect. A waif of the war, a distinguished German scholar, who had lived long in England before coming to America, did the work, and did it so well that his translation of *How the War Came to America*, and of the President's addresses, was adopted by some schools as substitutes for the sycophantic texts about modern Germany and its Hohenzollern readers. This man was a technical "enemy alien," but if any one doubts his spiritual kinship with the ideals of America and the Allies, they should read his own tragic story under the title, "A Man Without a Country," in *The Ladies' Home Journal* for September, 1917.

Besides these translations, special material was published for the foreign-language groups. In selecting this material we had the benefit of advice from our representatives abroad and our connection with the leaders of the patriotic groups of the foreign-born in the United States. While sternly revealing the methods and principles of Germany, we emphasized again the ideals of America, of the America that had drawn the foreigners to its shores, and that was the home of their children, for we knew that, whatever their own transplanted prejudices, the great mass of the foreign-born, like the native Americans, were loyal to the land of their children. An unwise use of the discretion granted us in presenting America's cause might easily have helped hammer these foreign groups into permanently aggrieved and hostile elements.

All in all, more than seventy-five million copies of these pamphlets went into American homes, each one a printed bullet that found its mark. This does not include the circulation given by the metropolitan dailies that printed many of the pamphlets in full. Nor does it take account of the hundreds of thousands of copies printed by state organizations such as the Department of Education in Michigan, or by private individuals at their own cost.

It is a matter of pride to the Committee on Public Information, as it should be to America, that the directors of English, French, and Italian propaganda were a unit in agreeing that our literature was remarkable above all others for its brilliant and concentrated effectiveness.

All this labor of preparation, publication, and distribution was heavy and exacting, but there is a gleam or two when I view it in retrospect. I thought at one time that we were in direct touch with all the people who knew how to win the war. The White House and the War Department may dispute this, but certainly all who thought the Germans could be overwhelmed with printer's ink or oratory landed on our door-step either in person or through the intermediacy of the postmen. What we did not get directly we got by reference from every other war agency in Washington. We had considerable faith in the power of the press, but it was all quite overtopped by the old German-American who pleaded with us to send him up to the front-line trenches accompanied by one man who could run a hand-press. Then there was the considerable number who felt sure that some poem or song or sermon —not infrequently of their own composition—would, if printed and distributed to the whole nation, set the people on fire with patriotic ardor.

Such material came in almost predictable waves, two weeks of poetry, then two weeks of sermons. If a vigorous article—especially one with a large element of imagination about a German invasion—appeared in some journal of wide circulation, we knew we would receive it, clipped and sent in from all quarters as the best possible thing to which we could give government sanction. Some of the more discriminating suggestions were helpful. Some of the material submitted was too valuable to lose and we sought always to direct the writer toward an effective avenue of publicity. We sought invariably to return the manuscript with a courteous acknowledgment, for we knew it came from people who really wanted to help—"to do their bit," was the phrase penned so often by hands that could never hope to handle a musket. I remember one woman who sent in a poem with a letter in which she told how two of her sons were in the army and she, at seventy, was earning her living by washing. Still, she wanted "to do her bit" and had written this poem. You may be sure that she had a special letter that convinced her we sometimes appreciated poetry by other standards than those of the Browning circle.

All these letters were of immense value to us, for they kept our hand on the pulse of the land, letting us know the tides of hope and earnest purpose that were surging through a great country. Often enough there was evidence of the rapid spread of idle or vicious rumors or of the baneful influence of some utterance of a picayune politician with a statesman's responsibilities, but this was a momentary phase or a purely surface matter, and the great mass of the nation responded over and over again to every appeal to their sturdy and enlightened patriotism.

I know the distressing illiteracy revealed by the draft and I am disturbed by all the inadequacies of the public-school system with its low salaries and immature and ever-changing teaching corps, but I also know that the press or politician who appeals to ignorance and prejudice is not reckoning on the reading and thinking and dominant mass of the American people. Great issues clearly put will always arouse them and there is no need to talk in words of one syllable to the man in the street. He wants the truth and will read to get it far more closely than many a man whom fortune has favored by putting him in a swivel-chair behind a glass-topped desk. I *know*, for we tried it out on a nation-wide scale, and that is why the publications of Professor Ford's division will remain a worthy evidence of the Committee's work in war education.

IX

"PERSHING'S CRUSADERS," "America's Answer," and "Under Four Flags" are feature films that will live long in the memory of the world, for they reached every country, and were not only the last word in photographic art, but epitomized in thrilling, dramatic sequence the war effort of America. Yet these pictures, important as they were, represented only a small portion of the work of the Division of Films, a work that played a vital part in the world-fight for public opinion. A steady output, ranging from one-reel subjects to seven-reel features, and covering every detail of American life, endeavor, and purpose, carried the call of the country to every community in the land, and then, captioned in all the various languages, went over the seas to inform and enthuse the peoples of Allied and neutral nations.

At the very outset, it was obvious that the motion picture had to be placed on the same plane of importance as the written and spoken word. There were, however, many obstacles in the way that prevented straightforward, driving action. In the first place, it was our original hope that we could put our reliance upon commercial producers, thus saving the time and expense that necessarily attended the creation of new machinery. This theory had to be abandoned, for the War Department issued a flat ruling that only the photographers in actual service would be permitted to take pictures of any kind either on the firing-

9

line in France or in the cantonments and other branches of the military establishment in the United States. Aside from the unwisdom of allowing individuals in private employ to have free run of aviation-fields and munition-factories, there was also the physical impossibility of handling the army of individual photographers that equitable representation would have demanded.

Going into the matter fully, we discovered that there was to be a photographic section of the Signal Corps, with first purpose to serve the fighting force and a second purpose to make pictures for the historical record desired by the War College. The Committee then went to the Secretary of War with representations as to the publicity value of much of the material that would be gathered. It was pointed out that since protection of military secrets barred private photographers, it was both wise and proper that we should have the right to go through the Signal Corps photographs, selecting such as were suitable for public exhibition. The contention was granted by Secretary Baker, and the Committee on Public Information was recognized by the War Department as the one authorized medium for the distribution of Signal Corps photographs, still pictures as well as "movies."

All of which seemed encouraging enough until investigation developed the sad news that the Photographic Section of the Signal Corps was a hope rather than a fact. Looking after film matters for the Committee at the time were Kendall Banning, formerly editor of *System*, and Mr. Lawrence E. Rubel, a young Chicago business man, both of the temperament that found inaction intolerable. The two made a survey of the photographers of the United States, motion and still, and urged selections upon the Signal Corps until an adequate force had been assembled for duty at home and abroad. Mr. Banning accepted a commission as major in the army, and as the distribution

F. DeSales Casey

Charles S. Hart

Charles Dana Gibson

L. E. Rubel

of still pictures occupied Mr. Rubel's full time, the motion-picture end was turned over to Mr. Louis B. Mack, a Chicago lawyer, and Mr. Walter Niebuhr, both volunteers. The routine, as finally worked out, was as follows: The negatives of still and motion pictures taken in France and in the United States by the uniformed photographers of the Signal Corps were delivered, undeveloped, to the Chief of Staff for transmission to the War College division. The material was "combed" and such part as was decided to be proper for public exhibition was then turned over to the Committee on Public Information in the form of duplicate negatives. The Committee, out of its own funds, made prints from these negatives.

Our first hope was to avoid all appearance of competition with the commercial producers, and as a consequence the bulk of material was distributed fairly and at a nominal price among the film-news weeklies. Experts were then engaged to put the remainder into feature form, and these pictures were handed over to the State Councils of Defense and to the various patriotic societies. They were not shown in motion-picture theaters, nor was admission charged except in the case of benefits for a particular purpose. Among the early features thus produced were:

The 1917 Recruit, 2 editions (training of the National Army).
The Second Liberty Loan.
Ready for the Fight (Artillery and Cavalry maneuvers).
Soldiers of the Sea (Marine Corps in training).
Torpedo-boat Destroyers (naval maneuvers).
Submarines.
Army and Navy Sports.
The Spirit of 1917 (the largest maneuver staged in America; an attack by the Jackies at Lake Bluff upon Fort Sheridan, Illinois).
In a Southern Camp (general army maneuvers).
The Lumber Jack (showing the growth of the Lumber Jack Regiment for reconstruction work in Europe).

The Medical Officers' Reserve Corps in Action (showing the development of the Medical Corps and training).

Fire and Gas (showing maneuvers of the new Thirtieth Engineer Regiment).

American Ambulances (complete display of ambulance work).

Labor's Part in Democracy's War (labor-union activities in the war).

Annapolis (naval officers in the making).

Shipbuilding (construction of all types of ships).

Making of Big Guns.

Making of Small Arms.

Making of Uniforms for the Soldiers.

Activities of the Engineers.

Woman's Part in the War.

The Conquest of the Air (airplane and balloon maneuvers)

As time went on, however, it was seen that this method of distribution not only put an unnecessary burden of expense upon the government, but that it was failing absolutely to place the pictorial record of America's war progress before more than a small percentage of the motion-picture audiences of the world. The growth of the Signal Corps's great Photographic Section was producing an enormous amount of material, both in the United States and France, possessed of the very highest propaganda value, and the existing arrangement wasted what it did not fritter away. Mr. Charles S. Hart, about to take a commission in the army, was persuaded to assume full charge of the work of reorganization, and too much credit cannot be given him for his accomplishment. He took an idea and a policy, and with courage, imagination, and driving genius he evolved a world machinery and built a business that handled millions, all without a single breakdown at any point.

One of Mr. Hart's first determinations was to take the cream of the material received from the Signal Corps, put it into great seven-reel features designed to set before the people a comprehensive record of war progress both in the United States and in France, and to *have the government itself present the pictures*. In plain, the Committee on Public Information went into the motion-picture business as a producer and exhibitor. The funds received from these sources were not to represent profit in any sense of the word. Every cent was to go to the manufacture and distribution of the huge amount of film that we were compelled to distribute without return in other countries as part of the educational campaign of the United States. Wherever possible this foreign distribution was made through the regular commercial channels, but there were various nations where these channels did not exist and where free showings were a necessity. It was also the case that we were put to heavy expense by the policy that sent all of the Committee's films, free of charge, to the encampments in the United States as well as to the picture-shows on the firing-line in France. The other belligerent countries all marketed their film. Why, then, was it not proper for the United States to use its own product in an effort to lighten the taxpayers' load, especially when commercial distribution meant 100 per cent. exhibition?

Our first feature-film was "Pershing's Crusaders," and at intervals of six weeks we produced "America's Answer" and "Under Four Flags." The policy decided upon was this: first, direct exhibition of the feature by the Committee itself in the larger cities in order to establish value and create demand; second, sale, lease, or rental of the feature to the local exhibitors. This activity was placed in the hands of Mr. George Bowles, an experienced theatrical and motion-picture manager, who had made a name for himself in exploiting "The Birth of a Nation." Mr. Bowles operated as many as eight road companies in different sections of the country at one time, each with its own advertising, advance sales, and business management.

The utmost care was taken with these "official showings," for what we sought was an impressiveness that would lift them out of the class of ordinary motion-picture productions in the minds of the public. L. S. Rothapfel, of the Rialto and Rivoli theaters in New York City, gave us his own aid and that of his experts in the matter of scenic accessories, orchestra, and incidental music, while for "America's Answer" Frank C. Yohn painted a great canvas, so much a thing of beauty and inspiration that it thrilled audiences into enthusiasm for the motion pictures that followed.

"Pershing's Crusaders" was officially presented in twenty-four cities, "America's Answer" in thirty-four, and "Under Four Flags" in nine. Each of these so-called official showings extended over the period of a week or more and was presented at municipal halls, well-known legitimate or motion-picture theaters centrally located in the respective cities. Wide and intensive publicity and advertising campaigns were conducted by representatives on the spot by means of department-store window and hotel-lobby displays, street-car cards, and banners and newspaper space donated by local advertisers, etc. This campaign, under the direction of Mr. Marcus A. Beeman, also included circularization and personal interviews with representatives, officials, and leading citizens, clubs, societies, and organizations, including large industrial plants and firms. Churches, schools, chambers of commerce, political and social clubs, Young Men's Christian Association, Red Cross, Liberty Loan, and fraternal organizations were among those included in the lists.

Taking, for example, the official presentations in New York City—"Pershing's Crusaders" was shown at the Lyric Theater; "America's Answer" was shown at the George M. Cohan Theater; "Under Four Flags" was shown simultaneously at the Rivoli and Rialto theaters on

Broadway. Each of these showings was preceded by a press campaign of about two weeks, several hundred twenty-four-sheet, three-sheet, and one-sheet posters were posted, and thousands of window-cards were displayed, invitations were sent to all local dignitaries, and the showings were attended by representatives of the French, British, and Italian High Commissions. In Washington, members of Congress, the President, his Cabinet, and many other officials attended, all of which facts were used extensively in advertising the features for general distribution.

As features did not consume the whole of the Signal Corps material by any means, we decided upon weekly releases, and in order to give this the highest interest as well as to emphasize the fact of partnership, we entered into co-operative arrangements with the representatives of England, France, and Italy. Each of the four nations contributed a fourth of the material and shared in the profits, and the joint product went forth as the Allied War Review.

Not one of the other governments, it may be explained, made free gifts of its pictures to private enterprise, but handled them upon commercial lines entirely, for in the motion-picture world revenue and circulation are synonymous. It was the first contention of the representatives of the English, French, and Italians that the War Review should be offered to the highest bidder, but the Committee on Public Information insisted that the four film-news weeklies of the United States should be given prior consideration. As a consequence, these four companies—the Hearst-Pathé, the Universal, the Mutual, and the Gaumont—were offered a weekly release of 2,000 feet of firing-line film at a flat rate of $5,000. The representatives of the Allied governments felt that this price robbed them of fair and demonstrated profits, but the Committee on Public Information gained its point through insistence.

At that period in the negotiations when the largest of

the weeklies had accepted the contract, one company addressed a series of letters to various officials of the government, complaining bitterly of the arrangement, not only insisting that the films should be given free of charge, but even hinting at a subsidy. As a consequence of this attitude, the Official War Review was offered to the motion-picture industry as a whole, as was the case with the feature-film. Every exchange was given an opportunity to bid, and the Pathé Exchange, Inc., was awarded the contract on these terms: Eighty per cent. of proceeds and a guaranty of showing in 25,000 theaters as a minimum.

Even after the making of the feature-films and the Official War Review there remained a certain amount of material that had as high publicity value as any of the other footage, and we placed this at the disposal of the news weeklies at the nominal cost of one dollar a foot, an equitable arrangement that worked.

With the tremendous advertising gained from these governmental showings in the principal cities we were then able to go direct to the exhibitor in the certainty of his keen interest. Our aim was to secure the widest possible distribution of the government films in the shortest possible time. To this end every effort was made to eliminate the competitive idea from the minds of exhibitors, and wherever possible to secure simultaneous showings in houses which ordinarily competed for pictures.

Mr. Denis Sullivan and his assistant, Mr. George Meeker, who were in charge of domestic distribution through motion-picture houses, inaugurated a proportionate selling plan whereby the rental charged every house was based on the average income derived from that particular house. By this method the small house as well as the large one could afford to run the government films. The result of these efforts to obtain the widest possible showing for government films was amazingly successful, and the showing of

"America's Answer" broke all records for range of distribution of any feature of any description ever marketed.

On the basis of twelve thousand motion-picture theaters in the United States, over one-half the total number of theaters in the country exhibited the Official War Review and nearly that portion of "America's Answer." In the film industry a booking of 40 per cent. of the theaters is considered as 100 per cent. distribution because of the close proximity of a great number of theaters, rendering them dependent on the same patronage—that is, theaters are plotted as available in zones rather than as individual theaters; thus three theaters in one zone present but one possible booking because of the identity of clientèle. Taking this into consideration, the distribution of government features approximated 80 per cent. and 90 per cent. rather than 50 per cent. distribution, although on "America's Answer," in certain territories such as New York and Seattle, the percentage of total theaters booked reached over 60 per cent. and 54 per cent., respectively, which on the above basis would equal 100 per cent. distribution.

The success of the feature-films and the Official War Review are best indicated by the following figures:

"Pershing's Crusaders"	$181,741 69
"America's Answer"	185,144 30
"Under Four Flags"	63,946 48
Official War Review	334,622 35
Our Bridge of Ships	992 41
U. S. A. Series	13,864 98
Our Colored Fighters	640 60
News Weekly	15,150 00
Miscellaneous sales	56,641 58
Total sales from films	$852,744 30

It was not only the case that the entire output of the Division of Films was handed over to the Foreign Section for circulation in the various countries of the world, but the Educational Department saw to it that all of the Committee pictures were furnished free of charge to every proper organization in the United States.

The films were loaned to army and navy stations, educational and patriotic institutions, without charge except transportation. Other organizations and individuals were usually charged one dollar per reel for each day used. When it is considered that the average reel costs forty dollars for raw stock and printing, and that the average life of a reel is about two hundred runs, it can be readily seen that this charge of one dollar per reel barely covered cost. For the purpose of comparison the leading motion-picture houses in New York pay as high as three thousand dollars for the use of one picture for one week's run.

On June 1, 1918, the Division of Films formed a scenario department to experiment with an interesting theory. The departments at Washington had been in the habit of contracting for the production of films on propaganda subjects and then making additional contracts to secure a more or less limited circulation of the pictures when produced. The general attitude of motion-picture exhibitors was that propaganda pictures were uninteresting to audiences and could have no regular place in their theaters. The theory of the Division of Films was that the fault lay in the fact that propaganda pictures had never been properly made, and that if skill and care were employed in the preparation of the scenarios the resultant pictures could secure place in regular motion-picture programs. Producers were at first skeptical, but in the end they agreed to undertake the production of one-reel pictures for which the division was to supply the scenario, the list of locations, and permits for filming the same, and to give every possible co-operation, all without charge. The finished picture became the sole property of the producer, who obligated himself merely to give it the widest possible circulation after it had been approved by the Division of Films. Mr. Rufus Steele was given charge of the new venture, and while many difficulties had to be overcome, the theory proved sound.

The following one-reel pictures were produced:

By the Paramount-Bray Pictograph:
  Says Uncle Sam: Keep 'Em Singing and Nothing Can Lick 'Em—the purpose and method of the vocal training of the army and the navy.
  Says Uncle Sam: I Run the Biggest Life-Insurance Company on Earth—story of the War Risk Insurance Bureau.
  Says Uncle Sam: A Girl's a Man for A' That—story of women in war-work.
  Says Uncle Sam: I'll Help Every Willing Worker Find a Job—story of the United States Employment Service.
By the Pathé Co.:
  Solving the Farm Problem of the Nation—story of the United States Boys' Working Reserve.
  Feeding the Fighter—how the army was supplied with food.
By the Universal Co.:
  Reclaiming the Soldiers' Duds—the salvage work of the War Department.
  The American Indian Gets Into the War Game—how the Indian took his place, both in the military forces and in food production.
By C. L. Chester:
  Schooling Our Fighting Mechanics—work of the Committee on Education and Special Training of the War Department.
  There Shall Be No Cripples—rehabilitation work of the Surgeon-General's Office.
  Colored Americans—activities of the negroes, both in the military forces and in war work at home.
  It's an Engineers' War—work of the Engineers' training-camps of the War Department.
  Finding and Fixing the Enemy—certain work of the Engineer Corps of the War Department.
  Waging War in Washington—the method of government operation.

All the Comforts of Home—methods of War Department in providing necessities and conveniences for soldiers.

Masters for the Merchant Marine—development of both officers and men for the new merchant navy.

The College for Camp Cooks—thorough training given men who were to prepare the food for the soldiers.

Rail-less Railroads—work of the Highway Transport Committee.

The following pictures, of more than one reel in length, were made by private producers from our scenarios and under our supervision:

By C. L. Chester:

"The Miracle of the Ships," a six-reel picture covering in detail the construction of the carrier ships at Hog Island and other yards, and showing every detail of construction.

By The W. W. Hodkinson Corporation:

"Made in America," an eight-reel picture telling the full story of the Liberty Army. It follows the soldier through every stage of the draft and through every step of his military, physical, and social development and into the actual combat overseas. Such a picture was greatly desired by General Munson, head of the Morale Branch of the War Department, for circulation in the army and among the people of the United States, as well as abroad. As this picture was to show the relation of the home life to the soldier, professional actors and actresses and much studio-work were required. The Morale Branch had no funds to pay for such a picture, and the Division of Films was able to work out a scenario of such promise that the Hodkinson Corporation agreed to produce the picture at their own expense, which they did at a cost exceeding forty thousand dollars.

Late in the summer of 1918, our system of production through outside concerns having worked out satisfactorily, it was decided to undertake production on our own account. Accordingly, scenarios were written, and the following six two-reel pictures were produced by the division:

THE BATTLE OF THE FILMS

"If Your Soldier's Hit," showing the operation of the regimental detachment and field hospital unit in getting wounded men off the front line, giving them first aid, and conveying them safely to recuperation bases. This picture was made in conjunction with the Surgeon-General's Office at the training-camp at Fort Riley, Kansas, and the scenes were supplemented by scenes from overseas.

"Our Wings of Victory," showing the complete processes of the manufacture and operation of airplanes for war purposes. The construction scenes were taken in the chief 'plane-factories and were supplemented by extraordinary scenes of flying.

"Our Horses of War," showing how the remount depots of the army obtain and train the horses and mules for cavalry and artillery purposes, and the feats performed by the animals so trained under the manipulation of the soldiers.

"Making the Nation Fit," showing how new recruits for the great army and the great navy were developed to a stage of physical fitness.

"The Storm of Steel," showing how twelve billions of the Liberty Loan money was being expended in the construction of guns and munitions. These scenes were taken in half a dozen of the chief gun-plants of the country and on the proving-grounds and are the most complete record in the government's possession of this undertaking.

"The Bath of Bullets," showing the development and use of machine-guns in this war.

A second series of six two-reel pictures had been laid out and the filming was about to proceed when the armistice caused the division to suspend all new undertakings.

The distribution of still pictures under the direction of Mr. Rubel and Mr. Harold E. Hecht also underwent a process of reorganization as time presented new needs and afforded new opportunities. One of the first of the new plans was the inauguration of the "permit system." While the military authorities were correct in refusing general admission to ordnance and airplane factories, to navy-yards and to certain cantonments where secret tests were being made, there was no good reason for barring private photographers from the majority of the camps and factories. Mr. Rubel, therefore, in consultation with the army and the navy, worked out a plan of permits that safeguarded military secrets even while it opened up the military effort to the cameras of civilians. Our procedure investigated each applicant and certified him to the camp commanders, and a "voluntary censorship" agreed to by the commercial photographers protected against indiscretion. Under this system, and as illustrative of its liberal provisions, the division issued more than six thousand permits, the daily applications ranging from ten to twenty-five.

This arrangement took care of domestic photographers, permitting Mr. Rubel to devote all his energy to the distribution of still pictures taken by the Signal Corps in France. In the first days, when the shipments were few, it was a simple matter to spread the photographs among the newspapers, but as great bundles commenced to be received, our simple machinery broke down. To meet the new demand, an arrangement was made with the Photographic Association, including such firms as Underwood & Underwood, International Film Service, Brown Bros., Paul Thompson, Kadel & Herbert, Harris & Ewing, Western Newspaper Union, the Newspaper Enterprise Association, and other firms that syndicated photographs nationally and internationally. Through organized effort these syndicate members placed our photographs in daily newspapers, weekly and monthly magazines, technical publications, and other mediums. To expedite production and delivery, a laboratory was secured in New York City and operated by the Signal Corps Photographic Division in conjunction with Columbia University. The prices fixed were nominal, designed only to cover expenses.

This department also furnished quantities of photographs each week to the Foreign Service Section of the

Committee for use in propaganda media in the Allied and neutral nations. Photographs were also furnished for publicity purposes for motion-picture features and we reproduced in hundreds of newspapers reaching millions of circulation. Another means of distribution of war photographs was to private collections, to universities, historical societies, state and municipal libraries, and any organization that could make use of pictures for future reference. Also, individuals who were interested in getting pictures of war activities, more especially those who had members of their families or friends directly connected with the war.

The Department of Slides was next added to the activities of the bureau and supplied a long-felt need for official and authentic photographs in stereopticon form for the use of ministers, lecturers, school-teachers, and others. Mr. Rubel and Mr. Hecht succeeded in putting out standard size balck and white slides of the finest workmanship at fifteen cents each, which price saved the user from 50 to 80 per cent. At first the production of slides was entirely dependent on the laboratory of the Signal Corps in Washington, which, as the orders increased in volume, proved inadequate to turn out sufficient quantity. The Committee on Public Information then built its own laboratory with ample production facilities. Out of this idea came another—that of illustrated war lectures. Taking the "Ruined Churches of France" as a first subject, for the original demand came from ministers for the most part, we prepared 50 slides, and accompanied them with a wonderful little lecture written movingly by Dr. John S. P. Tatlock of Leland Stanford University. Such was its enthusiastic reception that the following lectures were issued in rapid sequence: "Our Boys in France," 100 slides; "Building a Bridge of Ships to Pershing," 50 slides; "To Berlin *via* the Air Route," 50 slides;

"Making the American Army," 50 slides. About 700 of these sets were ordered by patriotic organizations and individuals, as well as churches and schools.

The next series of illustrated lectures to be distributed were as follows: "The Call to Arms," 58 slides; "Trenches and Trench Warfare," 73 slides; "Airplanes and How Made," 61 slides; "Flying for America," 54 slides; "The American Navy," 51 slides; "The Navy at Work," 36 slides; "Building a Bridge of Ships," 63 slides; "Transporting the Army to France," 63 slides; "Carrying the Home to the Camp," 61 slides. These sets were prepared and the lectures written by George F. Zook, professor of Modern European History in Pennsylvania State College. A total of 900 were ordered. While the greater number of orders came from various parts of this country, many were received from foreign countries.

In the year of existence the Department of Slides distributed a total of 200,000 slides.

X

THE "BATTLE OF THE FENCES"

IN some respects the Division of Pictorial Publicity was one of the most remarkable of the many forces called into being by the Committee on Public Information. Artists, from time immemorial, have been looked upon as an irresponsible lot, given over to dreams and impracticality and with little or no concern for the values that go to make up the every-day world. At America's call, however, painters, sculptors, designers, illustrators, and cartoonists rallied to the colors with instancy and enthusiasm, and no other class or profession excelled them in the devotion that took no account of sacrifice or drudgery. As a consequence, America had more posters than any other belligerent, and, what is more to the point, they were the *best*. They called to our own people from every hoarding like great clarions, and they went through the world, captioned in every language, carrying a message that thrilled and inspired.

Even in the rush of the first days, when we were calling writers and speakers and photographers into service, I had the conviction that the poster must play a great part in the fight for public opinion. The printed word might not be read, people might not choose to attend meetings or to watch motion pictures, but the billboard was something that caught even the most indifferent eye. The old-style poster, turned out by commercial artists as part of advertising routine, was miles away from our need, however. The current Washington idea that imagined art as a sort of slot-machine was a mistake that had to be rectified. What we wanted—what we had to have —was posters that represented the best work of the best artists—posters into which the masters of the pen and brush had poured heart and soul as well as genius. Looking the field over, we decided upon Charles Dana Gibson as the man best fitted to lead the army of artists, and on April 17, 1917, this splendid American entered the service as a volunteer. He called F. De Sales Casey to his right hand as vice-chairman and secretary, and the two formed these committees:

Associate chairmen—Herbert Adams, E. H. Blashfield, Ralph Clarkson, Cass Gilbert, Oliver D. Grover, Francis Jones, Arthur F. Matthews, Joseph Pennell, Edmond Tarbell, Douglas Volk.

Executive Committee—F. G. Cooper, N. Pousette-Dart, I. Doskow, F. E. Dayton, C. B. Falls, Albert E. Gallatin, Ray Greenleaf, Miss Malvina Hoffman, W. A. Rogers, Lieut. Henry Reuterdahl, U. S. N. R. F., H. Scott Train, H. D. Welsh, J. Thompson Willing, H. T. Webster, Walter Whitehead, Jack Sheridan.

Departmental captains—C. B. Falls, H. T. Webster, Walter Whitehead, Ray Greenleaf, I. Doskow, N. Pousette-Dart, H. Scott Train.

Headquarters were opened in New York, and within a month the organization had enlisted the great artists of America, and was working with speed and precision. H. Devitt Welsh of Philadelphia came to the office of the Committee in Washington to serve as "contact man." He went to the heads of all the war-making branches of government, telling them of the mobilization of the artists, and obtaining from each department its list of poster needs. This list was then sent to Mr. Gibson in New York, who made

CHICAGO WAR EXPOSITION

the assignments as would the art manager of a magazine, picking the artists best fitted for the particular need. The work, when finished, was hurried to Washington, and after approval was followed through the printing by experts. Not only this, but every man associated with Mr. Gibson submitted poster ideas of his own, so that governmental routines were soon broken up by the inrush of new and more vivid thought.

Strange as it may seem, the Division of Pictorial Publicity traveled no royal road to the favor of governmental heads. Many of these executives knew nothing at all about art or artists, and others, with greater knowledge, were products of the "chromo school." As a matter of fact, Mr. Gibson had to spend days in Washington actually begging for the privilege of *submitting sketches* from men and women whose names stood for all that was finest in American art. Through it all he held to his patience and enthusiasm, and at last the importance of the offering penetrated the official consciousness, and that which had been ignored came to be wildly pursued.

It was not only the case that the artists were subject to call, like so many members of a volunteer fire department, but they held regular weekly meetings at which the task was discussed as a whole, every one present contributing criticism, ideas, and inspiration. These meetings of the division developed into the most interesting series of dinners ever held in New York City. Under the magnetic leadership of Mr. Gibson, the dominant note was patriotic fervor. Everybody felt it a duty to come. The most celebrated men in every branch of art met for the first time at the same board with the younger men of their profession. This set the highest standard for the division and was an assurance to the government that it could expect the best that American art could give. It was also an inspiration to the younger men to be associated in such a notable league of artists, and made it a distinguished honor to succeed in the friendly competition for government acceptance of work.

The character of the division was best described in the words of Mr. Gibson himself when he said: "This is a schoolroom. All are welcome. We come here to learn from one another, to get inspiration and get religion for the great task the government has set for us. No artist is too great to come and give his best. We are fortunate to be alive at this time and be able to take advantage of the greatest opportunity ever presented to artists."

Being chosen to speak through their work to the millions of their countrymen, the artists felt a great sense of responsibility that bound them into a harmonious unit. All worked together in the common cause, sank personal considerations, gave and received advice. A fine spirit of helpfulness prevailed, the one aim—the highest excellence in all commissions executed. The steady appearance of the division's work became a feature of the war, not only stirring patriotism, but awakening in the public mind the importance of artists. It was a wholesale education to the country in that the division made the billboard "safe for art," the work standing out in sharp contrast to the commercial disfigurations of the past.

To increase the scope of the committee and to stimulate the personal interest of the artists outside of New York, sectional branches were formed, and Oliver Dennett Grover of Chicago became the chairman of the Western Committee, Mr. E. Tarbell and Mr. Arthur F. Matthews taking charge in Boston and San Francisco.

The full contribution of the artists of America to the national cause, as well as the reliance placed upon the Division of Pictorial Publicity by every department of government, is shown by the following record of achievement:

THE "BATTLE OF THE FENCES"

	Poster designs.	Car, bus, and window cards.	Newspaper and other advertising.	Cartoons.	Seals, buttons, banners, etc.
American Red Cross, Washington and New York	100	25	100	50	
War Savings Stamps	50	50	25	50	
Liberty Loan (Third)	3	10	15		
Liberty Loan (Fourth)	100		25		
Shipping Board	100			8	1
American Library Association	7		43		
War Camp Community Service	101	2	3		1
Ordnance Department	18	1	15	1	4
Training-camp Activities	10	1	3	10	
Food Administration	50	15	10	50	
Fuel Administration	25	10		23	
Department of Agriculture	11			1	1
War Department	11				1
Public Health Service	14	6	3		
Young Men's Christian Association	6		7		
Young Women's Christian Association	6		7		
Signal Corps	4		3	15	
Signal Corps, Aviation	1		2		1
Division of Films	33		4		1
Committee of Patriotic Societies			3		2
Turner Construction Co				20	
United States Boys' Working Reserve	5	1	2	7	
Committee on National Defense		1			3
Western Newspaper Union			2		
War Risk Insurance	2		2	1	
Committee on Public Information	4		6	5	
Division of Advertising	11		10	3	1
Squad A, Magazine Gun	2				
Mothers' Day	2				
Chain Stores	2				
Food for France	3				
Department of Labor	6				
Department of Interior	2		1		1
United States Tank Corps	1				
Salvation Army	5				
Treasure and Trinket Fund	1				
Boy Scouts	3		9		1
Jewish Welfare	5		1		
Trades for Disabled Soldiers	6		2		
Railroad Administration	8				
Motor Corps	1				
Southern Pine Association	1				
Federation of Neighborhood Associations			1		
Office of Chief of Staff	1				
International Arms & Fuse Co.	1				
Bastile Day	3			14	
Marine Corps	5				
Fifth Avenue Association	2				
American Poets' Committee	2				
Federal Food Board			3		
Rehabilitating Wounded Soldiers				2	2	1
Dewey Recreation Committee	1				
Italian War Work				1	
Mayor's Committee	1				
Official Bulletin	1				
Phonograph Recruiting Records	3			25	
Connecticut Defense Council	1				
Pelham Naval Station			1	1	
United War Work Campaign	5				

RECAPITULATION

Departments and committees requesting work....................................	58
Poster designs submitted..	700
Cards requested...	122
Newspaper and other advertising...	310
Cartoons submitted...	287
Seals, buttons, etc., executed...	19
Total material (drawings, designs, etc.).............................	1,438

In addition to the above, Lieut. Henry Reuterdahl and N. C. Wyeth worked on a painting ninety feet long, twenty-five feet high, which was placed at the Subtreasury Building for the Third Liberty Loan. Lieutenant Reuterdahl made also three paintings, each over twenty feet, for the publicity of the Fourth Liberty Loan in Washington, D. C.

During the United War Work Campaign the same plan was followed, seven artists painting on days assigned, in front of the Public Library, two others assigned in front of the Metropolitan Museum. This work was carried on by a committee of this division. These artists were:

F. D. Steele, Young Men's Christian Association.
Middleton Chambers, Knights of Columbus.
C. B. Falls, Salvation Army.
I. Olinsky, Jewish Welfare.
Denman Fink, Library Association.
Jean McLane, Young Women's Christian Association.
Howard Giles, War Camp Community Service.
Charles Chapman and Luis Mora, Metropolitan Museum.

As showing the manner in which the artists rose to high esteem, when General Pershing asked that the artists be sent to the firing-line in France, the task of selection was turned over to the Division of Pictorial Publicity and these men received commissions: Capts. J. Andre Smith, Ernest Peixotto, Harry Townsend, Wallace Morgan, George Harding, William J. Aylward, W. J. Duncan, and Harvey Dunn.

THE "BATTLE OF THE FENCES"

Almost three hundred drawings were received from them, which were framed and sent throughout the country for exhibition, and in addition to this the majority of them were given exquisite reproduction in the great magazines. The following characteristic comment, lifted out of a recent letter from Mr. Gibson, gives a hint of the spirit that made the Division of Pictorial Publicity a force and an inspiration:

It always struck me as more than fortunate that your telegram on the night of April 17, 1917, should have reached me when and where it did. It was at a dinner at the Hotel Majestic, the first gathering of artists after the declaration of war. We were there to offer our services to the country, but were in some doubt as to the method of procedure. We were sparring for an opening. Some of the speeches were about half over and some of them threatened to get us off the track, when just at the psychological moment your telegram was handed to me and we had a focusing-point. If it had all been prearranged it could not have happened better.

If I remember rightly, it was the following Sunday we met at your house, where the Division of Pictorial Publicity was formed. As you say, the division met some rough going in the early days, but for that matter so did every one who tried to elbow his way into the front trenches. I dare say no one knows this better than yourself. At any rate, it is easy to forget all those bumps now. In fact, the suspicion with which some of those in Washington looked upon the artists was not to be wondered at and bothered me less as I became better acquainted with the men I met down there. After all, we were offering something for nothing and that in itself was suspicious. We always felt that your experience was more or less like ours, only on a much larger scale, and you understood and were with us, so it was easy to wait. There is nothing like good company when the going is rough, and now that I look back upon it I dare say it really made the job more interesting.

The Associate Chairmen were most useful in allaying the fears of the heads of the different departments, and the work done by Casey was invaluable. He had great knowledge of the work and in addition possessed tact, even temper, and modesty.

HOW WE ADVERTISED AMERICA

There wasn't an artist in the country, man or woman, who didn't offer the best that was in him, and the single one who hesitated was a Quaker and he was only able to hold out for a short time.

THOUGHTS INSPIRED BY A WAR-TIME BILLBOARD

By Wallace Irwin

I stand by a fence on a peaceable street
    And gaze on the posters in colors of flame,
Historical documents, sheet upon sheet,
    Of our share in the war ere the armistice came.

And I think about Art as a Lady-at-Arms;
    She's a studio character most people say,
With a feminine trick of displaying her charms
    In a manner to puzzle the ignorant lay.

But now as I study that row upon row
    Of wind-blown engravings I feel satisfaction
Deep down in my star-spangled heart, for I know
    How Art put on khaki and went into action.

There are posters for drives—now triumphantly o'er—
    I look with a smile reminiscently fond
As mobilized Fishers and Christys implore
    In a feminine voice, "Win the War—Buy a Bond!"

There's a Jonas Lie shipbuilder, fit for a frame;
    Wallie Morg's· "Feed a Fighter" lurks deep in his trench;
There's Blashfield's Columbia setting her name
    In classical draperies, trimmed by the French.

Charles Livingston Bull in marine composition
    Exhorts us to Hooverize (portrait of bass).
Jack Sheridan tells us that Food's Ammunition—
    We've all tackled war biscuits under that class.

THE "BATTLE OF THE FENCES"

See the winged Polish warrior that Benda has wrought!
   Is he private or captain? I cannot tell which,
For printed below is the patriot thought
   Which Poles pronounce "Sladami Ojcow Naszych."

There's the Christy Girl wishing that she was a boy,
   There's Leyendecker coaling for Garfield in jeans,
There's the Montie Flagg guy with the air of fierce joy
   Inviting the public to Tell the Marines.

And the noble Six Thousand—they count up to that—
   Are marshaled before me in battered review.
They have uttered a thought that is All in One Hat
   In infinite shadings of red, white, and blue.

And if brave Uncle Sam—Dana Gibson, please bow—
   Has called for our labors as never before,
Let him stand in salute in acknowledgment now
   Of the fighters that trooped from the studio door.

THE WAR EXPOSITIONS

THE accidental quality that marked so many of our ideas was never more apparent than in the United States Government War Expositions that came to be one of the principal activities of the Committee on Public Information. These exhibitions, that had all the attraction of a circus and all the seriousness of a sermon, were given in twenty-one cities, were seen by more than 10,000,000 people, and earned a total income of $1,438,004.

In the spring of 1917, when the Committee was just getting under way, the representatives of the state fairs came to us and asked for a war exhibit. We took the matter up with the army and the navy and received assurance that the proper material would be provided. Unfortunately, however, the promise was lost sight of in the rush of more important things, and the Committee, as usual, received the full blame for the failure. In the early months of 1918 we entered into new communication with the state fairs and expositions, this time assuming full responsibility for the preparation of an exhibit. Capt. Joseph H. Hittinger was borrowed from the War Department, and co-operative arrangements were made with the departments of War, Navy, Agriculture, Commerce, Interior, and the Food Administration. From the army and the navy we secured guns of all kinds, hand-grenades, gas-masks, depth-bombs, mines, and hundreds of other things calculated to show the people how their money was being spent. The other departments joined in with exhibits of their own, all going to make up three carloads of material. Thirty-five state fairs and expositions were reached throughout the summer, soldiers and sailors accompanying exhibits and acting as lecturers.

In June, 1918, the Committee on Public Information was called before the Committee on Appropriations of the House to tell why it wanted money and to explain what it meant to do with the money. When I came to the item of the state fair exhibits, and explained the general idea of carrying the facts of war to the people of the United States, there was not only a very notable lack of enthusiasm, but even a distinct disposition to regard the idea as somewhat stupid and quite unnecessary. Here, for instance, is an excerpt from the printed report of the hearing:

THE CHAIRMAN. The question I am going to ask you does not express any opinion, but I am making the inquiry in order that you may express an opinion: What have you to say as to whether the fact that the mobilizing of men from nearly every family in the land of itself brings the war so directly home and in such a vital way as to make unnecessary this military propaganda work in order to interest the people in the war?

MR. CREEL. There are two sides to that. In the first place, the son in the service gives direct interest instantly, but that interest may be of a nature so tinged with anxiety that it lends itself to every rumor and every apprehension, and it is our duty to work for enthusiasm and against depression. That is important not only for the family, but for the boy who is fighting at the front. We know that every letter that is written to a soldier in a pessimistic tone tends to make him a poor soldier, and it is just as much the business of war to keep the home happy and ardent as it is to maintain courage on the firing-line.

We know from the experience of cantonments that the civilian morale is highest near those cantonments where the general in command has displayed his men most prominently, giving frequent drills at exhibitions, visiting near-by cities, and where he has made the most effective arrangements to bring the fathers and mothers to the cantonments to see the boys in action, to see how they are treated, to see how they look, and what they are doing. That is the way we feel, and I think that practically every member of the military establishment will tell you that it is of military value. The General Staff, as you know, is continually placing emphasis upon what they term "morale."

The sum eventually allowed us for War Expositions was five thousand dollars. A few days after this virtual rebuff, I was visited by Mr. W. C. D'Arcy, Mr. Llewellyn Pratt, and others, who explained that the Associated Advertising Clubs of the World would hold their annual convention in San Francisco, July 4th. What they wanted was a collection of war trophies in order to give the gathering a patriotic note. Going to the War Department, then to the English, French, and Italian Commissions, and finally to the Canadians, we collected every possible trophy and hurried them out to San Francisco. It was not much of an exhibition, even when viewed by the most enthusiastic eye, but the advertising clubs put themselves wholeheartedly behind the project and drove it through to success. Los Angeles then asked for the collection and we sent it there, doing even better with it than in San Francisco. Although the admission charge was small, in neither place did we lose money, a fact that gave us courage to disregard the smallness of the capital allowed us by Congress.

Making decision to go into the work on a huge scale, we turned the exposition idea over to Mr. Charles S. Hart of the Division of Films, who straightway gathered a staff of exhibit experts about him. Under the new plan we collected every possible trophy brought to this country either by the War Department or by the Allies, and to these we added everything that the army and navy could give that would let the people see the machinery of war.

THE WAR EXPOSITIONS

The Y. M. C. A., the Y. W. C. A., the Knights of Columbus, the Jewish Welfare Board, the American Library
Association, the War Camp Community Service, the Red
Cross, and every other voluntary agency were also induced
to prepare exhibits, all making up a great train of cars equal
in volume to a transcontinental circus.

Going into Chicago, we boldly took the Lake front and
proceeded to erect buildings and dig the trenches. Mr.
Samuel Insull, Chicago's dynamic public figure, was induced to lend his powerful aid, and he swung every one
of the civic associations into line. W. H. Rankin, the advertising expert, joined in the executive direction and
attended to the publicity. Having committed ourselves
to the hazard, no expense was spared, and on the day that
the United States Government War Exposition opened
our commitments were well over two hundred thousand
dollars, a radical advance indeed over the five thousand
dollars allowed by Congress, and one that meant disaster
if our conclusions were wrong.

The gates opened in a downpour of rain and the first
day's attendance was appallingly small. When the news
reached Washington over the long-distance telephone, a
more heart-sick group of people could not have been imagined. The sun came out, however, and in the two weeks
that followed more than two million people visited the
exposition, the average daily attendance being in excess
of that of the World's Fair. When the books were balanced it was seen that we had paid every cent of expense
and cleared for the government the sum of $318,000.

There was interest as well as inspiration in the exposition. Along the great stretches of promenade were distributed the trophies captured from the enemy by soldiers
of the United States and the Allies—great thirty-five-
thousand-pound guns taken in hand-to-hand struggle,
battered remnants of U-boats that sent women and chil-

dren to their death, reservoirs for poison-gas, German 'planes brought down as they hovered over villages and hospitals, helmets, gas-masks—all the paraphernalia of war. Our army and navy put on view all the varied manufactures that would permit people to grasp the extent of America's preparation, and from the Allies came types of their war material. In the booths that stretched in endless line all the various war organizations pictured the life of the soldier and the sailor, and showed what they were doing in the way of assistance and encouragement.

Through the generous co-operation of the army and the navy, a remarkable sham battle was staged every afternoon, and this daily spectacle of men going over the top to the rattle of rifles and machine-guns, and the roar of the navy ordnance, aroused the assembled thousands to the highest pitch of enthusiasm. Pleading military necessity, the army and the navy refused to lend us men after the Chicago Exposition, with the result that the sham battles had to be discontinued as one of our features. Even so, the tour continued with remarkable results. The following table, showing the cities visited and income received, should serve as an ample vindication of the Committee's decision:

San Francisco	$ 54,274 80
Los Angeles	65,375 75
Chicago	583,731 24
Cleveland	167,355 51
Waco	16,904 70
Pittsburgh	147,804 16
Kansas City	28,646 20
Cincinnati	66,541 20
Buffalo	60,354 27
St. Louis	23,570 40
New Orleans	14,439 20
Toledo	50,003 02
Detroit	63,470 74

THE WAR EXPOSITIONS

Houston	$22,684	05
Milwaukee	49,372	02
St. Paul (small exhibit)	9,065	34
Jackson (small exhibit)	5,169	29
Little Rock (small exhibit)	2,458	72
Oklahoma (small exhibit)	4,664	71
Great Falls (small exhibit)	996	07
Waterloo (small exhibit)	1,122	85
Total income, expositions	$1,438,004	24

Its financial success did not result from a high admission price, but was due to the appeal of the exposition itself. On the Pacific coast tickets were sold for 50 cents and were redeemable at the gate for a 25-cent War Saving Stamp in addition to an admission ticket. This plan was followed for the purpose of creating the War Saving Stamp habit in that territory. In Chicago and the other cities the tickets were sold in advance for 25 cents, children 2½ cents.

XII

THE United States, in the first months of the war, was an oratorical bedlam. More than a dozen national speakers' bureaus were being conducted by government departments and by associations which were seeking to promote the national interest. Scores of state speaking campaigns were being inaugurated under the auspices of Councils of Defense and other organizations. All these were competing for speakers, duplicating each other's activities, and failing to co-ordinate their efforts in an effective and comprehensive campaign. Nothing was more apparent than the need of some central clearing-house in Washington through which these various organizations, working for a great common purpose, but each with its special message, could be brought into touch with the affairs and facilities of other departments, and given the inspiration and information which came from the vital national interests involved.

In consideration of these needs, the Speaking Division of the Committee on Public Information was created September 25, 1917, the idea receiving the approval of the President in the following letter:

My dear Mr. Creel:

I heartily approve of the suggestion you have made that through your Committee some effort be made to co-ordinate the work of the various bureaus, departments, and agencies interested in presenting from the platform various phases of the national task. With the co-operation of the departments, the Food Administration, the Council of National Defense, and the Committee on Public Information, it would seem possible to enlist the many state and private organizations who have put the nation's cause above every other issue and stand ready to participate in a speaking campaign that shall give to the people that fullness of information which will enable and inspire each citizen to play intelligently his part in the greatest and most vital struggle ever undertaken by self-governing nations.

Your suggestion of Mr. Arthur E. Bestor, president of Chautauqua Institution, to direct this work is excellent. You are fortunate to be able to enlist one who has been so intimately connected with a great American educational institution devoted to popular instruction without prejudice or partizanship.

    Cordially and sincerely yours,

        WOODROW WILSON.

Certain general policies were followed from the very beginning with such modifications as from time to time became necessary. It was *not* the purpose of the division to attempt to combine the speakers' bureaus of the several departments or private organizations, nor to assume any responsibility for supervision over them, but rather to establish a bureau to co-ordinate their efforts where they related to common aims or activities. It *was* the purpose to seek co-operation among these speakers' bureaus by agreement and consultation; to offer a national clearing-house for speaking campaigns; to avoid duplication of effort and overlapping of territory; to supply speakers with usable information from government departments; to concentrate the attention of speakers during special periods upon different national needs; and to foster in all speakers a sense of the unity of the national purpose. There was never an attempt to control and supervise the speaking of the country—the problem was simply one of co-operation and co-ordination.

Through the medium of bulletins, conferences, and cor-

11   149

respondence, a direct relationship was maintained with every government department, patriotic society, Chamber of Commerce, Rotary Club, and similar associations, and by this means a machinery was created by which national speakers could be routed at short notice, with a certainty of large audiences.

It was in direct line with his work, though seemingly outside of it, that Mr. Bestor went from state to state in the interests of better organization. His first trips were concerned almost entirely with the State Councils of Defense, and, it was in consequence of these meetings that the great series of war conferences was held. Our idea was that the facts and necessities of war must be carried not only to every home in the cities and towns, but to hamlets and the most remote farm-houses as well.

Forty-five war conferences were held in thirty-seven states, and, in addition, local conferences were called in various sections. These official gatherings brought together all the effective war-workers in the state, usually occupied two days, and in addition to the general meetings addressed by the speakers sent out by the division there were sectional conferences held by federal and state officials who were carrying on war-work. These war conferences were oftentimes the greatest gatherings held within the states during the war. They had a profound effect upon public opinion and upon the efficient organization of state war-work. Usually the state-wide conferences were followed by county and town conferences of the same character.

A card catalogue of over ten thousand speakers and makers of public opinion was eventually gathered, and a select list of three hundred effective speakers. Whenever a request was made for an individual address, a list was prepared of those available for such service. This resulted in many appointments being made by organizations direct with speakers recommended by the division.

It became more and more the practice, however, for the division to assume entire charge of all tours. When some distinguished speaker volunteered his services for a week or a month, or even longer, it was the obvious dictate of common sense that his time and value should not be wasted. A steady and practical sequence of engagements had to be arranged, and this called for the central control and direction that only the Speaking Division was in a position to give.

In co-operation with the British War Mission, engagements were made for Sir Frederick E. Smith, the British Attorney-General; Sir Walter Lawrence, Sir George Adam Smith, Gen. H. D. Swinton, Col. A. C. Murray, Maj. Ian Hay Beith, Lieut. Hector MacQuarrie, Hon. Harald Smith, Maj. Robert Massie, and Maj. Laughlin McLean Watt. All were successes except Sir Frederick Smith, who proved only irritating and offensive.

Lieutenant MacQuarrie was a peculiarly effective speaker, giving ninety-three addresses in four months in nine states, everywhere arousing enthusiasm. Hon. Crawford Vaughan, ex-Premier of South Australia, a noted labor leader, was brought across the continent by the division, spoke at several of the war conferences, and gave in all twenty-two addresses under the auspices of the division until he became connected with the United States Shipping Board.

The French High Commission permitted us to make engagements for M. Maurice Casenave and M. Edouard de Billy, and placed at our disposal Countess Madeleine de Bryas, Captain Paul Perigord, and Lieutenant Wierzbicki for national tours. Of all those who spoke in America during the war, native or foreign, Captain Perigord, the warrior-priest, must be given first rank. This is not to be taken as disparagement of the others, for Captain Perigord was virtually in a class by himself. French by birth, the outbreak of the war found him a priest in St. Paul, serving in the Catholic University. Returning at once to his native land, he went into the ranks as a private, fought in battle after battle, and at Verdun won his commission, leading the charge of a few heroes when every officer had been killed. Blessed with a voice like an organ note, he was more than a great speaker; he seemed inspired. For seven months he went about the country, making 152 speeches in all, many of them to audiences that numbered thousands, only quitting when sheer exhaustion brought him to a sick-bed from which he liked not to have arisen.

Countess de Bryas was second only to Captain Perigord, for in addition to brains and real oratorical ability she had youth and beauty. Accompanied by her sister, the Countess Jacqueline, she toured America from Atlantic to Pacific, from North to South, speaking in cities and villages, before social and commercial organizations, in factories and churches, driving home the message of France, and making Americans realize America. She was peculiarly effective in factories, for her simplicity and sincerity went straight to the hearts of workers, and her proudest possession was a collection of grimy gloves made unwearable by the toil-stained hands of the hundreds who crowded around her at the close of every meeting. As in the case of Captain Perigord, Countess de Bryas broke under the strain imposed upon her, but, recovering after an illness of weeks, resumed her tour and carried it through to the agreed conclusion.

The Speaking Division also handled the engagements of the following officials of our own government:

Dr. Vernon Kellogg, Maj. W. L. Brown, Dr. Henry J. Waters, and Dr. Henry C. Culbertson, of the Food

Administration; and Dr. Anna Shaw and Miss Ida Tarbell, of the Woman's Committee of the Council of National Defense.

Hon. Wesley Frost, former consul at Queenstown, and the official reporter of eighty-one submarine sinkings, created profound sensation in his transcontinental tours, and from September to February gave sixty-three addresses in twenty-nine states for the Speaking Division.

Charles Edward Russell, a member of the President's Commission to Russia, who was particularly effective before labor audiences, gave fifty-eight addresses from October to February in all parts of the country. Congressman Albert Johnson, just back from the front, delivered nineteen addresses in nine states from December to February.

In co-operation with the Friends of German Democracy, Mr. Henry Riesenburg made twenty-seven addresses in nineteen states; Dr. Frank Bohn, nine addresses in three states; Dr. William H. Bohn, twenty-six addresses in three states; Dr. Karl Mathie, eighteen addresses in two states; and Prof. A. E. Koenig, nine addresses.

Some of the best features of the work were not the product of plan, but sprang entirely from lucky accident. One evening, at a dinner given by the French High Commission, Marquis Crequi Montfort de Courtivron asked me, in his precise English, if I knew where Richmond was. I gave him the necessary information and casually asked him why he wanted to know. He answered that his wife was a daughter of Prince Camille de Polignac, who had fought through the Civil War under the flag of the Confederacy, rising to the rank of general. On his death-bed in France the year before, General Prince de Polignac had asked his daughter to return his sword to the state of Virginia, and it was this sacred commission that the Marquis desired to discharge.

Here, as if made to order, was a splendid opportunity to reach the entire South with the message of France. Not only did the Marquise de Courtivron bear the sword of her father, but her husband was a distinguished French officer, and in the United States also was her cousin, the Marquis de Polignac, who had married an American woman, Mrs. James Eustace, of New York, only a short time before.

Getting in communication with the governor of Virginia, Mr. Bestor gained an official invitation for the party, and the governors of other Southern states, informed of the visit, begged that the itinerary might be extended to take in their capitals. By way of offsetting the titles in case of any such prejudice, we added Mr. Charles Edward Russell to the party, that distinguished Socialist, who was also one of the greatest speakers that ever addressed a patriotic audience. The trip, commencing in Richmond and ending in New Orleans, was a whirlwind of enthusiasm, and did as much as any one thing to drive home the facts of war.

Another feature was the American tour of Capt. Roald Amundsen, in many respects the most powerful individual in Scandinavia. We persuaded Captain Amundsen to go to the American lines in France for a visit of inspection, and then we managed to bring him to the United States, sending him to every part of the country where Scandinavian peoples were gathered in any quantity.

Inasmuch as the division had relations with state Councils of Defense in practically all the states and with various organizations like the Chambers of Commerce, Rotary Clubs, and others that had ready-made audiences, the division came more and more to be the organization to handle tours for patriotic purposes which were other than merely speaking tours. The French Blue Devils, for instance, were routed under the auspices of the division, and the 344 Belgian soldiers returning from Russia were brought across the continent by the division. The fifty American soldiers sent by General Pershing to aid in the Third Liberty Loan were, at the conclusion of that loan, routed by the division for one month and heard in practically all of the states.

Mr. Bestor's experience as president of the Chautauqua Institution, as well as his force and ability, was the principal factor in driving the work of the Speaking Division to complete success. Poor Bestor! No grand-opera impresario ever had greater difficulties, for many of our orators had all the temperament of a prima donna and had to be humored to a point where homicide appealed as necessary and justifiable. And the booking of an organization like the Blue Devils or Pershing's Veterans required as much work as the routing of a score of theatrical companies. Prof. J. J. Pettijohn, director of the extension division of Indiana University and head of the Indiana State Speakers' Bureau, became associate director of the division on May 6, 1918, and from June was in active charge in the absence of Mr. Bestor, until the consolidation of the division with the Four Minute Men, when he became the associate director of that division. His wide experience in popular education and his ability as an organizer were of great value to the division in the last months of its separate organization.

Prof. Thomas F. Moran of Purdue University was loaned to the division by that institution for service from January to April, and performed brilliant service in the editing of the bulletins and in addresses before the Southern war conferences and individual addresses before many audiences. Mr. W. Frank McClure, publicity director of the Redpath Bureau, Chicago, was another who rendered useful and devot'd service.

XIII

THE work of the Committee was so distinctly in the nature of an advertising campaign, though shot through and through with an evangelical quality, that we turned almost instinctively to the advertising profession for advice and assistance. As it happened, however, there was a sad lack of accord in the initial contacts between the government and the advertising experts. When the First Liberty Loan was announced a committee headed by Herbert Houston, William H. Rankin, and O. C. Harn came to Washington to urge a campaign based upon the outright purchase of advertising space in newspapers and other mediums.

There was no question as to the patriotism of the men, nor do I think that there was much doubt as to the value and efficiency of their plan. When one considers the disruption of business occasioned by each Liberty Loan and the appalling waste in stupid or misapplied energy, the conviction grows that paid advertising—controlled, authoritative, driving to its mark with the precision of a rifle-ball—would have been quicker, simpler, and in the end far cheaper.

It was in the first days of war enthusiasm, however, and there was a definite repugnance to any suggestion that savored of profit. "Voluntary" was the magic word, and even though it took five dollars to secure the gift of a

W. C. D'Arcy   H. S. Houston   L. B. Jones

W. H. Johns

Thomas Cusack   Jesse H. Neale   O. C. Harn

dime, there was a glamour about the donation that blinded every one to the economic waste. Aside from this, advertising was regarded as a business, not a profession, and the majority looked upon the advertising agent with suspicion, even when he was not viewed frankly as a plausible pirate belonging to the same school of endeavor as the édition-de-luxe book canvasser.

In any event, the advertising experts withdrew from Washington, feeling somewhat as though casualties had been sustained, but instead of sulking they proceeded to prove themselves and their theories by actual demonstration. Among other things, Mr. Rankin evolved what came to be known as the "Chicago Plan," being the purchase of space in the press by individuals or groups, and the donation of this space to the uses of government. As general director of a Red Cross drive in Chicago, for instance, he had induced a number of business men to stand the cost of thirty-five full-page advertisements in the daily papers, with the result that every dollar membership was secured at an expense of two and a half cents as opposed to an expense of twenty-three cents per member in New York, where all effort was "voluntary."

The "Chicago Plan" was applied to the First Liberty Loan by almost every advertising club and agent in the country, and it is safe to say that fully one million dollars were contributed to the campaign, the donated space being filled with effective appeals prepared by selling experts. In Muncie, Indiana, where full dependence was placed upon the Rankin idea, not a single solicitor being used to sell bonds, the city more than doubled its quota in record time.

The Second Liberty Loan saw much the same achievements on the part of the advertising fraternity, and the showing gave me opportunity, even as it afforded justification, for recognition of advertising as a real profession, and to include it as an honorable and integral part of the war-machinery of government. As a result of our recommendation the following executive order was issued:

> I hereby create, under the jurisdiction of the Committee on Public Information, heretofore established by executive order of April 14, 1917, a Division of Advertising for the purpose of receiving through the proper channels the generous offers of the advertising forces of the nation to support the effort of the government to inform public opinion properly and adequately.
>
> [Signed]   WOODROW WILSON.

This authority was instantly exercised by the appointment of a board of control composed of the following presidents of the leading advertising organizations:

Mr. William H. Johns, chairman, president of the American Association of Advertising Agencies, representing 115 leading firms of this kind in the country; Mr. Thomas Cusack, one of the acknowledged leaders of the poster and painted bulletin industry; Mr. W. C. D'Arcy, president of the Associated Advertising Clubs of the World, representing 180 advertising clubs with a combined membership of 17,000; Mr. O. C. Harn, chairman of the National Commission of the Associated Advertising Clubs of the World; Mr. Herbert S. Houston, formerly president of the Associated Advertising Clubs of the World; Mr. Lewis B. Jones, president of the Association of National Advertisers; and Mr. Jesse H. Neal, executive secretary of the Associated Business Papers, consisting of 500 leading trade and technical publications.

By this one stroke of President Wilson's pen every advertising man in the United States was enrolled in America's second line, and from the very moment of their enrolment we could feel the quickening of effort, the intensification of endeavor. Offices were taken in the

Metropolitan Tower in New York, a skilled force assembled, and from these headquarters the generals directed the energies of an army of experts.

A first effort, as a matter of course, was in connection with the advertising space, and donations of space, made by the publishers of national magazines, trade and agricultural papers, and theater programs in all the principal cities. Over 800 publishers of monthly and weekly periodicals gave space worth $159,275 per month for the duration of the war, and this was increasing monthly when the armistice terminated the arrangement. In addition, advertisers themselves purchased $340,981 worth of space in various nationally circulated periodicals and turned it over to the Division of Advertising to use for government purposes. These were definite purchases for 1918, but indications had already been given that renewals would follow in 1919. Figuring on a yearly basis, these donations totaled approximately $2,250,000, but only about $1,594,-000 was used, owing to the sudden cessation of activities. The same plan was used in connection with the billboards and painted signs, and while exact figures are not obtainable, a just estimate of these donations cannot be put under $250,000.

Never was there a machinery that operated with such automatic efficiency. Through its Washington representative, Mr. Carl Walberg, the division maintained direct contact with every branch of the American war effort, and whether it was the Treasury Department, the War Department, or the navy, the Shipping Board or the Food Administration, the Red Cross or the Fuel Administration, all that was necessary was the plain statement of the specific need. Mr. Johns and his associates did the rest. They studied the problem, planned the campaign, decided upon the agency best fitted to prepare the copy, or, as was more often the case, three or four agencies were instructed to turn in copy. When the selection had been made, the copy was turned over to the Division of Pictorial Publicity for illustration by some artist, then decision as to the publications best suited to the particular message, after which the plates went out.

Aside from newspaper and trade-press advertising, the use of billboards and the painted sign, another element of tremendous publicity value was contributed by the International Association of Display Men. This organization appointed a National War Service Committee on window displays, the chairman of which, Mr. C. J. Potter, took a desk in the New York offices of the Division of Advertising and not only turned over to the division the entire window-display resources of the association in six hundred cities, but directed the entire work of creating patriotic window displays throughout the country so that, timed to the minute, they supplemented the division's campaigns in the periodicals. The window-display committee was instrumental in the building of sixty thousand reported displays on various government subjects, and probably hundreds more unreported.

Perhaps a detailed description of one particular job will give a clearer conception of the energy, originality, and high value of the Committee's advertising associates and their organized method of work. For instance, it was the nation's task to register thirteen million men on September 12th. The enormous amount of detail compelled unavoidable delay, and as a result about two weeks were allowed to the office of the Provost-Marshal-General in which to reach every American between eighteen and forty-five with specific information and instructions.

Every resource of the Committee was put at the service of General Crowder, but the great burden of effort fell entirely upon the Division of Advertising. Through Mr. Walberg these men made a quick and authoritative study of the problem and outlined a nation-wide campaign that was altered in no detail, and that carried through the registration without a single hitch.

Expert copy-writers, working night and day, put the facts of registration in advertising form, the Division of Pictorial Publicity furnished illustrations, display experts put the product into type, and the whole was issued as an Advertising Service Bulletin and sent to every advertiser and advertising agent in the United States. Here, then, in form ready to use, was advertising copy in any space from one column to a page, suitable to any medium from a metropolitan daily to a country weekly, and through the generosity of local advertisers and the efforts of local advertising clubs these direct appeals went into the press of the United States. One full-page advertisement went to every agricultural, trade, and technical journal, while other class publications were dealt with in the same specialized manner.

The next publication was a Selective Service Register— a regular newspaper with one side of the sheet given over entirely to questions and answers, specific instructions, and general appeals; the other side a striking poster, blazoning the fundamental facts of registration. Newspapers and individuals, after reading or copying the stories, were then able to paste or hang up the sheet in such manner as to let the poster carry its message to every passer-by.

The Division of Distribution, augmenting its force and working day and night shifts, distributed some 20,-000,000 copies of the two publications to the following addresses: 18,000 newspapers, 11,000 national advertisers and agencies, 10,000 chambers of commerce and their members, 30,000 manufacturers' associations, 22,000 labor unions, 10,000 public libraries, 32,000 banks, 58,000 general stores, 3,500 Young Men's Christian Association branches, 10,000 members of the Council of National

Defense, 1,000 advertising clubs, 56,000 post-offices, 55,000 railroad station agents, 5,000 draft boards, 100,000 Red Cross organizations, 12,000 manufacturers' agents.

The foreign-language groups were reached by the establishment of direct contacts with 600 papers printed in nineteen different languages. Every advertisement, every instruction, and every appeal was translated into all of these tongues and the papers turned over their news and advertising columns with a generosity not surpassed by the native press. Fully 5,000,000 citizens were instructed in this direct fashion.

Another problem was the rural districts far from railroads and not reached by the press. A special mailing-card was devised and sent to 43,000 Rural Free Delivery routes, 18,000 of which were out on railroads. Other cards, brilliant and effective, were planned, printed, and put in the street-cars of the country, while almost overnight the poster and sign-board people swung into action and plastered the dead walls and boards of the nation with stirring appeals. Added to this, more than 37,000 registration posters were displayed in the store-windows of some 600 cities.

The output of the Division of Advertising, with its careful analysis of the details of registration, served also as ammunition for the Four Minute Men, and fifty thousand speakers backed up the printed word. Even the Division of Films was brought into the team-play.

The following excerpt from a letter addressed to the Division of Advertising may be accepted as the general attitude of the entire War Department:

Over and above the fine organization of the Committee staff, as a whole, what has impressed me particularly in your division is the thoroughness with which you have organized the patriotic assistance of private citizens in contributing to the public service rendered by the Committee. It is genuinely

American in its method—this voluntary union of individual citizens to accomplish these results which in some continental countries are left to the vast army of government officials.

[Signed]   E. H. CROWDER,
Provost-Marshal-General.

In similar fashion the division planned and prepared the Shipping Board's campaign for 250,000 shipyard volunteers, swung into line on the Third and Fourth Liberty Loans, and handled special drives for the Department of Agriculture, the Council of National Defense, the Fuel and Food Commissions, the United War Work Drive, and the Red Cross. It was the division, by the way, that conceived the idea of that wonderful drawing "The Greatest Mother in the World," since used as the official Red Cross symbol, and appealing to the heart of humanity from every dead wall in every country.

"Smileage" was another victory for the division. The Commission on Training Camp Activities, it may be remembered, devised a system of camp theaters to which a small admission fee was charged. Ticket-books, known as "Smileage," were issued with the idea that the civilian population should buy them and present them to the soldiers so that the boys might not be put even to a minimum of expense. The Division of Advertising, almost in the very first week of its existence, took hold of this moribund plan and breathed the breath of a new life into it. The Smileage advertiser was prepared and printed an eight-page publication containing every known kind and size of "display ad." attractively illustrated—and through donations of space by both press and merchants in each community these advertisements were reproduced until they reached the eye of virtually every American. Inside of three weeks the supply of printed books was sold out entirely and "Smileage," instead of sinking deeper into failure, rose to conspicuous success.

When the Department of Labor launched its plan of government employment offices, Mr. Walberg carried the idea to the Division of Advertising, and the result was another demonstration of efficiency. *The United States Employment Service Bulletin* was issued—sixteen pages of sample "ads."—and 60,000 copies were circulated to the press, manufacturers, and advertisers. More than 11,000 printed advertisements, ranging from one column to a page, were received by the Labor Department, showing the extent to which the contents of the bulletin had been copied.

With equal intelligence and enthusiasm, the division put itself back of the Committee in each and all of its undertakings. By way of experiment, the Committee sent some war trophies and war material to San Francisco, calling it the Allied War Exposition. The Division of Advertising saw its possibilities instantly, and it was due to its insistence, and a promise of its aid, that we changed the plan into the United States Government War Exposition, enlarging and broadening the exhibit, and sent it across the country from coast to coast. In Chicago, for instance, we took the entire Lake front, erected buildings and dug trenches, and in two weeks more than two million people entered the gates, our books showing a clean profit of $318,000 at the close.

As in every other activity of the Committee, there is no exact method by which the value of the division's services can be measured in terms of money. We have record of advertising space in national mediums to the amount of $1,594,000. We know that the contributions of street-car advertising, billboards, and painted signs totaled about $250,000. No approximation can be made, however, of the thousands of columns used in the daily press, scores of miscellaneous donations, and the almost weekly window displays in 600 cities. Nor is it possible to figure the value of the volunteer aid rendered by agencies and employees, for not only was every hour of time an absolute gift, but not one cent of charge was ever made for services, or even for materials. When all is said and done, it may be stated in perfect safety that the contributions of the Division of Advertising, had they been paid for, would have cost the government $5,000,000.

Money, however, is a poor measure of value in connection with the importances of life. Far above the donations of ability and space were the generous enthusiasms that every advertising man brought to bear upon the war effort of America. Had the Committee done nothing else, its existence would have been justified by the decision that gave advertising the dignity of a profession and incorporated its dynamic abilities in American team-play.

XIV

THERE is a certain sect in America that, for lack of a more forceful epithet, may be termed "Americanizers." It was particularly active in the months that followed April, 1917. With the passion for minding other people's business that is the distinguishing mark of the sect, some of its disciples descended upon the humble tenement home of a Bohemian family in Chicago during the first summer of the war.

"We are here," the spokesman announced, impressively, "in the interests of Americanization."

"I'm sorry," faltered the woman of the house, "but you'll have to come back next week."

"What!" The cry was a choice compound of protest and reproach. "You mean that you have no *time* for our message! That you want to put *off* your entrance into American *life?*"

"No, no!" The poor Bohemian woman fell straightway into a panic, for not even a policeman has the austere authoritativeness of those who elect themselves to be light-bringers. "We're *perfectly* willing to be Americanized. Why, we never turn *any* of them away. But there's nobody home but me. All the boys volunteered, my man's working on munitions, and all the rest are out selling Liberty Bonds. I don't want you to get mad, but *can't* you come back next week?"

This incident, true as gospel even if anecdotal, serves

the purpose of volumes in setting forth accurately the war attitudes of both native-born and immigrant aliens. On the part of the native American there was often a firm conviction that our declaration of war carried an instant knowledge of English with it, and that all who persisted in speaking any other tongue after April 6, 1917, were either actual or potential "disloyalists," objects of merited suspicion and distrust; on the part of the overwhelming majority of aliens there was an almost passionate desire to serve America that was impeded at every turn by the meannesses of chauvinism and the brutalities of prejudice, as well as the short-sightedness of ignorance.

Yet as long as history is read it will stand as a monument to the democratic experiment that in an hour of confusion and hysteria the American theory of unity stood the iron test of practice. For the most part, those of foreign birth or descent kept the faith in spite of every bitterness— the great mass of the native population held to justice in spite of every incitement to hatred and persecution. And out of the test emerged an America triumphant, strengthened, and unstained!

Speaking in terms of *percentage*, the amount of actual disloyalty was not large enough even to speck the shining patriotism of the millions of Americans that we refer to as "adopted." Nothing in the world was ever so smashed by developments as all those pre-war apprehensions that filled us with gloom. Who does not remember the fears of "wholesale disloyalty" that shook us daily? There were to be "revolutions" in Milwaukee, St. Louis, Cincinnati; armed uprisings here, there, and everywhere; small armies herding thousands of rebellious enemy aliens into huge internment camps; incendiarism, sabotage, explosions, murder, domestic riot. No imagination was too meager to paint a picture of America's adopted children turning faces of hatred to the motherland.

The President went before Congress, a state of war was accepted formally, and even as one army gathered in the cantonments, another went out over the land to watch, to search, to listen. The Department of Justice had already in the field a large, intelligent, and well-trained organization; there was also the Secret Service of the Treasury Department, and into being swiftly sprang Military Intelligence, Naval Intelligence, Shipping Board Intelligence, etc.; and, by way of climax, the American Protective League, an organization of *two hundred and fifty thousand* "citizen volunteers" formed with the sanction of the Attorney-General and operated under the direction of the Bureau of Investigation.

Never was a country so thoroughly contra-espionaged! Not a pin dropped in the home of any one with a foreign name but that it rang like thunder on the inner ear of some listening sleuth! And with what result?

A scientific system of registration, prescribed by law, revealed that there were about five hundred thousand German "enemy aliens" living in the United States, and between three and four million "Austro-Hungarian enemy aliens." These figures, as a matter of course, did not include the millions of naturalized citizens, or the sons and daughters of such millions. Out of this large number just *six* thousand were adjudged sufficiently disaffected to be detained under presidential warrants! Even a percentage of these, as a matter of common sense and justice, were eventually released from the army internment camps under a strict parole system.

As for criminal prosecutions, 1,532 persons were arrested under the provisions of the Espionage Act prohibiting disloyal utterance, propaganda, etc.; 65 persons for threats against the President; 10 persons for sabotage; and under the penal code, with relation to conspiracy, 908 indictments were returned, the last group including the I. W

W. cases. Even this does not spell guilt in every instance, for there have been acquittals as well as convictions, and many trials are yet to be held.

With full allowance for flagrant cases of intrigue and treachery, for the disloyalists that may have escaped the meshes of even so fine a net, for the disloyalty that cannot be measured in terms of jail and indictment—taken all in all, no belligerent country, not even those invaded, made as good a record of unity and loyalty.

After all the hubbub about "rebellion," "armed uprisings," "monster internment camps," etc., the showing was, to put it plainly, rather disappointing. In all of us there is a certain savage something that thrills to the man-hunt. People generally, and the press particularly, were keyed up to a high pitch, an excited distrust of our foreign population, and a percentage of editors and politicians were eager for a campaign of "hate" at home.

There is a simplicity about hate that makes it peculiarly attractive to a certain type of mind. It makes no demand on the mental processes, it does not require reading or thinking, estimate or analysis, and by reason of its instant removal of every doubt it gives an effect of decision, a sense of well-being. When the facts developed by the investigatory branches of government failed to provide sound foundation for a "hate campaign," these editors, politicians, and what not, commenced to build a little foundation of their own. Officials were arraigned for inefficiency and spinelessness, "firing-squads" were demanded with frequency and passion, and fake after fake was sprung, many of them laughable but for their appeals to prejudice and hysteria.

Take just one typical instance out of many: A man whose name need not be mentioned was arrested in December, 1917, and on the heels of his arrest these exaggerations were printed in rapid succession: that he was a former German officer of high rank; that he was a master spy known to have been in communication with Bernstorff, Boy-Ed, and other high German officers prior to our declaration of war; that he arrived in this country on the submarine *U-53*; that after the commencement of the European War he went back to Germany and later returned to the United States; that at times he disguised himself in the uniform of an American army officer; that he was arrested while in the act of lighting a fuse or match for an American army magazine; that a number of men were known to have been employed in his spy machinations; that money was advanced to him by the German spy system, etc. As a matter of fact, all the investigators and investigations failed to prove anything more than that he was a German reservist, in this country since 1910, and a poor sort, unable to hold any job long.

Every fire, every explosion in a munition-plant, every accident on land or sea, was straightway credited to the "spy system"; if the cut in a child's hand didn't heal quickly, then the "Germans" had put germs in all the court-plaster; if any experiment in submarine or aircraft factory failed, it was undoubtedly because the "spies" had tampered with delicate mechanism or dropped acid on the wires; if a woman's headache didn't yield to remedies, then the "Germans" had "doped" the particular pill or powder. I am not saying that none of these things happened; but what happened was out of all proportion to the dimensions of the mad rumors that swept the country; yet through it all the great, splendid majority of America's "aliens" stood fast, discharging their full duty to the United States in a manner that shamed the patriotism of many an heir to the traditions of Plymouth Rock.

In the year and a half of my chairmanship of the Committee on Public Information, a stream of people poured through the office daily, of all colors, creeds, and races;

THE "AMERICANIZERS"

and out of that nightmare of solicitation, selfish purposes, and personal aggrandizements I can recall with gratitude that never once did any foreign-born American come to me for any other purpose than an offer of service to the United States or some plan of sacrifice. When it comes to motives, of course, I am unable to estimate the possible weight of caution or fear; but the mere fact is too significant to be negligible.

Among the six thousand people interned were many Germans as full of disloyalty as an adder is full of venom. There were Germans, Austrians, and Hungarians in the United States not interned, who hid disloyalty in their hearts; nor may it be denied that there is still a great work to do among the German population to burn away entirely the last trace of Deutschtum. But against this minority must be balanced an overwhelming majority of Germans who offered their lives to cleanse the honor stained by the treachery and ingratitude of others.

It is estimated by military authorities that from 10 to 15 per cent. of the American Expeditionary Forces were men of German birth or origin. How they conducted themselves on the firing-line is a matter of history, for in the imperishable records of the War Department Americans of foreign birth and descent have written the story of their valor on every page. In the list of those cited for distinguished service by General Pershing, nothing is more significant than the fact that name after name betokens other than native origin. Here are a few illustrative samples:

Lieutenant Kuehlman, Field Engineers: "Sent on night of August fifth-sixth to make a reconnaissance of all possible means of crossing the river Vesle, near Fismes, France. It had been reported that the Germans had all retreated from the south bank of the river, but he found that such was not the case; they were there in force;

171

nevertheless, such was his bravery and determination that he crossed into and through the German lines, made a full reconnaissance, and returned with his report."

First Lieutenant Frank Baer, S. R. C. pilot, 103d Aero Pursuit Squadron: "For the following repeated acts of extraordinary heroism in action, April 5, 12, and 13, May 8 and 21, 1918, Lieutenant Baer is awarded a bronze oak leaf to be worn on the Distinguished Service Cross awarded him April 12, 1918. Lieutenant Baer brought down enemy 'planes on April 5, April 12, and on April 21, 1918. On May 4, 1918, he destroyed two German machines and on May 21st he destroyed his eighth enemy 'plane."

Private Bernard Schultheis: "When the infantry was advancing in a position exposed to cross-fire, volunteered and carried a message to advancing troops, informing them that the machine-gun barrage laid down on the enemy emplacements was friendly fire from a unit not in their support and acting without orders to cover the advance. He delivered the message, returned across an open field swept by enemy machine-guns, and thereby made it possible for the infantry unit to advance four hundred meters and gain its objective."

Sergeant John Blohm: "From a shell-hole in which he had taken shelter while returning from a successful daylight patrol across the Vesle River, Sergeant Blohm saw a corporal of his patrol dragging himself through the grass and bleeding profusely from a wound in his neck. He unhesitatingly left his shelter, carried the corporal behind a tree near the river-bank, dressed his wounds, and, using boughs from a fallen tree as an improvised raft, towed the injured man across the river and carried him two hundred yards over an open field to the American outpost line, all under continuous rifle and machine-gun fire."

The Distinguished Service Cross went posthumously to the following: Sergeant L. W. Pilcher, Corporal R.

McC. Fischer, Corporal Charles Auer, Corporal V. M. Schwab, Sergeant Bernard Werner.

As it was with our German-born, so it was in even larger degree with all the other foreign elements in our population.

Throughout its existence, the Committee on Public Information maintained intimate contact with over twenty foreign-language groups, and while this contact had its tremendous depression, there were also splendid inspirations. It was inspiring to see the passion of the immigrant peoples for freedom, their pathetic devotion to the professed ideals of America, their determination to be "real" Americans, and to watch their devotion persist in spite of persecution, neglect, and misunderstanding; it was depressing to discover how little America had done for them, how small a part the alien played in America's love and thought.

Nothing is more true than that people "do not live by bread alone." The great majority live on catch phrases. For years the United States had discharged its duty to the immigrant by glib reference to the melting-pot, and yet it has been years since the melting-pot has done any melting to speak of. These hopeful thousands, coming to the land of promise with their hearts in their hands, have been treated with every indifference, and only in the most haphazard way have they been brought into touch with the bright promise of American life.

Cheated by employers, lawyers, loan sharks, and employment agencies; excluded from American social and religious life as "wops," "Dagoes," and "hunkies"; given opportunity to learn English only at casual night-schools after brain-deadening days of toil; herded in ghettoes and foreign quarters by their poverties and ignorances; and then, after all this, when war brought these millions to our attention, we actually wondered why they had not been

"Americanized," and cried out against foreign languages, a "foreign press," and a "foreign pulpit" as evidences of disloyalty.

In spite of the past, with all of its cruelties and despairs, the foreign-born *were* loyal, and, what is even more inspiring, they *grew* in loyalty despite new persecutions initiated by mistaken patriotism. For instance, the governor of Iowa proclaimed the following rules:

"*First*—English should and must be the only medium of instruction in public, private, denominational, or other similar schools.

"*Second*—Conversation in public places, on trains, or over the telephone should be in the English language.

"*Third*—All public addresses should be in the English language.

"*Fourth*—Let those who cannot speak or understand the English language conduct their religious worship in their homes."

In other states, similar prohibitions were put into effect, and sudden and fundamental changes were worked not only in the schools, churches, and the press, but in the whole social structure. No effort at distinction was made —the language of Allied and neutral countries being put under the ban as well as enemy languages.

There can be no denial of the evil that was attempted to be cured. In our schools, our churches, our press, and in our social life, *English should be the one accepted language,* and this must of necessity be our goal. But it was criminal to let the ideal of to-morrow alter the facts of to-day. We faced the conditions that there were hundreds of thousands of foreigners in the United States who could not speak any language but their own—and through no fault of their own. The drive against the use of foreign languages, either written or spoken, merely shut off these thousands from contact with American life, with the danger of pushing them farther into ignorance and aloofness, and robbing us of the opportunity to win their understanding and co-operation.

The Czechoslovaks were the first to come to us with reports of the cruelties and injustices worked by these regulations in the various states. A great people indomitable, devoted! Over sixty thousand fought in the American army, thousands enlisting voluntarily at the outset of war; there were about thirty thousand in the Czechoslovak army in Italy, and about ninety thousand fought in Siberia. It will be news to many to learn that the first real blow against German and American intrigue in the United States was struck by the Bohemian National Alliance. With the assistance of some Czechoslovak officials at the Austrian consulates, and through a most remarkable machinery of espionage, the Bohemians defeated plot after plot against America and brought out the evidence that resulted in the recall of Dumba. The Czechoslovak societies were the only ones that adopted the rule that every member must own a Liberty bond.

Even these people, however, whose courage and loyalty have become proverbs, were not spared persecution by provincial ignorance. In one Texas town, virtually all the young men of the Czechoslovak colony volunteered, and their departure was made the occasion of a great demonstration. Many old people were there, and the speeches were in the native tongue. Without any attempt to inquire into the nature of the meeting, "native patriots" threw rocks in the window, attacked the audience, and drove them forth from the building as though they had been Huns caught in some atrocity.

In Iowa and Nebraska, meetings held to secure recruits for the Czechoslovak army were broken up because English was not used, and from scores of communities we received pathetic letters telling how Bohemian parents, who had given all their sons to the American army, were hounded as traitors because they could not speak English.

The Council of Defense for Seward County, Nebraska, requested all the churches in the district to conduct their services in English, except one for old people who could not understand English. The minister of the Danish Lutheran church of Staplehurst, one Hansen, asked the Council's permission to continue preaching in Danish because he was not young when he came to America, also because his bad ears had prevented him from learning English sufficiently well to preach in it. The Council denied his request and also refused him a year's grace while he found other work to support himself and his family.

The Danish Young People's Society of America changed a "loyalty convention" from Iowa because forbidden the use of Danish. Queerly enough, many of the members of the society speak and understand Danish but poorly, and, under ordinary circumstances, always use English among themselves. But as 85 per cent. of the members were serving in the United States army and navy, the members deeply resented the charge that the use of Danish in any way interfered with their patriotism.

Sheer stubbornness, of course, but exceedingly natural. The Danes, Norse, and Swedes are proud people, and very "set," and it stung them unbearably to be adjudged unpatriotic in any degree and to have their native tongues put under the ban along with German. But while they resented and protested, even working hard to remember a language half forgotten, they never failed to make themselves understood in every Liberty Loan drive, Red Cross rally, or at every recruiting station.

All the while the foreign-born, patiently, indomitably, were writing a record of devotion shot through with service and sacrifice. In Milwaukee a group of Polish women evolved an idea that spread all over the United States into every racial group. In order that their husbands might fight, these Polish women clubbed together by sixes and eights, rented a house, selected from among themselves a housekeeper who took care of the house and the children while the other five or seven went to work. In this way, their living expenses were cut down so that they could not only support themselves and relieve their husbands from any anxiety about them, but were even able to buy Liberty bonds from their savings.

The Italians in the United States are about 4 per cent. of the whole population, but the list of casualties shows a full 10 per cent. of Italian names. More than three hundred thousand Italians figured on the army list, and in defense of the inner lines as well as on the firing-lines they proved their devotion to their adopted country. There was no shipyard, ammunition - factory, airplane-factory, steel-mill, mine, lumber-camp, or docks in which the Italians did not play a large part, and often the most prominent part, in actual and efficient work. In some places, such as mines and docks, the Italians reached fully 30 per cent. of the total number of employees, working at all times with full and affectionate loyalty toward the government of the United States. For instance, when a strike was threatened in one of the big industrial centers, it was an Italian who jumped on a box and cried, "If you leave work now, it will be as though you were sneaking back out of a trench, abandoning your comrades at the time of a fight when they need you most." And the strike was averted.

The Lithuanians, of whom there are about one million in the United States, gave thirty thousand soldiers to the colors, 50 per cent. of them volunteers. At the close of the Fourth Liberty Loan, the leaders assured us that there was not a Lithuanian home in the United States in which the family savings had not been invested in bonds or War Savings Stamps.

There are about 15,000 Russians in the United States army and the total contribution of Russians to the Fourth Liberty Loan was $40,000,000.

The National Croatian Society, with a membership of 42,000, did these three things: adopted one of the most ringing declarations of loyalty ever penned; decreed expulsion for any member expressing a disloyal sentiment or attempting to evade military service; bought $300,000 of Liberty bonds, and donated over $50,000 to Red Cross work.

In the army were 60,000 men of Greek birth or descent, and it is estimated that the Greek purchase of Liberty bonds was well over $30,000,000 for the four drives, all coming in small amounts that represented sacrifice.

It is a record that could be stretched out into pages, for there is not a foreign-language group in the United States that did not answer America's call with devotion and understanding, pathetically proud of their Liberty bonds and their service flags, and feeling every individual instance of indifference or disloyalty as a stain and a shame. But never at any time were we able to fix this record in the consciousness of the American people or to induce the press of the United States to give it prominence or even recognition. It was infinite labor to get noted Americans to address the foreign-language groups, and great loyalty meetings of the foreign-born, where thousands pledged lives and money and love, either went unnoticed by the papers or were given an indifferent little note of two or three lines.

As if prejudice, indifference, and misguided patriotism were not handicaps enough in the fight for unity, politics also played an ugly part in the drama of confusion. Particularly was this true in the Northwest, where Scandinavians and Germans are in the majority among the farmers. There is no doubt that many of these people were pro-German at the outset, and, even after America's entrance, pro-Germanism persisted by reason of well-established lies and certain fundamental ignorances.

The Committee on Public Information, formed to fight disaffection, attacked the Northwest at once. Our pamphlets and motion pictures, received somewhat coldly at first, soon began to gain ground, and the next move was to send speakers, for there is nothing like the give and take of a public meeting to burn away misunderstanding. The one organization that we wanted most particularly to reach was the Nonpartisan League, for it had a membership that covered the Dakotas, Minnesota, Montana, and Idaho, and, more than any other, was impregnated with the lie about a "rich man's war."

The leaders of the Nonpartisan League came personally to Washington to ask the government to commence a campaign of patriotic education, and Minnesota was selected for the initiation of the drive. Our speakers, however, upon arrival in Minnesota, were informed by the State Public Safety Commission that they would not be allowed to address any meetings arranged by the Nonpartisan League or under its auspices. There was no quarrel with the men we sent, for the Commission asked permission to use them in its own speaking campaign.

As we tried to explain to them, however, the main purpose in sending speakers over the United States was not to address those already enthusiastic in the national service, but to reach and convert people out of touch and sympathy with American thought and aims. Even if the Nonpartisan League were disloyal, then the more reason why our speakers should smash at its membership with the truth. But the State Public Safety Commission stood like iron, barred our speakers absolutely, and inaugurated a campaign of terrorism that had its ugly reflex among the farmers and labor unions in every state.

In summer the proscribed farmers were compelled to hold Liberty Loan rallies or Red Cross meetings out in the fields under the blazing sun, and in winter they huddled in cowsheds and car-barns. Parades were stopped by Home Guards or broken up by townsmen. Old men and women were dragged from automobiles, and on one wretched occasion a baby of six months was torn from its mother's arms by the powerful stream from a fire-hose. Tar-and-feather "parties" were common, and even deportations took place, men being driven from their homes and from the very state because they had sons belonging to the League.

There is no doubt as to the political nature of the persecution. The Nonpartisan League had carried the state of North Dakota, and was showing such strength in Minnesota, South Dakota, Nebraska, Montana, and Idaho as to arouse the alarm of Democratic and Republican politicians. These leaders made no bones about confessing that the disloyalty issue was the means by which they hoped to crush and destroy the Nonpartisan League as a political organization.

Such is the seeming invincibility of the democratic ideal, however, that even campaigns of terrorism could not drive its membership, largely German and Scandinavian, into disloyalty. North Dakota, where the League elected every state officer, had a war record of which any state might be proud.

The State Councils of Defense did splendid work, as a rule, and the country owes much to them, but there were exceptions that aroused far more anger than loyalty, conducting themselves in a manner that would have been lawless in any other than a "patriotic" body. During Liberty Loan drives, for instance, it became a habit, in certain sections, to compel a regular income return from the foreign-born and the poorer classes. Men, claiming authority, would visit these homes, insist upon a statement of earnings, expenditures, savings, etc., and then calmly announce the amount of the contribution that the dazed victims were expected to make. Anything in the nature of resistance was set down as "slacking" and "disloyalty," and some of the penalties visited were expulsion from the community, personal ill treatment, or a pleasant little attention like painting the house yellow. Of all the bitternesses and disaffections reported to us, the majority proceeded from this sort of terrorism, and it had results that will be felt for years to come.

Another handicap in the fight for national unity soon presented itself in the form of those volunteer patriotic societies that sprang up over the land like mushrooms, all sincere and loyal enough, but demoralizing often by virtue of this very eagerness. These organizations collected their funds by public appeal, and as the most obvious justification of existence was furnished by publicity, their activities inevitably took such form as would earn the largest amount of newspaper space. As a consequence, their patriotism was a thing of screams, violence, and extremes; they outjingoed the worst of the jingoes, and their constant practice of extreme statement left a trail of anger, irritation, and resentment.

One instance may be cited as illustrative. Prof. Robert McNutt McElroy of the National Security League, returning from a three weeks' tour of the West, gave out a statement in which he said that he had known what it was "to face large bodies of young men clad in the uniform of the American army beneath which were concealed the souls of Prussians." Later, in *The New York Tribune*, he gave the University of Wisconsin as the place where he had encountered disloyalty. The basis of the

13   181

charge was the inattention of the audience throughout his speech, shuffling feet, snapping of rifle triggers, etc., and he told how, finally, to test the audience, he leaned forward and deliberately insulted them as "a bunch of damned traitors"; how, to his amazement, there was no resentment whatever of this or of his later reference to "a Prussian audience." "I hesitate to accuse an entire university of disloyalty," he said, "but to my mind that episode stands out as one of the most disgraceful things I have encountered."

Dr. Charles R. Van Hise, president of the university, John Bradley Winslow, Chief Justice of the Supreme Court of Wisconsin, and E. A. Birge of the College of Science and Letters were appointed as a committee of protest, and their report asserted that the address had been long; that the audience included the cadet regiment —students—who had marched two and a half miles in the rain and were wet and cold; that, being present under orders and unable to withdraw, they merely indicated their desire for an end to the long speech; that Professor McElroy's reflections on their loyalty were made in a tone so low that persons within twenty feet of him did not hear the words at all.

Thus, then, by reason of a speaker who failed to hold an audience of boys throughout an address of two hours, the loyalty of a state was impugned, the patriotism of a great university was besmirched, and a new element of anger and justifiable resentment introduced into the already delicate Wisconsin situation.

And so the story runs on drearily, volumes being necessary for any complete and circumstantial account of the obstacles thrown in the way of the millions of foreign birth or descent as they marched forward from every state in answer to the battle-call of their adopted country. The big fact is that they *continued* to march and that they *arrived*.

THE "AMERICANIZERS"

We are even now so close to the trees that we cannot see the forest. All that we have known is the underbrush of irritation, the tearing vines of prejudice, and the poison-ivy of politics. But when the day is come that we are on a hill, blessed with vision and perspective, it will be seen that the rallying of America was not sectional nor yet racial, but that it was the tremendous response of a unified whole, with men and women from other lands standing shoulder to shoulder with the native-born, serving and sacrificing with the same devotion, and in equal measure pouring their blood on the altar of freedom.

XV

THE loyalty of "our aliens," however, splendid as it was, had in it nothing of the spontaneous or the accidental. Results were obtained only by hard, driving work. The bitterness bred by years of neglect and injustice were not to be dissipated by any mere war-call, but had to be burned away by a continuous educational campaign. The *real* America had to be revealed to these foreign-language groups—its drama of hope and struggle, success and blunders—and their minds had to be filled with the tremendous truth that the fight against Germany was a fight for all that life has taught decent human beings to hold dear.

This campaign succeeded because the Committee avoided the professional "Americanizers," and steered clear of the accepted forms of "Americanization." We worked from the *inside*, not from the outside, aiding each group to develop its own loyalty league, and utilizing the natural and existing leaders, institutions, and machinery. We offered co-operation and supervision, and we gave counsel, not commands. As a consequence, each group had its own task, its own responsibility, and as soon as these facts were clearly understood the response was immediate.

Mr. Edwin Bjorkman, the auther and publicist, was selected to go to the Scandinavian group with the plan, and in a short while the Americans of Swedish birth and

ALEXANDER KONTA   JOSEPHINE ROCHE   JULIUS KOETTGEN

ROBERT E. LEE   DR. ANTONIO STELLA
                EDWIN BJORKMAN

descent organized the John Ericsson League of Patriotic Service with the following Executive Committee: Harry Olsen, president, Chicago, Ill.; Harry A. Lund, vice-president, Minneapolis, Minn.; Edwin Bjorkman, secretary, New York; Henry S. Henschen, treasurer, Chicago; Chas. S. Peterson, chairman Finance Committee, Chicago; Gustaf Andreen, Rock Island, Ill.; J. C. Bergquist, New York; J. E. Chilberg, Seattle, Wash.; Andrew Langquist, Chicago; Othelia Myhrman, Chicago; Eric Norton, St. Paul, Minn.; and Victor Olander, Chicago.

Then came the Jacob A. Riis League of Patriotic Service, formed by the Danes, with this Executive Board: Max Henius, president, Chicago; Sophus F. Neble, first vice-president, Omaha, Neb.; John C. Christensen, second vice-president, Chicago; Carl Antonsen, secretary, Chicago; Jens C. Hanse, treasurer and chairman Finance Committee, Chicago; Axel Hellrung, New York; Henry L. Hertz, Chicago; William Hovgaard, Washington, D. C.; Halvor Jacobsen, New York; and Truels P. Nielsen, Seattle, Wash.

Because of the large number of Norwegian-American clubs, societies, and fraternal organizations throughout the country, all busy with patriotic work and war activities, no separate Norwegian organization for this purpose was deemed advisable or necessary. Moreover, every prominent Norwegian-American stood ready at all times to assist with his counsel and influence, and among those of great service to the Committee may be mentioned Magnus Swensen, Madison, Wis., federal food administrator of Wisconsin, and Mr. Herbert Hoover's chief assistant in Northern Europe; Mr. Lauritz S. Swensen, Minneapolis, former United States Minister to Norway; Mr. John P. Howland, Chicago; Attorney Andrew Hummeland, Chicago; Birger Osland, Chicago, major in the United States army, attached to the American Legation, Christiania, Norway;

Joachim G. Giaver, president of the Chicago Norwegian Club, Chicago; Mr. Hauman G. Haugan, director of the State Bank of Chicago; Oscar M. Torrisen, Chicago; Louis M. Anderson, publisher of *Skandinaven*, Chicago; Mr. A. N. Rygg, vice-president of the Norwegian News Co., Brooklyn, N. Y.; the Rev. J. A. O. Stub, Minneapolis; and many others.

The Finns formed the Lincoln Loyalty League, with O. J. Larson as president and J. H. Jasberg as secretary.

The Roman Legion, under the brilliant leadership of Dr. Antonio Stella and Dr. Albert Bonaschi, proved a power among the Americans of Italian birth and descent, and I have always felt that it was this body, as much as any one other source of strength, that enabled Italy to make such an amazing recovery from the Caporetto disaster. In that hour of despair, cablegrams and letters were poured into Italy from the United States by the thousands, going from individuals, pastors, societies, and associations, calling upon the soldiers of Savoy to stand fast, that the Americans were coming and every dollar and every life in America was pledged to victory.

Charles Pergler, now representing the Republic of Czechoslovakia in Japan, was our reliance always in dealing with the peoples from Bohemia, Moravia, and Slovakia, and when Dr. Thomas Garrigues Masaryk came to the United States he put himself wholly and generously at our disposal.

For work among the Poles we had Paderewski, as a matter of course, wonderful in his devotions, enthusiasm, and genius for leadership, and there was also Sigismund Ivanowski, that great painter and even greater man. John Wedda, John Smulski, and many others, actuated by the same pure passions, were also sources of strength.

Then there were our close contacts with the Serbian Legation and the Japanese Embassy; with Captain Stoica, representing the Rumanians; with Doctor Hinkovic, representing the Jugoslavs, and with Doctor Szlupas of the Lithuanian National Council.

Work among the Hungarian population was intrusted to Mr. Alexander Konta of New York, who gave time, money, and finest faith to a difficult and thankless task. It was not only that certain vicious factional elements threw every possible obstacle in his path, but he was equally attacked by *The New York Tribune* and similar papers that made a business of chauvinism. Undismayed and undiscouraged, Mr. Konta continued the work, and the American-Hungarian Loyalty League played no small part in our national unity, for men of Magyar stock figured importantly in the coal and steel industries.

The American Friends of German Democracy was another organization that had to run the gantlet of secret disloyalty and a stupid chauvinism. The pro-Kaiser brand of German-America fought it as a matter of course, and murder threats were common. The word "democcracy" was an offense to the majority of the "better class," who derided the idea of a German republic as "imbecile" and "impudent." The chief enemies, however, were pseudo-patriots and hue-and-cry newspapers, none of them losing a chance to harass. Also, at regular intervals, some broken-arched representative of the Department of Justice would stalk into the office, convinced that he had unearthed a "nest of German spies."

I did not put the full force of the Committee behind the American Friends of German Democracy until its personnel and purposes had been subjected to every investigation, but only the intimacies of contact gave me full appreciation of the courage and patriotism of the men in charge of the movement. For instance, the president was Franz Sigel of New York, the son of that general of the same name who, after having fought for liberty in Germany, came to the United States and offered an exile's sword to Lincoln. Its honorary president was the late Dr. Abraham Jacobi, the famous physician who, after having been imprisoned for his liberal opinions by the Prussian government, fled to this country to become a beloved citizen and an honor to the medical profession. The most powerful spokesman of the movement was Rudolph Blankenburg, the former Mayor of Philadelphia, whose death in the spring of 1918 deprived America of one of its ablest and most honored public servants. J. Koettgen, the secretary, and the heart and soul of the movement, was another of those free minds who had long been fighting the Prussian system. He was of German birth and blood, but no heir to the traditions of Plymouth Rock had a finer, more virile conception of what it meant to be an American.

Among the men who helped most at all times were Dr. Frederick L. Hoffman, celebrated as a statistician; Dr. S. Adolphus Knopf, chosen by the War Department to instruct the American soldiers in France how to keep free from tuberculosis. In Chicago it was Mr. Otto C. Butz, who gathered round him all the actively patriotic Americans of German descent. In Wisconsin Mr. Karl Mathie did yeoman work for the cause of America and democracy. Some of the strongest supporters of the movement were business men like the late William Sleicher of Troy, N. Y., and Charles J. Schlegel of New York. From Cleveland, Ohio, a steady stream of personal letters, appeals, and pamphlets went out from Dr. Christian Sihler, the son of the German officer and clergyman who many decades ago came to Fort Wayne, Ind., to establish one of the most flourishing Lutheran communities. Miss K. Elizabeth Sihler seconded her brother's efforts in Fort Wayne. Dr. William Bohn addressed hundreds of meetings attended by people of German origin, and understood, as did few others, how to arouse the feeling of American loyalty. Mr. William Forster of New York and Mr. Richard Lieber of Indianapolis proved most convincing and effective speakers. Prof. Otta Manthey-Zorn, the son of a German missionary, who would not bow his knee to Bismarck and brought his band of missionaries into the free atmosphere of the United States, stirred the interest of the German-born in the New England States. Mr. Henry Riesenberg, a business man, formerly of Indianapolis, now of New York, employed all of his spare time in addressing public meetings.

The most effective work, however, was probably done by the host of plain men and women whose names are not widely known. There was, for instance, Mr. George Schauer of Indianapolis, who acted as organizer for Indiana. A Bavarian peasant who settled in the United States after having been ill-treated in the German army, Mr. Schauer attacked his task with rare enthusiasm and devotion, and soon became indispensable to all patriotic organizations in Indiana. Then there was Mr. William R. Bricker, the organizer for Pennsylvania, to whom the war provided the opportunity to prove his great organizing abilities.

The work of the organization was carried on through many activities. During the war, hundreds of meetings were held throughout the country. Among the bodies that gave the most powerful support must be mentioned the Turners, whose democratic origin and tendencies lined them up quite naturally on the side of the United States and its cobelligerents.

About a million pamphlets were distributed, chiefly to members of the thousands of clubs and benefit societies formed by the people of German blood. One of the most notable publications was the edition of Lichnowsky's famous memorandum, with an introduction by Mr. Koettgen. The pamphlet was republished in full by many German-language newspapers in this country, and proved itself an effective answer to the lies spread by German propaganda.

Throughout the war the German Bureau kept in closest touch with the German-language press of the United States. A weekly bulletin was published both in German and English. The German edition was sent to two hundred German-language newspapers and reached about two million readers. The English edition went to four hundred American newspapers published mainly in those parts of the country where the German population is numerous. The American newspapers expressed themselves in the most laudatory terms about this press service.

Some of the most interesting work was done abroad. Nearly every member of the American Friends of German Democracy was eager to send some word of good counsel to his blood-relations in Germany. The justice of America's cause was always emphasized, but the chief point would be that it was high time for the Germans to get rid of the Hohenzollerns and militarism. These documents were smuggled into Germany by the foreign representatives of the Committee on Public Information, a number of methods being used. Rather amusingly a splendid appeal written by Capt. A. L. Helwig, an American soldier born in Hamburg, Germany, and a member of the Executive Committee of the American Friends of German Democracy, was carried across the line quite openly. One day, in a certain Scandinavian country, the courier of the German Legation, just about to leave for Germany, was stopped by a very military-looking stranger who performed the Prussian kotow in the most approved fashion. This stranger, handing the courier a great bundle of pamphlets, stated that they were to be delivered to the newspapers and Socialist groups in Hamburg by orde of the German Minister. The courier carried out the commission and Helwig's appeal created no little furor in Hamburg.

The most effective contact, however, was with the German refugees in Switzerland, a brilliant, fearless group of radical democrats headed by such men as Doctor Greeling, author of *J'accuse*, Doctor Muehlon, and Doctor Rosenmeyer. These publicists, exiled from Germany by reason of their fight against Prussianism, published the *Freie Zeitung*, a biweekly paper that managed to slip across the line in considerable numbers. Dr. Frank Bohn, proceeding to Switzerland as the representative of the American Friends of German Democracy, established co-operation arrangements that continued until the armistice. A steady stream of articles went to the *Freie Zeitung* from the United States, and each week several thousand copies of the paper came to the United States for distribution among the German-language press, clubs, and societies.

At first the Germans pretended not to notice the American organization, but finally they could not contain their wrath. Some of the most prominent German newspapers published violent articles against the American Friends, and "dirty pigs" came to be a favorite epithet.

All these bodies worked well and successfully, but as time went on it was seen that more direct methods were necessary, and in May, 1918, the Division of Work Among the Foreign-born was formed. Miss Josephine Roche, in virtual charge of all these various activities from the first, was made director of the new division, and it is to her faith, vision, and rare devotions that the amazing results were due. Under Miss Roche, the government frankly established direct and continuous contact with fourteen racial groups through the following bureaus: the Italian, Hungarian, Lithuanian, Russian, Jugoslav, Czechoslovak, Polish,

German (American Friends of German Democracy), Ukrainian, Danish, Swedish, Norwegian, Finnish, Dutch, and the Foreign Information Service Bureau.

While the bureaus all had the same aim for their work, and all employed similar methods, each group presented problems entirely its own and demanded specialized attention. The press and the organizations, national and local, were the nucleus of the work, and in the cases of the Italian, the Czechoslovak, and the Scandinavian groups these activities met every need.

For other foreign-language groups, such as the Russian, Polish, Jugoslav, and Ukrainian, the press alone was not a sufficient means of contact: either it was not as widely distributed and influential among them or the considerable degree of illiteracy among the people made results from the written communication incomplete. The publication of pamphlets and considerable work through trips was therefore undertaken by these bureau managers. The Polish, Lithuanian, Hungarian, and Ukrainian bureaus did about an equal amount of their work through press and organization contacts and through field-work.

For the fourteen foreign-language groups there are approximately 865 foreign-language newspapers. About 745 of this number were issued regularly, and it was to these that the division sent its press services. Only 33 papers did not use the material, all but three of these being small papers of a highly specialized character; 96 per cent of the papers availed themselves extensively of the material. Very many papers used all but a few releases, and it was a frequent occurrence to have foreign-language papers come in carrying on their front page two or three columns of the bureaus' material.

National and local organizations, fraternal, educational, religious, beneficial, and social in type, are a powerful factor among the foreign-speaking groups. Their con ventions bring together hundreds of delegates from all the various centers of the foreign-language groups, and their activities are far-reaching. The information on government activities, prepared in the form of bulletins or circular letters by the bureaus, and sent to these organizations, was invariably given the most effective distribution to members. Draft and registration circulars, regulations issued by the Passport Control Division of the Department of State, income-tax provisions, were carefully and thoroughly distributed by them. They also gave most valuable and suggestive advice as to the needs and desires of their groups for instruction and understanding.

While there was no need to issue literature in any large quantity because of the facilities offered us for reaching foreign-language groups by their press organizations, the following pamphlets (in addition to the German) were printed as a result of a desire and need found to exist for them and had a distribution of about one hundred and twenty thousand: "America in War and Peace," in Ukrainian; "A Message to American-Hungarians," in Hungarian; "Abraham Lincoln," in Russian; "League of Nations," in Russian.

All bureau managers, either when initiating the work or at frequent intervals during its continuance, learned through personal conference the situation among their groups and gained complete confidence from their people in their work. Lectures were very popular, and the following letter received by a representative of the Russian bureau will give an idea of how eager these people were for the truth:

You have done very much for the Russian colony of the city of ——. You even made our Bolsheviki think and speak about education. I often think now that if we had in —— several people like you, many of the Russian workmen would have been saved from the Utopian Bolshevism, would not believe its idle promises, and would learn to govern themselves independently. Several of our members were present at the lecture and all were very much pleased and grateful to you. Our group has authorized me to ask you to come to live in ——. You are a man of science, and we have no educated people among us. You know that the mind of the Russian workmen has been moved from its former standpoint; it wants to go somewhere, but it does not know the way. If you, the intelligent people, will not help it to find the way, other unscrupulous people will take advantage of the occasion.

The Foreign Information Service, first directed by Mr. Donald Breed and after that by Mr. Barrett Clark, was designed to encourage the foreign-language groups of America by releasing stories telling of their co-operation with the government in such matters as the Liberty Loan, the Red Cross, etc., and to assist the foreign-language press not only in securing prompt and efficient co-operation with the government departments, but by informing the American people through the native-language press of the work that had been done and was now being done by the foreign-language press in helping the foreigner to become a better American. Over fifty such stories were released to thirty-three hundred American papers, these titles conveying the general idea: "The Jugoslav Club," "Greek-American Boys Are Genuine Patriots," "Lithuanians Support Fourth Liberty Loan," "The Czechoslovaks in America," "Ukrainians in America Eager for Education," and "Russian-Americans Aid America in Bond Sales." Fourteen "News Bulletins," giving a number of very brief accounts on the activities of the foreign-born, were also sent out. In addition to information service through press organizations, all bureaus did considerable translating of letters and articles for government departments and furnished them numerous reports concerning their group.

WORK AMONG THE FOREIGN-BORN

Highly intensive, as well as extensive, work was done in co-operation with the office of the Provost-Marshal-General. All the bureaus released for days before registration the fullest and clearest instructions which received columns of space daily in the press. Provost-Marshal-General Crowder wrote us the following letter in regard to the bureau's achievements:

I have already expressed to Mr. Creel my appreciation of the invaluable work done by all members of his staff in contributing to publicity on Registration Day. But I have an especial sentiment of gratitude to yourself, because the task of reaching the foreign-born, who are unfamiliar with our language, seemed to me to be one of the most difficult, and perhaps beyond power of achievement.

But as I read your report of the methods employed, I am convinced that the task was fully accomplished. The daily arrivals of newspapers in foreign languages show how wide-spread are the ramifications of influence of your office, and have revealed to me what a powerful and effective agency the government possesses. Your tact, energy, and ingenuity in utilizing this agency to its fullest command my admiration, and I offer my personal thanks.

Far more exhaustive was the work done in co-operation with the Internal Revenue Department in explaining and helping work out the provisions of the revenue bill affecting aliens. A most critical situation was created among the foreign-speaking people by the law's failure sufficiently to define the terms "resident" and "non-resident" aliens, and by its provision that employers should withhold 8 per cent. from the wages of their non-resident employees, their total tax being 12 per cent. as against the 6 per cent. paid by citizens and resident aliens. The matter came to the attention of our bureau managers through letters and personal appeals from their people all over the country. Altogether nearly 3,000 of these appeals came in, showing a state of complete bewilderment and wretchedness, and the two following, from different language groups, will give some idea of the situation:

RUSSIAN BUREAU: I, ——, beg the Russian Bureau to help me. The Russian immigrants are not able to pay the war [probably income] taxes. Some time ago I read in the papers that only those who earned more than $1,000 a year have to pay the tax and only on what they earned over $1,000; and I have paid $12.07. But now in the factory they withhold more, and tell that I myself must pay $145 for last year, and if I have to pay for this year also, I will have to pay more than $300. And so I have to work, but do not get money to live on. And I beg the Russian Bureau to answer my prayer, and to tell me what is going to become of the Russian immigrants.

GENTLEMEN: I wish to send my complaint against the —— in St. Joseph, Mo. I am a poor man, and working very hard for my living. I do not know who is wronging me, either United States government or the company. In the office they asked me whether I will go back to Europe; I answered yes. Then they told me that I have to pay the tax. I asked them what kind of a tax? For the year 1918. I said, all right, how much I have to pay? $25, they told me. I said, never mind! Then they withhold my one week and half wages. I thought that I would get the third week pay, so I could pay to the grocer and the storekeeper. But nevertheless they withheld the third pay. I was supposed to get $19.58, and they gave me only $3.80. What will I do; poor unfortunate man? I went to the superintendent and asked him for receipt. He refused. Now, whom shall I ask for it? I asked him whether I will get full pay for the fourth week? He said, no! To tell you the truth, I cried after I left the office. I really do not know how I can make a living.

Please accept my request, and help me in my grievance. Is it the same proceeding for everybody, or only for me? Does America allow the companies to exploit the poor people in such way?

Instead of withholding the tax on each pay-day, many employers took it in a lump sum, frequently amounting to an entire week's wages, or more. Many aliens in the resident class were considered non-residents because of their refusal to sign a "blue slip" stating intention of residence which they believed meant they could never go back to Europe for a visit, and was some sort of an enforced citizenship paper. An additional grievance was that receipts for wages thus withheld were rarely given.

In attempting to alleviate the various grave injustices, the Internal Revenue Department in Washington showed most unusual sympathy and breadth of vision. Treasury decisions were extensively revised and any number of regulations drawn up with the intent of bettering matters. Our bureaus released from ten to twenty explanatory articles and gave their attention and answers to all the individual inquiries.

Of equal importance with this work of reaching the foreign-speaking groups with information, as described, was what this work had revealed about these groups. The war gave a chance for a dramatic and striking manifestation of their services and loyalty to the country. After the armistice their interest and devotion was just as great in helping in the difficult transition and reconstruction problems. The same unreserved spirit with which they had enlisted in the army, and in the Liberty Loan and War Savings Stamp campaigns, marked their efforts in peace, in encouraging all their people to become citizens, to learn English, to carry out any suggestions coming from government sources. Numerous printing concerns offered to print and distribute among their people books on American history, civics, and the Constitution. Editors of several groups ran serials on citizenship and wished to carry translations of the best American stories in their papers. They asked us to suggest these and to get translation rights for them.

For years national unity and progress have demanded the release of the neglected potentialities of our millions of new Americans into a fuller participation in our country's

14   197

life. For this there is necessary a mutual process of education of native and foreign born. Full information on American life, opportunities, customs, and laws must reach the men and women coming here from foreign lands immediately upon their arrival. Necessarily it must be in their own language. The more they learn in this way of our fundamental democracy and the possibilities for them and their children in this country, the keener become their desire and efforts to learn "America's language." To withhold this information or delay it until, according to theoretic calculation, these immigrants have had time to acquire English, is deliberately to create a period of cruel bewilderment and false impressions for them which dampens whatever enthusiasm they had originally to study English. The numerous un-American conditions and injustices to which so many immigrants have fallen victims must be wiped out. Explanations and instruction about America given to the fullest extent carry little weight when individuals have been unjustly wronged.

The ignorance of many native-born Americans about European peoples and their contemptuous attitude toward persons with different customs from their own are just as serious obstacles to assimilation and unity as the tendency of some immigrants to cling to Old World ways; understanding must come, on our part, of the heritages of these new-comers, their suffering and struggles in Europe, and the contributions they bring us if we will only receive them.

The devotion of the men and women associated with Miss Roche was such that each deserves detailed mention, but space permits only this grateful record of their names:

Swedish Service.........First directed by Mr. Olaf P. Zethelius, and after his death in charge of Mr. H. Gude Grinndal
Norwegian Service........Mr. Sundby-Hansen

WORK AMONG THE FOREIGN-BORN

Danish Service...................Mr. Viggo C. Eberlin
Finnish Service..................Mr. Charles H. Hirsimaki
Dutch Service...................Mr. James J. Van Pernis
Polish Bureau...................Miss Wanda Wojcieszak
Ukrainian Bureau...............Mr. Nicholas Ceglinsky
Lithuanian Bureau..............Mr. Julius Kaupas
Czechoslovak Bureau............Mrs. Anna Tvrzicka
German Bureau.................Mr. Julius Koettgen
Hungarian Bureau..............Mr. Alfred Markus
Italian Bureau..................Dr. Albert C. Bonaschi
Russian Bureau.................Mr. Joseph Polonsky
Jugoslav Bureau................Mr. Peter Mladineo

XVI

WILL IRWIN had one of the great ideas of the war when he suggested that the Fourth of July, 1918, should be "turned over" to Americans of foreign birth and descent for such celebrations as might most fittingly manifest their loyalty to the United States and their devotion to free institutions. It was not only the case that the celebration of the day in this manner, if carried to success, meant a new unity and a larger enthusiasm, but there was also the influence that it would exert upon the public opinion of other countries. When the Central Powers heard that Germans, Austrians, and Turks were marching in public demonstration of their repudiation of the autocratic governments from which they came, and when the neutral nations saw men and women of their blood declaring a great faith in the ideals of America, our cause was bound to know a great strengthening. Through our various contacts we put the idea up to the thirty-three foreign-language groups, and on May 21st this petition went to the President of the United States:

To the President of the United States:

On the Fourth of July, 1776, the founders of this Republic began the movement for human liberty and the rights of nations to govern themselves. One hundred and forty-two years later we find the world democracy, of which this nation was a pioneer, formidably assailed by the powers of reaction and autocracy.

A WONDERFUL FOURTH OF JULY

We represent these peoples whose sons and daughters came to this land later than the founders of the Republic, but drawn by the same ideals. The nations and races and peoples which we represent are taking their part, in one way or another, in the struggle. Some, happily, enjoying a political entity, are fighting openly and with arms against the enemies of progress. Others, unhappily, submerged, can give but a passive opposition. Others have been forced against their will into the armies of the common enemy. Finally, a few still remain outside, hard pressed, threatened by the mailed fist, dreading alike to be drawn in and to be found apart from the rest when the hour of settlement comes. But all, through infinite suffering, struggle, either blindly or open-eyed, toward the same end, the right of peoples to govern themselves as they themselves see fit, and a just and lasting peace.

The higher interests of the races which we left behind have become identical, in this significant year, with the higher interests of the United States. We regard ourselves not only as members of an American commonwealth, one and indivisible, but of the world commonwealth, equally indivisible. United for the principles of that democratic world-state which is fighting now for its being on the battle-fields of Europe, we intend, on July 4, 1918, to manifest, by special celebrations, our loyalty to this country and to the cause for which we fight; and we respectfully request that you call the attention of your fellow-citizens to this fact, in order that they may join with us in commemorating this, the anniversary not only of national freedom, but of universal freedom.

From President Wilson came the sympathetic and favorable reply:

To Our Citizens of Foreign Extraction:

I have read with great sympathy the petition addressed to me by your representative bodies regarding your proposed celebration of Independence Day; and I wish to convey to you, in reply, my heartfelt appreciation for its expression of loyalty and good will. Nothing in this war has been more gratifying than the manner in which our foreign-born fellow-citizens, and the sons and daughters of the foreign-born, have risen to this greatest of all national emergencies. You have shown where you stand not only by your frequent professions of loyalty to the cause for which we fight, but by your eager response to calls to patriotic service, including the supreme sacrifice of offering life itself in battle for justice, freedom, and democracy. Before such devotion as you have shown all distinctions of race vanish; and we feel ourselves citizens in a Republic of free spirits.

I, therefore, take pleasure in calling your petition, with my hearty commendation, to the attention of all my fellow-countrymen, and I ask that they unite with you in making the Independence Day of this, the year when all the principles to which we stand pledged are on trial, the most significant in our national history.

As July 4, 1776, was the dawn of democracy for this nation, let us on July 4, 1918, celebrate the birth of a new and greater spirit of democracy by whose influence we hope and believe, what the signers of the Declaration of Independence dreamed of for themselves and their fellow-countrymen, shall be fulfilled for all mankind.

I have asked the Committee on Public Information to cooperate with you in any arrangements you may wish to make for this celebration.

WOODROW WILSON.

Mr. Irwin and Miss Josephine Roche threw themselves into the arrangements with enthusiasm, and under their stimulation governors and mayors issued proclamations similar to that of the President, and exactly thirty-three nationalities in the United States commenced to make plans that would insure their people's complete participation. No pains were spared to make the day all they longed to have it. Probably never were there such gigantic preparations throughout the entire country for Independence Day, and certainly never was there such an outpouring of the nation's millions of new citizens and citizens-to-be as on July 4, 1918.

Demonstrations of the thirty-three nationalities took place not only in all the cities and towns, but in practically every community where any of these people dwelt. Reports of parades, pageants, and mass-meetings, resolutions, declarations, and inscriptions on banners, could be enumerated for every foreign-born group and for each separate community, but it would be only a repetition of the story of their devotion.

The pilgrimage to Mount Vernon, so beautiful a feature of that inspiring Fourth of July, was *my* idea. I claim the credit and cling to it with fondness because the occasion stands out in the life of the Committee as one of the few events that swept from start to finish without attack, obstruction, or untoward happening. Everything in connection with the pilgrimage was dear and delightful, and lingers in memory as an inspiration. My first thought was merely to have the thirty-three foreign groups select representatives and send them to Washington, where the Committee would convey them to Mount Vernon by automobile to lay wreaths on the tomb of Washington and to make such speeches as befitted the occasion. And then it came to me that it was a time and place for the President himself not only to receive and greet the representatives of the foreign-born in the name of the country to which they were pledging their devotion, but also to make a new and explicit statement of America's ideals to the world.

At first the President refused flatly, for he felt that a speech at the tomb of Washington on the Fourth of July savored of presumption. When my own arguments proved unavailing I brought the foreign-born into play, and the message that he received made continued refusal an impossibility. When he consented finally it was with the completeness and generosity that never failed to mark his surrenders. For instance, he telephoned me a few days later, I remember, and remarked that if I had "no objections" to urge, he and Mrs. Wilson would be very glad to take the thirty-three representatives down to Mount Vernon as their guests on the *Mayflower*. I had no objections to urge. Albanians, Armenians, Assyrians, Belgians, Bulgarians, Chinese, Czechoslovaks, Costa-Ricans, Danes, Dutch, Ecuadorians, Finns, French, French-Canadians, Germans, Greeks, Hungarians, Italians, Japanese, Lithuanians, Mexicans, Norwegians, Poles, Filipinos, Russians, Venezuelans, Rumanians, Spaniards, Jugoslavs, Swedes, Swiss, Syrians, and Ukrainians were in the throng that flocked aboard the *Mayflower*.

With their Old World conceptions, built around kings and queens and courts, the majority of them wore silk hats, frock-coats, and expressions of the utmost solemnity. Within an hour the whole funereal aspect of the occasion changed to an unaffected joyousness. I have never known a man who had the gift of simplicity in greater degree than Woodrow Wilson or one with such a *human* note in the personal relation. He has dignity without effort, graciousness without condescension, interest without affectation, all expressions of a democracy that came from the heart, not merely from the lips. With Mrs. Wilson and Miss Margaret Wilson he moved from group to group, laughingly suggesting that they put their high silk hats to one side, as interested in them as they were in him, and giving every man and woman the feeling of being a sovereign citizen in a free country.

The scene at Mount Vernon was one that etched itself in memory. The shining stretches of the river, the walk up the winding path through the summer woods, the hillsides packed with people, the beat of their hands like the soft roar of a forest wind, the simple brick tomb of the Father of Our Country overhung with wistaria in all the glory of its purple bloom. A piano was tucked away behind a clump of cedars, and when John McCormack had somewhat recovered from his climb up the hill he sang "The Battle Hymn of the Republic," while each of the thirty-three representatives walked into the tomb, one by one, laid a wreath upon the grave, and offered a prayer to the "august shade of the departed." Easily, naturally, the group formed about the President, who stood on a grassy mound to the right of the vault, and Felix J. Stryckmans, Belgian-born, delivered the message bearing the signature of all the thirty-three representatives and expressing the feelings of the great masses of new Americans:

One hundred and forty-two years ago to-day a group of men animated with the same spirit as that of a man who lives here, founded the United States of America on the theory of free government with the consent of the governed. That was the beginning of America. As the years went on, and one century blended with another, men and women came from even the uttermost ends of the earth to join them. We have called them alien; but they were never alien. Though they spoke not a word of the language of this country, though they groped only dimly toward its institutions, they were already Americans in soul or they would never have come. We are the latest manifestation of that American soul.

We, who make this pilgrimage, are the offspring of thirty-three different nations—and Americans all. We come not alone. Behind us are millions of our people united to-day in pledging themselves to the cause of this country and of the free nations with which she is joined. From coast to coast, in city, town, and hamlet our citizens will be demonstrating that the oath they took upon their naturalization was not an empty form of words. Yes, more than that. When, to-morrow, the casualty list brings heaviness to some homes and a firm sense of resolution to all, we shall read upon the roll of honor Slavic names, Teutonic names, Latin names, Oriental names, to show that we have sealed our faith with the blood of our best youth. To this beloved shade we come to-day with the hopes of our races garnered in our hands.

The President, in answer, delivered the address that stands in my mind as one of the greatest that ever came from his lips. With the home of Washington on the hill above him, with the tomb of the warrior-statesman at his back, and with the purpose of America expressed by the thirty-three nationalities before him—made one by democracy—he challenged the world with these imperishable sentences:

There can be but one issue. The settlement must be final. There can be no compromise. No half-way decision would be tolerable. No half-way decision is conceivable. These are the ends for which the associated peoples of the world are fighting and which must be conceded them before there can be peace:

1. The destruction of every arbitrary power anywhere that can separately, secretly, and of its single choice disturb the peace of the world; or, if it cannot be presently destroyed, at the least its reduction to virtual impotence.

2. The settlement of every question, whether of territory, of sovereignty, of economic arrangements, or of political relationship, upon the basis of the free acceptance of that settlement by the people immediately concerned, and not upon the basis of the material interest or advantage of any other nation or people which may desire a different settlement for the sake of its own exterior influence or mastery.

3. The consent of all nations to be governed in their conduct toward each other by the same principles of honor and of respect for the common law of civilized society that govern the individual citizens of all modern states in their relations with one another to the end that all promises and covenants may be sacredly observed, no private plots or conspiracies hatched, no selfish injuries wrought with impunity, and a mutual trust established upon the handsome foundation of a mutual respect for right.

4. The establishment of an organization of peace which shall make it certain that the combined power of free nations will check every invasion of right and serve to make peace and justice the more secure by affording a definite tribunal of opinion to which all must submit and by which every international readjustment that cannot be amicably agreed upon by the peoples directly concerned shall be sanctioned.

These great objects can be put into a single sentence. What we seek is the reign of law, based upon the consent of the governed and sustained by the organized opinion of mankind.

John McCormack then sang "The Star-spangled Banner" as it was never sung before, and down we went to the river again, onto the *Mayflower* and back to Washington.

Great as were the meanings and hopes which the spirit of 1918's Fourth of July brought the foreign-born, of equal importance were the foundations it laid for an understanding by our "Americans for generations back" that these "Americans by choice" came here with the same hopes as did our Pilgrim ancestors, and willing, as they were, to make the supreme sacrifice for their nation's safe continuance, and knowing, as they did, the cost of freedom. From that day a new unity was manifest in the United States.

XVII

ALL credit for the *Official Bulletin* is due to the President. It was his conviction that the government should issue a daily gazette for the purpose of assuring full and authoritative publication of all official acts and proceedings, as well as serving as a chain of intelligence to link together the various branches of the war-making machinery of America. It was not an idea that appealed to me and as strongly as might be I dissented from it. The necessity of such a publication could not be denied, but I knew in my heart that it would be misrepresented, possibly to a degree that would destroy its usefulness. When the President insisted, however, I secured the services of Mr. E. S. Rochester, formerly managing editor of *The Washington Post*, and the *Official Bulletin* was launched in May, 1917, as economically as possible. It is a pleasure to be able to record that the President was absolutely right and that I was entirely wrong.

From its very first day, the *Official Bulletin* met a great need and discharged an important service, growing in popularity to a point that it became one of the great divisions of the Committee. As expected, the press attacked it viciously on the ground that it was a "government organ" designed to compete with private enterprise. The accusation was utterly without foundation in fact, for not one single item or article of any kind was ever

F. W. McReynolds

L. Ames Brown

Clara Sears Taylor

E. S. Rochester

printed in the *Official Bulletin* in advance of publication in the daily press. Nor did its columns ever contain an opinion or a conclusion, the contents being confined exclusively to official documents, statements, and orders.

When this attack fell to the ground of its own weight, the correspondents blithely changed from abuse to ridicule. Because the *Official Bulletin* did not express opinions it was branded as "dull," and because it did not print "exclusive stuff" it was derided as "useless." Yet neither slander nor jeers had power to stop a growth that proved almost resistless. In order to keep the circulation within official bounds, we fixed a subscription price of $5 a year, supposing that to be prohibitive, yet in November, 1918, we took in more than $10,000 in subscriptions, and on the day of suspension the books showed receipts of more than $80,000. Starting with a daily average circulation of 60,000 in May, 1917, a high-water mark of 118,000 was reached in August, 1918. If we had chosen to depart from our policy of repression at any time, the paid circulation could have been doubled and trebled.

What stood proved by the experiment was this: that there was an imperative demand from a large number of people for a publication that printed news without cutting or coloring. The newspaper practice is to cut down the story until it can be screamed in the head, and even these bald presentations of naked conclusions are changed according to the policies and politics of the paper. From every corner of the country the *Official Bulletin* was hailed with joy as the one publication that gave official information in full and without change.

There is humor in the fact that when we took the press at its word and cut newspapers from the free list, virtually every Washington correspondent sent in his five dollars to become a paid subscriber. Also, in the first months of attacks and ridicule, the metropolitan editors had a way of throwing the *Official Bulletin* into the waste-basket. As time went on, however, there dawned the realization that the *Official Bulletin* constituted the one full and accurate record of America's war progress, and we were deluged by letters begging us for complete sets or for back numbers to fill the gaps in files.

In the pages of the *Official Bulletin*, day after day, was printed every state paper, proclamation, executive order, and all statements, pronouncements, and addresses by the President since the entry of this government into the war; every order, pronouncement, and regulation issued by the heads of the great permanent government departments, the Food, Fuel, and Railroad Administrations, the War Industries Board, War Trade Board, Alien Property Custodian, War Labor Board, the Postmaster-General as Director-General of the Telephone, Telegraph, and Cable Systems, and all other independent agencies of the government. Important contracts awarded, texts of important laws, proceedings of the United States Supreme Court, a daily résumé of important actions of Congress, Treasury statements, etc., were also printed regularly.

The *Bulletin* printed all issued records to date of every casualty among our army and navy forces abroad and in the camps and cantonments in the United States; the name of every man taken prisoner, cited for bravery, or wounded on the field of battle, and every *communiqué* issued by General Pershing.

It was an immediate means of government communication with the business interests with which the government has been in contractual relations; with the offices of foreign governments here and abroad, with the consular service, and with the public desirous of information of a specific character. Its monetary value to the government in the clerical labor and supplies it conserved by anticipating nation-wide inquiries in its daily record of the facts represented an amount in excess of the cost of issuing the *Bulletin*.

It went to 56,000 post-offices throughout the country, to be posted, and was the voice of the Postmaster-General in communicating directly with 446,000 post-offices of the fourth class, to which the regular postal bulletin did not go.

It carried the official messages of government to every military post and station, to every ship and shore station of the navy, to every camp library at home and abroad, and Admiral Sims and General Pershing alike relied upon it for their own use and the use of their staffs.

No official organs were maintained by either the Food Administration or the Fuel Administration, by the War Trade Board, the War Industries Board, or the Council of National Defense, and these bodies reached their thousands of administrators and co-operative absentees through the instrumentality of the *Official Bulletin*.

When the government assumed control of the railroads of the country, the Director-General of Railroads had no other official medium than the *Official Bulletin* through which to reach the 2,000,000 employees of the great railroad systems. Copies of all orders, of course, were sent to the central railroad offices, but, as in the case of the Food and Fuel Administrations, there was no permanent printed record of such orders, except as they appeared in the *Official Bulletin*; and in all railroad offices of the country this publication was preserved religiously so that it might be referred to whenever matters of importance developed.

Even while Congress was attacking the *Official Bulletin* as useless expense, Senators and Representatives were hounding the Committee to have constituents placed on the free list, and when publication was suspended on April 1, 1919, there was not a voice raised except to beseech its continuance.

XVIII

EVEN had I not been an ardent suffragist, we could not have ignored the importance of women in connection with the war or failed to see the necessity of reaching them with our activities. There was a Woman's Committee of the Council of National Defense, however, headed by such brilliant personalities as Dr. Anna Howard Shaw, Mrs. Carrie Chapman Catt, and Miss Ida Tarbell, and it seemed a certainty that it would meet every need. What soon developed, unfortunately, was that the Woman's Committee had no money and was also expected to confine itself to "advising," the business of initiation having been placed in other hands.

By way of assistance, and at the request of Miss Tarbell, I attached Mrs. Clara Sears Taylor to the News Division and assigned her to the Woman's Committee as its general reporter. Lack of money and lack of authority joined to slacken effort very materially, and because an important work that *had* to be done was *not* being done I fell in with Mrs. Taylor's suggestion to form a Division of Women's War-work in the Committee on Public Information. Not only was Mrs. Taylor a person of tremendous energy and rare ability, but she had the gift of attracting women of similar type, and it was not long until a staff of twenty-two, many of them volunteers, were in full and effective swing.

DIVISION OF WOMEN'S WAR-WORK

What women were doing to help win the war was the one theme, and not only did they fill the women's pages in the daily press, as well as earning large space in magazine sections, but they fought their way to a place in the sun in the news columns. They went into the colleges where girls studied, into clubs of every kind, into ghettoes and foreign colonies, among the colored women of the country, giving information and arousing enthusiasm. Added to this, the division was a "question and answer" bureau that handled thousands of letters daily from women in every corner of the United States.

During the nine months of its existence, 2,305 stories were sent to 19,471 newspapers and women's publications. These releases included a wire and mail service, and were made up of news stories and feature articles. They were sent daily to 2,861 papers in seven columns a week, containing from twelve to twenty stories each. More than 10,000 cards were indexed on women's work, including the personnel of both organizations and individuals, and a collation of material of immense value to magazine and newspaper writers. Two hundred and ninety-two pictures were furnished newspapers, showing women actively engaged in war-work.

Weekly columns sent to newspapers and magazines included, first, war-work being done in national organizations; second, in governmental departments; third, in decentralized organizations throughout the United States; fourth, in schools and colleges; fifth, in churches; sixth, foreign co-operation; seventh, work being done by organizations of colored women.

Close co-operation was formed with the colleges, through representatives sent out by the collegiate alumni, and with fraternal organizations through representatives co-operating with the governmental departments through their international associations. The news for the foreign column was received by means of co-operation with the foreign embassies, legations, high commissions, and committees, and committees in foreign countries at war with Germany.

Mrs. Mary Holland Kinkaid, well-known magazine and newspaper editor and writer of New York, edited the columns of news which created an interchange in thought between the women war-workers of the world, culling from letters and other forms of communication the facts, figures, hopes, and ambitions that were woven into "stories." She handled also the copy brought in by trained reporters who had the governmental departments and national organizations in Washington for their "beats."

These reporters included women from many states and representing as many points of view. The War Department, with its thousands of women war-workers, was "covered" by Mrs. William A. Mundell (pen name Caroline Singer), a newspaper writer of San Francisco. News of the Woman's Committee of the Council of National Defense, which operated under the War Department, was collected by means of their own machinery, and prepared by them, and then distributed by the Committee on Public Information.

The State and Navy Departments' picturesque tales of the yeomanettes, women finger-print experts, etc., were gathered and written into magazine and newspaper stories by Miss Margaret Moses, who came to the division with recommendations from *The New York Times,* Columbia University, and Barnard College.

Miss Mildred Morris, of Denver and Chicago newspaper experience, invaded the Department of Labor, and from its statistical shelves and important war investigations and reports made available for the press much extremely valuable information. The labor-supply, depleted by the cutting off of immigration and by the military draft, necessitated calling into industrial services many women who had never before been wage-earners. The distribution of this information was extremely helpful in aiding to solve the problems which automatically arose from the advent of these women into industrial life. A clever feature-writer of Washington, Miss Helen Randall, assisted in this labor field, writing stories from the Agricultural Department.

Miss Dorothy Lewis Kitchen of Kansas City, Mo., a young woman who had been active in settlement and civic work and in the Consumers' League, had charge of the Interior Department, writing articles about teachers, librarians, and the many phases of work done in the Department of the Interior. Miss Kitchen compiled two brochures on "War-work of Women in Colleges." The issuance of these brochures was commenced in February, 1917, when the smaller colleges were more or less at sea as to the nature of the war-work best suited for them, and when the larger colleges were just establishing definite programs for more intensive work. The brochures were sent to colleges, schools, newspapers, magazines, women's organizations, and government officials. The effect was amazing. Every college in the country took advantage of the suggestive reports of every other college, and a vast amount of patriotic energy was utilized in a most effective manner. The news of this activity was immensely stimulating to other war-workers. An edition of twenty-five thousand copies was exhausted in a very short time, and thousands more were sent in response to requests from libraries, college officials, and individuals.

There was an appendix to this pamphlet called "Opportunities in War-work for Women," which was used so widely that it was later revised, and was just ready for the printer when the work of the division ceased. It contained a list of the chairmen of the Woman's Committee in each state, a list of civil service commissions, of farm-help specialists under the Department of Agriculture, and of the fourteen Red Cross divisions, besides definite ideas for war-work for trained and untrained college girls, for educated and uneducated—in fact, for every class of woman.

The Department of Agriculture, with all the war bodies associated with it, and with the women's organizations which functioned through it, was combed each day for news of women's war-work by Miss Constance Marguerite McGowan, now Mrs. C. B. Savage of New York. Mrs. Savage came from the Lindenwood College, where she was dean of journalism.

The Treasury, with its great Liberty-loan work by women, the Post Office, and the Department of Justice were reported by Mrs. Susan Hunter Walker, an able writer of wide experience.

Mrs. Florence Normile of the New York Public Library was given the Department of Commerce, the Fosdick Commission, and the Young Women's Christian Association.

This information, having been collected and written, was mimeographed, and "placed on the table" for distribution among the nine hundred and odd correspondents then in Washington. This number, of course, included the correspondents of the big press associations, so that every paper in the United States was reached. When the matter was not "spot" news—that is, when it was not of sufficient news importance to be carried by telegraph—the material was worked up into feature and special stories for news syndicates, or else was sent out in clip sheets. Many of the papers carried these columns in full, showing the interest felt all over the country in what was being done by women.

With respect to church news, Miss Elizabeth Gorton,

now Mrs. H. A. Adams, Jr., assembled this material into columns that gave information about organizations of every creed.

The highly dramatic story of the colored women's work was sent in from the four corners of the United States by their organizations, committees, and branches of national clubs. The Federation of Colored Women's Clubs found this information useful and effective, and the press of both races used the articles.

As the work expanded, inquiries poured in from public officials, special writers, speakers, magazine editors, school-teachers, college professors, grange officials, trade-unionists, and every class of woman from the most influential executive of an international activity to the humblest farm-worker.

The various departments in Washington and many Senators and Congressmen also got in the habit of sending women's letters to the Division of Women's War-work for answer. Thus the division, besides being a centralized medium of communication between writers, publicity bureaus, organization heads, and the government, soon became an important factor in the strengthening of the morale of women in America.

Miss Ellen Harvey, and later Mrs. Laura Miller of St. Louis, handled the bulk of this work, although Mrs. Taylor considered it of such great importance in sustaining the high morale of the work of the home that she gave it her personal attention, and insisted on the warm co-operation of every member of the staff in finding definite, accurate answers to the many questions asked.

These letters were the expressions of the very heart of American womanhood. The wording of an answer had power to determine whether or not a discontented and unhappy writer should form a center of agitation against the war. Some of these letters were addressed to the President, and many to the Secretary of War. The method employed was to answer the queries, and then to get the writer in touch with the group of women doing war-work in the vicinity of her home. In case of want, home-service workers were interested in the case. Often glowing expressions of patriotism followed a fiery protest against "sending my husband to war," or letters showing a new interest in life followed a suicide threat—"because you took my only son." Always, the idea was to interest these unhappy women in something real and vital.

Miss Helen M. Hogue of California, who was one of the assistants in this work, wrote from France, where she was doing war-work after leaving the committee: "The Division of Women's War-work has aroused patriotism, inspired courage, fostered self-sacrifice, and directed the surplus energies of women into sane channels. With a background of news releases, the correspondence was of inestimable importance. I sincerely believe that every letter, whether it goes to the dean of the college, who wants an outline for a thesis, or to the little war widow in Texas, struggling with her big plow and refractory mule, is a distinctly constructive factor in keeping up the morale of women, and through them of the men of America."

A report shows that over fifty thousand of these letters were answered. They went to wealthy women, who wanted to know how they or their organizations could be of service in spreading the truth about the war, to young women who wanted to offer their lives for their country as their brothers had, to mothers of soldiers on New England farms, or in mountain valleys cut off from all other government contact, and from wives or sweethearts of soldiers bewildered by the new conditions thrust upon them by the war.

To answer the queries successfully necessitated a careful

filing and cross-indexing of the material. "Make the files live and breathe" was the slogan of the librarian, Miss Helen Forbes, who left the New York Public Library to take charge of this work. So well did she carry out her program that she could give the names and addresses in Washington of every new-comer in national war-work of any prominence. She had at the ends of her capable fingers the cards that gave the history of virtually every woman war-worker of importance in America, every organization and its war plans, every new campaign among the women. A granddaughter of Abraham Lincoln, by the way, sent news of women's work in Cuba to these files.

Pictures were catalogued also, and the files contained a wonderful historical collection of actual scenes among the war-workers—the flying squadron pitching hay, the motor-drivers in action, Chinese women of San Francisco and Indian women of Oklahoma working around their tables, heaped up with Red Cross bandages and baby clothes—women working at strange trades and in strange occupations—logging-camps, machine-shops, etc. These pictures were accessible at all times to the magazine writers and to other seekers of information.

Miss Forbes also classified and made digests with indices of government documents pertaining to the war-work of women, reports of organizations, which were coming in from every part of the United States, circulars and other important mail matter, and newspaper clippings, making it possible to gather together everything in the files on a given subject. Miss Sue Schoolfield; Miss Eleanor Clark, who had been affiliated with the Public Education and Child Labor Association of Pittsburgh; Miss Antonio Thornton Jenkins Converse, daughter of Admiral Alexander Jenkins of the United States navy, and a writer of ability; Miss Catherine Connell; Miss Marguerite Jenison; Miss Cathrene H. Peebles, and Miss Gertrude R.

Wheeler assisted Miss Forbes in the heavy task of collating the mass of material and making it available for instant use.

No small part of the work of the division was the mailing and management of supplies. Miss Loretta Dowling took charge before the dissolution of the division, when the work became so strenuous that Miss Anna Maria Perrott Rose, a graduate of Vassar, joined the staff. Miss Rose, a student of printing and publishing, had taught typography in the night-school of the Pulitzer School of Journalism, had been head of the proof department in a large New York printing and publishing company, had done writing and dummying, and had worked in all of the mechanical departments of the plant to learn the machinery. Miss Rose was planning a series of brochures to follow the successful college booklet when the machinery stopped.

The work of the last month was concentrated largely upon the writing of the history of women in war-work. Mrs. Helen S. Wright of Pittsfield, Massachusetts, daughter of Rear-Admiral David Smith, of the United States navy, trained for twenty years in the science of compiling and assembling literary material, placed herself at the disposal of the woman's division. This author of *The Great White North*, *The Valley of Lebanon*, and *The Seventh Continent* worked early and late in the assembling of the events that told the vivid and dramatic history of American women in the war.

All this ended suddenly and even tragically. In June, 1918, I went before Congress for my appropriation. When it came to the Division of Women's War-work, Congress refused funds on the ground that we were trespassing upon a field "already occupied by the Woman's Committee of the Council of National Defense." Plain proof that this was not the case failed to secure a reversal of the decision, and Mrs. Taylor and her heartbroken associates were compelled to quit a great work that was just coming to the peak of its importance.

Strangely enough, the very dailies that were most derisive of the Committee printed columns and even pages in denunciation of the "arbitrary action" that ended an "invaluable agency," all taking care, however, to make it stand out as my personal fault.

XIX

THE Service Bureau was another of the many activities that were forced upon the Committee by proved necessities and a general demand. During the first six months of war the one great cry that rang through Washington was, "For Heaven's sake, don't send me to somebody else." It came from civilians eager to offer their services, business men with propositions to make, and even from officials themselves, all worn out with tramping from place to place, in every office receiving the answer, "I'm not the man. You'd better see—"

It is to be remembered that America's war machine came into being almost overnight, and not only was there a tremendous expansion in every department, but new boards and commissions were created daily. Housing was a bitter problem, and lack of quarters compelled a scattering that made it difficult for even executive heads to keep track of their bureaus. As a matter of course, there were delay and confusion in the transaction of the public business as a result of this lack of knowledge of the organization of the executive departments, of the distribution of the duties of each among its bureaus and divisions, of the personnel in charge, of the location of the many offices in which they were established, and of ready means of intercommunication.

To meet the situation, information bureaus were installed by the permanent departments like War and Navy, and elaborate organizations were also being planned by Food, Fuel, War Industry, War Trade, and other similar bodies. This was not a solution, however, and at a joint meeting it was decided that the Committee should establish one central service bureau to act for the entire war-machine. As a result of the decision the President issued the following executive order under date of March 19,1918:

I hereby create under the direction of the Committee on Public Information, created by Executive order of April 14, 1917, a Service Bureau, for the purpose of establishing a central office in the city of Washington, where complete information records may be available as to the function, location, and personnel of all government agencies.

I hereby ask the several departments of government, when so requested by the chairman of the Committee on Public Information, to detail such person or persons as may be necessary in gathering the information needed and carrying on the work of the bureau so far as it relates to such departments; to give opportunity to the director of the bureau, or such person as he may designate, to secure information from time to time for the purpose of keeping the records up to date; to supply the director of the bureau, on form cards furnished by him, with information as to personnel, function, and location.

WOODROW WILSON.

Prof. Frederick W. McReynolds was borrowed from Dartmouth College and quarters were taken in the very heart of Washington's business district. Every fact relating to the business of government in each of its several departments was gathered and indexed so that the Service Bureau stood ready to give instant and accurate information as to officials, councils, commissions, functions. Every detail of the war-machinery was at hand for inquiry and answer. When it is borne in mind that each day saw new bodies brought into being, and that the daily changes of personnel in established departments sometimes ran as high as five hundred, the magnitude of the task can be appreciated.

During the six months of its existence the Service Bureau answered over eighty-six thousand inquiries, made in person, by telephone, and by letter, and from the day of its creation there was a lessening of irritation and confusion. Hundreds of people took the trouble to return to compliment the bureau upon its efficiency, and even members of Congress were compelled to admit the value of the bureau. No one will ever be able to estimate the money saved by lifting the Bureau of Inquiries and Answers from the hard-driven departments of the government.

Professor McReynolds, after carrying the work to success, resigned to become a special agent of the Bureau of Internal Revenue, and Martin A. Morrison, who succeeded him, was subsequently appointed a Civil Service Commissioner by the President. Miss Marie Shick, office manager from the beginning, was then promoted to be director and at the time of the work's discontinuance was receiving offers from various other departments of government, which, while constituting an interference with the work, nevertheless stood as proof of the competent manner in which the bureau was administered.

A special word of commendation is due to Mr. F. E. Hackett and Mr. Arthur Klein, who made the initial survey of all the departments, and to Miss Emily A. Spilman, assistant librarian of the Department of Justice, who supervised the compiling of the directory.

Through the Division of Syndicate Features we enlisted the services of the leading novelists, essayists, and short-story writers of the United States, a picked group of men and women constituting a virtual staff that worked faithfully week after week in the preparation of brilliant articles that were sent by mail to the press of the country for release on given dates. Among those who gave so freely of their time and abilities were Samuel Hopkins Adams, Ellis Parker Butler, Booth Tarkington, Meredith Nicholson, Harvey O'Higgins, Herbert Quick, John Spargo, William English Walling, Mary Roberts Rinehart, Wallace Irwin, Richard Washburn Child, Samuel Merwin, Roland G. Usher, Ralph D. Paine, Martha Bensey Bruère, Edward Mott Wooley, John Reed Scott, Prof. John Erskine, Prof. Eugene Davenport, Crittenden Marriott, James H. Collins, Rex Beach, Virginia Frazer Boyle, and many others.

At first a good many personal pronouncements were used to make clear why we were at war, to explain the ideals for which we were fighting. Opinions of prominent people were in demand, though stories of our war activities were also used. But the character of the matter sent out changed as the war progressed. Our object was, in the newspaper phrase, to "sell the war," and we tried to furnish, dressed in acceptable newspaper style, the story of the war-machine in its thousands of phases, the story of our boys over there and over here, and the spirit that was back of the whole great adventure.

Mary Roberts Rinehart contributed timely articles based upon her own observations while visiting the various battle-fronts, and her story of an interview with the King of Belgium was a free feature that the papers advertised for days in advance. Samuel Hopkins Adams came to Washington at his own expense, and as a result of his skilful analysis of the papers taken from Von Igel by the Department of Justice, a page story went out that showed German intrigue down to the last sordid detail. James H. Collins wrote a wonderful series that made clear the work of new and little-understood departments; Herbert Quick fought regularly for the conquest of the agricultural mind; Ellis Parker Butler gave us a brilliant series which we syndicated in one hundred papers, and Harvey J. O'Higgins was such a success in answering the "German whisper" that we drafted him outright, and brought him to Washington to serve as associate chairman. The division did not confine itself wholly to fact stories and human interest stuff about army and navy workers. It dealt also with the larger aspects that were behind the immediate facts. It covered the racial, the social, the moral, and the financial aspects of the war written by specialists in these lines.

L. Ames Brown, transferred from the News Division for the purpose of inaugurating the plan of syndicate features, handled it brilliantly and well until he entered the army, and then, under the direction of William MacLeod Raine and Arthur MacFarlane, the stories were used from Florida to Alaska, from New York to California, reaching a circulation of about twelve million a month.

Then there was the Bureau of Cartoons to mobilize and direct the scattered cartoon power of the country for constructive war-work. I was never very enthusiastic over the idea and gave it a very grudging assent as well as a meager appropriation. But under Mr. George J. Hecht, capably assisted by Mr. Alfred M. Saperston and Miss Gretchen Leicht, a remarkable success was won. The principal activity of the bureau was the weekly publication of the *Bulletin for Cartoonists*. Every week the bureau obtained from all the chief departments of the government the announcements which they particularly wanted to transmit to the public, wrote them up in the bulletin, and sent them out to over seven hundred and fifty cartoonists. As general suggestions and advance-news "tips" were published rather than specific subjects for cartoons, there was no danger of cartoonists losing their individuality or originality. Cartoonists all over the nation followed out these suggestions. This made for timeliness and unity of cartoon power which developed into a stimulating and actively constructive force for shaping public opinion and winning the war.

XX

SHOWING AMERICA TO THE FOREIGN PRESS

IN many respects, one of the most effective ideas of the Committee on Public Information was the bringing to the United States, from time to time, of delegations of foreign newspaper men in order that they might "see with their own eyes, hear with their own ears," and upon their return be able to report fully on America's morale and effort. These trips were of incalculable value in our foreign educational work, for not only did the visitors send home daily reports by cable and by mail, but upon their return wrote series of articles and even went upon the lecture platform. Most important, everything was written on the basis of what had been seen by the eyes of the foreigners, with the individual correspondent's own interpretation of the facts in the manner that would most appeal to his own reading public.

Mexico was selected for the initial experiment in national entertaining, and Mr. Robert H. Murray, our resident commissioner, assembled the following representative group of Mexican editors:

From the City of Mexico, Señor Felix Palavacini of *El Universal*, Señor Manuel Carpio of *La Voz*, Señor Zamora Plowes of *A. B. C.*, Señor Manero of *El Economista*, and Señor Alducin of *El Excelsior*, and from other principal cities the correspondents of these papers: *El Dictámen*, Vera Cruz; *La Prensa*, Pueblo; *El Informador*, Saltillo; *El*

Liberal, Saltillo; *El Progreso*, *El Liberal*, and *Nueva Patria*, all of Monterey, La Prensa, and Tampico.

Lieut. P. S. O'Reilly, borrowed from the Cable Censorship by reason of a long association with Spanish-speaking peoples, took the party in charge for the Committee, and a tour was arranged that covered the United States.

Their itinerary included the following cities and points of interest: New Orleans, Louisiana; Atlanta, Georgia; Washington, D. C., where the delegation was received and addressed by President Wilson and where the Pan-American Bureau entertained it and the Mexicans were afforded an opportunity of seeing many governmental works; Annapolis, for inspection of the United States Naval Academy; Camp Meade, for inspection of a typical United States cantonment; Philadelphia, for a view of the Hog Island Shipbuilding Yard; South Bethlehem, for inspection of the Bethlehem Steel Works; New York City, for inspection of the United States Military Academy at West Point and numerous war factories in and around New York; Boston, for inspection of shipbuilding plants; Schenectady, for inspection of the plant of the General Electric Co.; Buffalo, for inspection of the Curtiss Aviation Co.; Detroit for view of various plants making Liberty motors and 'planes; Chicago, for view of various steel-plants, packing houses, etc.; St. Paul and Minneapolis, for study of the milling centers; Yakima, Washington, for a view of a United States reclamation project; Seattle, for study of west coast shipbuilding; Portland, for study of west-coast shipbuilding, and San Francisco for the same purpose; Los Angeles, and back to Mexico *via* San Antonio and Laredo.

The Mexicans came in distrust and suspicion, also in a vast and amazing ignorance of the extent and might of the United States. While Mr. Murray was working very effectively with the Committee's daily cable and mail service, literature, etc., it was still the case that the pro-

German press of Mexico had Republican attacks in the Senate to serve as a sort of answer, and the visiting editors were in doubt as to the exact facts. It was amusing to witness their surprise when they saw our cantonments, our ships, our aviation-fields, and great munition-plants.

"Why," exclaimed one of them, "we had been led to believe by your Senators that you did not have a ship or an airplane."

At every point we treated them with absolute frankness, showing everything, concealing nothing, and in the end they were enthusiastic believers not only in our power, but in our idealism.

Chambers of commerce, boards of trade, various other civic and business organizations and business firms and individuals throughout the country aided splendidly in making the Mexicans feel at home and in impressing them with the good will and friendship which the people of the United States felt for the people south of the Rio Grande. Many business firms and individuals entertained them and contributed not a little to making them, on their return to their native country, enthusiastic "boosters" for the United States. What won them absolutely, however, was the speech of the President, made to them simply and straightforwardly as they grouped about him in the White House, clear and ringing in its exposition of our ideals, aims, and purposes. This speech, more than any other one thing, killed the German lie in Latin America, for we gave it complete circulation in South and Central America as well as in Mexico.

The Swiss came next, and getting them to come was remarkable proof of the strength that Mrs. Whitehouse had acquired in Switzerland. The government itself had to approve the visit, also the personnel, and there were delicate questions of neutrality involved, as well as personal prejudices on the part of pro-German editors. The six men in the party were statesmen as well as journalists, and I have never seen a group that had fairer or more open minds. They saw and listened calmly and critically, and because of this judicial silence there were times when we felt that the trip was not a success. Mr. Norman de R. Whitehouse, however, who was conducting the party, having deserted his own affairs to render the service, assured us that all was going well, and his word came true. A night or two before they sailed the Swiss colony of New York gave a dinner in honor of the distinguished visitors, and not one of the six but made a speech that was ungrudging in its praise of America and its belief in our ideals.

The Italian journalist came next and Captain Merriman, in Rome, selected the following representative members of the Italian press: Aldo Cassuto of *Secolo*, Antonio Agresti of *Tribuna*, Paolo Cappa of *Avvenire d'Italia*, Orazio Pedrazzi of *Nuovo Giornale*, Franco Rainieri of *Giornale d'Italia*, Pietro Solari of *Tempo*, Leonardo Bitetti of *Idea Nazionale*.

The fourth group to arrive came from the Scandinavian countries and included representatives of the principal papers in Sweden, Denmark, and Norway. Not only did we show them America at war, but we made it a point to see that they came into contact with all those communities in which there were large Scandinavian populations. Mr Bjorkman handled the tour with rare judgment and carried it through to complete success. The armistice terminated our plans in this direction, and necessitated the cancelation of the invitations that had already been extended to the newspaper men of Holland and Spain. The itineraries arranged by the Italians, the Swiss, and the Scandinavians followed the same general plan as the one prepared for the Mexican editors.

There can be no question as to the signal success of these visits, for the effect of them was signal and lasting

The very fact that we were willing to let our war progress be seen and judged was impressive at the outset, and the magnitude of "America's Answer" did the rest. Countless columns in foreign newspapers were earned for us that could have been gained in no other way, and every column carried weight because it came from the pen of a writer in whom the readers had confidence.

Equally good results were obtained from similar visits to the American firing-line in France. The newspaper men of Spain, of Holland, of England, and of the Scandinavian countries were selected by the resident commissioners and on arrival in France were received by the Paris office and shown every detail of the American effort from landing-port to front-line trench. Every man of them carried back to his country the message, "America cannot lose."

The tours of the foreign editors having proved so wonderfully successful, it was decided that a like plan should be pursued with reference to the foreign correspondents on duty in the United States. Mr. Walter S. Rogers of the Foreign Cable Service took the matter up with them, and an association was formed that included these members: R. Bonnifield, Central News, London; P. P. Brown and E. W. Kelly, *Paris Herald;* W. F. Bullock, Henry N. Hall, and J. Andrew White, *London Times;* P. S. Bullen and S. J. Clarke, *London Daily Telegraph;* H. Delmas and Henri Collin Delavaud, Agence Havas, France; W. W. Davies, *La Nacion* of Buenos Aires; Frank Dilnot and J. W. Harding, *London Daily Chronicle;* Dr. F. Ferrera, *Corriere della Sera*, Rome; Sir John Foster Fraser, Scotch newspapers; Andrea Ferretti, *L'Idea Nazionale*, Rome; Leopold Grahame, *El Heraldo*, Cuba; Y. Hatada, *Asahi*, Japan; Frank Hillier, *London Daily Mail;* E. W. M. Hall, *Daily Sketch*, London; W. J. Herman, *Westminster Gazette*, London; Marcel Knecht, *Maison de la Presse*, Paris;

S. Lauzanne, A. Plottier, and Léon Levy, *Le Matin*, Paris; S. Levy Lawson and Wilmer Stuart, Reuters, Ltd., London; Capt. S. Loewy, *L'Information*, Paris; A. Maurice Low, *Morning Post*, London; Warren Mason, *London Daily Express;* Norman MacCallum, Canadian Press Association; Ernest Montenegro, *El Mercurio*, Chile; E. Rascovar, *Central News*, London; Romeo Ronconi, *La Prensa*, Buenos Aires; A. Rothman, Australian Press Association; Severo Salcedo, *La Nacion*, Santiago, Chile; Van Buren Thorne, *Mainichi*, Osaka, Japan; T. Walter Williams, *Daily Mirror*, London; P. W. Wilson, *London Daily News*.

Our first effort was to answer the German lie that America's shipbuilding was a "bluff." Permission for the unprecedented step of showing the secret processes of certain American shipbuilding yards was finally obtained from the government departments concerned, and the correspondents were taken on a tour which embraced the yards of the New York Shipbuilding Co., at Camden, N. J.; the American International plant at Hog Island, Pa.; the Squantum and Quincy plants of the Fore River Shipbuilding Co., outside of Boston, Mass.; the Brooklyn Navy Yard; and the Newark plant of the Submarine Boat Corporation. Each correspondent who made the trip was under no coercion as to the character of the matter he was to write, and the only pledges asked were with respect to certain secrets of construction.

Judging from the publicity to the American shipbuilding program which resulted, the trip was an immense success. All of the foreign correspondents were more than anxious to present America's viewpoint and more than enthusiastic over America's accomplishments. Matter written by these correspondents was published all over England, France, Italy, and South America, and reproduced in countries still more distant.

Necessary permission having been secured, the foreign

correspondents were next sent on a tour of the Middle West to study aviation progress. At Detroit the plant of the Packard Motor Co.—engaged in making Liberty motors —was thoroughly inspected, the first time that such a permission had been granted. The army authorities, thoroughly awake to the propaganda value of the plan, relaxed their stern rule against civilians and granted the correspondents fullest freedom at the special testing-field outside of Detroit. The plant of Henry Ford, making cylinders for the Liberty motors, was inspected.

The correspondents then traveled to Chicago. They were greatly interested in the Great Lakes Naval Training Station, were made to realize something of the gigantic responsibilities which the United States had shouldered in its self-assumed task of feeding the world by a detailed view of the Union Stock Yards and the great packing-plants of Chicago. One day was also spent in investigating the making of munitions at the plant of the International Harvester Co. Another day was spent visiting the great war plant of the Rock Island Arsenal.

The third trip undertaken was in response to earnest pleas from the correspondents that they be permitted to visit briefly with President Wilson himself. The President consented to receive the correspondents at the White House, and in a remarkable interview laid bare his own thought as well as his conception of the ideals of America. The correspondents were then taken to Old Point Comfort, where they saw the plant of the Newport News Shipbuilding Co., inspected the heavy-artillery school at Fortress Monroe, saw the training of naval aviators at Langley Field, Hampton Roads, and the vast embarkation works in and around that harbor.

The fourth trip was a corollary to the Detroit-Chicago-Rock Island inspection. It was designed to show the correspondents certain American aviation-plants in operation.

The correspondents were taken to Dayton, where they went over the plant of the Dayton-Wright Co., and as many as desired were afforded the opportunity of going aloft in a Liberty 'plane. The same inspection and the same opportunity were afforded them at Buffalo, where they went through the great plant of the Curtiss Co.

It was not only the case that each trip resulted in long cable stories and special articles sent by mail. From the very first tour a new note was apparent in the despatches —a note of enthusiasm, of courage, of victory. From what they had seen themselves they were able to discount the attacks of partizans, and "calamity howls" ceased to go out on the cables to alarm the Allies and frighten the neutrals.

It should be added that Mr. Perry Arnold, who conducted the correspondents on each trip, also prepared numerous articles covering what had been seen, which were extensively circulated in Europe and South America.

Part II
THE FOREIGN SECTION

I

THE domestic task was simple compared with the undertaking that faced the Committee on Public Information when it turned from the United States to make the fight for world opinion. It was not only that the people of the Allied Powers had to be strengthened with a message of encouragement, but there was the moral verdict of the neutral nations to be won and the stubborn problem of reaching the deluded soldiers and civilians of the Central Powers with the truths of the war. A prime importance was to preach the determination and military might of America and the certainty of victory, but it was equally necessary to teach the motives, purposes, and ideals of America so that friend, foe, and neutral alike might come to see us as a people without selfishness and in love with justice.

It was a task that looked almost hopeless. The United States, alone of the great nations of the world, had never conducted a propaganda movement. For years preceding the war Germany had been secretly building a vast publicity machine in every corner of the earth, designed to overwhelm all foreign peoples with pictures of Germany's vast power, her overwhelming pre-eminence in industry, commerce, and the arts. German agents, carefully selected from among her journalists and authors, neglected no opportunities for presenting Germany's case to readers of every language, and her commercial firms linked a propaganda of liberal credits with this newspaper campaign throughout the world.

Great Britain, through Reuters, likewise conducted a governmental propaganda. France had official connection with the Havas Agency. Both England and France, through ownership or liberal subsidy of certain great cable arteries, had long been able to direct currents of public opinion in channels favorable to themselves. Other nations had publicity machines of varying types.

America controlled no cables, manipulated no press associations, operated no propaganda machinery of any kind. We were, and always had been, dependent upon foreign press agencies for intercourse with the world. The volume of information that went from our shores was comparatively small, and after it had been filtered in London, or Paris, it grew smaller and smaller until it amounted to mere "flashes" when it reached a far country. Strangely enough, we were at once the best-known and the least-known people in the world. There was no corner of the globe in which America was not a familiar word, but as to our aims, our ideals, our social and industrial progress, our struggles and our achievements, there were the most absolute and disheartening misunderstandings and misconceptions. For instance, when the "gun-men" were executed in New York, papers in South America actually printed accounts that told of an admission fee being charged, with Governor Whitman taking tickets at the door. Into this situation the Germans projected themselves with vigor and decision. From the first, Berlin had an exact appreciation of the military value of public opinion, and it spent millions in its endeavor to win it or else to corrupt it. Just as the German propagandists worked in the United States during our period of neutrality, using every effort to prejudice Americans against

CARL BYOIR

WILL IRWIN

HARRY N. RICKEY

EDGAR G. SISSON

the Allies, so did they now attempt to poison the Allied and the neutral nations of the world against America.

It is impossible even to estimate the amount of money spent on propaganda by the Germans. Russians competent to judge assured us that the agents of Berlin spent $500,000,000 in that country alone in their work of corruption and destruction, and their expenditures in Spain were estimated at $60,000,000. Close to $5,000,000 went to Bolo Pasha for the corruption of the Paris press, and the sums spent in Mexico ran high into the millions. I know that they owned or subsidized dailies in most of the important cities of Spain, South America, the Orient, Scandinavia, Switzerland, and Holland; that their publications, issued in every language, ran from costly brochures to the most expensive books and albums; that they thought nothing of paying $25,000 for a hole-in-the-wall picturehouse, and that in every large city in every country their blackmailers and bribe-givers swarmed like carrion crows.

Their propaganda, while playing upon different points of prejudice in various countries, was much the same in all countries. As an initial proposition America's military strength was derided. By no possibility could the United States raise or train an army, and if, by some miracle, this did happen, the army could not be transported. America was a fat, loblolly nation, lacking courage, equipment, and ships, etc., etc. Working away from this pleasing premise, Americans were described as a nation of dollar-grabbers, devoid of ideals, and inordinate in their ambitions. Our war with Mexico was played up as a cold-blooded, evil conquest and our struggle with Spain painted as an effort of our financial masters to enter upon dreams of world imperialism; Cuba, the Philippines, and Porto Rico were pitied as "America's slave nations"; Pershing's expedition to Mexico was declared to be the start of a war of conquest that we were later forced to relinquish because our "cowardice" shrank before the "dauntless" courage of Carranza; the Colorado coal strike, the Lawrence strike, and the Paterson strikes were all treated in the utmost detail to prove America's "system of wage-slavery"; pictures were drawn of tremendous wealth on the one hand and peonage on the other; lynchings were exaggerated until it was made to appear that almost every tree in America was used for purposes of execution, and we were charged in every conceivable form and fashion with being the secret partner of one or the other of the Allies in commercial plans to control the trade of the world.

Where there was French sentiment, America was set down as the secret partner of England. Where English sentiment prevailed, we were the secret partner of France; and where Italian sentiment obtained, America, England, and France were assumed to be in a plot to destroy Italy.

In Spain every effort was made to revive the prejudices and passions of 1898, and the pro-German press ran daily lies in proof of "Yankee Contempt for the Spaniard." One falsehood was that a favorite American recruiting slogan was: "Enlist for the War! Remember the *Maine* and Spain."

In Switzerland we were accused of withholding grain shipments in order to starve the Swiss into alliance with us, and in South and Central America the Germans put full emphasis on the "Panama Canal rape" and the "conquest and annexation" of Haiti and Santo Domingo.

The German drive against us was particularly strong in Italy and France among the peasants, and weekly papers, printed in close imitation of French and Italian publications, were circulated by the thousands. The French were asked to believe that the high prices were entirely due to the selfishness and extravagance of the Americans in France, also that the docks and railroads and warehouses built by the Expeditionary Forces would be permanent American properties with a view to the commercial enslavement of France and the French.

Playing upon the fact that only a small number of American troops were in Italy, the German "fakes" kept up the continual cry: "Why is Italy deserted? A new and more terrific drive is on the way, but Foch keeps help from us. Pershing and the Americans are the dupes of the selfish French."

In France the *Gazette des Ardennes*, published in French printing-offices in the occupied district, deceived thousands, and Italian newspapers were also printed and distributed from captured cities. In both cases, the names of well-known French and Italian writers and artists were forged to articles and cartoons. A principal propaganda weapon, however, was *The Continental Times*, published in Berlin, with branch offices in Holland and Switzerland. Printed in English, edited by American and British renegades, and called "an independent cosmopolitan newspaper published in the interests of truth," the wretched sheet gave itself wholly to the dissemination of falsehood. It was peculiarly the medium used in attacking America, and in each issue there were columns devoted to the "failure" of our Liberty Loans, "armed resistance to the draft," the "utter breakdown" of our war preparations, and other like lies. In Russia particularly, but also among the labor and Socialist groups of all the neutral and Allied countries, exaggerated attention was paid to the Mooney trial, the imprisonment of Emma Goldman, the deportations in Arizona, and other matters intended to give the lying impression that there was an industrial autocracy in the United States more to be feared than the military autocracy of Germany.

The great wireless plant at Nauen was used almost exclusively for propaganda, from two to three thousand words being "broadcasted" each day as a lure to neutrals. The navy picked it up regularly for studying by various divisions of the government, in order that we might know what lies to fight.

Strangely enough, the Germans gathered much of their most effective material from our own press. From first to last American newspapers went to neutral countries without hindrance, and everything that they contained about "inefficiency," "graft," "delay," or "Wilson Bitterly Arraigned as Dictator" was seized upon by the German propagandists and played across the board. Mr. Roosevelt's articles, however conscientiously intended as constructive criticism, were among the chief weapons used by the Germans in their propaganda attack in every country. Senator La Follette's speeches were printed between red covers and broadcasted. No wonder that the thing that fairly stunned the visiting Mexican editors was their first sight of an aviation-field! They honestly believed, as a result of reports of Congressional debates, that there was not one airplane in America that could fly.

We were called upon to combat the prejudices of years, to buck a vast propaganda machinery with millions behind it, yet not only were we without equipment or agencies, but there was also the daily harassment of a press that refused to understand and the ignorances and partizanships of a Congress that counted the day lost that did not see some new obstacle thrown in the way of the Committee on Public Information.

Our one asset was the justice of our cause, our one hope the carrying power of truth, and not the least factor of our success in every neutral country was the honesty of our initial approach. We did not send agents secretly to carry on their work by stealth, but to each government we addressed an honest statement of purpose somewhat after this fashion:

242

THE FIGHT IN FOREIGN COUNTRIES

It is desired to establish in your country offices for the distribution of a wireless cable, and mail news service to the press; for the exhibition of motion pictures expressive of America's purpose and energies, for the assignment of speakers, for pamphlet distribution, and for other similar open activities. There will be no item nor pamphlet that we will not be willing to submit to the inspection of qualified officials, for our purpose is not the coercion of public opinion, but the information of public opinion to the end that there may be a better understanding between our two countries.

We desire to do these things openly, not only because it is the national policy to avoid secrecy, but because it is our desire to do nothing contrary to the wishes of your government or violative of the neutrality that we respect. It is not the idea of the United States to conduct propaganda in neutral countries in the sense of attacking the motives and methods of the enemy, or in the nature of argument designed to compel or to persuade certain courses of conduct. Our activities in every neutral country are open and aboveboard, confined always to a very frank exposition of America's war aims, the nation's ideals, and future hopes.

A news service was soon carrying several thousand words a day to the press of the world, a clarion as to America's war preparation and progress, America's purpose, thought, and aims. It was through this machinery that we were able to give universal circulation to the addresses of the President, putting them in every language within forty-eight hours of their delivery.

Under the direction of Ernest Poole, the author, a Foreign Mail Press Bureau was also formed that soon enlisted the services of many well-known writers and publicists in the United States. Week by week, a package went out to every one of our foreign representatives, carrying material designed to clear away all points of misunderstanding and misconception that prevailed, or might prevail, in foreign countries in regard to America, its life, work, ideals, and opinions; material in the shape

243

of editorial comment from newspapers, and original special articles prepared by accepted authorities, covering every phase of our national activity—education, agriculture, invention, co-operative ventures, modern machinery, rural free delivery, social legislation, etc., etc.

Charles Dana Gibson, at the head of the mobilized artists of the United States, and Charles S. Hart, director of the Film Division, worked closely with Mr. Poole, and through the Foreign Press Bureau went out posters, captioned in every language, millions of picture postals, and "still" photographs for purposes of display. In every country the show-windows of American business houses were commandeered and used for the display of posters, bulletins, and photographs, all changed at short intervals just as a theatrical offering is changed.

The problem of the spoken word was an awkward one to solve. At first we tried the experiment of selecting Americans of foreign birth, men of achievement in their particular trades and professions, and sending them back to their native lands for speaking tours. Certain patriotic Socialists, despatched to France and Italy, did splendid work along this line, and various other groups functioned very well. Speakers were not sent anywhere, however, unless they could be kept under careful observation, so that the use of oratory was therefore limited.

Capt. Charles E. Merriam finally evolved the idea of finding native Italians who knew America, filling them up with our latest facts and figures, and sending them out to talk to their own people. The scheme worked so well that we adopted it in some other countries, drawing impartially from the universities, shops, and farms. It was Captain Merriam, too, who thought of suggesting to General Pershing that wounded Americans of Italian birth or descent be invalided to Italy for convalescence. These men turned out to be our best propagandists, preaching the gospel of democracy with a fervor and understanding that would have shamed many an heir of Plymouth Rock.

James F. Kerney, in charge in France until the late summer of 1918, added to our working capital of experience by virtually mobilizing the French universities in the interests of America. French professors of standing who knew the United States were "educated" up to date, and these volunteers, proceeding from university to university, "educated" the various faculties, who in turn spread out over the communities with the truth about the United States and *L'effort américain.*

Reading-rooms were also established, with all the pamphlets, posters, and picture postals of the Committee for distribution, and with a full equipment of American books, newspapers, and magazines. Mr. Robert H. Murray, head of the work in Mexico, introduced a rather novel experiment in the shape of classes in English, American residents giving their time as teachers free of charge. These classes, ten a week, drew an average attendance of about eight hundred young men, and the instruction gave splendid opportunity to preach the history, aims, and ideals of America, with the result that every one of the eight hundred became an understanding champion of the United States.

The foreign-born, and those of foreign descent, played no small part in our educational effort. As I have related in previous chapters, the twenty-three principal foreign-language groups in the United States formed themselves into loyalty leagues and aided in the organization of great meetings from coast to coast that not only pledged the devotion of America's adopted sons to the President and the war, but also sent resolutions across the seas to strengthen the hearts of the firing-line and sustain the determination of the civilian population.

17   245

After the Caporetto disaster, when it seemed that Italy might have to be dismissed as a factor in the war, the Italians in America rallied as one man, and for weeks the cables were loaded down with messages, and the mails were filled with letters, all telling the preparations of America, pledging the aid of America, calling for courage and redoubled effort. The results were almost instantly apparent, and the Italian government has stated repeatedly that it was this cry of faith and command from the United States that stiffened the Italian defensive into a resistless offensive.

A feature of this phase of the work that had the most far-reaching effect probably was the great Fourth-of-July celebration, organized and handled by those of foreign birth or foreign descent. Each race in each city had its own story to send back to its country, its own set of motion pictures for distribution in its native land, and there was the great climax in the pilgrimage to Mount Vernon by representatives of the thirty-three foreign-language groups as the guests of the President. To this very day, in almost every country of the world, the stories of the Fourth of July are being printed, the pictures are being shown, and the speech of President Wilson has been translated into every language and has achieved wide use in the public schools.

So the work went on, each day forcing enlargements, each week witnessing progress, until at last there came the time when it was possible to say, "We have won." The things that we set out to do were done. The morale of the Allied fighting fronts had been galvanized, and faith and friendship had been substituted for dislike and distrust in the hearts of the civilian populations; the neutral nations had been brought to a conviction of American victory and a belief in American idealism, and the German censorship, breaking under our attack, let through the truth to soldiers and civilians a flood that crumbled the rotten structures of lies. Whatever may be the condition to-day after months of a Congress that brought to the surface all that was mean and despicable in American life, the fact remains that on the day of the armistice there was not a corner of earth that did not know us as we were —a people with failures behind us, but struggling indomitably to the heights; a people materialistic in achievement, but idealistic in every aspiration—and, knowing us, they liked and trusted us.

As chairman of the Committee on Public Information, keenly aware of the importancies and intricacies of these foreign activities, I exercised personal direction of all the work until the various trails were well blazed and when the need of undivided executive attention became imperative. Mr. Arthur Woods, former police commissioner of New York City, was decided upon as director of the Foreign Section, but within a week the aviation division of the army begged his services, and, knowing the bitter need for his type of genius, I released him. In January, 1918, at the height of our new search for the right man, Will Irwin dropped from heaven, *via* Europe, and volunteered for six months of service. He knew Western Europe intimately, was thoroughly familiar with German propaganda in all of its forms, and in addition to this knowledge he brought vision to the work, originality, and an enthusiasm that had the carry of a bullet.

He stayed his promised six months, carrying through the great Fourth-of-July celebration that was his idea, and after his return to his European work the post of director of the Foreign Section fell to Edgar G. Sisson, just back from Russia. At his right hand Mr. Sisson placed Carl Byoir as associate and business director, and Harry N. Rickey as assistant general director, and these three swept the program through to the end. Mr. Rickey, formerly executive head of the Newspaper Enterprise Association, had served as the Committee's representative in London, and brought experience to the aid of his rare ability. As for Mr. Byoir, he had, like Mr. Sisson, "grown up" with the Committee. Sacrificing his own business interests to serve, he soon came to be known among us as the "multiple director," for I used his organizing ability in division after division, moving him from one to the other, and, whether the activity was domestic or foreign, he showed equal skill in giving it efficiency, force, and direction.

The record would not be complete without recognition of the devoted and effective services of those who served the Foreign Section in the capitals of the world. In Russia Arthur Bullard, author and publicist, fought the fight from Petrograd to Vladivostok; Charles E. Merriam, of the University of Chicago, spread the gospel over Italy; James F. Kerney, editor of *The Trenton Times*, handled the difficult clearing-house job in France; Charles Edward Russell, Harry Rickey, and Paul Perry wrestled in turn with the English problem; George Edward Riis, son of Jacob Riis, went to Denmark, the home of his fathers; Eric Palmer, a first-class newspaper man of Swedish descent, and Guy Croswell Smith, in charge of films, were our representatives in Sweden; Mrs. Norman de R. Whitehouse carried the cause to victory in Switzerland; Henry Suydam, European correspondent of *The Brooklyn Eagle*, gave up his position to serve his country in Holland; Frank J. Marion, president of the Kalem Company, looked after Spain and Portugal; Robert H. Murray, for years the correspondent of *The New York World*, was our representative in Mexico; to Buenos Aires we sent Henry B. Sevier; to Chile, A. A. Preciado; in Peru we found C. V. Griffis, an American editing a powerful newspaper; in Brazil Ambassador Edwin V. Morgan was the real head of the work; S. P. Verner handled Central America, from

Panama; and in the Orient, Carl Crow, the American correspondent, achieved brilliantly, aided at all times by Paul Reinsch, our Minister to China, and Roland Morris, our Ambassador to Japan.

Each man went to his post with few assistants, usually a good news editor, a motion-picture expert, and perhaps a stenographer. Translators were expected to be engaged on the ground and from the American colony. Everywhere the consular corps gave intelligent, earnest aid. Too great credit cannot be given to the devoted drudgery of these small forces.

II

WHEN we first set about the creation of a news machinery to carry American facts to the world a natural reliance was placed upon cables, the one established medium for international communication. The cables, however, were virtually all foreign owned, the rates were prohibitive, and, what was even more conclusive, all were so overburdened as to endanger vital war business by their delays. Forced to look in some other direction, our eyes fell upon the wireless, taken over by the navy some time before and lying idle for a good part of the time. Without more ado, we placed our problem before Secretary Daniels, who, understanding and co-operative as always, put the wireless stations of the United States at our disposal, and likewise the expert navy personnel.

The next step was an organization, and in the very moment of need a gangling, youngish, Lincolnesque type walked into my office with a burst of conversation about "world communication." Others may collect stamps or coins, play golf or polo, but Walter S. Rogers of Chicago, as far as I know, is the only living man whose hobby is "news transmission," and it took a world war to get him his chance to ride it. It was his belief, and a sane one, that peoples best understand each other through the exchange of news, and he had just returned from a world tour devoted to a study of cable rates, press agencies, distributing machinery, etc.

PAUL KENNADAY

ERNEST POOLE

W. S. ROGERS

PERRY ARNOLD

Mr. Rogers was made director of the newly established Division of Wireless and Cable Service, and as his associate we were fortunate in the securement of Perry Arnold, cable editor of the United Press, and one of the ablest and most experienced men in the newspaper profession. Another piece of good luck was Capt. David W. Todd, Chief of Naval Communications, for aside from his brilliant specialized ability he gave a co-operation that was as helpful as it was enthusiastic.

Offices were taken in New York, a news force gathered, and in September, 1917, "Compub," as its code address soon advertised it to the world, commenced business. The first service was from Tuckerton to the wireless station at Lyons. From Lyons by arrangement with the French government it went to our office in Paris, and after translation and distribution to the press of France, Mr. Kerney relayed it to our offices in Switzerland, Italy, Spain, and Portugal.

The next step in the world dissemination of news came through arrangements heartily entered into by the British government. The same wireless report sent to Lyons was intercepted by navy operators at the American naval base, and relayed to London, where the representatives of the Committee received it, and distributed it to the English press.

The London office, in turn, relayed the service to the Committee's representative in The Hague for the Dutch press, a highly important operation in the machinery, as many Dutch papers managed to get past the German censorship. A further relay was to our offices in Copenhagen and Stockholm for translation and distribution to the newspapers of Denmark, Sweden, and Norway, and here again, particularly in the case of Copenhagen, we had a chance to beat the German censors. In Switzerland, too, we scored heavily against the Germans in the same fashion.

The service also went from London to Saloniki and other Greek points, for not only was Greece to be considered, but it was good ground from which to shoot into the Balkans.

Our first effort to serve Russia was by wireless, and after much experimentation under the direction of Captain Todd we were actually able to reach the Russian station at Moscow. When the Bolsheviki overthrew Kerensky, however, one of their first actions was to grab the wireless stations. The one at Moscow, either intentionally or through ignorance, they put out of operation. Cut off in this quarter, the Committee's representatives managed to obtain permission for a cable service, and this went from New York direct from three to five hundred words a day. When the President spoke or when some major action was taken, we shot it through as a "special."

With Europe accounted for, attention was next given to South and Central America. At first glance it seemed a simple enough proposition, for virtually every South and Central American country had a wireless station and each government agreed instantly to take our news service out of the air. Our representatives would then attend to the business of translation and distribution. It was not even the case that dependence had to be placed on the one wireless leap from Tuckerton, for there was our own high-power station on the Isthmus of Panama to act as a relay. What seemed easy in theory, however, proved impossible in practice. Only Brazil "made good," the other South American stations falling down completely. As a consequence Compub had to inaugurate a cable service from New York to the Argentine, but, fortunately enough, we were able to arrange a "drop copy" plan that gave the matter to Lima, Santiago, Valparaiso, and all other cities touched by the cable. Buenos Aires distributed to Uruguay and Paraguay, the Brazilian wireless took care of the north, and so in a few months South America was thoroughly covered.

Mr. John Collins, "borrowed" from the Panama Canal Board, handled Central America from Darien, broadcasting it for interception by the wireless stations of the United Fruit Company. There was also a special cable service circulated gratis through co-operation of the Haiti Cable Company. It consisted of a summary of the day's news, approximating four hundred words daily, which was prepared by this office and sent over cables of the Haitian Company to all their offices. By these offices it was posted in various Central American and Caribbean cities or sold by the cable company's agents to various newspapers, etc. In this way many cities and communities otherwise totally cut off from news of the world received adequate news summaries of the day's happenings and true news of America.

On studying Mexico, a distinct problem, we discovered that while the Associated Press served the Mexican morning newspapers, the afternoon press was not reached by any American agency. Compub, therefore, undertook a special service of its own, sending three hundred words daily to the City of Mexico for national distribution by Mr. Murray's office. A duplicate was generally sent to the American consular services along the Texas border, and very effective use was made of it.

The next link in the world chain was the Orient. Compub opened a branch office in San Francisco, and Mr. W. B. Clausen, "loaned" to us by the Associated Press, commenced the preparation of a daily service of particular interest to China, Japan, the Philippines, and Hawaii. The navy wireless station at San Diego flashed this to Pearl Harbor for distribution to the Hawaiian press, and from Pearl Harbor it went to the Philippines. Our original theory was that the Chinese and Japanese stations would receive from Manila, but owing to many mechanical difficulties it became necessary for our own station at Guam to take the service out of the air and put it on the cables to Tokio and to Shanghai. In China Mr. Crow, the Compub representative, distributed the service through a specially organized chain of newspapers, and in Japan we worked through the Kokusai and Nippon Dempo, the two principal news associations. Mr. Crow, in Shanghai, also relayed the service to Vladivostok, where our office gave it Siberian circulation. Distant Australia picked the service out of the air and used it. As the importance of the work became apparent, and as results were proved, the service increased its output. The regular wireless "report" was doubled and trebled in size, the navy's splendid efficiency in radio transmission permitting this expansion, and utilization was also made of the cables. Where some important official statement was released and publication desired abroad, Compub, with the co-operation of the foreign press associations and correspondents, sent such statements for simultaneous delivery and release.

This, then, was the ground-plan of America's world news service. When its strength and efficiency had been tested thoroughly, the machinery was augmented and improved at every possible point. Mr. Rogers and Mr. Arnold, selecting slowly and carefully, had gathered about them such newspaper men as Herman Suter, R. R. Reilly, Frank S. Gardner, Theodore Wallen, R. J. Rochon, E. F. Wilson, and Lieut. F. E. Ackerman and Lieut. P. S. O'Reilly (borrowed from the navy), constituting a force ready for any expansion.

Continued pressure upon the Italian government finally resulted in wireless improvements to such a degree that the station in Rome was able to receive directly from Tuckerton. This did away with the necessity of relay from Paris and enabled the New York office to pour a daily stream of news straight into Italy, an immediate contact to which the Italian press responded enthusiastically.

As Spain became more and more of a battle-ground, the relay service from Paris became insufficient, so a special cable service was sent to New York direct to Mr. Marion in Madrid, who worked out a splendid co-operative arrangement with Fabra, the official Spanish news agency, as well as serving Madrid papers directly, and issuing a news bulletin of his own.

The installation of Compub at Vladivostok, Harbin, Irkutsk, and Omsk in Siberia enabled us to send a direct Russian service from the wireless station at San Francisco. The naval vessel *Brooklyn* relayed the service at Vladivostok until a land wireless station was erected there. From London, in time, also went out several hundred words a day by cable to the American consul at Archangel, which were distributed to the American soldiers in that region as well as to the press.

London's importance as a clearing-house was recognized by the addition of a "localized" service of some six hundred words to the regular daily wireless. This included specialized news for England, Scotland, Wales, Ireland, Holland, Scandinavia, Greece, and other nations. *The Field*, a British periodical of large circulation, was induced through representatives of the Committee on duty in London to arrange for an "American Department." In this department the division furnished a great deal of American publicity matter, including, generally, a special cabled article weekly. Aside from the publicity obtained in this magazine, the editor, Sir Theodore Cook, a great admirer of America and of Americans, took a keen interest in circulation of American news, and through wide personal acquaintance with British editors and journalists got them frequently to reprint the American articles appearing in his periodical.

The National News organization was a British propaganda agency operating throughout the British Isles and particularly in Ireland. Many special news articles were prepared for this agency by Compub, and it proved a very effective medium of distribution. The Y. M. C. A. also gave a daily bulletin circulation among rest houses, camps, and clubs.

As the maintenance of Allied morale was one of Compub's fundamental purposes, naturally enough Compub was called upon to assist in the work of keeping up the morale of American soldiers in France. What the doughboys missed most, and wanted most, was news of home and home folks. What news was printed was mostly of national affairs or of the war. There was no newspaper in Europe which could afford the expense of cabling items of purely local interest to the boys from Helena, Mont., or of Milwaukee, or San Francisco, or Cincinnati, or scores of other American cities. What was wanted was tiny bits of "home news" for the soldier—little items which would keep him in touch with conditions in his home town, just as a letter from his chum, or his mother, brother, sister, or sweetheart, or wife would do.

To meet this need, Compub inaugurated a "home news" service, sending it by wireless to France in addition to the regular daily service.

The American press was combed by readers in the New York offices for "homey news," every effort being made to cover the whole of the United States, and a report of nearly fifteen hundred words daily was prepared from these small items of news, none of which in themselves averaged more than fifty words each. The wireless carried this, and, incidentally, the Paris edition of *The London Daily Mail*, and of *The New York Herald*, used this service daily.

In the distribution of this matter to the soldier overseas the Foreign Press Cable Service had the co-operation of all American welfare services—the Young Men's Christian Association, Red Cross, Knights of Columbus, Young Men's Hebrew Association, Salvation Army, and others— as well as the army authorities. The latter granted permission for transmission of these home-news items over army wires from Paris to the front. The welfare organizations received copies in the huts close to the front and posted them for the benefit of the soldiers. Several welfare organizations in London and Paris printed a daily "newspaper" composed of these items, and despatched copies by mail to all recreation centers, hospitals, canteens, huts, etc., within reach. American sailors received them, navy wireless operators copying them throughout the reach of the American wireless sending station.

Early in the summer of 1918, when American troops entered in the "great push," Compub was called upon to extend its services of information still farther. Perry Arnold was sent abroad to study methods of news distribution and to organize a "news from the American front" service. He inspected the Committee's offices in London, Paris, and Madrid, and employed Maximilian Foster, the well-known novelist and writer, as the Committee's representative at the front with the American army, after himself having started such a service.

This service from the front was cabled and wirelessed throughout the world, giving a daily analysis of what American troops were doing in the Great War. General Pershing's staff at American headquarters was at all times in full sympathy with a plan of telling the world exactly what American soldiers were doing, and Compub's representative was accorded the fullest facility in visiting the front and in transmitting his despatches *via* army wires.

The formation in New York of the local foreign correspondents in an association, one of Mr. Rogers's ideas, resulted in the doubling and trebling of the descriptive and interpretative matter that went out from the United States to the other countries of the world. As a result, a new and keener interest in America was aroused, and many of the European papers established "American departments." To meet this demand, Compub commenced a biweekly wireless service that carried feature matter and specialized material susceptible to illustration and editorial treatment.

Another duty of Compub was to keep in the closest possible touch with the trend of enemy propaganda. Its agents abroad reported on conditions frequently, and in the New York office certain employees were detailed regularly to read and analyze all German propaganda material received here—a great part of it being wireless matter sent by the great German wireless station at Nauen and intercepted by the United States Navy Communication station. By a co-operative arrangement with the publicity offices in America of the Allies, Compub likewise distributed to the American press all of the official British propaganda wireless material (intercepted by the American wireless stations) and on occasion special announcements "broadcasted" by the stations of the French and Italian governments.

In this manner, and scores of other ways, Compub expanded and improved, swift to take advantage of opportunity, keen to see new needs, and growing in strength certainty, and importance. At its peak no news organization in the world, or in history, equaled Compub in the sweep of its operations, for there was not a corner of the earth into which it did not flash America's message. What is more, it was a message that carried conviction, for at no time did Compub depart from its original purpose—*the presentation of facts*. It was not our idea to argue, but t inform, for such was the justice of America's case, the wonder of America's achievement, that we felt that information was in itself the most conclusive argument.

The most important of all Compub activities and the most dramatic was the universal circulation of the President's official addresses. From the day that he went before the Senate, asking it to recognize the existence of a state of war, the President was accepted by the Allies as the official spokesman, for his imperishable words cut through every confusion of controversy down to the very heart of truth and justice in human aspiration. Nevertheless, owing to the congestion of the cables and the enormous expense of cable tolls, the President's addresses were not printed in full in Europe, and in other countries of the world only trifling excerpts were given to the people. This opened the door to a double danger, for not only were the Allied Powers being deprived of an effective weapon, but the German propaganda machine took advantage of the situation to suppress, to distort, and even to circulate text, not alone in Germany, but in the neutral nations.

One of our first decisions was to give textual distribution of the President's speeches, not only to Europe but to every quarter of the civilized globe. This vast project could not have been carried through to success without the generous co-operation of the great world press agencies. Compub paid the cable and telegraph tolls on the speeches and messages plus a small overhead charge, but this only partially covered the immense expenditure of time and energy in the distribution.

Immediately upon the signing of the armistice, orders were given to close every division of the Committee on Public Information with the exception of the wireless and cable service and their necessary distributing offices. It was not only the case that there still remained the necessity of putting true reports of the Peace Conference before the people of the world, but the press of America itself demanded aid in telling the story of Paris to the people of the United States. The cables, already overburdened, became hopelessly jammed when an army of American newspaper men commenced to file daily despatches in Paris for quick transmission.

Mr. Rogers proceeded to France at once, and after conference with the Associated Press, the United Press, the International News Service, and the correspondents of metropolitan dailies, a plan was worked out that put Compub at the disposal of the newspapers of the United States.

III

AT the outset it was seen that the wireless and the cables, even used to the utmost, could not meet our foreign needs. It was not enough to give the world the daily news of America's war effort, our military progress, and the official declarations and expositions with respect to our war aims and determinations. There were lies of long standing that had to be met and defeated—lies that attacked America as "dollar-mad," that maligned our free institutions, that denied our liberty and our justice. What was needed were short descriptives of our development as a nation and a people; our social and industrial progress; our schools; our laws; our treatment of workers, women and children; a mail service, in fact, that could be taken by our foreign representatives, translated, rewritten if necessary, and pushed into the foreign press to the greatest possible extent.

Mr. Ernest Poole was given charge of this new undertaking, and, with the assistance of Mr. Paul Kennaday, he gathered about him a volunteer staff of brilliant men and women writers.

One feature that would have justified the work, had it stood alone, was a series of weekly or monthly letters by such well-known authors as Owen Wister, Booth Tarkington, Gertrude Atherton, William Shepard, Ellis Parker Butler, Henry Kitchell Webster, Robert Herrick, Arthur

18   261

Gleason, Will Payne, Mary Shipman Andrews, Anne O'Hagan Shinn, and Walter Prichard Eaton. Other distinguished contributors were William Dean Howells, Ida Tarbell, Wallace Irwin, Meredith Nicholson, Fannie Hurst, Edna Ferber, Samuel Merwin, and William Allen White, also scores of government experts, university and college professors, and men and women of specialized abilities. The Foreign Press Bureau was, in effect, a "feature service" operating on demand. Our foreign representatives would cable, "Can use to good advantage one thousand words on American lumber industry," or on equal suffrage, or on university extension, or on unions, or on free-milk depots, or on the use of the schoolhouse as a community center, or the co-operative marketing of dairy products in Wisconsin, or the "honor and trust" system of Colorado prisons, or the jury system of the United States, or municipal bath-houses, or free legal-aid bureaus, or a short history of the United States for children, etc. And straightway the home office would get in touch with "the" authorities on the various subjects, and have them turn out the signed articles. For instance, we made Booth Tarkington drop everything to write "American Facts and German Propaganda," an article so virile and attractive that after millions had read it in the English papers the British government made arrangements with our London representative to reprint, and at its own expense distributed eight hundred and fifty thousand pamphlets in England. It was also widely used in other countries.

In describing war aims and national activities the Foreign Press Bureau took the statements of the President, of the Secretary of State, and of other government officials, material from several hundred newspapers, weekly and monthly magazines, also the pronouncements of prominent citizens and organizations throughout the country, giving every shade of opinion.

About one-half of the service consisted of news and feature articles, government bulletins, etc., describing the activities of the army and navy—war preparations of all kinds, the recruiting of volunteers, the method and operation of the selective draft, the work in the cantonments, the going of our troops to France, and the many increasing activities there. Also the making of munitions, the building of ships, the vast work of the United States navy, and the rapidly deepening spirit all over the United States of unity and determination in the prosecution of the war.

In addition we dealt with various fields of activities, such as agriculture and food conservation, industry and finance, labor, education, religion, and medicine, in relation to the work of the war and the growth of our democracy. These articles were a means of reaching a wider public abroad—for owing to the lack of paper the foreign newspapers were greatly diminished in size, and although a large amount of our material did succeed in gaining a place in their columns, we felt it urgent to go farther, and by sending many special articles and getting them published in the trade and other special journals and magazines of each country, we gradually widened our circle of readers.

On the staff, or working as volunteer helpers from outside, were men and women with a special knowledge of England, France, Italy, Russia, Holland, Sweden, Norway, Denmark, Germany, Austria, Serbia, Spain, and Latin-American countries. With Hamilton Owens as editor-in-chief, it was their work to write or edit supplementary material of particular interest to each country. Prof. Arthur Livingston, the editor for Italy, could write colloquial Italian and had a good working knowledge of the principal newspapers in Italy. He wrote for such papers special news letters, which were sent by mail or cable, describing activities of Italians in this country, their support of the war, etc.; also editorial opinion here as it concerned our relations with Italy and the part that country played in the war; messages from administration officials here on Italian operations and comment from United States public men on Italian problems and events; also statements by various well-known Italians who visited this country during the war. The various official missions from Italy were in constant touch with this office; we supplemented the official programs arranged by other organizations, bringing the visitors into touch with people they desired to meet, getting publicity for them in various ways, and furnishing them with special material for use after their return to Europe. In this connection we instituted the plan for having a ship christened the *Piave* and for making the event an occasion for the exchange of official and popular expressions of esteem between the governments of Italy and of the United States.

More or less along these lines special articles were also sent to England, France, and Spain in large numbers, being written or edited either by staff editors or by volunteer helpers from outside. At first by Mr. Elias Tobenkin, and later by Dr. Francis Snow, similar work was done for Russia whenever that was possible, meeting Bolshevist and German statements against us by articles describing true conditions in this country, our democracy at home, and our purpose in the war, as well as the wide-spread friendliness here at first toward the Russian revolution and the willingness to support any effort which gave, in our opinion, hope of a real and lasting practical democracy there.

For Austria and Germany articles were obtained by Doctor Groszmann, of our staff, from prominent German-Americans here loyal to this country and making an appeal to the people of Germany and Austria to throw off their old rulers and begin to re-establish themselves in the good opinion of the world. Such articles made it plain that the warfare conducted by the German and Austrian governments had made these countries hated, not only by native Americans, but by those of German birth. In this connection we also ran various articles exposing German methods of propaganda.

For the Scandinavian countries and Holland, a bureau under Mr. Edwin Bjorkman did such good work that it soon became impossible to pick up a Scandinavian publication of any kind without finding references to America, indicating an eager desire to understand what this country stood for and what it intended to do in the future. It was through Sweden, among others, that some of our material directed to the Germans was sent after the signing of the armistice.

A pictorial service grew up in response to increased demands from our agents in foreign countries. Under the direction of Mr. W. H. Whitton and Mr. Frank Tuttle, it provided each week photographs, cuts, and mats to illustrate our articles, photographs to the number of fifteen hundred per week for display upon easels in shop-windows, and some sixty thousand large news pictorials to be placed in the many thousands of shop-windows in foreign countries which were available for our use. Seven hundred and fifty wooden easels were made, each carrying twelve pictures, and the resident commissioners distributed them and provided for the weekly change of photographs that gave each easel the attraction of a "show." The pictorial service also distributed widely the war posters of this country and millions of picture post-cards showing forth our war activities. The window hangers were sent out in sets of six each week with captions in various languages, such as English, French, Italian, Swedish, Portuguese, Spanish, Danish, Norwegian, and Dutch. Unimprinted display sheets were sent to Russia, China, Japan, Korea, some parts of India, etc. For the Oriental countries a special version was printed, with a wide margin on the right-hand side, thus allowing the space necessary for imprinting the language of the country receiving them. With all unimprinted material either English printed samples or English captions were inclosed.

Through various organizations of United States exporters to foreign countries an Export Service was established under Mr. Edward Bernays, beginning with Latin America and finally taking in a large part of Europe. Our articles and photographs were printed regularly in the several large export journals, and from our articles we made, in various languages, brief inserts telling of war aims and activities to be inclosed with business catalogues and also to be sent in tens of thousands of letters mailed weekly from the United States. In obtaining means of distribution, the confidential lists of many great commercial interests were used. The exporters put themselves solidly behind every resident commissioner, and the success of the pictorial service was entirely due to the fact that six hundred and fifty branches of American business houses scattered over the world put all their window space at the Committee's disposal.

The distribution of pamphlets was made by mail or direct delivery. Important utterances of the President and documents prepared in each country with a view to answering local questions were printed locally in numbers running from five to thirty thousand and distributed through co-operation with American, British, French, and Italian commercial and government organizations in each country.

The American reading-rooms opened by resident commissioners received their supplies from the Foreign Press Bureau, and lectures delivered in different countries by nationals were also based on material furnished by the home office. Data regarding the United States, including standard magazines, books, and periodicals, were furnished to public and private bodies and schools, and public libraries were supplied with American newspapers and periodicals, and in some cases particularly desirable books relating to public questions.

The Foreign Press Bureau, in conjunction with the Export Division, also devoted itself to the preparation of particular pamphlet and news material for South America, under the direction of Lieutenant Ackerman, U. S. N., attached to the staff. It furnished the headquarters in the different countries with posters from all the branches of the government devoted to war-work and aided the bureaus in forwarding campaigns for War Savings Stamps, Liberty Loan, and Red Cross, and other activities in each of their territories. It arranged for the publication in all magazines in the United States having foreign circulation for such articles and editorials indicating our attitude toward world questions. In addition to serving the accredited commissioners of the Committee on Public Information, a Bureau of Latin-American Affairs sent pamphlet and news material, pictures, cuts, mats, and the pictorial news service to a large number of volunteer distributors throughout Mexico and Central and South America.

The Foreign Press Bureau, while setting forth in detail the aims and ideals of America, the determinations and war efforts of a free people, also put great emphasis upon acquainting the rest of the world with the facts of American life. We wanted other nations to know us, to understand us, and in consequence the work concentrated in certain great fields. For instance, with respect to education, we endeavored to reach the hundreds of thousands of teachers in foreign countries through the press and to bind them together more closely in friendship and good will. They represented a great international force hitherto unmobilized, but united by multiple bonds of similar aims and activities. Throughout the neutral and Allied world enemy propagandists had circulated among them every conceivable distortion of our education and ideals. These needed to be counteracted by truthful interpretations, which, however, sought to avoid tendencies toward superlatives, and to allow accurate statements of fact to carry their own story.

Each week we sent out articles on education, edited by Dr. William H. Hirt, which were forwarded to some thirty-five foreign countries, where our representatives received, translated, and passed them on to the press of the country in question. There, as a rule, they appeared either in the public, the literary, or the technical educational press. Many of these articles were especially written for us on request by leading educators all over the United States.

Further, the educational press of the United States generously gave permission to use their current articles, and also signified a readiness to accept our proposed exchange service. This exchange program was based on the idea that only as people have things in common can they co-operate. Basic among these things is knowledge about one another. Unfortunately, the teachers of the world know little about one another. The great mass of the graded school-teachers have had little chance for travel or study of other peoples. So while we asked our educators to interpret our educational system and ideals and progress to others, we also asked foreign nations to interpret their systems to us, feeling that we had much to learn from these older cultures. In England, in Spain, and elsewhere the government authorized a native educator to mobilize such writings of his people for us.

For the purpose of translating such articles over here a large staff of volunteer translators offered their services without compensation. Special requests cabled from certain countries were met, and the articles, often illustrated with pictures of American school equipment and life, went by the next mail.

With respect to food, fuel, and textiles, our aim was to emphasize the position of the United States as the greatest source of the world's reserve supplies of food, fuels, and textiles, and to show this country's determination to keep the Allied fighting forces and civilian populations provided with the necessities of life. We emphasized throughout the patriotism, self-sacrifice, and good will toward Allied nations among the people of the United States as expressed in food and fuel production and conservation.

Also, at all times it was endeavored to reflect the spirit, progress, and development of the rural United States, especially in the direction of greater democracy, increased interest in co-operation, organization, and farmer representation in national affairs, and the application of principles of the larger internationalism to the life and interests of the farmers of America. Principles and measures whereby the government is co-operating with and assisting the farmer were also discussed, explained, and their significance pointed out.

The editor of this division, Mr. E. L. D. Seymour, sent out regular weekly letters on farm and crop conditions, Food Administration activities and achievements, and the fuel situation. Posters, administration bulletins, Department of Agriculture reports, and other illuminating publications were sent in considerable quantity.

With the generous co-operation of many trade and industrial journals and organizations, we set forth the manifold activities of the various trades and industries in support of the war. The editors of many of the leading trade journals in the country became regular volunteer contributors, giving us weekly or monthly reviews of the progress of war-work in their particular fields. These special news letters were sent to the foreign agents, together with a list of trade journals in each foreign country, asking our agents to try to place such special articles in special journals abroad.

In the field of finance, we described the financial strength of this country, the good will of the people, and the evidence of democracy in the various financial measures carried out by the government. We used reports from the Treasury Department, and also statements issued by that department from time to time; fully described the various Liberty Loan drives in popular news articles, and we obtained from the editor of *The American Bankers' Magazine*, Mr. Elmer Youngman, weekly financial articles, which in many foreign countries our agents readily placed in the financial columns of the foreign press. We also obtained from time to time statements especially written for us by well-known bankers and economists in this country.

From many angles the bureau established the warm support of the war by the labor elements in this country. Our editor, Mr. Norman Matson, used largely the reports and statements of government bodies dealing with labor, as well as those of the American Federation of Labor and various state and municipal bodies belonging to the federation. We ran statements of prominent labor leaders, and published articles describing labor activities in shipyards and other centers where war-work was carried on. We gave the workers' and the employers' sides, and showed the new relations and mutual understandings between employer and employed, which in many places were built up during the work of the war.

As for religion, Mrs. Shinn of our staff (better known as Anne O'Hagan) showed the churches of all denominations rallying to the support of the war. We made it a special point to answer in Catholic countries abroad the German false allegations that in this country the Catholic Church was being persecuted by the government and was hostile to the war. We ran statements by prominent men both in the Catholic and Protestant churches, and also by leaders of the Jewish religion. We described war activities of the churches, and ran extracts from sermons setting forth the ideals and war aims of this nation.

In medicine, we described both in popular and in more technical articles the activities of the medical profession in the war. Doctor Liber of our staff used largely the reports and statements from the Surgeon-General's office, also from the Red Cross, and from many non-government bodies having to do not only with strictly military work, but also with the public health.

The press material of the bureau, beginning with a weekly service of about 30,000 words and running as high as 80,000 in English and 20,000 in Spanish, was sent regularly to 17 foreign commissioners of the Committee, to 22 diplomatic and consular representatives in Countries where there were no Committee commissioners, to 10 United States citizens abroad co-operating as agents of the Committee, to the British ministry of labor, and to 18 accredited correspondents in this country of foreign newspapers. Close touch was maintained with all these commissioners and agents through letters sent out regularly once a week and through frequent cables. Advised through such correspondence of the openings in each country for articles along various lines, the service to each country became more and more specialized as the work continued. We were thus enabled, also, to serve as a clearing-house for methods of publicity that had been tried with success in each country, such as the distribution of quantities of small American flags, buttons carrying the flags of the United States and those of our allies, maps of Europe for window exhibition, showing the location of the American forces on the western front, sets of American band music,

American newspapers, magazines, and books for the equipment of small reading-rooms in connection with our foreign offices.

The extent to which our press material was printed in foreign newspapers and magazines week after week was remarkable, testifying at once to the new interest of the world in things American and to the ability with which this office was able to meet this demand with newspaper and magazine material prepared by a corps of experienced writers on our staff and by a large number of volunteers, who generously and repeatedly responded to our appeals for articles on special subjects.

IV

AS in the United States, motion pictures played a great part in the work of the Foreign Section, ranking as a major activity. To millions unable to read, to literate millions unreached by newspaper or magazine, to city audiences and village crowds, the screen carried the story of America, flashing the power of our army and navy, showing our natural resources, our industrial processes, our war spirit, and our national life. Our method of presentation was either to rent a theater outright, giving our own shows, or to rent the pictures themselves to exhibitors, although in many of the rural districts we put a projector on an automobile and traveled from village to village, delighting the rustic populace with "the wonders of America."

War pictures, as a matter of course, gave the point to every program. A steady stream of wonderful "fighting stuff" was poured into our foreign channels, so that the eyes of the world followed America's war progress from the cantonment to the ship, from St. Nazaire to the firing-line, along the firing-line from Château-Thierry to the Argonne, and saw America's war preparations from the shipyard to the sea, from the factory to the great supply depots in France. Great feature-films like "Pershing's Crusaders" and "America's Answer" could stand alone, but the majority of "war stuff" had to be accompanied by contrasting material. Not only this, but it was also the case that we wanted the world to see America "at home."

In the first days, Jules E. Brulatour, a pioneer in the motion-picture industry, and one of its fine, inspiring figures, came to the Committee as a volunteer, and it was his job to collect "educational stuff," meaning every sort of a movie that would show American cities, factories, and farms, our social progress, our industrial life, and our adventures in altruism and humanity. He knew exactly which of the great manufacturing concerns "went in" for motion pictures, and straightway commenced a begging tour that took in Henry Ford, the United States Steel Corporation, the International Harvester Company, Waterman's Pen, the Corn Products Company, the lumber companies, coal companies, etc., until he had thousands of reels showing every phase of American industry. Then he went to the Bureau of Parks and got "nature stuff," to the Department of Agriculture for scientific farming pictures, to the Bureau of Education for "school stuff," to the Public Health Service for "sanitation stuff," and on down the line until he had everything that the government possessed in the way of an educational film. An arrangement with the film-news weeklies permitted us to comb their releases, and from them we bought footage that showed patriotic celebrations, women voting, Labor Day parades, seashore scenes, baby contests, stock shows, athletic games, and everything else that threw any light on us as a people.

All of the manufacturers were generous in the extreme, giving us a full set of positives without debate, although Henry Ford led all others in princely donations that totaled thousands of dollars. The task of duplication was Mr. Brulatour's, also the hard, tedious job of putting the titles into the various languages. It was a remarkable task that Mr. Brulatour carried to success, although a very

LLEWELLYN THOMAS   JULES BRULATOUR   GUY CROSWELL SMITH

E. L. STARR   WILBUR H. HART
LT. JOHN TUERK

enthusiastic word must be said for Lieut. John Tuerk, borrowed from the army by reason of his wide experience in the motion-picture field. The old Kalem studio on West Twenty-third Street in New York was taken over, and hummed night and day with the rush of picture selection and picture shipping.

Later, when the Foreign Section was fully organized, Mr. Hart's Division of Films became the source of supply, and Mr. Byoir was placed in charge of operations. As a result of these combined activities, the foreign commissioners were able to present a well-balanced program, starting out with pictures of an American city or some national park, following with typical American scenes, then showing schools, model farms, welfare work in factories, a shipyard or munitions-factory, and then finishing strong with an American cantonment, the grand fleet, the arrival in France, and "over the top with the Yanks."

All of which was very fine as far as it went, but upon investigation we found that it did not go far enough. What the war-weary foreigners liked and demanded was American comedy and dramatic film. They had to have their Mary Pickford and Douglas Fairbanks and Charlie Chaplin and Norma Talmadge. The Germans, either by outright purchase of picture-houses or else by subsidizing exhibitors, were largely in control in every neutral country, and used American entertainment film to put across their propaganda material. As a result, we stood to be left out in the cold.

Looking around, we discovered that no film of any kind could be sent out of the United States without a license from the War Trade Board. Without waste of time, we saw Vance McCormick, the chairman, and secured from him a ruling to the effect that every application for a license must bear the indorsement of the Committee on Public Information. The rest was simple.

Calling a meeting of all the film supporters, we explained the situation in detail, and while promising that the Committee would use all of its influence to expedite film shipments, we demanded in return that the motion-picture industry should come to the aid of the Committee in equal degree. As a result of negotiations this arrangement was worked out:

(1) That every shipment for entertainment film from the United States should contain at least 20 per cent. "educational matter."

(2) That not a single foot of American entertainment film would be sold to any exhibitor who refused to show the Committee's war pictures.

(3) That no American pictures of any kind would be sold to houses where any sort of German film was being used.

This method shut the German film out of Sweden and Norway in a few weeks after the adoption. With respect to Switzerland and Holland, where the German control was virtually complete, the Committee adopted an even more drastic mode of procedure. It was asked of the leading film-producers, and agreed to by them, that the representatives of the Committee should have the absolute and unquestioned disposition of every foot of commercial film that went into the two countries. As a consequence of this air-tight arrangement, Mrs. Whitehouse and Mr. Suydam were not only in possession of the Committee's war and educational pictures, but also had entire charge of every comedy and dramatic picture that went out from the shores of the United States. No motion-picture house could do business without our product, and it was very soon the case that the Germans were being run out of both fields. In Switzerland, where they held most tenaciously, the lid was falling relentlessly when the armistice came.

In France, England, and Italy the initial showing of

our picture films was always an event, the high officials of government attending formally, and even in the neutral countries we were able eventually to make our own productions on an impressive scale. Our most glittering success, perhaps, was in The Hague, where the police had to stop one performance of "America's Answer" owing to "the great pro-American demonstrations that it aroused." In Mexico, however, much the same result was achieved.

As the work grew, and as the fight took on greater intensity, it became apparent that film experts would have to be despatched to aid the resident commissioners, also that we would have to install our own laboratories in certain countries and export our own raw material and equipment. The success of Guy Croswell Smith in Scandinavia had shown that this should be the method. Coming out of Russia with Mr. Sisson in March, 1918, he took film charge of Sweden, Norway, and Denmark immediately.

In furtherance of the general plan, H. C. Hoagland went to France, where he established intimate contact with the Signal Corps, enlarging laboratories, vitalizing procedure, and generally increasing and improving the output. He handled the Italian situation also, making arrangements in Rome for the national exhibition of American programs. Llewellyn R. Thomas, sent to The Hague, handled 306,000 feet of dramatics, 52,000 feet of comedies, 12,000 feet of Committee war film, 92 reels of news pictures, and 200,000 feet of raw stock. He operated fifty eight-reel programs, and his speed, ability, and enthusiasm dazzled the Dutch and routed the Germans. From the very outset our "movie" work in Russia was attended by every difficulty. The fall of Kerensky made Russian consignments a problem, and to meet this situation we made arrangements with the Y. M. C. A. by which its representatives would carry film to the Committee's representatives in Petrograd and Moscow. In the fall of 1917 we assembled thousands of

19   277

reels, covering every field of American activity, and intrusted them to A. C. Harte, who was proceeding to Russia for the Y. M. C. A. Through various unforeseen changes in Mr. Harte's plans, he turned back at Stockholm, and, as the Russian frontier was closed, our pictures continued to rest in Sweden. Another effort was made through the agency of Herman Bernstein, the war correspondent of *The New York Herald*, who took with him many cases of film, and who also agreed, if he found it possible, to pick up the shipment left in Stockholm by Mr. Harte. Mr. Bernstein's chance to get into Russia came suddenly and he had to travel without impediment of any kind; the films that he carried took their place in storage alongside of those left by Mr. Harte.

As a consequence, Mr. Sisson and Mr. Bullard were compelled to rely entirely upon the small amount of film already possessed, and while they used it over and over again with remarkable results, there was always the sense of bitter disappointment. When the Bolsheviki finally threw pretense aside and came out as open enemies of America, the Committee changed its basis of operation from Moscow and Petrograd to Archangel and Vladivostok.

To Vladivostok, the center of east Siberian motion-picture trade, the Committee sent carloads of equipment, including six-B cameragraphs, delco light plants, monoplane lamps, rewinders, motors, etc., motion-picture film-printing machines, motion-picture rheostats, screens, etc. This permitted the installation of our laboratory with full titling facilities, and as a consequence the Committee was able to ship continuously and in quantity. As in other countries, arrangements were made with the commercial producers for exclusive rights, and feature dramas and comedies soon joined with the Committee's war and industrial film for the presentation of well-balanced eight-reel programs.

Charles Philip Norton and H. Y. Barnes handled the motion-picture campaign for Mr. Bullard, and under their direction the Committee showed pictures throughout Siberia. Not only were our programs presented in picture-houses, but through the co-operation of the Red Cross, the Young Men's Christian Association, and the Military and Naval Association we reached the firing-line, the churches, the rural communities, and other places where the Russian peasants assembled in any number. Read Lewis, the Committee's commissioner at Archangel, had been supplying one motion-picture theater in Archangel, and two in a suburb, with programs, and in conjunction with the Young Men's Christian Association was furnishing three reels of features and comedies and two reels of educationals. Harry P. Inman, ordered to Archangel to assist Mr. Lewis, carried with him a laboratory outfit for the manufacture and exhibition of motion pictures, also a large amount of negative and positive raw stock, 42 reels of feature dramas, 16 reels of good comedies, 26 reels of news weeklies, and all our official film, including "Pershing's Crusaders," "America's Answer," "Bridge of Ships," "Official War Review." Not the least of Mr. Inman's many successful undertakings was an arrangement with the educational department of the Russian Co-operative Unions (which is recognized by the present Archangel government) for films to be released in towns within a two-hundred-mile radius of Archangel. Wilbur H. Hart, sent to China, found that distribution through established theaters was not feasible, inasmuch as less than 2 per cent. of their entire attendance was Chinese. In many of the principal theaters in Shanghai and in Pekin he presented the feature-films of the Committee with success and followed up with special presentations of various kinds in an effort to reach the purely Chinese population. Japan was comparatively simple, as we dealt with a well-established system of exchanges. E. L. Starr, the motion-picture expert despatched to South America, made a very complete survey and worked out a plan that gave maximum results. In Buenos Aires a theater was taken for official showing of the Committee's feature-films, after which a commercial arrangement was made with the leading distributor in the Argentine. In Brazil the motion-picture industry was controlled almost entirely by the French and Italians, and Mr. Starr made arrangements for distribution through the American Embassy at Rio de Janeiro. Mr. Morgan, the Ambassador, gave the matter his personal supervision, and as a result it was not long before American films held highest place in the favor of the Brazilian people.

In Peru the motion-picture theaters were found to be crude and unsatisfactory, the greater portion of the Peruvian population being Indian and entirely illiterate. Railroads reached some of the more important mining and agricultural sections, but a vast amount of this territory was accessible only by burro through mountain trails. The distribution of motion pictures for Peru, Bolivia, and Ecuador, made through Lima, was based, therefore, on a system worked out by C. V. Griffis, commissioner of the Committee in Peru, head of the American Society, and editor of the only English weekly on the west coast. Mr. Griffis owed much to the assistance of Mr. Handley, American consul-general at Lima.

Arrangements were made for the showing of the films in Peru through the Peru chapter of the American Red Cross in each of the cities and towns having a Red Cross branch. After this showing the films were turned over to the only important distributing corporation in the country, the Impreso de Teatros y Cinemas, Limitada, which agreed to play the films in every city and town having a cinema theater (26 towns and cities with a total of 34 theaters). That gave us over a period of time a very efficient distribution. Bolivia had five towns in which we made the same arrangement as in Peru. Ecuador likewise had eight towns in which the same arrangement for distribution was effected.

In Chile the official films of the Committee were turned over to Mr. Sevier, the Compub commissioner, and in the larger cities they were shown in conjunction with various charities. In the American mining towns and camps the films were shown by the American Red Cross under the auspices of the local chapters, and at the completion of these showings the Southern Pacific Paramount Company released these pictures in two or three reel lengths, in every city and town and camp having a cinema theater.

It was not only that the Committee put motion pictures into foreign countries. Just as important was the work of keeping certain motion pictures *out* of these countries. As a matter of bitter fact, much of the misconception about America before the war was due to American motion pictures portraying the lives and exploits of New York's gun-men, Western bandits, and wild days of the old frontier, all of which were accepted in many parts of the world as representative of American life.

What we wanted to get into foreign countries were pictures that presented the wholesome life of America, giving fair ideas of our people and our institutions. What we wanted to keep out of world circulation were the "thrillers," that gave entirely false impressions of American life and morals. Film dramas portraying the exploits of "Gyp the Blood," or "Jesse James," were bound to prejudice our fight for the good opinion of neutral nations.

Our arrangements with the War Trade Board gave us power and we exercised it. Under the direction of Lieutenant Tuerk, offices were opened in New York, and when applications for export licenses were made the pictures themselves were examined by competent committees in which tne army, the navy, and the customs were equally represented. As the motion-picture industry commenced to understand our purpose and realized that we stood ready to expedite all proper licenses, as well as to make the fight for shipping space, the co-operation became enthusiastic. Not only was it the case that all harmful film was barred from export, but producers became more and more willing to incorporate a large percentage of "educational pictures" in their shipments. "Educational" in our sense of the word meant film that showed our schools, our industrial life, our war preparations, our natural resources, and our social progress.

The spirit of co-operation reduced the element of friction to a minimum. Oftentimes it was the case that a picture could be made helpful by a change in title or the elimination of a scene, and in no instance did a producer fail to make the alterations suggested. During its existence, according to the report of Lieutenant Tuerk, more than eight thousand motion pictures were reviewed, the greater percentage of which went forward into foreign countries with the true message from America.

V

BREAKING THROUGH THE ENEMY CENSORSHIP

THE Germans were not whipped by man-power alone. No grain of credit is to be taken away from the courage of the Allies or the heroic, decisive charges of the Americans at Château-Thierry, St. Mihiel, and Belleau Wood, but there are certain facts that prove the importance of other compulsions than major force.

On the day that the Germans signed the armistice, accepting defeat as overwhelming as their ambitions had been colossal they had two million men under arms on the western front alone. This army was well equipped with supplies and munitions, and behind it still stretched line after line almost impregnable by reason of natural strength and military science. Not one inch of German territory knew the feet of an invading force, and to the east there were the armies of Mackensen and von Sanders. Nothing is more apparent than that a defensive warfare could have been waged for months, taking a tremendous toll in Allied and American lives. In 1870, even after Sedan, without an army, food, or munitions, the French fought on, Paris standing a siege of six months.

What happened to the Germans was an utter spiritual collapse, a disintegration of morale both on the firing-line and among the civilian population. Slowly at first, but always more swiftly, the truth made its way into Germany, sapping a foundation of lies laid carefully through long years. People and fighting-men alike commenced to feel the loathing of the world, came to understand the might arrayed against them, the inevitability of defeat, and when French, English, Italians, Serbians, and Americans began to deal the sledge-hammer blows directed by Foch, apprehension turned to certainty, fear became panic, and the whole rotten structure went tumbling into ruins.

Getting the truth into Germany and Austria-Hungary was as hard a battle as any fought in France. A censorship cunningly conceived and rigidly enforced not only guarded the frontiers, but crushed every internal attempt to speak or write honestly. Soldiers and civilians were drugged with lies about "Germany's defensive war," the "cruel purposes" of the enemy, the collapse of the Allies, the utter inability of America to train or transport troops, and the near approach of a tremendous victory that would mean world mastery.

These lies had all the force of divisions and it was as necessary to destroy them as though each had been a machine-gun nest. The Committee fought the German censorship on every front, attacking from France, Italy, Greece, Russia, and from such border nations as Switzerland, Holland, and Denmark. From the very first, the Paris office of the Committee worked in close co-operation with the French department of enemy propaganda. Mr. Kerney, our commissioner, was assisted by Lieut. Harry A. Franck of the Intelligence Section of the A. E. F., an officer with intimate knowledge of the German language and the German people.

As the importance of the work came to be recognized many efforts were made to bring about a single command so that resources might be pooled and confusion avoided. The Committee was at all times eager for co-operation and designated Mr. James Keeley, editor of *The Chicago Herald*, as our representative in the various conferences called by Lord Northcliffe and participated in by all the Allied

Powers. Aside from a very valuable exchange of ideas, nothing ever came of these efforts and the Committee continued to go its own way, working hand in hand with the Intelligence Section of the A. E. F. An office was opened in Padua for an attack upon the morale of Austria, and from France and Italy we managed to maintain a reasonable flow of American facts into the Central Powers. German and Austrian newspapers were carefully studied and their misrepresentations met with leaflets.

As the American Expeditionary Force grew in size and power it became increasingly apparent that American propaganda was the best wedge to drive it to the German censorship. The French bureau was reorganized and Commandant Chaix, a thoroughgoing business man, placed at its head with full power to work intimately with the Paris office of the Committee. A most efficient equipment was assembled, and documents were given a genuine German appearance as to paper, type, typesetting, and the fine points of German diction. The printers were German prisoners chosen for this particular task. For the troops, special matter was prepared according to nationalities. The military authorities, as soon as they noted the presence in certain trenches of Jugoslav, Polish, or other elements, or of German troops from disaffected districts, at once conveyed the information to the end that material specially designed to appeal to these respective forces might be despatched.

While it was easy enough to write and print the "shrapnel," it was always difficult to determine the most effective way to fire it. The most obvious method of distribution was by airplanes, of course, and over firing-lines, towns, and cities the sky rained single sheets that told the truth in short, sharp sentences. But the demand was so great for 'planes for the more imperative purposes of war that they could not be obtained in sufficient numbers for propaganda use and other and additional means of distribution had to be found.

The French introduced a rifle grenade that carried leaflets about six hundred feet in a favoring wind, and a 75-shell that carried four or five miles. The British developed a six-inch gun that carried ten or twelve miles and scattered several thousand leaflets from each shell. The Italians used rockets for close work on the front, each rocket carrying forty or fifty leaflets. The obvious smash at German morale was through America's aims and swift war progress, and for this reason the Allies used the President's speeches and our military facts freely and sometimes even exclusively.

To reach farther behind the lines, all fronts used paper balloons filled with coal-gas. They would remain in the air a minimum of twenty hours, so as to make a trip of six hundred miles in a thirty-mile wind. On a Belgian fête-day such balloons carried four hundred thousand greetings into Belgium, and some flew clear across Belgium. Fabric balloons, carrying seventeen or eighteen pounds of leaflets, were also employed, but with all the balloons the uncertainty of the wind made the work haphazard. A paper balloon, with propaganda intended for Alsace, came down in Kent, and a French balloon intended to reach the Rhine towns came down in Geneva.

The attempt was made to fly kites over the trenches and drop leaflets from traveling containers that were run up the kite wire, but this method could be used only on fronts where airplanes were not active, because the wires were a menace to the 'planes. The paper used in the leaflets was chemically treated so that they would not spoil if they lay out in the rain.

An American invention that gave promise of supplanting all others was a balloon that carried a tin container holding about ten thousand sheets. The Committee of

Public Information carried the inventor and his idea to the War Department, and provided the money for tests and experimentation that proved encouragingly successful, but the armistice prevented full firing-line use. A clock attachment governed the climb of the balloon, it had a sailing range of from six to eight hundred miles, and the mechanism could be set in such a manner as to have the pamphlets dropped in a bunch or one at a time at regular intervals, the whole business blowing up conclusively with the descent of the last printed "bullet."

At the end of June and during early July, when some of the German newspapers began to wake up to the fact that there really was more than a million American troops in France and that they were fighters, there appeared articles indicating war-weariness and hints that all might not be going so well on the western front. This material was quickly reproduced in Paris and spread among the German troops. It was along in July that the first genuine effects of the enemy propaganda were felt. On July 18, 1918, a conference of heads of the British, French, Belgian, and American services was held in the Paris office of the Committee on Public Information. It was the frank consensus of opinion that the place for concentrated effective work was in front of the American lines, then shortly to be very greatly extended. General Nolan, Major James, and Capt. Mark Watson of the Intelligence Section, A. E. F., attended the conference, and soon thereafter a special group of experts, under the immediate direction of Major James, took over the American end of the work.

All this was on the western front. In the East, up to the Brest-Litovsk treaty, the problem was merely one of printing and distribution, and with due appreciation of the Bolshevik surrender that was on the way, we strove mightily during the days of opportunity. Edgar G.

Sisson and Arthur Bullard, in charge of the Committee's educational work in Russia, put the speeches of President Wilson into German and into Magyar (the latter for Hungarians) and secured distribution from Russia across the line into the enemy's country by the hundreds of thousands. Even when the Germans advanced into Russia they found the walls of the towns freshly plastered with the President's Fourteen Points speech, printed in German for the information of the German soldiers.

The preparation of the material, no matter what the front, followed a set plan. At first all time and space was devoted to the causes that drove the United States to war—the brutal purposes of Germany, her plots and intrigues, her record of bloody cruelty—the absolute disinterestedness of America, and the great truth that the free world we fought for was a victory in which the wretched victims of the Prussian military machine would be permitted to share. The second step was to preach the doctrine of American achievement; the selective service law, the miracle of cantonments and training-schools, the building of ships and 'planes, the rush of men across the sea, the mighty resources of America, and the inevitability of German defeat and of Allied victory.

And always the speeches of President Wilson! They were our most effective weapons and it was easy to mark their progress through the enemy country by the trail of ferment and disaffection that each one left. Never at any time did the German censorship dare to kill a Wilson speech outright, but the first addresses were invariably cut in such manner as to distort and misrepresent the meaning. What we did was to have the entire speech printed in German, playing up all deleted words and passages and then, with the varied devices, begin to pound in upon the German people the new deceits practised upon them by their government. It was this backfire that compelled the Germans eventually to publish the President's addresses in their entirety.

The first proof of effectiveness was an order issued by the German General Staff establishing death as a penalty for all those seen picking up our matter or found with it in their possession. And even before this Austria-Hungary had given orders to shoot or imprison all soldiers or citizens guilty of the abominable crime of reading "printed lies" against the government.

Accounts of trials and cruel sentences contained in Austrian papers proved conclusively that there was no "bluff" about it as far as the Dual Monarchy was concerned; but it is very questionable whether the Germans went very far in enforcement of the orders. Eight prisoners out of every ten captured by the Americans had our "stuff" in their pockets, and reports united in declaring the literature "well thumbed."

A medium of attack wider in effect, even if less direct, was through the press of Switzerland, Denmark, and Holland. Through methods that will be described later, the public opinion of these countries was won for America, and our material was given daily place in the newspapers. It was under this strain that the German censorship began to crack, breaking at last with a loud report, and letting in daylight with a rush.

VI

FRANCE, ENGLAND, AND ITALY

NATURALLY enough, the Allied countries were first consideration in the matter of intensive activities, for the maintenance of French, English, and Italian morale was of the supremest importance. It was not that either soldiers or civilians lacked courage or were lessening in determination, but war-weariness had sapped ardor and enthusiasm, and there was the ever-present consciousness that the enemy advanced in spite of every resistance. "Can America come in time?" This was a question in every heart, if not on every lip, and the Germans answered it by sneering assertions that America had neither troops, transports, nor munitions. It was the job of the Committee to answer this lie by daily report on America's war progress, so that on every firing-line, and back of them, there might be understanding of the invincibility of the United States, the speed of its preparations, and the certainty of swift and decisive aid.

France was not only of peculiar importance in itself, but Paris was the clearing-house for our cable and wireless service, the center from which Switzerland, Italy, Spain, and Portugal drew direct information. To this important post we sent James Kerney, editor of *The Trenton Evening Times*, a choice for which I was blamed no little in the first days. Mr. Kerney did not know Europe, did not speak French, and had no familiarity with diplomatic usage, and these lacks were assumed to unfit him

JAMES F. KERNEY

ROBERT H. MURRAY

CHARLES E. MERRIAM

PAUL PERRY

HENRY SUYDAM

for the task in hand. As a matter of fact, these supposed qualifications were always of minor importance in our calculations. We did not want a commissioner who had the European point of view, or one who fancied himself a diplomat, but we wanted an American who thought regularly and enthusiastically in terms of America and who would worry over his job, not over his dignity. That was why we selected "Jim" Kerney, a first-class newspaper man, a dynamo of energy and originality, an enthusiast with an unfailing supply of optimism, and, above all, a real American. Not only did he fulfil every hope in the discharge of his duties, but, humorously enough, the French took him to their hearts at once, and he enjoyed a popularity that was never attained by the careful, precise gentlemen who "knew Europe, spoke French, and were familiar with diplomatic usage."

At the very outset Mr. Kerney established close working relations with Ambassador Sharp, General Pershing, and Admiral Wilson, linked up with the Maison de la Presse, the French propaganda bureau, and gained intimate contacts with the editors of the provincial press as well as the great Paris dailies. It was soon the case that the French press and reviews were filled with American news, and a smooth-running machinery took care of the relay of the wireless service to Berne, Rome, Madrid, and Lisbon.

A next step was "American front stuff," not the usual *communiqué*, but live news stories, day by day, that would give the Allies and the neutral nations a vivid understanding of how the Yankees were massing, preparing, and fighting. Martin Egan, at General Pershing's headquarters, was of invaluable aid in putting across the plan, and before long this service was in operation, Maximilian Foster roaming the fighting front, his author's eye quick to see, his artist's hand keen to write.

Not only were there American objections to overcome, but there was the French censorship itself that the new firing-line service had to buck up against. Mr. Kerney saw Premier Clemenceau personally, and as a result the rules were modified in such manner as to permit free relation of the wonderful story of "America in France." The Foster *communiqués*, as they came to be called, were not only added to the Committee's news service for Europe, but became an integral part of the world service as well, doing their work in South America and the Orient as well as in Holland and Scandinavia.

As a further use for the Committee's wireless service, Mr. Kerney relayed it by telegraph to American headquarters and the various American bases in France for the information of the A. E. F., and also put it in the offices of the Paris editions of *The London Daily Mail*, *The New York Herald*, *The Chicago Tribune*, and *The Stars and Stripes*. As a matter of fact, the bulk of the American news that appeared in these papers was furnished by the Committee on Public Information, and certainly it was the principal source of the "home news" that meant so much to the individual doughboy.

As in the case of so many other foreign commissioners, Mr. Kerney was hurried to Paris with instructions to find his force "on the ground," for even had there been time for the selection of assistance, there was the objection that he could not know what personnel he needed until he found out exactly what it was that he had to do. The building of his organization is not only a matter of interest in itself, but it may give some idea of how the Committee, driving always at top speed, was forced to rely upon its representatives and to trust to good fortune in the securement of expert assistance.

One of Mr. Kerney's first acquisitions was Madame Edith Bagues, the American wife of a distinguished French officer, who entered the Committee's office to serve as executive secretary. Speaking French like a native, knowing France intimately, and blessed with brains as well as beauty, Madame Bagues was a voice, a right hand, a rudder, and an inspiration. Frank M. Mansfield and A. Brace, two competent American newspaper men, were located and put in charge of the wireless service, Wilmot H. Lewis, a cosmopolitan correspondent, handled all contacts with the French press, and two clever French journalists, M. Claude Berton and M. Beryl, were assigned to the task of translation. James Hazen Hyde, long resident in Paris, was finding Red Cross work an insufficient outlet for his eager patriotism and tremendous energies, and Mr. Kerney soon captured him. It can safely be said that Mr. Hyde knew everybody in France who was worth knowing, and he put his time entirely at the service of the Committee, rendering aid of inestimable value. Marquise de Polignac, formerly Mrs. "Jimmy" Eustis of New York, was another American that Mr. Kerney pressed into service, and Marquis de Polignac himself was also used vigorously in the work of distributing specially prepared leaflets to the peasants of France.

Maj. A. L. James, Jr., chief of the press and censorship division of the Intelligence Section, took offices immediately adjoining those of the Committee, and in addition Mr. Kerney won to close and understanding contact with Gen. Dennis E. Nolan, chief of the Intelligence Section, and with Gen, Edgar E. Russel, chief of the Signal Corps. Whether it was in connection with pictures, the relay of news, or getting our matter in the German territory, these officers never failed to put men and facilities at Mr. Kerney's disposal.

Edgar B. Hatrick, a film expert in France in the interests of the Red Cross, was taken over by Mr. Kerney, and not only planned productions, but organized channels for the flow of pictures from the Signal Corps to the Committee. In order to save time, all firing-line photographs were sent to the European offices of the Committee directly from Paris, going out in weekly shipments. Under the direction of Mr. Hatrick, a great feature-film was assembled under the title of "America's Answer to the Hun," and the Gaumont Palace in Paris was rented for a presentation. It was witnessed by the members of the Senate and Chamber of Deputies, the diplomatic representatives of Great Britain, Italy, and Japan, as well as many of the Allied military and naval chiefs, and was given a mighty reception. This film in four reels depicted the protection afforded by the American navy to transports, disembarking of troops, our construction and installations at ports and along the lines of communication right up to the fighting front, the ambulance and supply services. It concluded with a number of scenes showing the American fighters in action at Château-Thierry, and one section of the theater was reserved for wounded doughboys from the hospitals in and about Paris. Columns of space were devoted to the event in the newspapers of France and England, and copies of the film were promptly sent to all the Allied and neutral countries for showing there. The big commercial producers, Gaumont and Pathé, arranged at once to send it into all their houses in France, and it was used most successfully among the troops, in factories, universities, schools, etc.

This feature-film, brought to the United States, was enriched with the cantonment scenes and pictures of the shipyards and the navy, and released under the title of "America's Answer."

One of the most enduring features of Mr. Kerney's work was a system of university and university extension lectures. Shortly after his arrival he met the presidents of all the French universities and presented to them a plan aimed at combating the wide-spread anti-American propaganda throughout France, by making known the spirit and extent of America's part in the war. These lectures were further framed to put the story of America's greatness, in some permanent form, into the minds of the local leaders of thought, as well as into the minds of the people. The Committee was able to get into personal touch with more than two hundred qualified lecturers, furnishing them with literature and documents, as well as lantern slides, with the result that practically every part of France was reached. The presidents of the universities gave their heartiest co-operation, and one hundred and fifty thousand copies of a pamphlet containing a summarization of American information were distributed to the school-teachers. The university presidents, together with the Ministry of Public Instruction, agreed upon M. Firman Roz of the University of Paris as a man most eminently fitted to inaugurate the American lectures. M. Roz, together with some other university representatives and writers, was taken over the American lines of communication and supplies, as well as to the front lines. The series of lectures began at the Sorbonne, M. Lucien Poincaré, brother of the President of the Republic, presiding, and immediately after this initial lecture M. Firman Roz began his tour of the universities, speaking at Bordeaux, Toulouse, Montpellier, Marseilles, Grenoble, Chambery, Lyons, Dijon, Besançon, Caen, Rennes, Poitiers, and Clermont-Ferrand.

These lectures gave America much publicity in the provincial press and had an especially good influence on the editorial columns. The presidents of the respective universities had invited to the lectures leading professors from each town in the educational district under the control of the university. In this way the university extension lectures were developed, the local professors organizing lecture centers. A complete list of these lecturers was kept in Paris and fresh literature, giving the latest information about America, regularly mailed to them. Local lectures were also given in many of the big provincial towns, the Committee receiving fine co-operation on the part of American consular representatives. Through the consulates everywhere printed matter was distributed, and in the larger centers, such as Havre, Cherbourg, Marseilles, Nantes, Tours, St. Nazaire, Lyons, Boulogne, Franco-American demonstrations, including lectures and production of movie films, were provided.

At the urgent request of the French Minister of Munitions, lectures on the American participation in the war were given in the various industrial plants in France engaged in manufacturing war-supplies, the purpose being to stem the unrest constantly cropping up. These lectures were given by Dr. Herbert Adams Gibbons, the American writer who had been in France since before the outbreak of the war, and who gladly turned his time and abilities over to Mr. Kerney. Both the French government officials and the manufacturers pronounced this work as highly valuable in its effect on the industrial situation. The proprietors and managers of the big steel and munitions plants were brought together in Paris on July 5th, the meeting being presided over by M. Loucher, Minister of Munitions, who dwelt upon the importance of the lecture and cinematographic work of the Committee in France.

Doctor Gibbons's first lecture in this unique course was at the factory of Louis Renault, where airplane motors, motor-trucks, tanks, cannon, and shells were being produced. The lecture was given twice in this plant, being recorded both stenographically and on the phonograph in order that it might get the most complete distribution among the twenty-five thousand employees. M. Renault subsequently declared that this exposition of America's part insured his plant against any labor disturbances for at least six months. The film was shown and the lecture given in all of the large plants engaged in the manufacture of war materials throughout France. Upward of one hundred thousand copies of the lecture were printed at the expense of the manufacturers for distribution among their employees.

On the invitation of the official French Propaganda Bureau, Doctor Gibbons spent several days lecturing in the mining country and, at the instance of the same organization, went for ten days into Alsace, explaining the American situation to the populations of the reconquered regions and, in turn, explaining the Alsatian question to the American troops occupying sectors on that front.

At our suggestion, Mr. Kerney established a "visitors' bureau" for the purpose of taking American correspondents on trips to the various fighting fronts, and Mr. Kerney soon broadened this original purpose by invitations to the correspondents of every country.

Leading writers for the French dailies, magazines, and reviews, with illustrators, were taken to the American front, and the publications were soon crowded with the remarkable accomplishments of our army and navy. This liberal treatment of the work continued until accounts of the glorious conduct of the troops at the fighting front produced the finest propaganda that ever appeared in any country. Writers from Spain, Switzerland, Italy, Holland, and the Scandinavian countries were brought to France and shown over the sectors in which the Americans were operating, and the reports they published were exceedingly useful in their effect not only in their home countries, but upon the civilian morale of Germany. This was particularly the case with the publication of American news in Switzerland, which occupied the most advantageous position in the matter of enemy propaganda. Photographs of the

American work and of the American fighters were supplied in great quantities, through the Signal Corps of the army, and were likewise despatched weekly to the Committee's representatives all over Europe, with the result that American pictures and American news filled the reviews and journals everywhere.

The English situation was never very bothersome, coming to be handled almost as a matter of routine. The great London dailies maintained correspondents in New York and Washington, and in addition to this the British government made it a practice to invite groups of prominent Americans for English tours. While the purpose, of course, was to have England's story brought back to the United States in the interests of better understanding, it was equally the case that these Americans put the facts of our own accomplishments before the people of England.

Mr. Harry N. Rickey, formerly head of the Newspaper Enterprise Association, was our first London representative, opening the office and remaining until called back to the United States to assist in the direction of the Foreign Section. By reason of his ability, experience, and personality, Mr. Rickey put the work on firm foundations. He was succeeded by Charles Edward Russell, who gave most of his time to public speaking, while his son, John Russell, looked after the office routine. Mr. Russell was too valuable in the speaking field to be kept on a single job for any length of time, and he was soon moved to France and Italy, where he put the motives and purposes of America before the workers of the two countries. Paul Perry followed Mr. Russell as head of the London office, serving with distinction to the end.

Had the English situation presented any real problem, as in the case of other countries, the way of the Committee would have been difficult. Lord Northcliffe was in charge of enemy propaganda, there was a press bureau under the

direction of Sir Frederick Cook and Sir Frederick Swetten-
han, the Foreign Office held certain propaganda functions
and claimed a right of general control, Wellington House
prepared and distributed pamphlets, Sir William Jury had
a motion-picture organization of his own, and the Board
of Naval Control possessed censorship powers that were
autocratic and varied. Intelligent co-operation was an
impossibility and the many changes in personnel, the endless jealousies, the continuous confliction between authorities, oftentimes resulted in confusion and failure. For
the most part, therefore, we used England as a clearing-
house, avoiding as far as possible any contact with the pull
and haul of the various organizations.

Italy, on the other hand, was a distinct problem, for
German propaganda not only poured in from the outside,
but worked with equal vigor from the inside. On looking
the field over for a fit representative, we learned that
Prof. Charles E. Merriam of the University of Chicago
was a captain in the army and engaged in some comparatively unimportant work in one of the Southern camps.
Here was not only a professor and economist and a sociolo-
gist, but also a man with a wide and varied experience in
public life, and by personal appeal to Secretary Baker
the army was induced to lend him to us.

Just as we were fortunate in securing Captain Merriam,
so was he fortunate in finding John Hearley, in Rome.
Aside from his very remarkable natural ability, Mr. Hearley
had served as Italian correspondent for the United Press
and at the time of Captain Merriam's arrival was operating an American news bureau under the direction of Ambassador Page. Due to the energy and vision of these
two men, thirteen thousand cities and towns in Italy were
brought to thorough understanding of America and the
army itself was fired to the old hope, the old enthusiasm.

Lieut. Walter Wanger was borrowed from the American

air service to act as liaison officer with the Italian army, Miss Gertrude Barr, an American of rare executive capacity, was drafted as executive secretary, and Capt. Piero Tozzi and Lieut. Albert Peccorini of the Italian army came into the office to serve as expert advisers. Miss Alice Rohe, the well-known writer, was another valuable volunteer by reason of her intimate knowledge of Italy, and others who gave time and effort unflaggingly were Kingsley Moses, E. Q. Cordner, and Byron M. Nester.

Mr. Hearley, assisted by Kenneth Durant, sent over from the Washington office for this particular purpose, gave first attention to the news service. By arrangement with the Agenzia Stefani, Italy's largest press association, every paper in Italy received the Committee's daily cable and wireless service, and in addition to this a daily news bulletin was printed for direct distribution in military, journalistic, educational, and governmental circles. The Poole service was turned over to Miss Rohe and Mr. Moses, who prepared illustrated feature articles for the daily press and the periodical press. The people of Italy were almost childishly eager for American news, and both services were enthusiastic and given columns in every publication.

At the suggestion of Captain Merriam, the Committee made a selection in the United States of certain men calculated to have influence in Italy, and among those sent over were Dr. Rudolph Altrocchi from the Chicago University, Senator Salvatore Cotillo of the New York State legislature, Judge Ben B. Lindsey, and Arthur Bennington, the Italian authority of *The New York World*. It was also our good fortune to secure Captain Fiorello from the army, as he proved a forceful and convincing speaker. Judge Cravates, United States judge at Cairo, was also brought to Italy, and from native sources Captain Merriam gained the assistance of Agostino d'Isernia, Doctor Professor Satorio,

Doctor Professor Penunzio, Signor Poggiolini, and the thirteen-year-old Alberto Gelpi. Besides, Professoressa Gugliesmina Ronconi, a prominent Italian social worker, and her several associates were attached to this department. These concerned themselves with the women workers, peasant women, and school-children, holding frequent morale and educational conferences or discussions for them in popular halls, workshops, and farm centers.

Whenever possible, American moving pictures or lantern slides were used to illustrate all these discourses.

The native speakers did a splendid work, but Italian enthusiasm was reserved for those who came to them from the United States. The cities and towns turned out *en masse* to hear them, and in many of the villages the people drew the carriage through the streets and rained flowers on the flattered occupant.

Mr. Hoagland, proceeding to Italy from France, established a laboratory and worked with Lieutenant Wanger and Mr. Cordner in the building of the machinery that carried the Committee's pictures to every corner of the nation.

The perfected films with Italian captions were shown to both military and civilian populations, at the front and behind the lines, aid being received from private and public agencies, such as Italian cinema houses, patriotic associations, schools, Italian offices of naval and military propaganda, the American Young Men's Christian Association.

Once a week the Committee supplied the Inter-Allied Weekly, a war-time Pathé of the Italian government, with appropriate American film material for display in theaters throughout Italy.

More peculiarly than any other people, the Italians loved picture-cards and little gimcracks of all kinds, and under Mr. Nester's direction the Committee distributed 4,500,500 post-cards bearing American war pictures; American flag bow-pins, Italo-American ribbons and buttons, 154,854; President Wilson posters, 68,574; assorted American war posters, 66,640; American flags in paper, 200,000; American flags in cloth, 30; sheet music, "The Star-spangled Banner," 33,300; booklets containing extracts from President Wilson's speeches, 326,650; pamphlets containing American war statistics and other information, 364,235; United States maps, 200; President Wilson photographs, 500; President Wilson engravings, 35.

Reprints from American photographic displays were exhibited in three thousand Italian towns and cities. In some form or other American educational information was disseminated through sixteen thousand towns and cities of Italy by this department alone.

VII

MR. ROBERT H. MURRAY, for years the correspondent of *The New York World* in the City of
Mexico, and a man of proved ability, courage, and honor,
was selected to have charge of the Committee's activities
in Mexico. His report is given in full, not only that Mr.
Murray's own achievement may be estimated, but because
his clear, concise chronicle will permit readers to understand the nature of the work done by all foreign commissioners, thereby obviating the necessity of complete reports in every case.

In the beginning, elements confronted the Mexico Section
which rendered its task peculiarly difficult and, to a certain
extent, unique. With the possible exception of Spain, in no
other country outside of Mexico did the German propaganda
attain such vigor and proportion, and nowhere was it waged
with more determination and vicious mendacity. Events and
conditions, which it is unnecessary to recapitulate, had caused
the people and the government of Mexico to become highly
responsive to overt or covert propaganda directed against the
United States and in favor of Germany. The people, especially the masses, reacted favorably almost to a unit to the
specious and insidious endeavors of the Germans to deceive
them into believing that the triumph of the arms of the United
States spelled menace and disaster to Mexico, and that a German
victory would insure for them and their country every manner
of political and economic benefit.

Thus the German propaganda thrived upon fruitful soil. It appealed to a ready-made, receptively sympathetic audience. Nevertheless, as the writer prophesied early in February, 1918, in a résumé of the Mexican situation which he furnished to Chairman Creel, the German propaganda up to that time had not been successful in creating anything substantial or lasting commensurate with the effort and money expended. Nor did it later. This was proved when, as a result of the defeat of the German military power, the German propaganda in Mexico collapsed almost overnight, leaving nothing save a faint and rapidly disappearing impression upon the Mexican public to show for the expenditure of more than four years' time and intensive effort and at least 10,000,000 marks in German money. The German propaganda failed in Mexico, as elsewhere, because, as a writer in *The Journal of the American Chamber in Mexico* expressed it in the November number of that publication:

"It is, and always has been, a propaganda of lies. Because it deals exclusively in lies. Because it is composed of lies. Because it is organized and managed by arch liars who work with intent to lie and to deceive. But the German propaganda has failed principally because, in the long run, truth will beat lies every time."

Whatever success the Mexico Section attained may be attributed, in the main, to the fact that it dealt from the beginning to the end exclusively in truth. Its sole mission in Mexico was to tell the Mexicans the truth, not only about the United States, why it went to war, what it was doing in the war, and what the real attitude of the people and of the government of the United States was toward Mexico, but also what German militarism actually stood for, what the conduct of German statesmen, soldiers, and sailors had been in the war, and what were the sinister aims of the Kaiser and his accomplices toward democracy and free governments of free peoples.

The fight to win Mexico, or at least to obtain for the common cause an adequate hearing before the Mexican people, was essentially our fight. And this quite regardless of whatever interest any other nation embattled against the Germans might have held in the way of impressing their cause and their point of view upon the Mexicans. That the Mexican fight was our fight became apparent from the fact that it was only from the day we declared war that the German propaganda in Mexico really began to flourish. The Germans were cunning enough

ERIC PALMER

GEORGE RIIS

H. H. SEVIER

FRANK J. MARION

VIRA B. WHITEHOUSE

immediately thereafter to play upon the anti-American string. That was their best asset in Mexico, and they omitted no effort or expense to capitalize and profit by it.

This had been going on for almost a year when the Mexico Section was created. The Germans had organized well. For the most part, their propaganda was financed by loans made to the German Minister in Mexico by wealthy German commercial houses and individuals. These provided the Minister with unlimited funds in Mexican currency with which to corrupt public sentiment in Mexico, and which they loaned upon drafts upon the German government. In passing, it may be said that none of these drafts has yet been paid. No source of revenue of this nature was available to the Mexico Section. The only financial support, with one exception, which this office received from American nationals was indirect. It came through newspaper advertising from American business houses, which was provided for the support and encouragement of legitimate newspapers who championed the cause of the United States and of the Allies. This movement, although it was originated before the Mexico Section came into being, was latterly revived and placed upon a more effective basis through the influence of this office, with the assistance in various members of the American Chamber of Commerce in Mexico, notably William L. Vail, who volunteered to take charge of the work.

Details of the operation of the propaganda of the enemy did not differ materially from those employed in every neutral country. The basis of their work was conventional, practical, and sound. Upon that, however, they had reared a structure of falsification, misrepresentation, and chicanery. It was upheld, on the part of those among the Mexicans whom they drew to their support, not because of conscientious conviction of the justice of the cause which they were espousing, but solely because they were paid for what they did with copious moneys dealt out by the German information service. Authenticated documents from the records of the German information service, which are in possession of this office, show that the Germans were paying subsidies aggregating nearly $25,000 United States currency monthly to twenty-three newspapers and periodicals, besides supplying them with free paper and an alleged "cable" service made in Mexico. At a conservative estimate the press activities alone of the Germans in subsidies, paper, telegraph service, and tolls must have cost them not far from $50,000 United States currency monthly.

It is a significant fact, and one which redounds to the credit of the reputable, honorable journalists of Mexico, that during the war there was not a single newspaper or periodical in the Republic which pleaded the German cause that was self-sustaining. All were subsidized with German gold. On the other hand, there was not one pro-American Ally newspaper or periodical which was not self-sustaining. The Mexico Section, directly or indirectly, did not subsidize any publication

When the work of this office began the Germans had the field virtually to themselves. With rare exceptions the newspapers which were not avowedly pro-German gave the cause of the United States and of the Allies languid and indifferent support. Largely the fault for this condition was ours. Until we started our work no organized, adequate, authoritative channels for obtaining information regarding the purposes and the acts of the United States at war were available to newspapers or individuals who were inclined to be friendly. The reverse was impressively, emphatically, and, to us, reproachfully true, so far as the Germans were concerned.

But this initial handicap was speedily overcome. From the outset it was assumed that the Mexican press and public, or at least that portion of it which was not debauched by German money and German lies, was fair and receptive. This was almost instantaneously proved. We worked always in the open. Official notice was served upon the Mexican government of the establishment of the offices of the Committee in the City of Mexico and of the purpose of the Committee in extending its operations into Mexico. We hid nothing from public view. There was nothing to hide. Incidentally this principle was laid down and maintained to the point that the director felt free to declare, and still does declare, that there is not a document, record, payment, or act of the Mexico Section which is not open to the full and unrestricted scrutiny of any person in or out of Mexico.

From the beginning this office stressed the fact and gave it the widest proper publicity, that the Mexico Section spoke and functioned officially for the government of the United States, and that the government of the United States stood back of every statement contained in every cable report or piece of literature issued by us. Our challenge of responsibility for word and deed, both on behalf of our government and of this office, was not once questioned or accepted by those who opposed us.

Our sole mission was to inform the people of Mexico. It has been said that we did this adequately. All things considered— the remoteness of many of the populous parts of the Republic from our headquarters in the City of Mexico, the regrettable delay in commencing our work, the vast numerical preponderance of the illiterate over the literate among the population of Mexico, their latent antagonism to, and suspicion of, the United States, and the modest sum available for the purpose of the Committee in Mexico—one feels that inspection of the record of the Mexico Section may safely be invited from any critics, friendly or unfriendly.

The director was fortunate in being able to surround himself with a corps of assistants—Americans for the greater part, but including Mexicans, British, Russians, and French— who gave him efficient, loyal, and patriotic support. He owes much to them, and he takes pleasure in acknowledging that obligation with deep thanks. The always constructive, appreciated, and helpful interest and co-operation of the American Ambassador, Henry Prather Fletcher, Esq., contributed immeasurably to the success of the work of the Committee in Mexico. Enthusiastic and invaluable aid was also rendered, almost without exception, by the members of the consul corps of the United States in Mexico. Equally important service was given by volunteer correspondents in all parts of the Republic, who included not only Americans, but Mexican citizens and nationals of substantially every country on earth which either militantly or sentimentally were alined on the side of justice and democracy against despotism and ruthless force.

Two dominant facts stand out clearly as a result of the experience: One is that much was accomplished in acquainting the people of Mexico with the power, the resources in national crises, the righteously militant spirit, the ideals, the underlying altruism of their neighbors to the north. The obvious reply to this, of course, is that, considering the close geographical, commercial, and political ties of the two countries, the Mexican people should have known all this before. Which is quite true. But they didn't. It had never been the business of any one to enlighten them systematically, purposefully, and truthfully. The other fact is that much of permanent benefit to the United States and Mexico could and should be built upon the foundation laid by the Committee on Public Information.

Two expressions of judgment upon the work of the Mexico Section may properly be included in this report. The first is in the form of a resolution adopted by the American Chamber of Commerce in Mexico, as follows:

"*Resolved*, That this chamber commends in the highest terms the work accomplished by the Committee on Public Information in Mexico under the direction of Mr. Robert H. Murray, it being its judgment that a decided change for the better in the attitude of the Mexican people has been brought about through its efficient work.

"*Resolved*, That copies of the resolution be sent to the American Ambassador, American Consul-General in Mexico, Mr. George Creel, chairman of the Committee on Public Information in Washington, and to Mr. Robert H. Murray, director of the Mexican Section."

The second is an editorial published in *La Prensa*, a daily newspaper printed in the city of Puebla, on December 24, 1918.

"Varied and contradictory were the notices which during the terrible European War were circulated by the foreign information agencies established in the capital of the Republic, news emanating from the battle-fields according to the events occurring and sent to Mexico from the very countries at war. The effect of all this on the various parties is past history, each group wishing success for the side they sympathized with. The time is also past of uneasy expectation on the part of neutral nations, who anxiously followed the march of events as given out by the respective agencies, and who, while regretting the bloodshed and destruction of war, thought, as they still do, uneasily about the future of the world in respect to commercial relations and that state of peace which was to form a league of nations.

"Now that the great struggle has been solved by an armistice which will lead to the basis of a lasting peace; now with the disappearance of the powerful empire of the autocratic and warlike German Kaiser, who carried destruction and extermination into France and Belgium, and that the European nations breathe freely again; and now, also, that we can appreciate present events, as deductions from the past great battles, we see clearly that the reports of some foreign agencies were not true as to the course of events in the theaters of war, since we remember that for many days after the German failure and the abdication of a conquered William II, the pro-German papers and agencies continued to deny these events for a purpose the ultimate end of which would be ridicule, as actually happened in the case of these agencies.

"We must confess, however, because facts have so proved this, that the agency in the capital of the Committee on Public Information of the United States government in charge of Mr. Robert H. Murray never diverged from the truth and never tried to alter the telegrams which it received, whether they were favorable or adverse to the nation to which it belonged. Its reports were an exact statement and a truthful one of events, and its straightforward conduct must be valued for its true worth, if we remember those days of anxiety, of expectation, and of worry as to the results of the world struggle which had no equal in the centuries."

"We have always relied upon the reports issued by Mr. Murray's agency; we always received them with pleasure and entire confidence, and in repeating them to the public as received we invariably did so with the conviction of truth-bearers as to the terrible events happening overseas in which all Europe was involved.

The organization of the Mexico Section was arranged by subdivisions, according to the nature of the work. To the director fell the general executive functions. Next in authority came the office manager, Mr. Arthur de Lima, followed by the managers of the Editorial Department, the Motion Picture Department, the Still Picture Department, the Reading Room and School, and the Mailing Department. Each department had the necessary corps of translators, editors, teachers, clerks, stenographers, messengers, and office-boys. At no time did the entire force of the executive office exceed 40 persons. Salaries ranged downward from 100 pesos (substantially $50 United States currency), which was the highest paid. Our salaries as a rule were lower than paid for similar service by commercial houses. Preference in employment, so far as possible, was given to American citizens.

Thanks to the co-operation of Compub in New York, an excellent and carefully selected general war-news service which ran as high as 1,000 words daily, according to the importance and interest of the occurrences at home and abroad, was received in the City of Mexico by cable, *via* Galveston. Translators reduced the cables to Spanish. Copies were transmitted by messenger, or land-telegraph wires, to 31 newspapers, 9 in the capital and 22 in the interior. In many instances the newspapers gave the Committee's cable service preference in display to despatches of their own special correspondents, or those of regular news agencies. At frequent intervals the newspapers in the capital issued extra afternoon editions on the war news furnished them by the Committee.

Implicit confidence was placed upon the authenticity of our news—so much so, in fact, that several newspapers which had been printing the alleged news despatches of the German information service abandoned them and instead used those of the Committee.

It was notorious that the German news service was fabricated in Mexico and that the Germans did not receive a word of cable news from without the Republic. German agents stationed at border points, notably Nuevo Laredo and Juarez, rewrote cable news clipped from the United States newspapers and stolen from news bureaus' and special correspondents' despatches sent to Mexican newspapers, distorted them to suit the purposes of the Germans, and distributed them to their dupes and subsidized newspapers as "special" cable or "wireless" messages.

Approximately 4,433,000 words of our daily cable service were distributed to the Mexican newspapers during the eleven months of the existence of the Mexico Section. Mimeographed copies of the daily despatches were prepared and a total of 35,000 of them were distributed in the City of Mexico among business firms, which displayed them in show windows, to the foreign legations, Mexican government officials, and individuals.

Spanish translations of special articles prepared by the Foreign Press Bureau of the Committee in New York, and made suitable by careful editing and revision for the Mexican field and the limited space of the newspapers, were sent daily to the 65 newspapers and periodicals on our list. The record shows that nearly 60 per cent. of this material was used. On an average 300 articles monthly, or 3,300 in all, were distributed. The supply was not equal to the demand, the same being true of cuts and matrices. Of the latter more than 2,000 were used.

To the newspapers also supplementary daily news letters (virtually a complete telegraphic service) were mailed, the total being

178,000. For the benefit of persons outside of Mexico, who were interested in Mexican affairs, it was deemed expedient, and within the functions of the Committee, to issue a weekly news bulletin in English. In this bulletin appeared only matter relating to official Mexican government activities and topics connected with reconstruction, industry, development, etc. This was sent by mail to 1,000 individuals and firms in the United States. Eighteen editions were published with a total circulation of 20,000. The bulletin met with appreciative reception and comment from hundreds of persons among those who received it, including members of the United States Congress, the Librarian of Congress, and other officials of our government and corporations and individuals having investment interests in Mexico. Requests for this bulletin were received in almost every mail and from parts as distant as England, Canada, and Japan. Franking privileges were granted by the Mexican government for both the news letter and the English bulletin.

Several months before the war closed it was found advisable to issue a weekly publication devoted exclusively to the interests and war activities of our government. This bore the title, *America in the War*. It consisted of sixteen illustrated pages, well edited and attractively arranged and printed. Its success was instantaneous and it developed into one of the most effective elements of our educational campaign. Especially was it valuable in inspiring and maintaining interest and enthusiasm among our correspondents, and bringing them more intimately in touch with this office. Of *America in the War* more than 100,000 were circulated in weekly editions of from 4,000 to 5,000 copies. We also bought and distributed not far from 500,000 copies of various publications containing special articles in support of the cause of the United States, or throwing light upon the friendly attitude of the United States toward the Mexican people and government.

Mr. George F. Weeks was manager of the Editorial Department.

With respect to literature, the chief difficulty encountered was not to find channels and outlets for carrying the word to the people, but to obtain enough material with which to satisfy their demands. We distributed a total of 985,000 pieces of literature of all descriptions—pamphlets, posters, folders, post-cards, not counting between 50,000 and 75,000 Liberty Loan and other war posters and half-tone window hangers, consigned to us from

Washington and New York. Not less than 75 per cent. of our correspondents filed repeat orders for substantially every shipment of literature sent them. It was impossible to meet all of these requisitions. Double the amount of literature could have been circulated had it been available. Travelers constantly brought us word of having seen in remote places copies of the more popular of the pamphlets, President Wilson's Fourteen Points, his address to the Mexican editors who visited him at the White House, his war speeches to the Congress, a condensation of Brand Whitlock's story of Belgium, the circumstantial accounts of the German atrocities, and Prince Lichnowsky's pillorying of his government for precipitating the war, which had been passed from hand to hand and read and reread until the pages were in tatters.

In general, the literature was circulated in two ways—by the correspondents in their respective districts and by mail directly from headquarters. A mailing-list was prepared which contained nearly 20,000 names of professional men, government officials, school-teachers, merchants, clergymen, labor leaders, farmers, and others in the middle and higher walks of life. Many hundreds of letters were received from the persons who obtained literature, expressing their thanks, asking for more, and not seldom inclosing the names of friends to whom they wished pamphlets mailed. So far as possible, pamphlets were prepared which contained matter calculated to appeal especially to sundry classes, such as working-men, the clergy, educators, etc. Whenever the text permitted, they were embellished with illustrations.

Posters were effective and we used them freely. Care was taken to phrase them tersely and simply.

No literature was issued anonymously. We officially stood sponsor for everything. Each piece of printed matter bore the imprint of the Committee and the slogan of the office: "The War: Remember, The United States *Cannot* Lose!" Constant and indefatigable reiteration of this phrase eventually elevated it to the dignity of an impressive and confident prophecy. It was effective—so much so that for a time it enjoyed ephemeral life as a popular catchword in the streets and on the stage of the capital. In their heyday the Germans made it the subject of sarcastic jest.

It goes without saying that among a population in which illiterates unfortunately predominate motion pictures possess an enormous influence as a medium for conveying impressions and creating sentiment where the printed word is without value. In Mexico the motion-picture films proved to be one of our greatest assets. The pictures "got over" and won converts to our cause where other mediums would inevitably have failed. Our motion-picture campaign was successful. But at first it was uphill work. German agents saw to it diligently in the beginning that displays of war pictures of American soldiers, in the camp or in the field, of our preparations in every branch of our mobilizations of the industrial, military, naval, and social forces which the government brought to bear in the conflict, met with an uproariously hostile reception from the audiences to which they were shown. Frequently the police were summoned to restore order. Complaints to the authorities were made by our opponents that our pictures were inciting riots and that the screening of portraits of the President, General Pershing, and other notable personages, and of the American flag floating at the forefront of marching troops or at the masthead of naval units, constituted an insult to the Mexican government and people and were in violation of Mexico's neutrality. On various occasions our displays were halted until the local authorities could be convinced by tactful explanations, and by private exhibitions given for their benefit, that the pictures might properly be allowed on view.

Gradually the demonstrations lessened, and finally ceased. The pictures won their way. The attitude of the public altered until after a few months we were repaid for our persistence by reports from our agents telling of cheering and applause in place of hoots and yells, and even of *vivas* being given for the flag, the President, American war-vessels, and American soldiers.

American industrial films, with which we were freely supplied, aroused a disappointing volume of interest. The public appetite would be satisfied with nothing less tame than actual war pictures or commercial films telling stories to Germany's discredit. Measurably successful exhibitions of the industrial films were given in the open air, in schools, and before selected audiences.

On the circuit organized by the Motion Picture Department, of which Dr. M. L. Espinosa was in charge, our films were shown in 68 houses throughout the Republic, and to audiences which, according to our carefully kept reports, aggregated 4,500,000 persons.

Effective use was made of the still pictures sent us from Washington. Boards were provided which had space for twelve pictures, each with an explanatory caption in Spanish. The boards were attractively made and painted and bore in Spanish, "The Committee on Public Information, Mexico Section," in addition to printed cards, which were frequently changed, with educational references to what the United States was doing in the war. These pictures were changed weekly. The boards were exhibited in shop-windows and other conspicuous places. They amply supplemented the appeal of the motion pictures, and, probably to the same extent as the latter, impressed through the medium of the eye the might and resources which the United States arrayed against German military despotism. Altogether there were displayed in this manner 116,256 separate still pictures. Mr. L. Kuhn was manager of the Still Picture Department.

Two experiments which were approached with a degree of caution and doubt—our Reading Room and School in the City of Mexico—proved to be among the most successful and effective branches of the work. The Reading Room was designed as a popular center for general dissemination of information. It became all of that and more. Quarters were obtained in a large store-room on one of the most frequented thoroughfares in the business heart of the capital. Appropriate equipment of tables, chairs, etc., was provided. With flags, bunting, pictures of American and Allied notables, posters, etc., the room was attractively decorated. Files were kept of the Mexican newspapers and periodicals and also of the principal American newspapers and illustrated magazines.

An abundant supply of Spanish-printed literature, including all of the publications of the Committee, was available, both for reading and on the premises and for distribution.

Our daily cable news was displayed on bulletin-boards, inside and outside of the Reading Room. Free toilet conveniences, a dressing-room for women, telephone, and writing-paper were included in the equipment. From the beginning the Reading Room was patronized to capacity day and evening. The visitors came from all ranks of citizens, artisans, laborers, shopkeepers, professional men, women, flocking there for enlightenment as to the issues and progress of the war, and to exchange views on the situation. Spirited discussions took place. Several times weekly lectures or talks upon the war, the United States, Mexican affairs, and kindred topics were given. Occasionally the discussions were illustrated by motion pictures. During the seven and a half months in which the Reading Room was open the number of visitors, by actual count, totaled 106,868.

Encouraged by the reception given the Reading Room, it was determined to take advantage of the wide-spread demand, indicated frequently among the visitors, to open a school for instruction in English. A shop adjoining the Reading Room was rented and furnished with desks, benches, and blackboards.

From the initial session, the capacity of the school was taxed. English was the most eagerly sought-for study, but French, bookkeeping, and stenography classes were well patronized. A corps of teachers, volunteers or paid, labored diligently, intelligently, and successfully. Instruction was free and many pupils were drawn from institutions where tuition fees were charged because, as they said, more practical and effective teaching was given in the Committee's school than in the others. The zest of the pupils to acquire English was amazing. Their curiosity regarding the government of the United States, its history, art, literature, and the customs of our people, was evinced to a degree which the management, owing to the limitations imposed upon it, found difficult to satisfy.

In age the students ranged from boys and girls of sixteen to elderly men and women. The working-classes predominated. With few exceptions those who entered studied hard and persistently. Uninterested pupils were weeded out, and their places given to the more ambitious and serious applicants. When the school closed 1,127 individual pupils were registered. The total school-day attendance was nearly 30,000. Sixteen English classes were in operation with an average of 65 pupils, two French classes with an average of 103 pupils, and four special English and two special classes with an average of 12 pupils.

No one who watched the operation of the school and appreciated by observation the zest of the students to learn English, and the sympathetic mental trend toward the United States inspired among them in the process, could fail to regret that the classes might not have been continued permanently, and that some arrangement might not be made for extending on a larger scale throughout Mexico what the Committee accomplished in an experimental way in the capital.

Through the efforts of the section six reading-rooms were

established and successfully conducted outside of the capital, in Guadalajara, Vera Cruz, Aguascalientes, Leon, Durango, and Irapuato.

Mr. J. B. Frisbie was manager of the Reading Room and School.

A trial shipment of 50,000 celluloid buttons bearing the flags of the United States and of the Spanish-American Republics which entered the war against Germany, and the legend, "Allied in Honor," proved so popular that 100,000 more were obtained. The end of the war rendered it unnecessary to continue this distribution.

The Liberty Truth Committee, composed of representatives of the American Chamber of Commerce in Mexico, and operating in close co-operation with the section, aided vitally in our newspaper campaign by obtaining advertising appropriations from American business concerns for the legitimate encouragement of newspapers and other publications which supported our cause.

The Advertising Section bought and used freely advertising space, plainly marked as such, in newspapers and magazines. Its appropriation for this purpose was inadequate, but profitable reaction resulted from what expenditures it was able to make. Especially effective was a series of full-page and half-page advertisements announcing the heavy oversubscription to the Fourth Liberty Loan which were printed to counteract the intensive and desperate efforts of the Germans to delude the Mexican public into believing that the American people had repudiated the war through failure to subscribe the full amount of the loan.

With the exception of a few sparsely settled and remote points operations extended through the entire Republic. Representatives of the Committee were stationed in every city and important town in the country. When the armistice—the date upon which the work of the section was at flood-tide—was signed on November 11, 1918, the Mexico Section had 222 individual correspondents, who covered 165 points.

VIII

SWITZERLAND was a notable victory and full credit must go to Mrs. Norman de R. Whitehouse, in charge from bitter first to happy last. It was a new thing to place a woman in such a position of absolutely international importance, but behind her was a record of achievement that made the appointment wise and necessary. Equal suffrage in New York after its defeat in 1915 was apparently "dead," but Mrs. Whitehouse accepted the office of state chairman, galvanized the movement, gave it new force and enthusiasm, and drove it through to victory. It proved rare understanding of people and their prejudices; it meant technical knowledge of every medium of appeal, and, above all, it showed the translation of devotion into terms of energy and actual drudgery. Mrs. Whitehouse's job was to put America across in Switzerland just as she had put equal suffrage across in New York.

We knew that she was doing well, by our study of the Swiss papers, and we knew that she was winning when the German press commenced to attack her and the work with hysterical bitterness; but it remained for the six Swiss journalists, arriving in the United States as our guests, to tell the whole story of accomplishment.

"She has changed the whole attitude of Switzerland," they joined in declaring. "It was never the case that we were pro-Germans, but rather that we did not know America. This was the knowledge that she gave us, openly, honestly, and with rare intelligence, overcoming suspicions, climbing over a hundred and one obstacles, and reaching the heart and mind of Switzerland in a manner never approached by the agent of any other country."

With the exception of those owned by Germans, there was not a paper that she failed to influence fairly; her ultimate control of the motion-picture situation was complete; her use of speakers and literature was without an ounce of waste, and effective to the last degree was her inspiration of the German radical group in Switzerland, a band of enthusiasts who preached the gospel of democracy in the days when the world did not dream that the Hohenzollern could be divorced from his asserted union with divinity.

It was no easy task to which Mrs. Whitehouse was assigned. Switzerland, right under the German fist, lived in fear of meeting Belgium's fate, and there was a further compelling consideration in that the Swiss were dependent upon German coal for their railroads and industries. In addition to all this, German propaganda had been developing in Switzerland for thirty or forty years and was conducted by a corps of trained experts. It was common gossip that there were between eight and twelve hundred German diplomatic representatives, a large majority of whom had no other function than to praise Germany and to attack her enemies. A fundamental feature of the German policy was to buy or subsidize Swiss newspapers and news agencies and leave them under the Swiss directors. They also had a system of paying the smaller papers throughout Switzerland for every published paragraph or item sent out by German-owned news agencies.

The majority of the motion-picture houses in German-

Switzerland were either owned outright or controlled by the German government. The same conditions applied to theaters, opera-houses, commercial establishments, and even to the news-stands. Aside from these controls, German agents had a very complete, accurate, and efficient system of circulation, and as a result Switzerland was inundated not only by pro-German propaganda, but with anti-Ally and especially anti-American propaganda.

"On my arrival," to quote from the report of Mrs. Whitehouse, "I found that the Germans were maintaining that America could not raise an army in spite of her draft law, that she could not train it, could not arm it, could not transport it to Europe, and that if she did, the untrained soldiers could not face the German heroes. They tried to persuade the Swiss that America was going to invade Switzerland in order to attack Germany. They agitated a great deal about a secret treaty, which was supposed to exist between the United States and Great Britain in regard to Japan. They tried to show our weakness at home by reporting that our difficulties on the Mexican border amounted to our being at war with that country and they insinuated that we meant to annex it. They tried to create difficulties between the Allies by articles showing that the Americans had invaded France to the latter country's disadvantage. They harped upon our supposed effort to steal Great Britain's place as the leader of commerce on the seas, and particularly did they exaggerate every delay in grain shipments from America, charging a Yankee effort to 'starve poor Switzerland.'"

Nowhere was there a single agency interested in presenting America's position or the American effort. The French and the English were concerned only with their own persuasions, and the news services sent out by Reuters and Havas contained few American items. The importance of Switzerland to us as a news center was that it was the only neutral nation whose newspapers are printed in the German language, and all of them had a free and large circulation in Austria and Germany. They were not only read by Germans, but the German press quoted from them freely, the liberal papers especially following everything that appeared in the Swiss papers. Getting our news into the German-Swiss press was the best way of getting it into Germany. It was also the case that Switzerland was filled with Germans and Austrians seeking escape from the privations of war, and these were naturally influenced by the Swiss papers that they read. In addition a great number of Germans came back and forth into Switzerland very freely and in large numbers, forming a virtual messenger service. It is therefore easy to be seen that Switzerland was a "first-line trench" in our drive against the morale of the German people.

It can be said truthfully that never at any time did Mrs. Whitehouse receive the assistance to which she was entitled. In the first place, Mr. Stovall, the American Minister, while a very delightful gentleman, was a Southerner with all the traditions of the South, and he had the very deep conviction that "woman's place is the home." In the second place, just before Mrs. Whitehouse sailed, *The New York Times* printed a story to the effect that she was proceeding to Switzerland as a representative of the President and giving the idea that her mission was diplomatic in its nature. This wretched canard, copied in the Swiss press, caused certain unpleasant reactions in all circles, and shortly before Mrs. Whitehouse's arrival an announcement was made to the effect that her work in Switzerland would be concerned with "women and children."

These misunderstandings were straightened out eventually by the frank statement of purpose that was our invariable policy. The President defined Mrs. Whitehouse's functions and the Swiss government, when it understood the true nature of her errand, gave full approval and all assistance. Even then, however, obstacles arose to embarrass and impede. As the real work had to be done in German-Switzerland, Mrs. Whitehouse's needs were translators and assistants who knew the German language in all of its dialects and idioms, and quite naturally this need could only be met by men and women of German birth. We searched the country over for this type of American and succeeded in finding several who possessed the necessary qualifications as well as having records for loyalty that were above question. No passports could be issued without the approval of Military Intelligence, and the officers of this division refused to let our selections go to Switzerland until after weeks and weeks of tedious investigation. Even when every test had been met, and when permission to sail had been granted, the French came forward with objections, and additional months had to be taken to convince them that the people we were sending were loyal Americans and not spies. All the while Mrs. Whitehouse was without this very necessary assistance, so that a great burden of unnecessary drudgery fell upon her own shoulders.

Unable to secure proper offices, lacking an office force, and compelled to work under every inconvenience, Mrs. Whitehouse drove ahead with unflagging energy. Borrowing Mr. George B. Fife from the Red Cross, her first activity was the translation and distribution of the daily cable and wireless service received from her office in Paris. To quote from her report:

Our service arrived early in the morning. It was rewritten in simple English, translated into French and German and delivered to the Agence Télégraphique Suisse, the official Swiss news agency, which distributed it for us to the Swiss press. This agency was reported to be unsympathetic, and whether because of this fact or not, we found that mistakes were made in our figures and that sometimes important items were overlooked. This compelled us to take pains in confirming and reconfirming by telephone and by letter all figures, and in order to avoid any oversight in distributing important news items we ourselves would telegraph or telephone such items directly to the papers.

In August I was able to report to the Committee on Public Information in Washington that an estimated minimum of 2,000 paragraphs of our service was being published weekly in the Swiss papers. All of the President's speeches and notes were translated in full and sent both in English and German, or English and French, to every newspaper. Previously only extracts had been carried by Havas and Reuter. In addition, the News Service Department sent weekly bulletins directly to the editorial offices of all the papers, reviewing the American events of greatest interest of the past week, and commenting upon their significance.

The news items from our service aroused great public interest and discussion, and as a result both Havas and Reuter commenced to include a larger amount of American news in their daily releases. We believe that to this fact is due the enormously increased use of the Havas and Reuter items on American events.

From the Foreign Press Bureau in New York we received special articles and feature stories through the diplomatic pouch. These articles we found of great value, but they presented enormous difficulties. They had to be rewritten and edited from the Swiss point of view and connected with events in Switzerland, before they were translated. Until the armistice negotiations began to absorb public attention, we placed almost 100 per cent. of these articles which we succeeded in having translated. Extracts from the Foreign Press Bureau were useful as news items also, although they were many weeks old when we received them.

We also sent a biweekly inform ationservice to the editorial staffs of the newspapers, including in this service such material as Secretary Baker's military report, the Shipping Board's report, navy reports on naval constructions, etc. Many extracts from them were printed in the press and they furnished good material for editorials.

The Mittel Presse, an agency which served a collection of small German-Swiss papers, formerly considered pro-German, accepted a service of special articles from us three times a week

A number of pamphlets were issued and circulated, including the Bolshevik revelations, President Wilson's speeches, and one on America's achievement in the first year of the war. These pamphlets were printed in comparatively small numbers—about 10,000 in the first edition. They were distributed free to men of prominence and influence and put on sale at bookshops and news-stands at a nominal price.

It was in connection with pamphlet distribution that Mrs. Whitehouse gave most convincing proof of her executive intelligence. It had been the habit of the Allied propagandists to print pamphlets in huge quantities, giving them circulation without reference to readers. Mrs. Whitehouse made a survey of Switzerland that established the number of Swiss that spoke German, the number that spoke French, the number of men and women who could read, and the number of illiterates. As a consequence she issued ten thousand pamphlets instead of a million and had a mark for every one of her "paper bullets."

From a score of sources we learned of her tirelessness and courage. If she could not get a passenger-train she traveled on a freight. She made personal trips to every city and town, visited every editor, established relations with all the business and social organizations, and not the least of her achievements was the manner in which she enlisted the services of the university professors. William E. Rappard of the University of Geneva, one of Switzerland's most distinguished scholars, gave wonderful assistance, and so unselfish and unremitting were his efforts that it might almost be said that he became a part of the organization itself.

It may be remembered that President Wilson sent a message direct to the people of the Austro-Hungarian Empire, a great word of encouragement that had the force of a military offensive. It was most important that the

President's address should reach the people for whom it was intended, and without thought of danger or privation Mrs. Whitehouse herself crossed the frontier and placed the message in the proper channels for thorough circulation.

In the matter of motion pictures, the Allied propagandists recognized that this was an important field of propaganda and appointed an inter-Allied committee to work out a plan of co-operation. The mere report of joint action caused one of the German-owned companies to offer for sale their large chain of houses, but in spite of this indication of power, the Allies could agree to no plans except that Allied film of commercial value should not be sold except on condition that a certain per cent. of news or propaganda film should be shown with it. In the mean time the British and French disputed that the Committee's propaganda films should be shown with American films of commercial value. The British claimed that all American commercial films were British property because the accepted business method was to sell American films to British firms, who reproduced them in England on British material. The French claimed they were French property because the method of renting them in Europe was through French firms with right for other countries.

Mrs. Whitehouse cut this Gordian knot by asking the Committee in Washington to obtain for her the exclusive rights for the distribution of all American commercial film in Switzerland, and not only did we do this, but we sent such film directly to her in the diplomatic pouch. It was also the case that the Paris office sent her battle-front film direct each week. Without further reference to the French and English, she prepared her own programs, combining the Committee's pictures with comedies and drama films, and gave them a circulation that soon covered the entire field.

With respect to photographs, Mrs. Whitehouse filled

the shop-windows in Switzerland with them, and also
arranged a system of glass display cases in which the pictures were changed weekly. In one month alone more
than 2,000 enlarged photographs of 127 different kinds
were on exhibition in 77 places, in 33 towns.

It was Mrs. Whitehouse who suggested that the Committee, in the name of the government of the United
States, should invite the representative editors of Switzerland for the inspection of our war effort, and proof of the
standing that she had gained in Switzerland was furnished
by the fact that the delegation was virtually selected by
the government itself and was almost official in its character. The tour of these six journalists was the finishing
blow in our fight for the public opinion of Switzerland.
Not only was it the case that each man ʼent back daily
cables that increased in enthusiasm regularly, but upon
their return they told the story of our resolve and invincibility in such direct phrases as to convince Switzerland
that Germany was beaten and that the free peoples of
the world had nothing to fear from our victory, but could
look to it with hope and rejoicing.

There is no finer comment upon the work of Mrs.
Whitehouse than the following editorial, written by the
Swiss Middle Press News Bureau, anti-American in the
beginning, and printed in scores of papers that had been
pro-German at the start:

It is stated that the American Committee on Public Information at Berne will close its bureau and discontinue its news
service on February 22d.

This announcement cannot be passed over in silence. The
American press service in Switzerland, as no other bureau which
supplied the Swiss press with news and articles, has from the
start taken a position which placed it far above the usual standard of propaganda. In this respect it formed a counterpart to
the Swiss Mission, which not long ago went to America and was
accompanied by Minister Sulzer, because it made it its principal

object to explain to the Swiss the true conditions and intentions of America and to bring the two republics to a better mutual understanding. Just because of this high interpretation of its task, it has fulfilled its purpose. As far as its activity concerned the war, it was anything but an imperialistic war agitation; rather has it carried on only propaganda for a just and lasting peace and thereby gained the full appreciation of Switzerland. There is probably no state and no statesman so highly esteemed and regarded with so much confidence in Switzerland as the North American Union and its President Wilson.

The following editorial from the *Berner Tageblatt* is also significant:

As we are informed, the American "Committee of Public Information" in Berne will close its offices and discontinue its news service. On this occasion, the recognition is due to this Press Bureau that its practice has been to give real information and not one-sided colored propaganda, as has been conspicuously the custom of similar foreign enterprises.

If I have seemed to deal too briefly with the Swiss achievement, it is because Mrs. Whitehouse has written her own story. *A Year As a Government Agent*, published by Harper & Brothers, sets down her experiences in careful and fascinating detail.

IX

HOLLAND must be regarded as having offered the main avenue of attack upon the public opinion of the German masses. It was not, like other neutral countries adjacent to German territory, the scene of international conferences or sinister outside influences, but presented a clear and homogeneous field for the dissemination of information. The information provided was therefore designed to gain direct circulation in Holland, but the content was always chosen with regard to the ultimate effect on the German masses.

Henry Suydam, European correspondent for *The Brooklyn Eagle*, was the man decided upon to serve as commissioner for Holland. It was not only that his work stood out by reason of its strength, breadth, and analytical keenness, but personal reports placed even larger emphasis upon his personality. It was a difficult post to which Mr. Suydam was called, and it is a deserved tribute to say that he carried the work forward to success without a single blunder. The following excerpts from his report will show the manner in which the Dutch situation was handled:

The general problem confronting the Committee on Public Information in the Netherlands was twofold: (1) To enlighten Dutch public opinion with regard to the fairness and detachment of the United States, as well as to provide an adequate picture of American war effort as a factor in international affairs, and

(2) to use Holland, as far as that might legitimately be done without committing a belligerent act, as a means of approach to all classes of Germans, who were to be convinced that the United States was strong and would use that strength for the common good. The effort was to obtain facts emphasizing these points, and to present these facts to Dutch and Germans with due force and precision.

When my work in Holland began, the Dutch press—through which the German press maintained a large degree of contact with the United States—was without adequate American news. American editorial comment appeared in the Dutch press when it furthered the peculiar interests of some foreign news agency, and not often otherwise. American news was frequently selected by these agencies for interested reasons. Reuter and Havas were, in the opinion of Dutch editors, nothing more than the mouthpieces of the British and French governments, and as such, little better, in effect, than the German Wolff Bureau. It was perhaps unavoidable, but none the less unfortunate, that many of the earlier of President Wilson's speeches reached the Germans first through these agencies. With the co-operation of John W. Garrett, American Minister at The Hague, I never ceased to insist that these speeches should reach the Germans first either through an American or Dutch source. In two or three instances the text of such speeches was telegraphed direct to me, and distributed to a Dutch news agency, which either telegraphed the text direct to the German press or handed it to German correspondents, who telegraphed it to their newspapers, as notably in the case of the *Frankfort Gazette*. The *Frankfort Gazette* was the organ of the Reichstag majority parties, and publication of the President's speeches therein, in correct text, some hours previous to publication in the semi-official German government organs, such as the *North German Gazette* and the *Cologne Gazette*, forced them to publish accurate, unaltered versions. This method not only purveyed them to the German masses without outside interference, but often had the effect of forcing the German government to issue the full text. When the method was finally adopted of issuing the President's speeches on the American wireless, the text appeared fully and quickly in both the Dutch and German press, and the question was solved.

Although Reuter's Telegraph Agency offered very great and very unstinted assistance at all times, I felt that, however irreproachable its motive for the common cause, it had identified its service too exactly with the British government to be of exclusive value to the United States in a neutral country, and therefore, although I did not discriminate against it, I saw no reason why Reuter should be favored over the two Dutch agencies. These were the Hollandsche Nieuws Bureau (The Hague) and the Persbureau M. S. Vas Dias (Amsterdam), and although the former especially was under some suspicion as having too close German connections, I felt that its full use for our own purposes was justifiable, especially as it was the one Dutch news service of consequence. A regular service of American news, selected by the Committee on Public Information in New York, under my constant correction and advice, was telegraphed to me daily, together with a special service from general headquarters of the American Expeditionary Forces. Both of these services were edited and issued, in various forms and through various means, direct to the Dutch press. I was also furnished with a daily copy of the American news wireless from a Dutch receiving station, and issued sections of these items to such Dutch agencies as did not operate a wireless receiving station and, in many instances, to Reuter as well.

Although there were no Dutch newspaper men in the United States, all the larger Dutch dailies maintained men in London and Paris. It was my plan to have these men in close touch with American official sources of information in those capitals. While in England on an official mission, I gave a dinner, in the mess of the American Embassy in London, to the four Dutch editors resident in England (representing *Nieuwe Rotterdamsche Courant*, *Handelsblad* and *Telegraaf* of Amsterdam, and *Nieuws van den Dag* of The Hague. There were present representatives of the American army and navy and of all other departments of the government functioning in England, all of whom expressed willingness to provide information for the Dutch editors on demand. From subsequent information coming from official sources I learned that the effect of this entertainment on the Dutch editors was to give them a new conception of Americans and Americanism.

The advantage thus gained was quickly followed up. On June 5, 1918, I escorted Dr. Peter Geyl, editor in England of *Nieuwe Rotterdamsche Courant*, and Mr. E. W. de Jong, editor in England of *Handelsblad* (Amsterdam), to Queenstown for an inspection of the American destroyer base, engaged in convoy and anti-submarine work. Upon returning from Queenstown, the correspondents had a long interview with Admiral Sims, who explained with great frankness the methods and policies of our anti-submarine campaign. On June 14th we arrived in Paris, proceeding thence to the French coast at St. Nazaire, and following the American lines of communication to the front in Lorraine. Thus the representatives of the two most important newspapers in Holland had followed the course of an American soldier from the moment his transport was picked up by the convoys until he had arrived in a front-line trench. From this trip, which was one of the first excursions of neutral editors to the American front, there resulted nineteen long telegrams and eight mail stories in the Dutch press, all of which were copied extensively in the German press, and thus provided the first independent neutral testimony of the size of American effort. The interview with Admiral Sims on the success of our anti-submarine measures provoked much protest from German naval experts, and Mr. de Jong's telegram, "The American phase of the war has begun," was produced in all the important German newspapers and circulated by the semi-official Wolff Bureau.

From confidential information which reached me through a direct source which I do not feel can yet be disclosed, I learned about August 1, 1918, that when Mr. de Jong's figures regarding the size of the American establishment in France were published, both the German Foreign Office and the General Staff summoned the Berlin correspondent of the *Handelsblad* and demanded to know whether Mr. de Jong was the type of man who would allow himself to be bought by the American government. It was apparent that the German authorities were simply staggered at the direct revelations made as the result of this excursion, which I regard as one of the most important single contributions of our whole work in the Netherlands.

Arrangements were later made for the Dutch editors in Paris to make similar trips, under the auspices of the Paris office of the Committee on Public Information.

To summarize, then, our solution of the problem of providing adequate American news to the Dutch press, through Dutch or American sources, I was able to accomplish the following: (1) To provide direct telegraphic and wireless news and comment from the United States to Dutch news agencies and newspapers;

(2) to establish contact between Dutch editors in Great Britain and France with American news sources, and, furthermore, (3) to maintain close personal contact with the more important Dutch editors in Holland; and (4) later to issue, in the form of a daily bulletin, translations of the more significant news items and comment appearing in the American press during each twenty-four hours—a service that was sent regularly to some seventy-six Dutch newspapers. Through these means I was not only able to reduce the suspicion of Dutch editors of American news served through non-American sources and censorship, but to establish direct news communication be een the two countries.

The German government—whether the Imperial government before the armistice or the Republican government afterward—maintained a very elaborate organization on which millions of marks were expended. It was, of course, impossible for me to fight such an organization with its own weapons. Frequent attacks, however, were made on the United States, either by means of deliberate lies or perversions of the truth. These were constantly contradicted in the Dutch press by means of special information telegraphed from Washington, at my request, from the government department concerned. The German propaganda fell into well-reorganized lines of policies, such as questioning the intellectual sincerity of American war aims, belittling our physical effort, and attempting to corrupt relations between the Allied and Associated Governments. We were able to fight the Germans along these same lines, and by insisting, time after time, on a given point, to induce them ultimately to abandon the gesture as worthless.

The German so-called "intellectual propaganda" in Holland was very effective. Prof. Hans Delbrueck, professor in the University of Berlin, and leader of a group of German Moderates, made frequent excursions to Holland, for the purpose of lecturing at the universities and talking with prominent Dutchmen. He was usually accompanied by Kurt Hahn, a young German educated in England, who was believed to provide the lines of attack to the German "intellectual propagandists" in Holland.

This form of German propaganda was very successful. Although my remedy for this—the establishment of a two-year lectureship at the University of Leyden in American history, held by a prominent American academician, who was to have

revived historical Holland-American unity with a living sentiment—was not adopted, we were able to make considerable
progress. Lieut. Leonard van Noppen, U. S. N. R. F., former
Queen Wilhelmina Professor of Dutch in Columbia University,
and assistant naval attaché at The Hague, was of very great
service in reaching the intellectual aristocracy of Holland. I
myself made it a point to know as many important Dutchmen
as possible, to meet them frequently, and to set them right, in
short conversations, on many points of American policy which
they professed to misunderstand. John C. Wiley, second secretary of the American Legation in The Hague, and Paul L. Edwards, commercial attaché, were of very great assistance in this
difficult work.

Although the use of the pamphlet as an educational measure
had been very general in Europe during the war, I was convinced
that, for our work, the extensive printing of such matter would
be a waste of money. We issued only one booklet—a collection
of the pronouncements of President Wilson concerning the League
of Nations, comprising excerpts from his speeches and statements
from February 1, 1916, to September 27, 1918. Of these, ten
thousand copies were printed, and distributed to universities,
schools, public libraries, editors, members of both Houses of
Parliament, members of the government, and other persons of
importance. The residue, after such distribution, was sent to
various persons on the mailing-list of the German propaganda in
Holland, a copy of which had come into my hands.

Special articles on various American subjects from American
magazines and reviews were translated, however, and issued
to the Dutch press or to individual editors, and these, in my
opinion, were of far greater value than any cheap pleading by
pamphlets scattered about in barber shops and bars.

The second most important aspect of our work was education
by means of motion pictures. Upon my arrival in Holland
from England I found several consignments of very old and un-
suitable films, dealing mostly with current events in the United
States. Furthermore, there was no co-operation between the
British, French, and Italians. Mr. George F. Steward, representative of the British Ministry of Information in Holland, aided
me in establishing an inter-Allied cinema committee, which
functioned in connection with an inter-Allied blockade committee,
composed of the commercial attachés of the four Allied legations.

THE WORK IN HOLLAND

As the Dutch exhibitors, to say nothing of the Dutch audiences, had been subject to war films for almost four years when the Committee on Public Information in Holland arrived on the scene, it was my conviction that only the most unusual American war films would have effect. Moreover, it was our opinion that straight American commercial films of superior sort would be a new and invaluable form of education for the Dutch public. I therefore cabled to Washington, pointing out the shortage of good Allied war films, together with the dangers arising from an adequate German supply, and requesting a large consignment of straight commercial films as well. As a result of this telegram, Mr. Llewellyn R. Thomas of New York, a motion-picture expert, was despatched to The Hague, and arrived with several hundred thousand feet of war, educational, and commercial film, all of which was sold, not given, to the Dutch exhibitors, for the total sum of $57,340.80, with a very considerable profit to the American producers, for whose future benefit, moreover, an American market was thus established.

On November 4, 1918, a private performance of "America's Answer" was given to the general staffs of the Dutch army and navy in The Hague. The Dutch officers expressed themselves as greatly impressed, and many in the audience showed their appreciation by rising when President Wilson and General Pershing were thrown on the screen.

A regular supply of photographs dealing with American war-making was received from Washington and general headquarters of the American Expeditionary Forces. These were exhibited in shop-windows in the larger cities and towns throughout Holland. They were regularly sent to Dutch photographic agencies and published in the Dutch illustrated press. The Dutch agencies also sent them to German agencies in Berlin and Vienna, and many of them were printed in the German illustrated journals.

There was a noticeable absence of books and magazines in the Dutch libraries concerning American topics. Apart from the distribution of American newspapers, reviews, magazines, and trade publications, four complete sets of books were obtained from the Foreign Section of the Committee on Public Information in Washington. These books, written by American experts in international law, politics, history, economics, social conditions, and various other aspects of Americanism, were presented to the Nieuwe of Litteraire Societeit, the largest club in Holland, situated in The Hague, and frequented by all important governmental officers and business men, to the Royal Library in The Hague, to the University of Leyden, and to the State University of Amsterdam. There were about twenty-five volumes in each set.

It was a settled policy to act in very close co-operation with the Legation, and more especially with Mr. John W. Garrett, the Minister in The Hague. As the Committee on Public Information was in a general sense the mouthpiece of the United States government in Holland, I considered it of the utmost importance to acquaint myself with the general business of the Legation as far as it affected relations between the two countries. Although the Committee on Public Information was a separate organization, I maintained close contact with the diplomatic situation as conceived by the Legation, and in return received the advice and assistance of the Minister. Our relations were always most cordial, and both of us were able to perform services for the other which ordinarily would have lain outside our regular duties.

Through the kindness of the Minister in allowing us to install a motion-picture projector in his residence, we were able to reach many of the influential members of the Dutch government and of the Allied and neutral diplomatic corps who otherwise would never have been available for our motion-picture educational campaign.

I wish to record my own opinion that the activities of the Foreign Section of the Committee on Public Information had throughout a certain definite constructive value in helping to create that firmest assurance against the sudden passionate crises that so often lead to war—namely, mutual understanding and sympathy between Europe and America, based upon the freest possible interchange of exact and continuous information, in the form of news. This, it seemed to me, was an effort that could be made incredibly inspiring. That it often proved so in the case of important official and non-official Hollanders to whom I presented Holland-American questions, and indeed the general international situation, in that light, was sufficient justification of my own policy of stating *facts* about the United States, instead of resorting to the essentially weaker European method of special pleading.

In conclusion, I wish to state that the work of the Committee on Public Information in Holland was designed to show to the Dutch, and, as might be, to the Germans, what Americanism, as a moral force in operation, really meant. My work started at a very critical time, when neither the dignity of President Wilson's position nor the strength of our Americanism that supported it was credited either in Holland or within the German borders. The details of what was accomplished remain a matter of record. In giving to the Dutch public an array of facts through *American* sources, we appealed to both their reason and sentiment—not through a blatant propaganda, but through restrained presentation of the truth—to a degree which must have lasting effect on the good relations between the Netherlands and the United States.

X

THE situation in Spain, no less than in Mexico, was a very ugly one indeed. The German penetration was evident in every department of Spanish activity, particularly in the army, and many of the most important Spanish papers were receiving German subsidies and pouring out a steady stream of untruths against America. Every effort was made to revive the passions of 1898, and nowhere in the whole country was there a single voice that spoke for America. The following extracts from Madrid papers will show the lengths to which the Germans went in their campaign of vilification:

In my last article I gave a brief account of the horrible crime committed by Wilson against Nicaragua. If this were not more than enough to show that the Yankee President is disqualified in law and in equity to speak to us Europeans in such words as he uses in his answer to the Pope—if the moral opinion of the world had not been excited against the cynicism and unequaled perversities of Wilson, who, though on trial for *lèse-humanité*, has tried to constitute himself the judge of Europe and America, unfortunately there still exist, to the shame of humanity and the dishonor of civilization, other monstrous deeds done by Wilson, against which the world has not protested. . . . No: we must tear the mask from the hypocrite, Wilson.

After having carefully examined the sinister chapters of Yankee imperialistic history, each and every one of which is a crime whose principal author is the actual President Wilson, our heart rebels against this man, against this Puritan, who has the bare-faced insolence to appear as a mediator between nations. This is his rôle in his speeches and proclamations, but his deeds are those of brute force, of war without quarter, of inconceivable extermination and devastation. Blushing at the sight of the repulsive creature, we ask ourselves the question whether the moral sense of humanity has been perverted when it listens to the words of the false and evil Wilson.

In addition to the aspersion of motives there was a continual flood of lies into the news columns as a means of convincing the Spanish people that Germany was winning and that America and the Allies were meeting with disastrous defeats. By way of example, the following is taken from a Barcelona paper of November 10, 1917:

News comes from Halifax *via* New York that the North American battleship *Texas* and other units of the North American fleet were sunk by a German U-boat 75 miles from the Island of Guernsey and 120 miles from Cherbourg at the entrance of the Channel, the latter part of September of last year. Eleven thousand men found their death in the waves; only 3,260 soldiers and 2,585 men of the crew were saved.

The counter-attack of the Allies had failed utterly. Not only were the efforts ill-advised, but there was a natural Spanish prejudice against England on account of Gibraltar, and as a Catholic country Spain looked upon France as a land of "Jacobins and libertines."

The first efforts of the Committee were in connection with "movies," and the work was intrusted to Frank J. Marion, president of the Kalem Company and one of the outstanding figures in the motion-picture industry. He carried with him a large stock of films, showing America at work as well as America at war. Upon arrival in Spain he found that neither France nor England was permitted to show their motion pictures in public, but by sheer force of personality and skilful emphasis upon the "movies" that showed agriculture and industry Mr. Marion succeeded in having his entire stock passed by the Spanish censors. An arrangement was made with a great distributing house that sent our film throughout Spain, and from the theaters Mr. Marion expanded to the schools and colleges, eventually giving open-air shows in cities and villages. Some of the audiences ran as high as nine thousand people, and when the Spanish garrisons asked to see the pictures Mr. Marion was justified in feeling that he had succeeded.

The original plan was to have Mr. Marion inaugurate the motion-picture work in Spain and then proceed to Italy. No sooner had he left Spain, however, than a flood of cables commenced to pour in that convinced us that Mr. Marion was the man above all men for the Spanish job. As a consequence he was ordered back from Rome, appointed commissioner for Spain, and given full authority to launch a complete campaign. The fight was a long one, and bitterly difficult, but when the tide turned it turned with a vengeance. Malaga and Barcelona extended the rights of citizenship to President Wilson, city after city in Spain changed the name of some principal thoroughfare to that of President Wilson, and the Declaration of Independence and the addresses of President Wilson were used in the public schools of Spain for the reading-classes.

The following excerpts from Mr. Marion's report, while giving little idea of the genius with which he overcame obstacles, nevertheless indicate somewhat the sweep of his activities:

Before the commencement of the Committee's work, the amount of American news printed in Spanish papers was not only small, but concerned entirely with epidemics, disasters, and lynchings. We learned later that these lynching items were very generously furnished to the Spanish press by the German propaganda office.

From the first gun of the war the enemy had been maintaining a wireless service from Nauen, which was distributed to the Spanish press free of charge. England, France, and Italy were maintaining a so-called news service through their embassies, but the propaganda element was so strong as to make them worthless. The material was sent to the newspapers on embassy letter-heads in embassy envelopes by uniformed embassy messengers, and in almost every instance the embassies received a bill for the printing at a substantial figure per line.

Most of the leading papers in Spain were under regular subsidy from the German Embassy, and I was told by my French colleagues that space could not be secured in the Spanish press without paying for it. A very large sum was suggested as necessary to carry out the plan. However, I was convinced that truthful news items from America would be welcomed by all the progressive papers and that the system then in vogue of sending out "official" *communiqués* from the various embassies virtually compelled the treatment of the material as advertising.

Looking around, I discovered the Fabra Agency, a Spanish press association doing a small business, and I laid before the managers a plan to incorporate our cable services into their daily "flimsy." I had no difficulty in procuring complete cooperation, even to the extent of having their news editor come to my office each day so that the translations might be made under my direction.

The venture was a success from the start. As a matter of fact, our news service was printed in papers known to be under German subsidy. The point of it was that it was real news, and interesting news from a newspaper point of view. It was what Spain had wanted from America for years, and when the service was finally discontinued there was a storm of protest from the leading Spanish papers.

However, the Fabra Agency was not furnishing the service to the smaller papers of the provinces which could not afford to pay the telegraph tolls, because of the high cost of print paper and the scarcity of advertising. Accordingly, with the aid of Captain Decker, the naval attaché, who placed his various secret agents throughout Spain at my disposal, I organized my own distributing system and within a short time had the satisfaction of seeing the entire press of Spain printing more news from America than from the Allied countries combined.

Following the establishment of the Foreign Press Bureau of the Committee in New York my office commenced to receive regular weekly instalments of special articles, photographs, posters, window-display cards, etc. This material necessitated further expansion. Very little that appears in the Spanish newspaper carries any influence unless it is signed with the name of a writer of acknowledged standing. As a consequence, none of the hundreds of special articles that were sent us was put out over the names of the American authors responsible for them. Each article was given as an exclusive fund of material to some Spanish writer, who would rewrite it in his own particular style. It would then be published in the Spanish papers over his name and with his authority. We were suspected of paying these distinguished literary lights for the work, but not a cent ever went to a single one of them. My chief translator, Señor José Armas, for many years correspondent of *The New York Herald*, and Señorita Raquel Alonzo, formerly of the Gulick School for Girls, performed prodigies of labor and could always be relied upon to give not only accurate translations, but translations of a high literary style.

One of our original beliefs was in the value of pamphlets. A visit to the offices of the British, Italian, and French organizations soon convinced me that if there had ever been any advantage in this phase of work, it had completely disappeared, for in nearly every instance the pamphlets, which had been prepared at the home offices to be distributed in Spain, were used to keep fires going in the grates. The main trouble was defective Spanish. A pamphlet which was prepared by my own committee in Washington, and sent to me as a sample, was so full of errors as to be absolutely useless. Later when large window-display photographs were sent to me lettered in Spanish, many of these were found to be useless for a similar reason.

While attending the propaganda conference in Paris, I became convinced that the strongest arguments in behalf of the Allied cause were embodied in the various official utterances of President Wilson, and following that conviction, we used every effort to give them widest possible publicity. Not only were they published immediately in the Spanish press, but they were printed in pamphlet form as well and sent under letter postage to upward of ten thousand prominent Spaniards. So accurate and elegant in its diction was Prof. Romero-Navarro's translation of the President's famous Fourteen Points speech that it was adopted as a literary text-book by one of the leading schools for boys in Madrid. In the distribution of this and other material we were greatly assisted by Señor Amato of the Fabra Agency. As a general proposition, pamphleteering had been overdone in Spain by both the Allies and the enemy embassies and we did not deem it advisable to enter to any great extent into this branch of work.

Every center of population in Spain from the tiny mountain pueblo to the capital city has its atheneum. This is a civic center. For the purpose of taking advantage of these forums, Prof. M. Romero-Navarro of the Department of Romance Languages in the University of Pennsylvania, a Castilian by birth and education, and still a Spanish citizen, was persuaded to give up his collegiate work and come to Spain for the purpose of giving an extended series of lectures. Professor Navarro lectured on Spanish artistic, literary, and historic influences in America, and against this background painted a splendid picture of America's idealism, unselfishness, and military invincibility.

A Spaniard likes to have things visualized and the illustrated papers were all eager for American photographs. The Committee offices in Washington, New York, and Paris sent us a weekly supply well selected as to subject and excellent as to photographic quality, and as a result we had a virtual monopoly of the illustrated press in Spain. It was not at all unusual for us to have two-thirds of the pictures in one illustrated paper. None of these pictures was distributed from our own office. We employed a local agent, who peddled them from paper to paper as his own stock and sold them on their own merits to pro-German as well as to pro-Ally papers.

The poster situation presented one of our greatest problems. The German posters were scurrilous and indecent. One most widely circulated in Spain purported to represent typical soldiers of the various armies opposed to Germany, and in each case the type was as brutal and degenerate as the German mind could conceive. It would have been easy to plaster Spain with our own posters showing the American idea of the Prussian face, but we decided that the best answer was to fill the illustrated papers and the store-windows with photographs of our manly doughboys at the front so that the Spaniard could judge for himself.

For our window-display campaign we started by securing the co-operation of American firms doing business in Spain. These were very few indeed, but one alone, the Singer Sewing Machine Company, put the windows of some seven hundred branch stores in Spain at our disposition, saw to the trimming of the windows, the display of the material, and even took care of the transportation expenses. All we had to do was to deliver our material at the main office of this patriotic concern and the rest was attended to better than we could have done it ourselves.

The Eastman Kodak Company and the Æolian Company were two other American concerns which gave us the continual use of their window-display space without cost.

The central feature of all of our window-display work was a handsomely framed group of photographs covering both the preparations in America and behind the line scenes in France. Hundreds of frames were made up and kept in continuous circulation, and our own personal observation shows that they invariably attracted a great deal of attention and favorable comment. On at least two occasions the Eastman Kodak's window display of our materials in their handsome store on the Puerta del Sol nearly blockaded traffic.

Quite a notable success was made with the exhibition of Joseph Pennell drawings. One of the stanchest friends of America in Spain was Sorolla, the great painter. Señor Sorolla personally took charge of this collection, patronized its exhibitions throughout the leading cities of Spain, and finally saw to it that the collection was properly housed in the National Academy of Modern Arts in Madrid as the gift of Mr. Pennell to the Spanish government. These magnificent pictures showed various phases of our preparatory work in shipyards and munition-plants. If they had been exhibited in the ordinary way as propaganda they would have come under the ban of Spanish censorship, but shown as a pure art exhibit under the patronage of Sorolla, they met with no objection and everywhere attracted favorable comment from the press.

In July, 1918, we started the publication of a weekly bulletin in English, the *American News*, which was distributed free of charge to all Americans whose names we could secure in Spain and Portugal. The purpose of this bulletin in the form of a small eight-page newspaper was to put the facts of our war preparations and achievements into the hands of Americans to be disseminated by them in their contact with the Spanish people. The editor of this paper was Seward B. Collins, a Princeton student unable to get into the army or navy, but eager to serve. In many respects this was one of our most important activities.

The spy system maintained by the Germans, and by the Allies as well, may only be described as a "scream." After about six months' residence in Madrid I happened in at an out-of-the-way café and met a reliable Spanish friend.

"What are you doing here?" he asked.

"Having a cup of coffee."

"Don't you know what sort of a place you are in?"

"No, I don't. Tell me."

"This is the place," he said, "where all the spies get together at four o'clock every afternoon and exchange lies to be reported to the various embassies the following morning. The German spies hand a bunch of inside information from their embassy to their friends who are working for the Allies, and in return receive a mess of stuff which they hand back to the Germans. Thus both sides are satisfied and a prosperous business is established."

My friend then pointed out to me the agents of the various embassies, enemy agents and Allied agents chatting like the best of friends. Scarcely a day went by but that a half-dozen men would call upon us to tell the same kind of story; that they had been employed by the German Embassy, that they were poor but honest men, that their hearts were really with the Allies, and if we would pay them a little more money they would come to us and tell us secrets of the greatest importance.

A book might be written on this phase of outside war-work alone. From the standpoint of an American I want to go on record as being of the opinion that the spy system as I saw it in operation in Spain for eighteen months, both enemy and the Ally, is "bunk." There is no other word that so adequately expresses it.

Jack Johnson, the ex-champion, was generally understood to be a spy in the employ of the Germans. He claimed to have access to the German Embassy, and offered to make a night entry and rob it of all its files if by doing so he could only get back to his "dear old U. S. A." again. He was told that the best way to do that would be to go to France and enlist, upon which he faded away. Johnson posed in Spain as a typical American, claiming that he was still champion of the world, and was one of the worst elements of negative propaganda in Spain. There seemed to be little doubt that he was being paid by the Germans to keep in a prominent position, and there was seldom a gala performance at the opera that did not see Johnson in full evening dress seated directly in front of the royal box. There was murder in the hearts of all Americans, but there was nothing we could do.

The Palace Hotel, where Johnson made his headquarters, was a nest of German spies. Every employee of the hotel was a German spy. I arrived in Madrid at two o'clock one fine afternoon, with Mr. David Harrell of the War Trade Board, Mrs. Harrell, and their son David, a lad of seventeen. David stayed behind for a minute as we went down the hall, and before we had time to round the corner a German spy was in the room, ransacking our bags. David reached out of the bathroom door, grabbed the man by the collar, and sprawled him headlong into the hall. The man struck his head so hard that David was afraid he had hurt him, so he gave him two pesetas to square himself and then came down and told us about it. During the two weeks we were compelled to stay at the hotel, our every step was dogged and our every word was listened to. None of us had any information of the slightest use to the enemy, but the sleuths were set on us just the same.

Most of the German propaganda was as stupid as their spy system. A typical specimen of their work was a comic picture book printed in Barcelona by the German propaganda office. This was gotten up like our five-cent story editions of *Puss in Boots* or *Jack the Giant Killer*—fifteen or twenty pages of grotesque figures in color with verses. The title of the book was *Kings Without a Throne*, and a page was devoted to each of the petty European rulers who had lost his crown because of defying the wrath of the all-powerful one in Berlin. This book was printed in enormous numbers and distributed to the children as they came out of school. The object-lesson, of course, was that if the King of Spain did not recognize German might, he, too, would lose his throne. Many of the pictures in this book were positively obscene. The German cartoon of President

Wilson found everywhere in Spain in the form of picture post-
cards was that of a lantern-jawed maniac. Always in the German window displays the central feature would be the Kaiser,
Ludendorff, and Hindenburg, portrayed as magnificent and inspiring specimens of manhood, while the representatives of the
Allies were pictured as degenerates.

Another example of stupidity was the insertion of a paid
article in one or two papers in all the principal cities that the
American army was irreligious, that no Catholic priest was allowed to function in his sacred vestments, that Pershing and his
staff were all members of the Liberty Lodge of Masons in Brooklyn, and that the American army in France was being directed
by the Masonic order, its real purpose the crushing of Cathol-
icism in Europe. Our answer to this, in illustrated papers and
window displays, was a magnificent picture of six thousand
soldiers in uniform attending an open-air mass near the front
lines in France.

Of course, the principal accusation against the Americans
was that all our claims were Yankee bluff, that we had no army,
couldn't raise an army, couldn't train an army if we could raise
one, had no officers, and even if we could raise and train an army
we couldn't transport them, because we had no ships, and even
if we did get ships, the German submarines would take care of
them. We sent a delegation of prominent Spanish newspaper
men to France, headed by the Marquis Valleglesias, owner
and editor of *Epoca,* and this delegation returned to Madrid
after ten days with our troops and announced that, instead of
bluffing, the Americans had not told one tenth of the story.

We had so many different schemes at work at the same time that
the Germans finally became rather bewildered. Prince Ratibor
and his daughters, the Princesses of Taxis and Thurn, went to a
ball at the Ritz one night and had a wonderful time dancing to the
music of "Over There" and all our popular war songs. We were
supplied with orchestrations of all this music from our foreign service department in New York, and for the last six months of the
war we had all the bands in Spain playing American music.

The educational campaign in Spain was not conducted by the
representative of the Committee on Public Information alone
and unassisted. In the first place the need of the work was
recognized by Capt. Benton C. Decker, Chief of Naval Intelligence, of Spain. When I arrived in Spain every facility of

Captain Decker's office was put at my disposal. Although ordered by the Ambassador to refrain from assisting or helping the Committee on Public Information in any way, Captain Decker, with a high sense of patriotic duty, insisted upon doing so, and was recalled at the request of Ambassador Willard in May, 1918. From that time on the work of the Committee on Public Information was entirely detached from all other American agencies, but the utmost encouragement and all needed help were given by Captain Crossley, succeeding Captain Decker, and later by Capt. Chester Wells, succeeding Captain Crossley. Both the Madrid and Barcelona branches of the War Trade Board, headed by Mr. Waldmar Chadbourne of the former office and Mr. David Harrell, of the latter, were in the warmest sympathy with our work, and gave every possible assistance and encouragement. Preston Morris Smith of the War Trade Board did almost as much work for the Committee on Public Information as for his own department, all without recompense and for the good of the cause.

Among the Spanish gentlemen who aided the cause in many and varied ways may be named Señor I. DeMora of *The Pictorial Review;* Senator Paloma of Seville; Sorolla, the painter Azorin, Ariquistain, and Aznar, three of the most famous editorial writers; the entire personnel of the Fabra News Agency headed by Señor A. Mato; and Ledesma and Villeseca, the motion-picture distributors.

On my own staff particular credit is due to my secretary and personal representative, Señor José M. Gay, an American citizen of Filipino descent, a lawyer and a thorough patriot. Next to Señor Gay I am indebted to Mr. Collins and to Prof. Romero Navarro.

Every American in Spain loyally assisted, but particular service was rendered by the gentlemen of the American Chamber of Commerce of Barcelona, headed by Messrs. Brewer, van Tress and Preston M. Smith, all of whom could be relied upon to do any work that seemed necessary in their territory. And above all, the most effective argument was the work of our army and navy. As our campaign progressed, the pro-German tendency of Spain began perceptibly to fade, and when Spain sent its peremptory note to Germany regarding the sinking of Spanish merchant-ships we felt that the climax of our efforts had been reached.

THE WORK IN SPAIN

As evidencing the value of the Committee's work in Spain, carried forward under the direction of Mr. Marion, the Madrid correspondent of *The Christian Science Monitor* wrote as follows under date of October 23, 1918:

A development of the popular attitude that has been most marked in recent months, and has become a significant feature of Spanish inclination, has been a sincere, anxious, and deep interest that Spain has begun to take in all that concerns the United States, and especially on her productive and industrial side. . . . Demonstrations by cinema pictures and in other ways of how things are done in America have been greatly appreciated. So have the object-lessons of what the Americans have been doing in the way of metamorphosis in France in various directions. An indication of the new state of interest that Spain feels in regard to American institutions, systems, and so forth, is furnished by the long articles that continually appear about them in some of the daily newspapers, especially in the newer journals. Lectures on similar subjects are increasingly popular, and multitudinous papers have been read before the members of literary and scientific institutions concerning different aspects of American development.

In this connection it is of special interest to point out that at the present time Señor Miguel-Navarro, professor of Spanish language and literature at the University of Pennsylvania, is in the country and has been delivering some pointed discourses which have received close attention and have been reported in detail in the newspapers.

And on December 11, 1918, *The Monitor* said:

What may be called the Wilson cult is truly making astonishing progress in Spain, as shall be shown. Three months ago the President of the United States was known but little to the general community. To-day there is hardly a city of any consequence in Spain whose newspapers are not devoting innumerable columns to articles upon his career, his views in general, and his present actions, with occasional personal details.

XI

THE WORK IN SCANDINAVIA

FROM the very beginning of the World War, Sweden was a paradise for the German propagandists, many natural causes creating a very intense sympathy for the Kaiser's cause both among the people generally and in the government itself. Norway, by reason of the destruction of her shipping by German submarines, was strongly pro-Ally, but in Denmark the situation was almost as bad as in Sweden. In the first place there was the delicacy of Denmark's position proceeding from geographical considerations that made her absolutely helpless. When Denmark lost Schleswig, and the Kiel Canal was built, there disappeared the last hope of successfully defending Copenhagen from attack by the Germans. A fleet of airships sailing from Warnemunde, the German Baltic port, could lay Copenhagen in ruins in five hours. German big guns could bombard Copenhagen from the Baltic. They could also sweep the peninsula of Jutland from one side to the other. Therein was the secret of the Danish fear.

The Germans had been unloading propaganda on Denmark for three years, working through a strong organization that included a number of young authors who had been unsuccessful in having their works published. The Germans tempted them by telling them they would see their names in print and offered free publication for the books they wrote. In among these books were cleverly sandwiched others full of German propaganda. These books were issued from a large publishing-house and later another smaller firm was added. They had a clientèle of from one hundred thousand to one hundred and fifty thousand. The Germans also tempted newspapers which were known to be in financial difficulties, by offering them paying advertising contracts and a supply of printing paper at considerably less cost than they were able to get it from Allied sources. This paper was to be delivered free at the plant, and ink and printing-machines were also offered. The leader of the German propaganda was Louis vom Kohl, of an old Danish family, and a clever author. He and his associates bought up a chain of eight Danish magazines, and while none of the more influential ones fell into their clutches, the publicity influence wielded by the group was very real.

To Denmark we sent George Edward Waldemar Riis, an able newspaper man himself, but possessing added values by being the son of that great Danish-American, Jacob Riis. When Mr. Riis arrived in Denmark he found no adequate conception of America's motives of the goal we sought to attain, of what we were capable of doing under pressure of great necessity, and what our participation and final triumph would mean to the small nations of Europe. When his work ceased Denmark understood us as never before. America's work had been carried into every nook and corner of the kingdom. The spirit of America had been photographed for the Danes by word of mouth, by written article, and by picture, so that they saw us clearly and comprehended us. Mr. Riis found them looking through glasses darkly. He left them with a new vision of our people, our activities, and the lofty principles which governed us. Our material appeared in every publication of any importance in the land and our

pictures were displayed in towns which had never seen
American war film. He won powerful newspapers to our
side; he made people our lasting friends, for he taught
them that our fight was for Denmark as well as ourselves;
that America had no ax to grind; that we sought gain of
neither land nor gold; that we strove to attain only peace
and universal justice. An idea of the activities may be
gained by these extracts from the report of Mr. Riis:

Denmark was tired of propaganda when I came and if we had
attempted to put out material plainly tagged as such it would
have gone into the waste-basket. I adopted a new line of endeavor. I went to the editors and told them frankly what we
were aiming at. I hid nothing. I said we were conducting a
news bureau. Before I did that I went to the chief censor, Mr.
Marinus Yde (one of the fairest, ablest men I ever met), and was
perfectly frank with him. I showed him our files and said he
might come back and look at our office at any time. We strove
to, and we did, convince the people that we were there not so
much to advertise our wares as to bring about a better relationship, a mutual understanding between our country and theirs
as to the aims, objects, and purposes of each. Frankness on
our part begot frankness on their part.

We did not feed the Danes cut-and-dried propaganda. We
carefully selected those articles which we knew the Danish publications would be eager for. In this I had the invaluable aid
of Mr. Herman Bente, my assistant director, who knew the likes
and dislikes of the Danish press all through the land. We let
the Danish editors know that we were running a straight news
bureau—that we had news of interest about America and what
was going on behind the scenes there. We did not urge it on
them. They could take it or leave it, as they chose. They
took it and called for more. At first we went to them. Then
they came to us. We put the breath of life in dry material.
We put an American journalistic punch in it. We aimed to tell
the story of the pictures in short, crisp sentences so that they
would hit the reader between the eyes. When we were sending
over three hundred thousand troops a month I figured out how
many men that would mean departing from our shores every
minute, and wrote a short story stating that every minute so

many men were going out from the States to serve under the flag. There was need of this. The Germans had said that we were not able to send an army. They said that such troops as we had were ill equipped. We were able to convince the Danes to the contrary.

When the great American offensive at St. Mihiel began we received, just in time, a picture of Pershing, but no written matter with it. The people of Denmark were unable to visualize Pershing. What manner of man was he? What was his previous military experience? What had he done that he had earned the right to lead the American armies? From my material I wrote a column story which appeared, along with the picture, on the first page of the second largest newspaper in Denmark, *Berlingske Tidende*, the time of the publication fitting in with the beginning of the offensive.

When I found, on first coming, that nobody knew just what was going on behind the scenes at home, I sat down and wrote an article telling what I had seen of the strength and power of our war preparations, letting them know that we did not want this war, but when we found that it had to be fought we became one great workshop in which all the people were working unitedly to end the war as quickly and as effectively as possible. When I found that the Danes had only an imperfect idea of President Wilson, how he rose to fame, what he meant in the life of the people, how he was trying to interpret the spirit of his country, just what he stood for and what he strove to attain, I wrote a three-column story, "Wilson, Hope of the World," in which I endeavored properly to interpret him and his principles. Along with it I tried to mirror the spirit of my people. That story was favorably commented on all over Denmark. It was not only printed in one of the largest of the Copenhagen newspapers, *Berlingske Tidende*, but ran the rounds of the provincial press. It was published in four provincial papers, four of the leading papers, and among others in the leading newspaper of Ribe, three miles from the German border. That was just where I wanted to get it.

I made several speeches in Copenhagen and in the provinces after they had asked me to do so. I delivered one at a large concentration camp for soldiers at Sandholm. I was asked to, and did, deliver one in the auditorium of the chief Copenhagen newspaper, *Politiken*, just before I left. I made myself a personal friend of the editors. I called on some of them almost daily. I went to the provinces, and to the editors there I explained what we were trying to do. These calls were followed by an encouraging result in the greater use of our material.

We kept careful track of what the newspapers were saying, either to our detriment or to our credit. When they said anything which was incorrect, and we knew it to be incorrect, we went after them. When one newspaper, which had been printing erroneous reports about us, wrote vicious subheads on a news article dealing with an address delivered by the President and referred to him as the "Trustland's President," I called them to account, and the second editor came to my office and apologized. He did more. A two-column article was written praising our work. The newspaper swung over so that it took with eagerness articles sent out by us, attributing them to our Committee. This newspaper published two columns of Justice Clark's important decision on the eight-hour law and credited it to our Committee. The story went the rounds of the Social Democratic papers.

Every magazine of any prominence using pictures published ours. We had more pictures in the magazines than any of the other Allied bureaus were able to show. Sometimes half a dozen such pictures would appear in an issue of a single magazine having a circulation of 200,000. Many hundreds of pictures were sent out by us through the Pressens Illustrations Bureau, which serves between 200 and 300 publications in Scandinavia, and this material, sent out in Copenhagen, was published in Norway as well.

Copenhagen was filled with our pictures. They were posted in places conveniently located. The Germans afterward followed us up and put up pictures where we did. We put them up on side-streets where pictures had not been shown before and in outlying districts. We sent them to provincial towns, such as Aarhus, Esbjerg, Ribe, Kallundborg, Roskilde, and other places. We grouped them so that people could see the gradual development of small-arms manufacture, of the progress of the Browning machine-gun, of the flying-machine, and we put red-lettered captions and stories under them which conveyed a ready lesson to the man in the street. These pictures were viewed daily by thousands.

We gave pictures to the British Legation to be used in their illustrated booklets, and to lecturers. We even paid for lantern slides for such men as Winding, one of the prominent journalists on the staff of *Politiken*, who had been a correspondent at the front and who afterward delivered lectures telling what American troops were doing in the war, what they were like, and the spirit which actuated them.

We furnished school-teachers with printed material in the shape of articles or pamphlets, likewise writers. We sent a volume of President Wilson's messages to a large publishing-house, which got them out in Danish.

We took up the Schleswig question at a time when scores of persons came to see me to ask that the United States help to adjust the Schleswig problem on a basis of justice to the Danes, and I sent home cables, articles, and pamphlets dealing exhaustively with the entire Schleswig question. I wrote home about it, and even sent a letter to the President, pointing out that the people of the small neutral nation which had suffered so grievously looked to him in the wistful hope that he would right an ancient wrong and strike off the shackles of the Danes in Schleswig who for fifty long years had felt the tyranny and oppression of Prussian rule.

When Mr. Edgar Sisson's Bolshevist disclosures first reached Denmark by cable, I got the complete text, and that night I called a meeting of my staff and instructed them to go get out the entire text on our duplicating machine first thing in the morning. I invited the chief censor to sit in on our talk. It was not necessary for us to get it out on the duplicating machine, for the newspapers were impressed with its extreme importance as news and the next day all the Danish newspapers gave it all the space that was possible. The *Social-Demokraten*, the strongest organ among the Socialists of Denmark, alone published eight columns of the revelations. The newspapers continued to publish the story for three days. Later we got rid of between ten thousand and fifteen thousand copies of the disclosures printed in pamphlet form, part in Danish and part in Russian. The Russians who were combating Bolshevism snapped them up eagerly.

We published three pamphlets in Denmark. One was by Booth Tarkington, dealing with our awakening; another was by Ernest Poole and described the spirit of the army; a third was an appeal to the reason of the German people written by a Captain Helwig, born in Germany, but an American serving as a captain in our army.

The last-named pamphlet was published in German. It was distributed in the last months of the war. From one place alone we received reports that it had been given into the hands of about three hundred Germans. Copies of that pamphlet were left at all hotels and restaurants frequented by Germans. We sent many into Germany.

I suggested and helped to arrange the visit to our country of the twelve Scandinavian journalists. That visit did much to cement the friendly relations between ourselves, Norway, Sweden, and Denmark. When they returned they wrote many admirable articles showing a ready understanding of our people and our spirit and correcting such impressions as that we were a dollar-chasing land engrossed merely in our own selfish considerations. Emil Marot, one of the Danes and a member of Parliament, gave, on his return, a series of twenty-five lectures in which he explained us to his people.

I have seen a change of feeling come over people who had not understood us before. I have seen a new understanding of President Wilson come into the minds of the Danes, so that they placed him on a plane beside their greatest national heroes. I have known them to cut out the photographs of him sent out by us, which appeared in Danish papers, and place them in a sort of family shrine. Yes, I have known the rough farmers to do that on the lonely heath lands. I know that the people of the small neutral nations of Europe, soul-sick with war, yearning for an enduring peace, have looked to him in the hour of trial as the great deliverer, the Moses in a wilderness of trouble. They looked to him to lead them to the light, to lasting peace, to bind the nations in the great brotherhood of which so many millions dream. They believed in him and in us when I left.

Mr. Eric Palmer, the Committee's news representative in Sweden and Norway, won to success, as did Mr. Riis, and from first to last enjoyed the powerful and intelligent support of the American Minister, Mr. Ira Nelson Morris. Finland also came within the scope of Mr. Palmer's activities, and the following tribute from Thornwell Haynes, our consul at Helsingfors, is not without its own interest:

THE WORK IN SCANDINAVIA

So far the results in Finland of the work of the Committee on Public Information have been most gratifying, especially considering the irritating obstacles to be overcome in the way of pre-existing German propaganda. In whatever direction the faces of the Finns were turned, there flourished German articles and maps and pictures, German books and newspapers, even little Finns toddling in and out of newly established German kindergartens. Bookstore windows contained more German literature than Swedish or Finnish, and such superior German war maps were broadcasted that even Allied consulates bought them for reference. A daily paper, printed in German and receiving financial support from the Finnish Treasury, made its appearance in the capital every evening. German uniforms were seen everywhere, Finnish-German clubs were formed and German banks established. In fact, as far as propaganda was concerned, Finland was a German vassal state.

The work done by the Committee on Public Information, though single-handed and alone, has contributed wonderfully toward saving the situation. In this respect I consider the discrimination shown in the selection of the news by far the most deserving. It has been done so as to create no irritation, and yet quietly demonstrated its force in supplanting William by Wilson and Militarism by America.

While of course the turning of battle on the western front was the immediate cause of the turning of public opinion in Finland toward the Entente, the work done by the Committee has most effectively cleared the way and prepared a suitable soil wherein the unwillingly changed public opinion can reasonably and conscientiously grow.

Guy Croswell Smith, just out of Russia, was left in Stockholm by Mr. Sisson in 1918 and given charge of film distribution in Sweden, Norway, and Denmark. This brief extract from his report will indicate the manner in which he handled his problem:

Upon investigation of the situation I found that an immense amount of German propaganda and drama films was being presented in the picture theaters throughout these countries. The Scandinavians like films very much and to the large attendance at the five hundred-odd theaters was constantly being conveyed a broad influence—always, of course, for the German point of view. The propaganda films showed the success of the Germans and Austrians, scenes in German cities, munition-factories, etc., all tending to demonstrate how Germany was winning the war. And there was absolutely no representation as to what the United States was doing. In Sweden particularly the German film propaganda was especially damaging toward the existence of any ideas of fair neutrality for the reason that the Swedes were practically all inclined to be pro-German and the influence of these films was a constant stimulus in the same direction. I foresaw that our films would have to be forced upon the theaters and distributing companies in the same way.

The supply of American drama films in the country was limited on account of the embargo that had existed, which for a time had excluded the possibility of importing films from the United States. This condition had made it easy for the German film-producers to get in their product, but they sold only with the provision that some German propaganda subjects would be taken with the drama films.

Shortly before my arrival in Stockholm, the export prohibition on American drama films had been provisionally raised and shipments again began to come, addressed to the American legations in the various countries. Before releasing these to the consignees, they signed agreements that the films would never be shown in any program with a German drama or propaganda film and that one reel of American "war stuff" would always be shown with them. This agreement they in turn made with the theaters before distributing. The largest three companies controlling theaters in Scandinavia further agreed that they would never permit any films previously received to be shown in the same program with German subjects. Inasmuch as American films were much more popular with the public on account of their superiority, the effect of these agreements was quickly evident. German films were gradually forced out to such an extent that in three months after my arrival it was difficult to find a theater showing German drama films, and the German propaganda films had been completely driven out and replaced by our official films. I kept close check on the programs throughout the three countries and in the few instances where theaters did not keep their agreement and showed a German film their ability to get American film was discontinued. During the eight months I was in Scandinavia I distributed about one hundred thousand feet of official films. This included American industrial subjects; Hearst-Pathé and Universal weeklies showing the Allies' war activities and events in the United States; "Pershing's Crusaders" and the Allied War Review. These pictures were first shown in the best theaters of the capitals—Stockholm, Christiania, and Copenhagen—and then went in rotation to the smaller houses in these cities and afterward throughout the other cities and towns of the three countries. Thus, where previously this immense number of theater-goers had seen the war news only through German eyes, they now saw America and Americans—at home, at work, and under arms, laying aside the pursuits of peace to fight in defense of freedom.

24

XII

CHINESE dislike of England and Chinese hatred of Japan pointed clearly to the fact that the Allied fight for public opinion in China would have to be made by America and Americans. The Germans had carried on a very extensive and expensive propaganda, and, while unmarked by any particular cleverness, the work swept forward to success on the wave of anti-Japanese, anti-British feeling. A principal feature of the Hun activity was a news agency that supplied a daily cable service from Berlin to the Chinese press. Pay was taken in the form of advertising space, which in turn was allotted to the German houses doing business in China. As a consequence, both news and advertising columns were regularly poisoned, and China stood in danger of seeing the World War through Hun spectacles only.

Reuters, the official news agency, was in control of the field as far as Allied information was concerned. All American news, for instance, went into China by way of London, and the part sent on by Reuters dealt mainly with our crimes, corruptions, and commercial hypocrisies. Our policies were never referred to except when British interests were affected. In addition to Reuters there was a separate propaganda organization that seemed to have no other object than to preach Great Britain's preponderating part in the war. This work was directed from three headquarters: (a) the British colony of Hongkong; (b) the British Legation in Peking; (c) the British consulate in Shanghai. Through the four years of the war these three agencies worked at cross-purposes, often in opposition to one another, and at the end of the war were still quarreling over which one of the three should run the show.

Under these circumstances, the plan of campaign was different in each place. In Shanghai the work was turned over to a clerk in the consulate, who worked under the direction of Reuters' agent and the British consul. In the early part of the war they established a daily Chinese newspaper in Shanghai, at a cost said to be about $125,000. A great deal of British advertising was diverted to this paper, but it was not a financial success and reverted to Chinese ownership after the armistice. They also published a fortnightly war magazine, distributed through British firms. In the establishment of these publications the British ignored existing mediums and created more or less resentment among Chinese publishers. A daily résumé of war events was made and telegraphed to some fifty or sixty points in the Yangtze Valley to Britishers, who undertook the work of translating these messages and securing their publication in the Chinese press. This résumé was also published in handbill form and seven thousand distributed in Shanghai each afternoon. In Peking a similar résumé was sent to the newspapers and once a week a poster was issued giving the résumé of the week's news. This poster was put up by the police in Peking and was posted in the waiting-rooms of the British-controlled railways. The Hongkong committee published daily an official bulletin in English giving all Reuters' telegrams. This was sent to Chinese officials.

Through a connection between Reuters and the Kokusai (the official Japanese news agency) the Japanese were able to present their views in China, as news sent from Tokio is distributed by Reuters. This means that when there was a controversial issue between Japan and America, Japanese views were given the widest publicity in China, while American opinions were learned only after they had been edited in London. This arrangement between the Kokusai and Reuters was similar to that between the Associated Press and Reuters, with this important difference—that Japanese news was sent direct to China, while American news sent by the Associated Press had to come through London.

In addition to this arrangement with Reuters, the Japanese originated a semi-official news agency which supplied Far Eastern news to Chinese publications. Japanese consuls acted as correspondents for this agency, the despatches being sent in code. In the treaty ports the Japanese adopted the policy of registering Chinese newspapers at the Japanese consulate, thereby giving them protection against Chinese officials, and gaining more or less control over the papers. In addition the Japanese owned a number of Chinese papers and secretly controlled several English-language papers by means of loans and subsidies. None of the Japanese propaganda was directed toward creating a sentiment favorable to the Allies, but to the furtherance of Japan's aims in China.

French propaganda was directed from Shanghai and consisted principally in the publication of a fortnightly magazine of about sixteen pages, containing pictures and articles about the war. Several posters were issued. About two months before the signing of the armistice the French wireless station in Shanghai got in touch with the Lyons wireless station and received French *communiqués* daily. These were handed to Reuters for distribution to the English-language press and were translated into Chinese by the French consulate and sent out to a list of about thirty Chinese papers.

THE WORK IN THE ORIENT

For reasons that must be obvious, Allied propaganda had failed when we entered the field. Our first approach was through Dr. Paul Reinsch, our Minister in Peking, one of the five or six members of the diplomatic service that gave the Committee unfailing assistance instead of enmity and sabotage. Through his arrangement, our wireless service was taken out of the air by the legation station in Peking, and was also intercepted at Shanghai by the French municipal wireless station. In both places the service was handed to Reuters for distribution, but we soon discovered that this distribution was anything but adequate. Mr. Carl Crow, a brilliant correspondent and a man who knew China and the Chinese intimately and sympathetically, was soon appointed to be the Committee's commissioner, and these excerpts from his report tell the story of his conquest of the problem.

After a survey of the situation and consultation with a number of Americans we came to the conclusion (1) that Reuters, because of its attitude toward American news and its indifference to the Chinese press, could not be depended on to give the American wireless news any wide distribution; (2) that while the publication of the American news in the English-language press of the Far East is of comparatively little importance, it is of the very greatest importance that it be published in Chinese newspapers; (3) that there was no existing agency for the distribution of the news to the Chinese press and that one must be created.

In carrying out the above program a company of American business and professional men organized the Chinese-American News Agency (Oriental News Agency) for work with the Chinese press. In the mean time I engaged a staff of translators and trained them to the very difficult work of preparing translations of American war news which would be intelligible to the average newspaper reader. In due time the news agency began sending out its daily report, which included the American wireless news, special articles, Chinese news, etc. The report went to more than three hundred Chinese papers and was published in part in practically all of them. There was no other news agency of a national character in China and this agency developed into an organization occupying the Chinese field as fully as the Associated Press occupies the field at home. The only aid given the agency by the Committee on Public Information was to supply it with the translations for distribution to the newspapers and to pay it for the performance of specific functions (distribution of pictures, presidential addresses, etc.) which the agency could perform economically. In working out the above plans I was in close co-operation with Doctor Reinsch and Mr. J. B. Powell, with whom I consulted regarding every phase of my work.

In order to distribute literature and collect information about Chinese in the interior it was necessary to secure the co-operation of a number of volunteer agents. These were secured, about four hundred in number, from the ranks of the American missionaries, teachers, and Standard Oil employees. These men undertook their work with great enthusiasm and constituted an active body of agents of tremendous value. It would have been impossible for any other country to organize a body of this sort because no other country was so ably represented in the interior of China.

Through the courtesy of the Standard Oil Company, the British-American Tobacco Company, the Singer Sewing Machine Company, and other American concerns in China, we had at our disposal several thousand stations where pictures and posters could be displayed. These stations were the sales agencies of the above concerns in almost every town and village in the country, exceptionally well located on busy streets where pictures received the greatest possible attention.

I collected the principal addresses of President Wilson and gave them to the Commercial Press, a large Chinese publishing-house, with the suggestion that they bring out a Chinese edition. This was published, and the first edition was all sold out in two weeks, compelling a second edition. This volume became the best seller in China, and the Commercial Press is pushing the sale of the book to Chinese schools.

As a means of promptly reaching the ruling class in China, it was decided to compile a mailing-list, which would comprise the names of the real Chinese leaders of thought in each community. The help of the volunteer agents mentioned above was enlisted and the work of compiling the list went forward rapidly. I included the names and addresses of all members of the Provincial Assembly, all members of the Chamber of Commerce, all officials of or above the rank of magistrate, and all Chinese scholars. In the end we had the most valuable mailing-list in China, consisting of about twenty-five thousand names. As far as funds at our disposal permitted, I sent to each name on this list a copy of President Wilson's addresses.

It will be noted that the program of work outlined above contemplated propaganda among the ruling classes. It did not take into consideration the student classes, because funds were not sufficient for work in both. The students are more easily reached and influenced, and if it were possible to plan and carry out a program to extend over a period of years, great good would result from it in the future. The most obvious and direct way of reaching the students would be by distribution of literature in both English and Chinese to mission and government schools. There are great possibilities in a sustained program among the students. The text-book publishing industry is at present undeveloped and it would be possible to secure the use in Chinese schools of text-books planned and edited by Americans. This would not involve any expenditures for publication, as the books would be published and their use developed by Chinese publishing-houses. Some American university should send a man to China for several years to make a study of this situation. He should be supplied with funds enough to enable him to organize a translation bureau. The result of his studies would doubtless disclose many ways in which America can be of benefit to China in developing her educational system. Several American text-book companies have interested themselves in this field, but chiefly as a market for English text-books.

Japan, strangely enough, presented few problems. In the first place, Ambassador Morris put his personal and official influence behind the Committee at the very outset and drove through an arrangement that worked splendidly. The daily Compub service was turned over to the Kokusai, the official Japanese news agency, for translation and distribution to the Japanese press. A clipping bureau maintained a constant check on the operation and never at any time did we have cause to complain, either as to the distribution itself or with respect to the manner in which the Japanese newspapers printed it.

In the matter of films, we found that the Universal Company had built up a good Oriental business, and the Ambassador entered into a working agreement with its representative, Mr. Cochran, that gave us the services of an established organization. Mr. Cochran gave generously of his time and effort and the Committee's pictures became feature attractions in the provinces as well as in the cities.

XIII

SOUTH AMERICA and Central America, like Mexico and Spain, were parade-grounds for the agents of Germany. Colombia and Venezuela were bitterly hostile, and in every other country there was a distinct distrust of our sincerity and a very lively fear of our strength. In every city and in every town Germans were prominent in business, and the constant stream of money from Berlin subsidized newspapers and individuals to make a daily and direct attack upon the United States.

Lieut. F. E. Ackerman, a newspaper man of wide experience, was borrowed from the navy and sent on a tour of South America to study methods of news distribution and to organize offices for the Committee. He visited Pernambuco, Rio de Janeiro, Santiago, Lima, Valparaiso, Buenos Aires, and numerous other South American cities, and with the hearty co-operation of American diplomatic and consular officials soon had an intensive publicity campaign on throughout South America.

The commissioner selected for Argentina, Uruguay, and Paraguay was H. H. Sevier, a newspaper man of Austin, Texas, and from his headquarters in Buenos Aires he planned and perfected a publicity organization that swept through the cities and reached down to the very villages. There is not space for the whole report of Mr. Sevier, but organization and results may be gathered from the following excerpts:

HOW WE ADVERTISED AMERICA

The value and importance of such a service may be more fully appreciated if it is understood that before the advent of your Committee the amount of news of any character concerning the United States carried by South American publications was practically negligible. The European news agencies occupied the field without opposition of consequence. The French and English associations naturally devoted their services to the interests of their own countries. The affairs of the United States, even our war activities, were treated lightly. Under subsidies of the German government and German capitalists three daily newspapers were published in Buenos Aires. One, written in the Spanish language, was a positive force, because of the skill with which it distorted the facts and the cleverness of its editorial misrepresentation of the cause of the Allies. The other two, printed in German, gave aid and comfort to the Teutonic element.

The percentage of literacy in Argentina and Uruguay, particularly, is remarkably high, and every newspaper of any importance at all in those countries has a considerable following. The good will and co-operation of the leading journals were secured at the beginning, and within a reasonable length of time 90 per cent. of the publications, of all classes in the countries named, were receiving and using our service. The newspapers of the cities and towns carried daily a specially prepared cable service covering official announcements from Washington, the development of our war preparations, and the extent of our participation in the actual fighting; the progress of our ship-building, munitions manufacture, and the financial, moral, and other aid extended to our allies. These news stories were frequently played up with illustrations of our air and sea craft, our camps, cantonments, and trenches, our factories, and our guns; and with photographs of our statesmen, soldiers, and citizen workers in every branch of war activity.

Weekly and class publications were regularly supplied with special articles and illustrations, carefully prepared to meet their particular requirements and style. The triweekly, semi-weekly, and weekly press of the provinces was furnished with condensed news stories assembled from the more important developments of the period between publication.

It should be mentioned that all news stories and special articles were translated by experts in our offices, and always in the language of the publication receiving our service. During the periods of important military operations and through the exciting times preceding the armistice a day and night service was maintained, with our offices in constant touch with the great newspapers of the three countries. In submitting our matter we invariably stipulated that it was offered for reproduction either in total or in part, at the discretion of the editor, and that no credit to the Committee was necessary. In many instances, however, our credit line was carried, and in no instance, to our knowledge, was our matter garbled or falsely construed.

An important feature of the work of your Buenos Aires office was the preparation, printing, and distribution of pamphlets, posters, circulars, etc. A list of all American business concerns was secured. A card index indicated how much matter each could effectively distribute. The packing-houses, banks, shippers, merchants, and selling agencies cheerfully agreed to inclose our literature in their daily correspondence. Many patriotic institutions and individuals took from us copies of the speeches of President Wilson and other leaders by the thousands, forwarding them to their representatives and customers in all sections of the country. The ever-increasing demand from these sources indicated the interest with which America's message was being received.

The photograpns sent from Washington were captioned and catalogued on their arrival. They were used in profusion in newspapers and magazines both with and without explanatory articles. In addition, and perhaps most effective, were the exhibitions of the pictures in public places. For such displays some one hundred or more light, attractive frames were designed, each frame carrying twelve photographs. These were placed in the show windows of the largest business houses, the lobbies of the leading hotels, and the reading-rooms of various social, commercial, and working-men's clubs. In every city or town of any importance one or more of these frames was conspicuously located. By a carefully worked-out system we were able to change these displays once a week.

In the offices of the Committee files of such American newspapers, magazines, trade journals, etc., as were sent us or could be purchased were kept. These, together with our government reports, the *Official Bulletin*, authoritative articles on banking, industrial, manufacturing, agricultural, and other subjects by

American experts, were at the disposition of the general public. From them data were obtained by educators, journalists, and students. We wrote articles on given subjects and assembled facts and figures for addresses delivered to various organizations and societies. Editors of Argentine, Spanish, French, Italian, and British publications were constantly supplied with material which was desired in order to answer statements of enemy writers.

Personal association with leaders of South American thought was not overlooked or neglected. Your commissioner was frequently extended the privilege of addressing the universities and schools in response to requests from the student bodies for information concerning "North America." A sincere desire on the part of many students to attend universities in the United States, in order that they might perfect themselves in the English or "North American" language and study our life, our laws, and our business methods, was developed, and at the suggestion and with the assistance of Dr. Ernesto Nelson of Buenos Aires and Doctor Galves of the University of Chile a plan for an exchange of North American for South American students was worked out and about to be placed in operation when the activities of the Committee were suspended.

Your commissioner is under obligations to Mr. Frederico Crocker of Montevideo, who acted as local representative in Paraguay; to William Dawson, Esq., American consul at Montevideo, and to the American colony of Uruguay in general. The assistance of Hon. Daniel Mooney, American Minister, and the American residents of Ascension, was of much value in our efforts in Paraguay.

For the work in Peru, Ecuador, and Bolivia the Committee was fortunate in securing the services of C. V. Griffis, a resident of Lima for six years, and the head of an established publicity organization in the form of *The West Coast Leader*, an Anglo-American newspaper. Aside from Mr. Griffis's own ability and expert knowledge, he placed the services of the *Leader* organization—its agents, correspondents, and friends—entirely at the disposition of the Committee, obtaining for its material a comprehensive circulation in territory which would otherwise have been difficult and expensive to cover. Thus in addition to telegraph and mail service reaching the important centers, such as Lima and Arequipa in Peru, La Paz and Oruro in Bolivia, and Guayaquil and Quito in Ecuador, the pamphlet and pictorial publications were sent broadcast through the more remote provinces of the three republics —to the isolated mining-camps, the scattered estates— to points as widely separated and as difficult to reach as Santa Cruz de la Sierra and Trinidad in Bolivia, Moyobamba and the Chanchamayo Valley in Peru, Esmeraldas and Cuenca in Ecuador.

To quote from the report of Mr. Griffis:

It is not my desire in any way to overestimate the importance of the results obtained by the work conducted in this territory. Accurate analysis of these results is, of course, impossible. Yet it cannot be denied that, as a result of the few months' intensive work undertaken by the Committee in this field, the mass of people in all sections of the country have acquired a far more graphic and comprehensive idea of the power and position of the United States, as well as the policies and ideals of the American people, than they ever had before. These conceptions could not possibly have been obtained through ordinary channels, and it is safe to say that the Peruvians and their neighbors have a much clearer idea of the war efforts and achievements of the States than they have of the efforts and achievements of any of our European allies, though the latter were engaged in the war for a much longer period. This clearer conception is due almost wholly to Compub activities, for other agencies of intercommunication made no radical departure in their established policies to meet the radically altered conditions.

What I regard as concrete evidence of some of the statements made in the above paragraph is supplied by the magnificent response of Lima, a city of less than 200,000 inhabitants, to the Fourth Liberty Loan, with a total of $700,000. Lima is far from being a wealthy city, and this subscription was $400,000 more than the maximum set by the committee in charge of the sale of bonds. But the investing public here had become thoroughly convinced of the boundless resources and impregnable economic strength of the States. They could not evade absorbing that impression. The Committee photographs setting forth American industrial resources were constantly surrounded by interesting crowds, while the morning and afternoon papers invariably carried their columns of supplementary data. As a first-hand observer of Latin-American opinion during the past few years I would say that the old conception of the United States held in 1913, an admixture of Mexican and Colombian suspicions and general distrust, has given entirely way in 1919 to a wholly new conception and realization of the full magnitude of American power and policy.

The most important and perhaps the most influential feature of the Compub service from the point of view of this particular field was the daily cable service. Owing to arrangements effected by cable, railway telegraph, and wireless communication two trunk systems were thrown out from the central office in Lima, covering a wide stretch of territory at a very low cost.

The first system was south from Lima, wireless messages being filed at the San Christobal (Lima) radiographic station, which were picked up by the Cachendo wireless station, located near Arequipa on the Southern Railway of Peru. Through arrangement with Mr. L. S. Blaisdell, manager of the Southern, an experienced telegraph operator received the messages from the state wireless service and sent them out over the railway telegraph line to Mollendo, Cuzco, Arequipa, Puno, and La Paz, and intermediate points. At all of these points the messages were given full publicity. Arrangements were being made for a farther extension of this southern trunk line by sending out the messages from La Paz over all of the Bolivian railway telegraph lines, but, owing to the signing of the armistice shortly after this office was opened and the falling off of cable service, no regular service was ever established on the Bolivian railways, though many of the more important messages were given publicity throughout Bolivia in this manner.

The second line was north from Lima, by Central & South American Cable Company, to Payta, Peru, and Guayaquil, Ecuador. At the latter point the messages were filed free of charge on the Guayaquil & Quito Railway telegraph line to Quito, Ecuador, and intermediate points.

The sub-agents co-operating with this office on the southern line wire service were L. S. Blaisdell, manager of the Southern

Railway, at Arequipa, and Mr. Victor Tyree, of Denniston & Company, at La Paz.

Those co-operating with this office on the northern wire service were C. W. Copeland, of the American consulate, Guayaquil, and Prof. E. S. Brown, of the Allied committee at Quito. Expenditure in connection with this service is duly set forth in the accounts of the Lima office, which have been submitted.

By means of the foregoing service the daily cables of the Committee were distributed and published in all of the more important newspapers of Peru, Bolivia, and Ecuador.

In addition to the newspapers, there were many small communities, particularly mining-camps, along the line of the Central Railway of Peru, where no newspapers existed, but where this telegraphic news was received and placed on bulletin-boards. The same condition applied to the Southern Railway system in southern Peru and the Guayaquil & Quito Railway in Ecuador, over which Compub telegrams were transmitted.

As stated in the previous report of the pamphlets received by this office for distribution, some 40 per cent. were retained in Peru, 30 per cent. shipped to Ecuador, and 30 per cent. shipped to Bolivia. Of the amount retained in Peru practically all were sent into the smaller towns and provinces. This was owing to the fact that in the metropolitan centers the daily press and other abundant reading material nullified to a considerable degree the propaganda value of the pamphlet; whereas in the provinces reading matter is exceedingly scarce and difficult to secure and even patent-medicine almanacs are read religiously through. My experience has been that even the most attractive pamphlets, though they may be carefully conserved by their recipients, are rarely if ever read through in the metropolitan centers. Vast sums of money were spent by British propaganda on costly lithographed pamphlets, but it is now generally admitted that this money was inadvisably spent and that more effective results could have been secured by other means. Were it not for the provincial outlet, I personally would have advised the suspension of pamphlet distribution. It might have reached the mark in a few individual cases, but in Lima wide-spread pamphlet distribution would have done more harm than good. For four years pamphlets, British, French, Belgian, and German, had been raining from the heavens, the public were surfeited with them, and pamphlets were actually creating prejudice against their distributors.

HOW WE ADVERTISED AMERICA

The Photographic Service was, beyond question, one of the most effective divisions of Compub activities. The appeal of the picture service was instantaneous, not so much to the press as to the general public. It has been my experience that average newspaper illustrations do not hold a reader's attention very long, while high-quality engravings or preferably original photographs catch and hold the eye of people in every walk of society. Certainly the 12 bulletin-boards which we placed throughout Lima, each carrying 40 to 50 photographs, were never lacking an audience. This system of photographic distribution was highly satisfactory in its results. After rotating on the 12 Lima boards, sets of photographs were sent up the line of the Central Railway to be shown at the various stations and camps, and were also sent out into the provinces and were kept track of until lost or worn out. In this manner each photograph passed before several thousand pairs of eyes, while out of the abundant supply the newspapers were provided with all they could use. The wastage in photographic publicity material was therefore practically *nil*. The poster reproduction of photographs with Spanish captions were also exceedingly popular and permitted us to reach certain provincial districts where the use of photographs would have been prohibitive from the viewpoint of cost. All of the photographic enlargements were suitably framed, and after being exhibited for several weeks in shop-windows were distributed among various leading clubs and other institutions.

The activities of the Committee in other South American countries followed the same lines as those described by Mr. Sevier and Mr. Griffis. In Brazil Ambassador Edwin V. Morgan maintained constant supervision over the work and his success was entirely due to his force and vision. Mr. A. A. Preciado was in charge in Chile, and in Venezuela the American Minister, Mr. Preston McGoodwin, was the directing mind. Mr. S. P. Verner, in the government service in the Panama Canal, gave executive supervision as far as the whole of Central America was concerned. Mr. John Collins, borrowed from the Panama Canal Board, was in charge of the distribution of the Compub service, taking it out of the air at Darien and translating and relaying it to many cities in Central America where no other news was received from any source.

Fortunately, there are now two American news associations—the Associated Press and the United Press—operating successfully in South America with a rapidly increasing clientèle. They are furnishing an excellent and comprehensive service and will undoubtedly prove indispensable in carrying on the campaign for the permanent establishment of mutual knowledge, understanding, and friendship which the Committee conceived and placed in operation.

25

XIV

THROUGHOUT the summer of 1917, while the Foreign
Section was building, we sent a daily cable service to
Petrograd for distribution through Vestnik, the official
news association. For contact work we were forced to
depend upon the activities and influences of such American
organizations as the Red Cross, Young Men's Christian
Association, and volunteer groups formed by the American colonies in Petrograd and Moscow for the specific
purpose of "making Russia understand America."

The temporary nature of the Root mission, and the
erratic activities of the various "volunteer groups," brought
home to us the imperative need of a continuous educational
campaign under a central control, and Mr. Sisson, detached
from his duties as associate chairman, was sent to Russia
with full authority to work out a complete Committee
organization. He sailed on October 27th, reaching Petrograd November 25, 1917, and his report tells the story
pointedly and concisely:

The Bolshevik-Proletarian revolution had begun November
7th, and the city was still under the closest Red Guard military
control. I was told by the Americans on the scene that there
was no possibility of any open governmental activity. This
did not seem logical to me, but it necessitated a careful preliminary survey.

In a week's time I had convinced myself not only that it was

MALCOLM W. DAVIS

GRAHAM R. TAYLOR

ARTHUR BULLARD

READ LEWIS

possible to go ahead, but that the best way was to go ahead openly. This plan, however, required the use of the mechanical facilities wholly in the control of the Bolshevik government—telegraph agencies, printing-shops, and, to a lesser degree, distributing agencies.

As an example of the chaotic condition of affairs, the Bolsheviki had suppressed all the existing and opposing bourgeois newspapers, leaving for the chief publications in Petrograd their official newspapers, the *Isvestia* and the *Pravda*. Such other newspapers as appeared were being obliged to change their names almost with each issue, so fast did the suppressions come.

When I left the United States our cable service was supposed to be ready to begin to feed into the Russian governmental distributing organization, the Petrograd Telegraph Agency, which in Russia corresponds to the Associated Press in the United States. The revolution, however, had broken the service. Efforts to replace it had been made by the use of the wireless station at Lyons, France, the receiving station being at Moscow. The project failed because the Moscow station itself was almost immediately put out of commission. In Russia we would not have known of the effort had not a few sentences of one garbled message been picked up a few days before inefficient operators (or intent) finally wrecked the instruments at the station.

The first job, therefore, was to restore the cable service. This was done after an interchange of cables with Washington, and after finding that the Petrograd Telegraph Agency desired to have and would use the cables.

I called Arthur Bullard up from Moscow, where of his own initiative he had been acting as a volunteer in the consul's office in preparing a mail service for provincial papers, and made him the director of the Russian News Division of the Committee. I also commandeered Graham Taylor, Jr., who had been engaged on work in the German prison-camps in Russia until we went to war, and put him in charge of the Petrograd office. This was done in order to enable Mr. Bullard to return to Moscow and organize an office there.

We opened an office at 4 Gorokovaya for the receipt of cable messages, and put in a translating force. The messages, as soon as translated, were fed into the Petrograd Telegraph Agency in Petrograd and theoretically were telegraphed all over Russia, as well as released to the Petrograd newspapers. Such was the disorganization of the telegraph lines, however, that in practice we found it at once necessary to install a courier service to Moscow, and to make the larger part of the national distribution from there. In both places we also released direct as exigencies required.

In Moscow each week we assembled the cable material in pamphlet form, added to it educational mail and article material and distributed the pamphlets to the provincial press, and to organizations where we deemed it useful.

We adopted for ourselves the Russian name Amerikansky Bureau Pachata (the American Press Bureau), and attached a governmental symbol to indicate its official nature.

Both the British and the French did their publicity work as private organizations, and it was a matter of interest to me that the head of the French department came to me before I left Petrograd and said that ours was the right way. The British organization, Cosmos, was raided and closed by the Bolsheviki the last week in December. The French never put out anything openly. We were not seriously interfered with throughout the winter.

The middle of December found our news organization in operation. One of the first impressions I had got of Petrograd was of its billboard possibilities. Every street, including the Nevsky, was papered up and down with placards and proclamations, mostly emanating from the Soviet. The first of President Wilson's Russian messages came in early December. As I feared, after reading it, the official newspapers refused to print it in full, and misused and misinterpreted such parts as they did print. Other papers also used it insufficiently, so I made up my mind to put it on the billboard. I was advised this would be regarded as a challenge by the Bolshevik government, but this view did not appear reasonable to me. I went about the matter openly, gave the job of printing to the biggest government printing establishment in Petrograd, a plant that would compare favorably with all but a few in the United States, and negotiated with a bill-poster agency to put up the message. The bill-posting man was the only person to show any fear of the outcome, but he needed the business and decided to take a chance. He played "safety first," and hired soldiers to do the pasting. The result was that fifty thousand copies of the President's message were posted one morning throughout Petrograd without any hindrance whatever. This posting was followed by a street hand distribution of three hundred thousand copies—in the street-cars, in the theaters, hotels, stores, and to the street crowds.

Similar plans were started in Moscow, but rioting broke out and prevented success. The third process of printing, the turning of the speech to pamphlet use, was done at Moscow.

The experience with this message enabled us to do the big job on the President's message of January 8th, with its statement of terms of any possible peace. We had learned the machinery. The speech began to reach us January 10th, but did not come complete until January 11th. A successful maneuver enabled us to get it used in full in the *Isvestia*, the direct organ of the Soviets. This in itself gave a complete all-Russia circulation among the Soviets. There was liberal use of the message in nearly all of the newspapers.

The Petrograd posters were up January 13th. The street distribution, again of three hundred thousand, followed a few days later. The Moscow distribution was done almost simultaneously.

On this message German distribution was essential. One million copies were printed in German. Of this quantity three hundred thousand were put across the northern line into the German line, and two hundred thousand similarly at the central and the southern front. A half-million went to German prison-camps in Russia, for the reason that these prisoners were expected soon to return to Germany.

The German distribution was done by an organization of soldiers through the help of Jerome Davis, of the Young Men's Christian Association, who had used them for package distribution. The Young Men's Christian Association as a body had nothing to do with the work. This soldiers' organization was later made a part of our own machinery, and was used with high effectiveness in the distribution of German and Hungarian versions of President Wilson's speech of February 11th. It worked along the line of the German advance into Russia, and fulfilled its instructions to scatter the messages in territory about to be occupied by the German army. The head of this organization was B. Morgenstern.

Had the Germans entered Petrograd in late February they would have been greeted by posters in German, of the President's messages of January 8th and February 11th. One hundred thousand copies of the former were run the middle of February to provide for this contingency.

In the last week in February we encountered our first definite Bolshevik stoppage. The colored cartoon poster, showing the arm of German force stabbing the people's hand and tramping upon the people's banner of liberty, was confiscated on the press by order of the Bolshevik government.

Why?

Smolny laughed at us when we asked it.

We asked in order to see whether Smolny would laugh.

The News Division moved into larger quarters on the Nevsky the last week in February, the week that saw the exit from Petrograd of the embassies, consulates, and the missions, including the American Embassy, the American consul, the American Military Mission, and the American Red Cross. The change had been planned for weeks earlier. We concluded to be found going ahead until we could go no farther. So large American flags were draped across the windows, and the division moved in.

The Film Division headquarters were on the Kazansky, half a block from the Nevsky, facing the cathedral. They were in charge of Guy Croswell Smith as director. The machine stood ready to receive new films by January 1st. The failure of Hart, of the Young Men's Christian Association, to bring through a quarter of a million feet of film intended for us kept us from saturating Russia with American films in the early winter. The second allotment of films given into the custody of Bernstein had reached Stockholm when the Finnish revolution of the last days of January closed the gates into Russia. No couriers came into Petrograd after February 1st.

Smith and I found both Hart and the Bernstein films still in Scandinavia in April.

With such films as he had on hand Mr. Smith did fine work. The "Uncle Sam Immigrant" film was put out with a camouflage title, "All for Peace." The finished title would have read "All for Peace Through War," but we left it to the audiences to find that out for themselves. The biggest moving-picture theater in Petrograd ran both films, and they fed rapidly throughout the whole of Russia. We traced them from the Arctic Ocean to the Black Sea and far into Siberia.

I arranged for an option on a Petrograd theater, and the purpose was to lease similarly in Moscow, and after a run for advertising purposes, to turn the films into trade channels, to add incentive to circulation. It is the method to use in Russia and, in general, nearly everywhere.

In my opinion, the best individual work done in Russia for the United States was that of Arthur Bullard in writing the pamphlet, "Letters to a Russian Friend," an interpretation of the highest order of America. We published it in Russian as a Red, White, and Blue Book. Three hundred thousand copies were distributed.

The Moscow office continued the distribution of the January and February messages in the remote sections of Russia after March 1st. The total distribution of the Fourteen Points speech, including the Hungarian and German text, was more than four million. Three hundred thousand handbills containing both messages were distributed ahead of the German advance in Ukraine. The President's Baltimore speech was printed in Irkutsk, Omsk, Samara, Petrograd, Moscow, and Ekaterinburg.

A few weeks after my own departure from Russia, in the spring of 1918, it became definitely clear to me that the purpose of the Germans and of the Russian Bolsheviks was to bring about an untenable situation in Russia for all officials and citizens of Entente countries. The purpose was to limit their freedom and their activities more and more, and finally to expel them. It was my hope that all countries would see this and get their nationals out of Russia before they should be thrown out humiliatingly. But at that time the international political world could not believe that this outcome was inevitable.

I was sure, however, that within a few weeks it would be impossible to get material into European Russia. Accordingly, I took the responsibility of ordering Mr. Bullard and his American group, save one man, to remove themselves from the Bolshevik area of Russia. Our chief office at Moscow, and even the office at Petrograd, remained open, the former in charge of Read Lewis, and the latter in charge of a Russian assistant. The Moscow office was finally raided and closed by the Bolsheviks the first week in September, 1918.

It was necessary to shift the organization as a whole to a place where it could have a dependable base of supplies. Obviously, this place was Siberia, affording the opportunity for a sound and steady penetration along the line of the Siberian railroad as fast as order was restored along this railroad line. The eventual goal would be Moscow.

This whole project of transfer was successfully carried out. Two men, Malcolm Davis and William Adams Brown, worked their way out through Siberia, and in the early summer had opened new offices at Harbin and Vladivostok.

Meantime Mr. Bullard, accompanied by Mr. George Bakeman, Mr. Otto Glaman, and Mr. Taylor, secured passage from Archangel to Halifax and about July 1st reached the United States. This nucleus was at once equipped for the remainder of the journey around the world. The additional staff, made up of newspaper men, translators, teachers, moving-picture experts, and office helpers, included Dr. Joshua Rosett, Franklin Clarkin, Edwin Schoonmaker, Robert Winters, George Bothwell, Sid Evans, Prof. William Russell, William Carnes, Lem A. Dever, Phil Norton, Dennis J. Haggerty, and H. Y. Barnes. Seven hundred and fifty thousand feet of the best moving-picture film were sent, together with high-powered projecting machines. Four weeks after he set foot on American soil Mr. Bullard was sailing with the first contingent from a Pacific port.[1]

Too great credit cannot be given to the representatives of the Committee who stayed with the work from bitter first to bitter last, enduring every hardship, running every risk, and called upon at every turn to fight overwhelming difficulties. Arthur Bullard, in full charge after Mr. Sisson's departure, not only gave a full measure of devotion and ability, but also his health. It is not possible in this brief space to print the full record of effort and accomplishment, but the following summaries will serve to convey some idea of the campaign carried forward entirely by individual courage and initiative. Mr. Read Lewis was in charge of the work in Moscow and Petrograd until the offices were closed by the Soviet, and despite civil war, governmental opposition, and his inability to receive our cable and mail services he fought on. To quote:

[1] Mr. Sisson's report on the German-Bolshevik conspiracy is a separate publication of the Committee on Public Information.

THE RUSSIAN CAMPAIGN

During July and August the principal work of the Russian Press Division was the publication and distribution of the *American Bulletin*. This sixteen-page pamphlet, designed for the general reading public, was issued weekly and distributed free of charge to a mailing-list of forty thousand names. The bulletin contained the cable news despatches, so long as they were received, and articles and paragraphs descriptive of the different phases of American life. The bulletin mailing-list included all newspapers and publications, eight hundred co-operative unions and their more than ten thousand constituent societies, thousands of schools and libraries, all the Soviet and government institutions of the country, trade unions, teachers' associations, the old zemstvos, commercial and manufacturing associations, many business houses and individuals. The building up of this mailing-list was a matter of continuous and careful work. Our attempt was to reach not only the sources of public opinion, but at least some part of the people themselves. Not a day went by without at least one letter from a provincial Soviet, or one of its departments, expressing interest in our work, forwarding names of local organizations, and requesting sometimes as many as fifty copies of each issue for its use. Thus, despite the territory impossible to reach on account of civil war, we were distributing fifty thousand copies of each issue of the bulletin.

In addition to the *American Bulletin* the bureau also issued during the summer a translation of "How the War Came to America," and a pamphlet collecting several of the speeches of President Wilson, principally those of January 8th on terms of general peace, of February 11th replying to the Central Powers, and of April 7th at Baltimore. Of each of these two pamphlets one hundred thousand copies had been printed and were being distributed. We continued to print and distribute the very successful "Letters of an American Friend." Of this four hundred thousand copies had been printed and distributed and a new order was on the press. In the form of leaflets we issued and distributed both the President's Red Cross speech of May 18th in New York and his speech of June 11th to the Mexican editors. Four million copies, indeed, of the speech of January 8th were distributed throughout the country and at the front. Copies of it for posting had been sent to all railroad stations in Russia. In default of a greater variety of literature for general distribution we printed of the last several issues of the bulletin a second fifty thousand for distribution outside of its regular mailing-list. To pamphlets like "Letters of an American Friend" and the speeches of President Wilson, the bureau aimed to give a far more general distribution than to the weekly bulletin. Copies of such pamphlets were of course sent to the bulletin mailing-list. In addition the bureau maintained a staff of eleven couriers and messengers for the work of distribution. Two, for example, devoted their entire time to daily distribution at the railroad stations in Moscow; two more to distribution at the factories and co-operative societies in the Moscow district. A special effort was made to reach personally with our literature each of the many congresses and conferences with their delegates from different parts of the country. To these meetings and conventions our messengers carried subscription lists and in this way were able to add to the bulletin mailing-list. The rest of our courier staff were employed in making regular trips to the provinces. The complete breakdown of the transportation system in Russia made it essential, if we were consistently to reach the provincial cities and districts with our literature, that we should have our own system of distribution. The trips for our provincial messengers were carefully planned, each man being given a list of the organizations, factories, persons, etc., to which he was to distribute literature in the several cities which he was to visit. Nearly all men engaged in this department of our work were members of the Society of Escaped Prisoners—that is, they had been common soldiers in the Russian army and subsequently prisoners in Germany, from which they had escaped.

Through its department of distribution the bureau had thus distributed, during the month from July 15th to August 15th, 10,112 pieces of literature at congresses and conventions; 51,600 at railroad stations in Moscow; 55,951 at factories, to works committees and trade unions; 38,007 to co-operative societies and shops in Moscow and vicinity; and 167,950 in the provinces by the bureau's couriers. This, in addition to a small miscellaneous distribution at the offices of the committee in Petrograd and Moscow and in addition to the distribution of the bulletin by post, made the total distribution for the month 479,333.

It is obvious, of course, that if we could have supplied to and had published by the Russian newspapers the same or material equivalent to that which we ourselves printed and distributed, we should have employed a far more economical and extensive method of publication and distribution. The publication of our own pamphlets, and especially of our weekly paper, however, seemed essential, not only because of the utter demoralization of the Russian press, but as a concrete evidence and expression of America's policy of friendship and helpful co-operation with the Russian people. Following the assassination of Ambassador Mirbach early in July, all of the bourgeois press was permanently closed, and until I left Moscow, August 28, 1918, none but a few Bolshevik newspapers appeared.

All through July and part of August, while the Russian press was fuming at Anglo-French imperialists, never a word was said about America, although it was well known that we were also parties with England and France to the treaty with the Murmansk Soviet. The different attitude which the Russian newspapers and government have taken toward America, as distinguished from the other allies, has been due not only to what America is, but also, I believe, to our propaganda, and the efforts we have made to make America understood. It has been due to the fact that our propaganda was distinguished from that of the English and French, has aimed at reaching the broad masses of the Russian people. We have tried to make friends with the people themselves. That we have at least in a small measure succeeded is attested by many letters of appreciation received from simple people, often from scarcely literate peasants and working-men.

As soon as Mr. Lewis reached Stockholm in September, 1918, he was ordered to Archangel and remained on duty there until the late winter of 1919, a notable contribution of citizen service.

Malcolm Davis and William Adams Brown opened telegraph and wireless-receiving offices at Vladivostok and Harbin in June, 1918. Arthur Bullard and the staff of reinforcements joined them in the late summer. The organization was approaching the top of its stride in February, 1919, when its demobilization order came. All the staff recognized the inevitability of the ending of the work and understood the reasons for it, yet there was not a member of the organization who did not feel that it came at a most unfortunate time, considered from the point of view of Siberia and of Russian relationship generally. Other nations were developing energetic propaganda campaigns, and the American engineers were finally taking up the task of railroad reorganization and the American Red Cross extending its relief activities. These considerations, together with the fact that it was a critical time in the discussion of Russian-Allied relations, made the withdrawal of the American Information Bureau regrettable. That this was not merely the feeling of men engaged in the work, but that it was a view shared by impartial representatives of the government of the United States of America as well as by Russians and by representatives of some of the other Allies, is evidenced by the messages to Washington of Ambassador Morris, who was in Vladivostok on a special mission from Tokio, from Consul-General Harris and all his consular staff, by the telegram of Motosada Zuomoto, head of the Japanese Information Bureau, and by letters from Russians, all urging the continuance of the work, if possible.

Mr. Davis and Mr. Brown originally left Moscow for a survey of Siberia in March, 1918. To quote from the report of Mr. Davis:

We found the press under the strict control of the Bolshevik régime. No papers with a political color were being published in any town visited except the official Bolshevik organ and one or two others of the most radical Socialist revolutionary tendencies. In general, there was less freedom for the press in Siberia under the Bolshevik régime than in Petrograd and Moscow under the same régime. The separate peace had just been concluded between the German government and the "Russian Federated Socialistic Soviet Republic."

We proceeded on the same policy which had won a measure of success in Moscow and Petrograd, since we were under orders to attempt to continue publicity in Bolshevik Russia and Siberia.

THE RUSSIAN CAMPAIGN

It had been decided not to attack Bolshevism or discuss political questions in Russia directly, and to get across as much information as possible about the principles of democratic government, the aims of America and the Allies, the war organization of America and the growing supremacy of the Allied arms, the actions of the German government in Russia and other occupied territories and spheres of influence, and as much general news and special-article material as possible about political and social conditions and ideas in the United States. This work was regarded as tending to strengthen every sane democratic movement existing in the country, to give information that might serve as a basis for working out new problems of government in the country, and to create as much of friendly feeling and understanding as possible among the common people in Russia.

We met with varying attitudes on the part of the editors and of the leaders of the soviets or councils which were in charge of affairs everywhere. While frankly antagonistic to America as a "capitalists' country," they had no objection to our carrying on a campaign of information so long as they were sure they knew what we were doing and that we were not doing anything directly against Bolshevist organization.

We had at this time the war anniversary speech of President Wilson, and this we had printed as a wall poster, in fifty thousand copies, for posting in and around Omsk and for mail distribution. The circulation was carried out, after our departure, by a Russian assistant whom we engaged, under the supervision of American Consul Thomson. An additional ten thousand copies of this poster were later sent to Vice-Consul Thomas in Krasnoyarsk for display and distribution there. We also arranged at once for the distribution of about fifteen thousand copies each of Mr. Bullard's pamphlet "Letters of an American Friend," which had been very successful, and also of the weekly *American Bulletin* from the Moscow office.

Going on to Krasnoyarsk, we stayed long enough to form an impression of all the editors and Soviet leaders there, and to engage a local Russian representative, who was to work in contact with the American vice-consul. We also arranged for the circulation of material through the co-operative unions; and for the regular forwarding of telegraphic news and printed literature from the central offices in Moscow. In order to circulate copies of the President's speeches at all, we had to get the official permission of the Irkutsk commissars, who were determining entirely what should be published in the city at the time. We went to call on Yanson, the commissar for foreign affairs of the Siberian administration, which was located in Irkutsk. He was at first absolutely opposed to publication of anything representing an American or Allied point of view.

"You know," said the commissar, "we regard all established governments with antagonism, for we aim at a world-wide revolution which will overthrow the power of the capitalists everywhere."

"Do you mean," asked we, "that you recognize no difference between such a government as the government of the United States of America and the Prussian military government of Germany?"

"Absolutely none," replied the commissar. "America is one financial imperialism and Germany is another. Both systematically exploit the working-class and the people. So far as we are concerned they are one and the same; and we are against them both!"

We pointed out to him that the address which we proposed to publish and to circulate in and around Irkutsk was an official utterance of the Chief Executive of our nation, that it represented the point of view of the government of one of the great Powers both with regard to the issues of the war in general and with regard to Russia, and that as such it should be published as news, not as propaganda. We got the necessary rubber-stamped permission to circulate the copies of the address on the strength of this argument, and proceeded to plaster the town with copies of the address.

In the course of doing the work in Siberia we got constant evidence of friendly feeling for America and confidence in her intentions on the part of the common people not allied with the Bolsheviks. These people were completely suppressed for the time being, however, and they could not make their point of view effective, since the Bolsheviks had all the guns. They did take our material and circulate it. We got such expressions of feeling from the railroad men along the Trans-Siberian line, and from the students, members of professional unions, and coöperative society workers in cities where we stopped. This feeling was also evidenced in an incident which occurred after we left Irkutsk. We had left all our printed material and special-article material with the American consul, asking him to give it as much circulation as possible, since we were ordered out of the region. He gave the material to a representative of an American firm in Irkutsk. There the material was displayed on a counter, and in a very short time it was all gone. The consul afterward related to us how people would come in and ask for copies and also for permission to circulate them among their friends. Representatives of the railroad workers' unions also came in and asked for permission to reprint at their own cost some of the material about America, for distribution among their members.

Having discharged their task completely, Mr. Davis and Mr. Brown were now faced with the problem of getting out of Bolshevik Siberia. Three days' travel by train and then a boat trip up the Selenga River brought them to the border, where they slipped across, after which Ford automobiles carried them through Mongolia and across the Gobi Desert. Peking was reached on May 31st, where they received instructions to proceed to Harbin, Manchuria, on the line of the Chinese Eastern Railway, managed by a Russian directorate and forming an important link on the Trans-Siberian line from the west to Vladivostok. The city of Harbin at that time formed what might be called the external political capital of Russia, having as residents influential members of the Russian business and political groups most strongly opposed to the Bolshevik régime. It therefore offered a very fertile field for publicity, combining in its population the elements above mentioned with the Russian workers in the large railroad repair-shops of the Chinese Eastern Railway.

Purchasing a few office supplies in Peking, and assembling all available material, Mr. Davis and Mr. Brown started for Harbin on June 10th, arriving two days later. Mr. Davis's report continues as follows:

The state of public opinion in Harbin and in the general section around it and reached by its newspapers was very uncertain. The German advance on the western front was still in full progress, and the fresh forces of the American army had not yet been thrown into action. The submarine campaign was continuing, and the facts of American shipbuilding were not known as they needed to be known in this part of the world. The Allies had not yet adopted a policy of active aid to loyal Russians against the Bolsheviks and German-Magyar ex-prisoner forces, so no one knew what would be the issue of the political situation in Siberia and Russia. Consequently, there were a great many people who were listening to the incessant German propaganda that the Russian Bolshevik revolution had destroyed the last chance of the Allies to win, that the entrance of America into the war was too late to save the situation, that at least the Allies would be forced to a compromise peace in which Germany would gain the main advantages or else that Germany would actually win the decisive victory in the war and thus dominate the international situation. In Russian circles there were many who believed that a monarchy supported by an alliance with the Prussian monarchy would be the best thing for Russia; and there were many others who believed that any force which could bring order in Russia would be beneficial, and who, consequently, were ready to turn to Germany for that result.

We had arranged before leaving Peking for the forwarding from the American Legation there of the daily news cable service of the Committee on Public Information from Washington. We also found in the American consulate's care some cases of motion-picture films, about sixty different films in all, some of them in duplicate and triplicate. There were also some books and pamphlets from America about American conditions and war organization, sent by the Committee in Washington. The Committee had also sent to the American consul, Mr. Moser, the sum of five thousand dollars to finance a campaign of publicity in and around Harbin, and Mr. Moser, working under great pressure in the complicated situation in Harbin, had engaged H. Curtis Vezey, formerly editor of *The Russian Daily News* in Petrograd, to act as publicity agent. We retained Mr. Vezey as an assistant, moved into the temporary office which he had engaged, and started to work at the job of changing public opinion regarding the war.

We began to flood the newspapers with telegrams, translated ready into Russian and furnished free, regarding the numbers of American troops being transported each month to France, the numbers of new ships being built for the battle-fleet and merchant marine, amounts of Liberty Loans and other subscriptions for the war, amounts of foodstuffs shipped to the Allies, and refutations of rumors about paralyzing strikes in the United States and proofs of the unity of the people in the effort against the Central Empires. Fortunately, the newspapers were either friendly to the Allies or open-minded; and further, they were comparatively poor and had no good telegraph news service. The appearance of the free American service was a boon to them and they printed nearly every line of news that we gave to them.

We also began to translate special articles on American national institutions and organizations, on labor conditions and the labor movement, and the reasons why labor was supporting the government in the war and would continue to support it, on various aspects of the life of the people in America, political, social, economic, tending to show what advantages they already have and what powers they have to change conditions constantly for the better, all intended to show the reasons for American unity and loyalty. Many of these articles were also printed, despite the comparatively small size of Russian newspapers. The changed tone of editorial utterances regarding the war showed the cumulative effect of the propaganda. All utterances by the President were also translated and sent to the papers, and they were invariably published and commented on.

During all of this period our assistant, Mr. Vezey, whom we employed on a part-time arrangement, was publishing our news in English in his *Russian Daily News*, Occasionally, when especially important news arrived, an evening telegraph bulletin in Russian was gotten out by *The Russian Daily News* and sold on the streets, which made a very useful and effective form of quick-action publicity.

We sorted our motion-picture films into programs and arranged for a week of American official motion pictures in one of the Harbin theaters for the benefit of the Russian Red Cross. The pictures which we had were mainly military and industrial, with a few travel pictures of America and some weekly news review films. We had the excellent film, "The Remaking of a Nation," and also much other film showing army-training in the United States. We divided the films off into programs as well balanced as possible; and then covered the town with advertisements

26

and distributed handbills for the week's program, which we entitled "America for the Allies."

The pictures were well attended by mixed audiences and made a considerable impression. Those showing the efficient drilling of the new army of America and the power of the battle-fleet, however, seemed to impress them most of all. The impression which we were trying to make constantly was that America was with the Allies, and for them, heart and soul, and that she was throwing into the fight every bit of strength and resource that she could make effective, a fact which was making the ultimate triumph of the Allied arms sure. The pictures also served as an excellent prelude to the news which we were able to give shortly afterward about the first victorious American drive at Château-Thierry, and the turning of the tide of battle which developed into victory.

The pictures had English flash titles, so we arranged to show them with a lecturer, who explained each picture in Russian and who answered any questions about it from the audience. After finishing the showings in Harbin, the pictures were sent out along the line of the Chinese Eastern Railroad in Manchuria to the Russian theaters in Tsitsikar, Hailar, and Manchuria Station. On their return they were sent to the office which had by that time been opened in Vladivostok to have Russian titles put in.

When we first arrived in Harbin the lines to Vladivostok and to Siberia were, of course, closed. The Bolsheviks were still in control and fighting between them and Semenov was going on along the line between Manchuria Station and Chita. The Harbin newspapers, however, were the only ones in Russian in Manchuria, and were sent to every Russian community. Consequently, by placing material in these papers we were reaching all Russian newspaper readers. The Harbin papers were also sent through whenever possible, by various individual ways, to Vladivostok, to Habarovsk, to Blagovestchensk, and to Chita; and there they were read and often reprinted by the editors of local papers. In this way, consequently, we were reaching as much of the Siberian field as possible at the moment. When a paper was established at Manchuria Station, we started sending our telegrams and special articles there; and when another was started in Sakhalin, just across the river in Manchuria from Blagovestchensk, we began sending material there.

The President's speech at Mount Vernon, which we printed

in a pamphlet to the number of ten thousand copies in Harbin, in addition to securing publication in the newspapers, was distributed in Harbin and through Manchuria in these various ways.

The American proclamation of August 3d, regarding Russia, caused a very animated discussion in the Harbin press. We printed twenty thousand copies of the statement and distributed them as well as possible in Harbin and Manchuria, sending some to Sakhalin for Blagovestchensk, and some to Vladivostok. In this distribution, the American Railroad Mission was very helpful. We also had selections from the announcement made into plates for projection on the moving-picture screen and showed them in two motion-picture theaters. From the large number of photographs sent us from Washington by the Committee, twenty-five were selected, and after some difficulty we arranged to have cuts made of them and have them printed in the form of post-cards for sale in railroad stations and stationery stores.

The triumph of the Czechoslovaks in the summer opened up the Siberian Railroad, first from Harbin to Vladivostok, and afterward through to the Urals, giving the Committee a chance for general Siberian work. For some time Admiral Knight, commander of the cruiser *Brooklyn* off Vladivostok, had been receiving the Committee's wireless reports and giving them to the American consulate for distribution, so that the field was not entirely virgin. Mr. Brown, going from Harbin to Vladivostok with motion pictures, opened the campaign with successful showings of our films, and Mr. Davis, following him, established the usual Committee office. A staff was picked up on the ground and authorized translations of the daily news service as well as the special articles contained in the Poole service commenced to flow steadily into the press. Printing arrangements were made for the pamphlet, "Letters of an American Friend," and a daily bulletin in English was issued for the information of the Allied consulates and officials. This bulletin also went to the French Red Cross for translation for the French troops and was also put into Russian for courier transmission to papers not reached by wire. Mr. Carl Kranz, given authority to secure offices and an office force, did his work so well that when Mr. Bullard and his party arrived in Vladivostok he found a publicity machine of such smoothness and power that he was enabled instantly to make Vladivostok his headquarters, turning Harbin into a subsidiary.

A film campaign that reached from the theaters to the schools, the churches, and the homes was at once begun, and these exhibitions were a powerful factor in our appeal to the Siberian masses. Some of the difficulties under which the Committee labored are set forth in the following memorandum filed by G. S. Bothwell, technical director of the Motion Picture Division:

The building we worked in is like most other buildings in Vladivostok. It has neither water-supply nor sewerage systems, as this is almost unknown in this place. In order to turn out any quantity of these titles we found it necessary to have running water, and at an expense of twenty-five thousand rubles we put in a water-supply and sewerage system which meets all requirements of the city laws. However, after this system was completed and all arrangements had been agreed upon, the city authorities refused to turn water on and kept us three weeks or more without running water.

We found it necessary to establish a machine-shop, and as the Russian government had many lathes lying on the wharves rusting and fast becoming worthless, we tried to requisition one. We were switched from one party to another by the Russian authorities until we were fighting-mad and at last pinned them down to facts. We were informed that if we deposited sixteen thousand rubles in a bank a commission would let us know how much they would charge us for a lathe worth at the most fifty dollars. Despite these obstacles, for the past month we have been turning out about twenty-five hundred feet of completed titles each day, quite a number of still pictures, and some motion pictures, both negative and positive.

About the middle of October we received our shipment of machines and film that we brought to Japan and the Japanese held up when we reshipped from Kobe to Vladivostok. This is a long story, and it is not possible to exactly place the responsibility.

However, after we received this film we made many attempts to get distribution and found it most discouraging. The picture-houses would not use these pictures without Russian titles and graciously offered to show them for us if we would insert good Russian titles and pay them for exhibiting first-class American films.

We then got the Vladivostok Zemstvo (Russian self-government for local districts) interested, with fine results. They agreed to take our industrial and educational pictures throughout Siberia and show them in the towns and villages if we would supply the complete outfit, consisting of generator, motion-picture machine, etc., which we gladly did, and the results were most satisfactory. The first show was for the agricultural districts and the reports were simply great. The village commune is common all over Siberia, and these people in many instances want to buy tractors and other farming implements collectively. They ask no end of questions and beg for farming instructors from America. We now handle all the educational work through the Vladivostok Zemstvo with gratifying success. Our Russian titles are real Russian and they like them.

Mr. Glaman had the same obstacles to overcome in the matter of printing. It was difficult to find presses, and the shortage of paper compelled him to buy old stock in Shanghai and Japan. The same difficulties were encountered by the publication department, directed editorially by Malcolm Davis and Graham Taylor, and under the business management of Mr. Glaman. Despite every discouragement, the work went on, as the following list of publications will show:

The Friendly Word.—A weekly magazine; 14 issues totaling 288 pages and 522,350 copies. Some of this material was drawn from the cable service of the Committee on Public Information, particularly the texts of the notes exchanged between the various nations leading up to the armistice, and the speeches of President Wilson. The main portion of the material was received from the Foreign Press Bureau and included many articles and news notes which were used in full, others which were shortened or condensed, and others which were used as the basis for the preparation of material adapted to meet space conditions or the interest of the Siberian public. All of the illustrations appearing in *The Friendly Word* are from half-tones or photographs which were sent by the Foreign Press Bureau.

The remaining portion of the material used in *The Friendly Word* was almost wholly written by members of the staff of the Russian Division. This included various editorial notes and articles; the articles on American Activity in Siberia, by Arthur Bullard; the series of articles by Prof. W. F. Russell on the Development of Education in America; a series of four articles on the League of Nations, by E. D. Schoonmaker, and a series of four articles on health—Typhus, Tuberculosis, Milk, and Infant Feeding—by Dr. Joshua Rosett.

This distribution was greatly facilitated by the generous co-operation of the Czechoslovak authorities in permitting the shipment of bundles of copies in the weekly mail-car operated by the Czechoslovaks on the Trans-Siberian Railroad.

From each of the offices of the Committee copies were sent, as far as possible, to individual addresses. The mailing-lists included governmental and local officials, libraries, reading-rooms, universities and schools, officers and members of zemstvos, co-operative societies and peasant unions, persons who wrote letters expressing interest and requesting copies, etc. In many cases organizations such as zemstvos, co-operative societies, peasant unions, teachers' organizations, literary societies, and commercial and industrial bodies took an active interest in distributing copies to their members.

Letters of an American Friend.—Of this pamphlet of 24 pages, written by Arthur Bullard, director of the Russian Division, expressing the friendly interest of America in the democratic progress of the Russian people and explaining the principles of American democracy, there were published 150,000 copies.

American Activity in Siberia.—This pamphlet of 8 pages, containing a reprint of an article by Arthur Bullard, director of the Russian Division, which originally appeared in *The Friendly Word*, was published in an edition of 100,000 copies.

America and Peace.—This pamphlet of 16 pages, compiled by

THE RUSSIAN CAMPAIGN

M. W. Davis, containing, with an introduction, the texts of notes exchanged between the various nations in the negotiations leading up to the armistice, and passages from President Wilson's speeches bearing on peace, was published in an edition of 100,550.

The German Plot to Control Russia.—This pamphlet of 16 pages, by M. W. Davis, after consultation with Mr. Bullard, containing the substance of the documents in the Sisson report made public by the Committee on Public Information to show the character of German activity in Russia, was published in an edition of 100,000 copies.

Typhus handbill.—This handbill, containing a reprint of an article in *The Friendly Word*, designed to give information in popular form concerning ways whereby each individual and family could help combat the epidemic of typhus in Siberia, was printed in an edition of 24,000.

Development of Education in the United States.—This booklet of 64 pages, containing a reprint of the 14 educational articles by Prof. W. F. Russell of the State University of Iowa which were originally published in *The Friendly Word*, was printed in an edition of 50,000 and, in accordance with instructions from the main office of the Committee in Washington, the entire edition, issued just prior to the termination of the Committee's work in Siberia, was turned over to the American consul in Vladivostok for distribution under the supervision of the various consular officers in Siberia.

Speeches of President Wilson.—This booklet of 48 pages was published in an edition of 100,000 copies, 7,000 on a good quality of paper for distribution to libraries, reading-rooms, schools, universities, and officials, and 93,000 on cheap paper for popular distribution.

It is regrettable indeed that there is not space for publication of the entire report by Mr. Davis on the Siberian work, but his closing chapters pay some deserved tributes and contain some very valuable observations. To quote:

The scope of this report does not give opportunity to include the reports of the individual field men in Chita, Irkutsk, Omsk, Ekaterinburg, and Chelyabinsk, which contain much interesting detail. They worked loyally and hard in the service, with a spirit of co-operation which made the whole relationship a pleasure. Special notice is due to the service of W. A. Brown, Jr., who had the hardest physical conditions to face. He traveled on freight-cars and crowded third and fourth-class cars constantly, and never complained of hardship if a piece of work could be done. He went to Perm as soon as possible after its capture from the Bolsheviks, and had literature dropped across their lines from airplanes.

The daily telegraph news service was extended to reach nearly all Siberian papers through an agreement with the Russian Telegraph Agency at Omsk, reached through R. E. Winters, our representative there.

In addition, our bulletins in English were sent by American headquarters at Vladivostok to Chita and relayed by our man there to the other field men, so that each would have the service in full. The field men also received weekly packages by mail, with special articles already translated for the press, and full sets of the bulletin accompanying a regular service letter.

Early in January Otto T. Glaman, business manager, and I started out for a tour of the field to get in touch with the men in the several offices and to co-ordinate their activities further if necessary. We traveled in a freight-car, which had been made over into an office car, with a sleeping compartment and a kitchen and a brakeman's compartment, specially for this purpose by the American Railway Mission. We also had a smaller freight-car as trailer, with a stock of literature and of fuel and food supplies for ourselves and the field men.

In Irkutsk we received the demobilization orders, and from there on the original purpose of the trip was automatically changed. We went to Omsk, where we took Brown from Ekaterinburg, and Winters from Omsk, office manager, on board with us and started back for Vladivostok on March 2d. Bakeman, the Irkutsk manager, returned in a consulate car, and Clarkin, from Chita, with us.

To estimate the results and the consequent value of a campaign of public information which could not be completed is both difficult and problematical. Nevertheless, I am confident in saying that all of the men engaged in the work, and also men in other official American services, felt at the close that the effort had justified itself and been worth while.

The telegraph news service alone, reaching one hundred and fifty Siberian papers by our arrangement with the Russian Telegraph Agency in Omsk, was a great influence.

When the division was ordered to demobilize, the friendly attitude of other American agencies, and especially the cordial co-operation of the headquarters of the American Expeditionary Forces and of the consulate general and branch consulates, were evidence that useful work had been accomplished. This evidence was reinforced by many expressions from Russians, samples of whose letters are given at the end of the report.

Summing up the results of the work, I should say that the most valuable effect was the creation of a new sense of acquaintance with America and with the spirit of the American people. As one Siberian editor wrote, "I think that I am not mistaken when I say that, owing to the activities of the representatives of the American Press Bureau, democratic America will never again become a strange country of industrial kings to the population of Siberia."

This establishment of a knowledge of the life and character of the rank and file of the American people, and of the broad range of their interests and activities, together with a sense of mutual sympathetic interest in common ideals and aspirations, is the most important achievement of the Siberian Department. The circulation of our material on the organization and growth of a modern democracy, with its creative principles of constructive change and development, may also do much to clear up the confusion existing in many Russian minds challenged for the first time with the problem of working out their own difficulties. All the evidence is that the work has laid a basis of friendly interest which will remain for future relations of co-operative good will.

Coupled with this broader result and contributing to it are certain very specific things which the Siberian Department did. By circulating broadcast information about American war organization and activity, it helped to convince the public mind in Siberia of the potential power of America and its promise of victory during the critical days when the issue of the war was still in doubt in 1918. By circulating information about the American peace program and the League of Nations proposal, embodied in the addresses of President Wilson, it helped to establish confidence in the genuine disinterested sincerity of America as a nation and as a democracy in matters of international policy.

HOW WE ADVERTISED AMERICA

By circulating information regarding the American policy concerning Russia, it served to create confidence in America as a country not seeking for internal control in Russia and Siberia and truly interested in free and fair play for Russians in the settlement of their own affairs. The circulation of information regarding the activities of American relief agencies, such as the American Red Cross, the American Railway Mission, and the American War Trade Board, as well as regarding the interest taken by Americans at home in Russian affairs and the progress of the Russian people in their struggle for a better order under free institutions, has at the same time kept alive the sense of American friendship and sympathy. Circulation of information regarding American methods of agriculture and industry and regarding the life of the American farmer and the efforts for betterment of the conditions of life of the worker, regarding the activities of the American government in the interest of the people, and regarding the powers and opportunities which the people of the United States have for changing and perfecting their institutions, have both corrected many false impressions of America and tended to develop new standards in Russian minds for their own national life and system of government.

Part III

DEMOBILIZATION

I

THE Peace Treaty has been attacked from many sides as a "failure in advertising." I agree. There can be no question that the Paris proceedings have never been placed before the people of the United States with any degree of clearness or in such manner as to put public opinion in possession of the truth, the whole truth, and nothing but the truth.

When it is charged, however, that the failure is the fault of the Committee on Public Information because we did not conduct a "vigorous campaign," I disagree absolutely and unalterably. Nothing would have been more instantly attacked, and *justly* attacked, than the use of governmental machinery and public funds for any such purpose. Bad as conditions are to-day, they would be infinitely worse had the President attempted to support his cause by "press-agenting" with the people's money. As for the Committee on Public Information, its duties ceased automatically when fighting ceased.

Within twenty-four hours from the signing of the armistice orders were issued for the immediate cessation of every domestic activity of the Committee on Public Information. Many of the divisions had a continuing value, but I had the deep conviction that the Committee was a *war organization* only, and that it was without proper place in the national life in time of peace. War is a simple fact,

401

with victory as its one objective. Peace is far from simple, and has as many objectives as there are parties and political aims and prejudices. No matter how honest its intent or pure its purpose, a Committee on Public Information operating in peace-times would be caught inevitably in the net of controversy, affording the highly improper spectacle of a government organization using public moneys to advance the contentions of one side or the other. The President was in thorough agreement with me and the order for domestic demobilization had his explicit approval.

On November 14th announcement was made of the discontinuance of the volunteer censorship agreement.

On November 15th a formal statement was issued to the effect that all press censorship in connection with cables and mails had been discontinued.

The question that next arose was in connection with publicity arrangements for the Peace Conference in Paris. There was a general assumption that the government would exercise certain authorities and controls, and that I would act as administrative agent. It was against this assumption that I entered immediate and vigorous protest, taking the matter straight to the President. What I insisted upon was the government's immediate and complete surrender of every supervisory function as far as news was concerned and the restoration to the press of every power, liberty, and independence. This course, in my opinion, was dictated by common sense as well as by propriety. The Republican papers, as a matter of course, were insistent that the Administration should abandon all publicity effort, but it was also the case that the press, as a whole, was flatly in favor of the step. From every quarter came the demand for full release from restraint, suggestion, or "interference" of any kind. There was also Congress to be considered.

The League of Nations was the chief issue to be fought out in the Peace Conference and the Republican majority in the Senate was already serving notice that it would be regarded as a controversial and political question. Any attempt at government supervision, regardless of its honesty and helpfulness, was sure to be seized upon by the Republican Senators and by the Republican press as an effort of the Administration to "muzzle the press" and to give the people no other information than that favorable to the President's cause.

What I urged was the lifting of every barrier, full permission and aid for every American newspaper man desiring to go to Paris, open sessions of the Peace Conference, and instant demand upon England and France that American news should be exempted from censorship of any kind.

The President stated that he stood unqualifiedly for open sessions, authorized the announcement that all passport regulations would be lifted in the case of accredited newspaper men, and in the course of a few days informed me that the governments of France and England had acceded to his request that the despatches of American correspondents should not be subjected to censorship. These facts were duly given to the press, and all was "quiet along the Potomac."

With Peace Conference publicity disposed of presumably, and with the domestic activities of the Committee in process of settlement, there then remained only the Foreign Section with its representatives in every capital, its intricate machinery, and with hundreds of thousands of dollars involved in the adjustment of assets and liabilities. Paris was the one logical center for this demobilization and the President believed that the importance of this liquidation required my personal attention. At the same time, with his usual kindliness of thought, he asked me to be his guest on the *George Washington* if I could make my plans coincide with his sailing date. This, then, was why I went to Paris, and how I happened to be on the *George Washington.* The wisdom of my course in taking a stand against "salesmanship" was soon demonstrated in conclusive fashion.

To assist in the heavy detail of checking the books of the European offices, in paying bills, selling assets, and collecting money due, I sent an advance delegation to Paris, consisting of Mr. Edgar G. Sisson, director of the Foreign Section; his associate, Mr. Carl Byoir; and a force of accountants and stenographers. *The New York World,* on the alleged authority of some member of the party whose name was not given, announced that these purely clerical employees constituted "The United States Official Press Mission to the Peace Conference."

At almost the same time the Postmaster-General announced the taking over of the cables, an action as remote as the moon from my authority and duties. Straightway the inevitable Senate group — Reed, Watson, Hiram Johnson, Sherman, and New—started off with their full-mouthed baying, and the press, with equal recklessness and enthusiasm, joined in the hue and cry. The President, Mr. Burleson, and I were in a deep and dark conspiracy to gag, stifle, muzzle, and throttle. With the cables in our clutches, *mine* was to be the task of censorship in Paris, *my* autocratic whim would decide what news of the Peace Conference should reach the people of the United States, and *my* "interpretations" would be forced upon suffering correspondents.

As a matter of course, no Senator made the slightest effort to ascertain the facts, the press carried their fulminations with glaring head-lines, and editors thundered against the hapless stenographers composing "The United States Official Press Mission" and denounced my "iniquitous pact" with Mr. Burleson. The following statement was issued on November 21st in an effort to stem the tide of absurdity and falsehood:

With respect to my charged connection with the cables and cable censorship, there is no such connection, nor will there be any.

On November 14th announcement was made by the Committee on Public Information of the discontinuance of the volunteer censorship agreement under which the press of the United States has operated with the government.

On November 15th a formal statement was issued to the effect that all press censorship in connection with cables and mails would be discontinued forthwith.

There is, therefore, no press censorship of any kind existing in the United States to-day. No plan of resumption has been suggested or even contemplated.

The whole domestic machinery of the Committee on Public Information is being dismantled and will cease operation by December 15th at the very latest. As for my work in Europe, and that of the Committee on Public Information, it will have absolutely no connection whatsoever with the control of the cables, any form of censorship, or any supervision over the press.

The charge that I will have control of all publicity in connection with the Peace Commission has no base in fact. The policy decided upon is that there shall be no selection or discrimination in the matter of the representation of the press either in the matter of passports or in foreign arrangements. Any responsible newspaper man is entitled to go and equally entitled to fair and impartial treatment abroad.

These men, on the ground and with every right and chance to observe, estimate, and interview, will write as they please and with their usual independence. As for press arrangements, conveniences, and privileges, these matters will necessarily be governed in large degree by the desires of the authorities of the country in which the Peace Conference is held.

The one proper effort of the Committee on Public Information will be to open every means of communication to the press of America without dictation, without supervision, and with no other desire than to facilitate in every manner the fullest and freest flow of news.

27   405

This statement clarified the atmosphere in some degree, but attack continued from many quarters, and as late as November 29th Mr. Roosevelt, in public print, accepted the story that my stenographers and accountants were "The United States Official Press Mission to the Peace Conference," added that these men and women had been sent by the President himself, and asserted that the whole purpose was the determination of the President to "make the news sent out from the Peace Conference to ourselves, our allies, and our enemies what they desire to have told from their own standpoint, and nothing more."

On November 23d, or thereabouts, a committee of the Washington correspondents came to me to learn my plans for "handling them." It was an amazing situation that had more humor in it than irritation. Before me were the very men who had been most insistent that "Creel must take his hands off," that there must be "no interference with correspondents," and as a consequence of their clamor I had issued a public statement binding myself to avoid even an appearance of supervision.

It developed, however, that none of them had taken the trouble to engage passage or to apply for passports, and that unless authoritative help came quickly they stood small chance of getting to France in time. At the request of these correspondents, and acting entirely in a personal capacity, I went to the President and begged him to let the newspaper group travel with him on the *George Washington*. He pointed out that there was no way by which any fair discrimination could be made, and that if one correspondent were given the privilege, the same invitation would necessarily have to be extended to every other correspondent in the United States. He explained further that the accommodations on the *George Washington* were not unlimited, as every one seemed to suppose, and that the inclusion of the Peace Commission, the scores of experts attached to the commission, the State Department group, etc., had already brought about a condition of congestion. With the full approval of the correspondents I then devoted my efforts to placing the representatives of the Associated Press, United Press, and the International News Service on the *George Washington*, and these three men were asked by the President as his guests. This done, I took up with the War Department the question of securing a transport for the use of such correspondents as desired to go to France. The *Orizaba* happened to be the one boat available, and while it was not a Cunarder, it was a good seaworthy boat, and at the time there was no quarrel with it whatsoever, only a great thanksgiving that a ship of any kind had been secured. These activities on my part, undertaken entirely at the request of the correspondents themselves, aroused a new outcry in the Senate, and even in some of the newspapers that I was trying to serve, and on November 27th the following statement was issued:

It has been arranged that the representatives of the press associations will travel with the President and the official party.

With the approval of the President, the Secretary of War has set aside the transport *Orizaba* to carry duly accredited newspaper correspondents to France. The *Orizaba* will leave the Hoboken dock at twelve o'clock noon Sunday, December 1st. All passengers will report to General McManus at the port of embarkation, Pier 3.

In the matter of the sailing-list no discrimination will be made or special privilege granted. All newspaper men duly accredited by responsible newspapers are entitled to passage.

Passports have to be viséd by the various consuls in New York. Applications that have not yet been made should be filed at once and reported to me. Likewise, applications that have been made but have not yet been acted upon. The State Department is extending every aid in the interest of expedition, and press passports will be lifted out of the regular routine.

It is requested, and hoped, that correction will be made of

the very untrue report that any attempt will be made to interfere in any manner with the free flow of news from America to Europe, or from Europe to America. The whole effort of government, from the first, has been to assure adequate and authoritative representation of the press at the Peace Conference and to assist news distribution in every possible way.

There is no press censorship of any kind in the United States to-day, and at the personal request of the President the French and English governments have lifted all censorship regulations bearing upon American press matters.

The widely circulated rumor that George Creel, chairman of the Committee on Public Information, will have control of official publicity in connection with the Peace Conference is absolutely without foundation. There will be no such control, and the situation itself precludes any such control. The Peace Conference itself will undoubtedly decide upon the manner of announcing its deliberations and decisions, and the right of correspondents to free movement and interviews is, of course, one that cannot be abridged in any degree.

The Postmaster-General is maintaining a study of the cables, with a view to aiding the press in every possible way, and will shortly make his own statement.

Mr. Creel, who has made all arrangements for the discontinuance of the domestic work of the Committee on Public Information, is proceeding to Europe to wind up the work of the Foreign Section. He has no connection whatsoever with the Peace Commission.

The representatives of the Committee on Public Information who sailed last week did not in any manner constitute an official Peace Conference press mission. They were stenographers, accountants, film men, and division heads, not one of whom will have connection with the Peace Conference or with the preparation of the Conference's press matter. Their sole duties will be the completion of the Committee's foreign work and settlement of contracts and business details incident to the absolute cessation of activity.

The Departments of State and War threw down all barriers in the matter of passports, the embarkation officials at Hoboken worked overtime, and through a dreary Sunday I sat wearily signing credentials asking foreign governments to show the bearers every possible courtesy, privilege, consideration, etc. Conservative, radical, Democratic, and Republican, all went down into the *Orizaba* in the order of their application, and the one joy that I had out of it was to know that the correspondents of reactionary papers like the *Sun* and *Tribune* were to travel for seven days with Abraham Cahan of the *Vorwärts*, and Reuben Spink of the Socialist *Call*.

On December 4th I sailed on the *George Washington*, but even the sea afforded no refuge. Two days after my departure, a Paris despatch charged that the Committee on Public Information would take control of the European cables, "ration" space to the correspondents; and that all official communications to the press from the Paris Conference would pass through my hands. I was the one person with authority to make such an announcement; I was on the sea and had left behind me flat statements that guaranteed the absolute freedom of the press. Upon arrival in Paris, investigation disclosed that the despatch had no base whatsoever save in the imagination of the correspondent that sent it. Yet Senator Hiram Johnson and the others of his ilk accepted the lie without question, and *The Philadelphia North American* even printed this infamous attack:

Some indication of the course to be pursued was given to-day when Senate anger again found expression as the result of the cabled information from Paris that George Creel is to decide how much news matter each newspaper correspondent may file for cable transmission each day, and is to pass upon every official statement that is to be given out from the American delegation.

This announcement is in direct conflict with the statement made by President Wilson in his speech on Monday that there was to be no censorship or restriction imposed by the government upon the information to be sent from the Peace Conference to this country, and that in the interest of publicity he had induced

409

the governments of Great Britain and France to lift their censorship news.

It is an absolute exposure of the falsity of the statement made by George Creel that he has gone to France to wind up the affairs of the Public Information Committee and will have nothing to do with preparation or transmission of information concerning the conferences.

In fact, Congress and the public have every reason to feel that both the President and Creel made statements to the American public which were deliberately planned to deceive, and the uncomfortable inference suggests itself that since these statements are shown to have been untrue, no other statements they may issue can the public accept with absolute confidence of their reliability.

Johnson cried, "What a sad thing it is that Creel should ration the news which is to be received by the American people—the news concerning developments that may mean the whole future of our Republic." New of Indiana even went into figures, stating that the press allotment on the cables, as fixed by me, would be twenty-eight thousand words a day, a limit that he boldly branded as "ridiculous." Even when the report stood proved as a lie and when it became indisputably apparent that the attacks were false, not one word of retraction or apology ever came from the Senators or from *The North American* and such other papers as had spread the slanders.

Another charge made freely to-day is that "Creel's Committee might have done something to provide for the comfort and convenience of the newspaper workers in Paris and so saved its scalp." Under this head the principal complaint is that the correspondents were not "housed in their own American club, led, guided, stimulated at every step of the Conference proceedings." To make the case more conclusive, it is stated that a business man of large affairs made an offer to lease a hotel or apartment-house in Paris for the American correspondents where they would be lodged and fed, provided with every working convenience, and informed at regular intervals by prominent Americans and internationalists as to the problems upon which the new treaty would be founded. This man, invariably anonymous, was ready to under-write such a scheme up to a quarter of a million dollars, but "the Committee on Public Information laughed at this offer and promptly proceeded to ignore it."

No such offer was ever made to me or to any other executive of the Committee. Knowing the difficulties under which the correspondents would labor in Paris, I took the chance of instructing Mr. Sisson to engage and equip working quarters for the American press, and he took the old James Gordon Bennett apartments on the Champs-Élysées and fitted them up with desks and type-writers. Almost instantly despatches commenced to go back to the United States declaring that we were squander-ing government money in a secret attempt to control the press, and, finally convinced that any effort to help the correspondents directly would be misinterpreted, I gave orders to surrender the lease and dismantle the place.

As evidence of my own shortcomings and the superior propaganda genius of the French, many correspondents glowingly described "the remarkable international press club which the French government set up in the Champs-Élysées." This is really humorous. When I saw that it would not be possible for the American government to do anything of its own initiative, I went to M. Tardieu and M. Aubert, with whom I had been closely associated in Washington during their service in the French High Commission, and the three of us made the plans for the establishment of the French press club in the Hôtel Dufayal. On a bitter winter morning M. Aubert and I tramped through the chilly palace, deciding upon general arrange-ment and specific quarters, and it was the Committee that furnished a large part of the desks and typewriters. It was planned that this should be a home for all correspondents and that the prominent men of all nations would be invited there to talk over Peace Conference problems for the information of the writers. I might say that the failure of the plan constituted one of the French government's bitter disappointments. The last thing that the correspondents wanted was to be guided and instructed and stimulated. What they were after was *news*, and the Peace Conference itself was the one news source.

Various correspondents are also ardent in this admiration of the French for the manner in which they conducted visitors over the devastated areas, for "compared with it the best of our American efforts were almost as nothing." During the war, when it was our business to impress the world with the power of America, our Paris office maintained smooth-working machinery for the exploitation of the American effort in France. In conjunction with the army, the newspaper men of Spain, Holland, England, Scandinavia, Italy, and all other nations, were taken on tours that covered the entire activities of the A. E. F. With the armistice this work ended naturally, and nothing would have been more improper and unwise than for the American government to take correspondents over the devastated area in competition with the French.

As a matter of fact, however, the Committee was the moving spirit behind most of the trips on which the correspondents were taken. Not only did we work with the French government on such plans, but through Mr. Frederick H. Wile, Lord Northcliffe's representative, it was arranged that all the American correspondents should be the guests of the British government during the President's visit in England. From the Italian government I secured a similar invitation, along with a special train and an offer to take the entire group of American correspondents over the Italian battle-front.

When the President decided to spend Christmas Day at Chaumont, it was the Committee that arranged for a special train for the correspondents and it was the Committee that paid for it.

What with all these arrangements, and especially the Italian trip, which had to be planned in conjunction with a grand-opera tenor in uniform, I was compelled to stay in Paris when the President went to London, and by way of showing a delicate and restrained appreciation of my efforts, *The New York Sun* correspondent sent a despatch from London that I was not with the President because I had quarreled with him and that I was making plans to leave at once for the United States.

Praise has been given, and very properly, to the helpfulness of Mr. Ray Stannard Baker, also to the President's agreement that the correspondents should have a daily conference each morning with the American members of the Peace Commission. On the second day after my arrival in Paris I took up with the President this matter of a daily conference and secured his consent to it. It was at my request, joined in by Colonel House, that the President signed the order attaching Mr. Baker to the Peace Commission to act as its press representative. From the first I begged the President to meet regularly with the correspondents and it was his sincere desire to do this, and it would have been done but for the back-breaking burdens that he bore, the demands that took every second of his time, and the constantly changing situation that made it impossible to talk with any degree of certainty.

These things done, I had the feeling that the Committee, as far as was properly in its power, had discharged its full duty in aiding the press of America to *obtain* the news. What remained to be done was to help the correspondents

413

to transmit the news with the greatest possible degree of speed. The cables were abnormally congested. Not only was the press of the world assembled in Paris, but the war had left only four transatlantic cables available for use, and as a consequence incredible delays developed unavoidably. To meet the situation, Mr. Walter S. Rogers, director of the Committee's Foreign Wireless and Cable Service, was placed unreservedly at the disposal of the correspondents and directed to find a "way out." As a first measure to lighten the cable load, the Committee agreed to transmit to the United States all formal statements, speeches of the President, and other like matter requiring textual sending, and to make simultaneous delivery in New York to the three press associations. Even when the matter had to be sent by cable, two additional sendings were saved, and when flashed by wireless the entire load was lifted from the cable.

A second step was in the direction of aid to individual correspondents. The navy, in charge of the wireless, was forbidden by law to charge tolls, nor could it even receive private messages; but in view of the importance of giving the American public all possible news of the peace deliberations it was agreed that the Committee on Public Information might undertake the delivery of the matter to the American press.

After many negotiations the French government and the United States navy entered into an arrangement through which the Committee was able to offer thirty-five hundred words daily on the wireless, absolutely free of charge, to the American correspondents in Paris. The correspondents themselves, formed into an association, allotted the wordage as they saw fit, handed copy to the Committee in Paris, and from our office it went over the American army wires to the French wireless station at Lyons and from Lyons to the Committee's office in New York for distribution.

AFTER THE ARMISTICE

At no time did the Foreign Press Cable Service undertake to deliver analytical articles or "propaganda matter" to the American press. The matter sent for simultaneous release consisted solely of official statements, speeches, and announcements, and merely the bare text of these. We construed our service to be the delivery of these documents textually, leaving it to the newspapers to draw conclusions or to describe the events in connection with the issuance of such statements. Emphasis should also be laid on the fact that this division at no time exercised any censorship on any articles prepared by any correspondents for American newspapers.

The consummation of these arrangements marked the limit of proper effort on the part of the Committee. England, France, and Italy were the hosts of the American press; every battle-front was to be shown the correspondents; an incredibly magnificent press club stood provided for them; daily contacts with the American peace commissioners were being held; cable and wireless facilities, free of charge, were at their disposal, and no censorship stood in the way.

Future arrangements were entirely and absolutely in the hands of the Peace Conference itself. There was no other way. Nothing stands so clear as that it would have been suicidal for the President to have used a single government dollar or a piece of government machinery for publicity purposes in connection with the Peace Conference. If plain downright lies had the power to stir the Republican press and the Republican Senators into rage and abuse, imagine the storm that would have been aroused had any of the reports of press-agenting been based upon fact. In the very nature of the case, dependence had to be placed upon the activities of the Conference itself and upon the spirit in which the correspondents reported and interpreted these activities.

This spirit was bad. The Peace Treaty failed because the press itself failed in its duty of proper information, and the press failed because it interested itself only in the personal and obvious, not in the educational and interpretative. And the reason for this misplaced emphasis goes back to the bitter fact that partizans made the Peace Treaty a party question instead of letting it shine out as a nation's pledge.

II

THROUGHOUT these two weeks of press arrangements the work of dismantling the Foreign Section was proceeding steadily. Orders went out to the Committee's commissioners in every country to "close shop," settle accounts, and make the best possible disposition of furniture, fixtures, films, and all other assets. The only offices kept alive were those in Paris and New York, and these were skeleton organizations for news distribution.

It was my deep desire to make a clean sweep, but the American Peace Commission was of the opinion that some machinery should be left to assure the proper world distribution of official policies and positions in times of crisis. There was also our agreement with the American correspondents in the matter of the wireless and cable accommodations. Walter Rogers and Herman Suter, therefore, "stayed on the job" in Paris, handling the daily service for the press, and at the disposal of the Peace Commission for putting official statements into the channels of world-communication.

With demobilization in full swing, but one constructive task remained to be discharged. While much of our matter had penetrated Middle Europe during the war, it was still the case that enemy censorship had prevented any complete approach. What we wanted to do, the thing that we felt it necessary to do, was to drive home, once and for all, the idealism of America and the blood-guilt of

Germany. Poles, Czechs, Austrians, Hungarians, and Jugoslavs were crystallizing into new political shapes, and nothing seemed more desirable than that they should have the *facts in the case* in order that their determinations might form along lines acceptable to the new world.

In accordance with an arrangement made previously with President Masaryk it was decided that Prague should be our headquarters, and from the Division of Military Intelligence we borrowed Capt. Emanuel Voska, a man who fitted our plans as skin fits the hand. A native of Bohemia and an ardent patriot from his boyhood, Captain Voska had been compelled to find safety in exile when still a young man, and in 1914 was the head of a prosperous business. He saw in the World War the chance for Bohemian independence, and, quitting everything, he began the task of turning the Bohemian National Alliance into a war body. Undoubtedly he will tell his own story some day. It must suffice at this time to say that it was Captain Voska, more than any other one man, who defeated German intrigue in the United States and worked the exposure of Dumba and von Bernstorff. Czechs, speaking German perfectly, were placed in Austrian consulates and in every like office, so that every move of the plotters was known to Captain Voska in its inception. At first he worked in connection with the British Secret Service, but when America entered the war he put himself and his organization at the disposal of the War Department and joined the Military Intelligence with the rank of captain.

It was this man that we wanted to help us now. As his assistants Captain Voska selected five Czechs from the American army and borrowed five Czechoslovak legionaries from the French—men who spoke Czech, Polish, Magyar, German, and the various tongues of Jugoslavia. One was a radio expert. It was not only our plan to print selected publications in the various tongues, but to make arrangements to put the various wireless stations in touch with the wireless station at Lyons.

On January 1st I left Paris for Rome with the President and was joined there a few days later by Mr. Byoir. Mr. Sisson, going by way of Berne, wound up our affairs in Switzerland and reached Rome on January 8th. By that time Mr. Byoir and I had finished the Italian settlement with Mr. Hearley and the three of us set out that night for Padua, where Captain Voska and his party were waiting for us.

There was no passenger service of any kind between Italy and Bohemia, and Captain Voska had arranged that we were to travel to Prague with a troop-train of Czecho-slovak legionaries. There were about one thousand of them—veterans who had seen fighting on many fronts— and with their horses and guns and baggage they filled thirty-five freight-cars. For our own accommodation we managed to secure a battered passenger-coach, stripped of all upholstery and indescribably dirty. To add to con-gestion our party of fourteen was asked to share this car with Colonel Phillippe, the French officer in charge of the legionaries, also his aides, and with the newly ap-pointed British *chargé d'affaires* who was trying to reach Prague at the earliest possible moment.

The journey to Prague from Padua took almost four days, a weary crawl through the devastated Piave plain and over the Alps, with never a chance to get the bitter cold out of one's marrow. We took off nothing but our hats when we slept on the narrow seats, and aside from hot coffee, made over charcoal braziers, we ate out of mail-sacks that we had filled with dried apricots, Italian bread, "bully beef," and canned stuff. Heaven only knows what would have happened to us but for the blankets loaned in Padua by the American Red Cross! The stations in Austria were closed as we passed, owing to fear of trouble, and all that we saw of the people were sullen faces peering at us through railings or from the hills. They looked well fed and fat, the villages were whole and the land unravaged—all in sharp contrast to the hunger and devastation of France and Italy. I knew, as every one must know, that the peace of the world depended upon just treatment of these defeated enemies, but I could not help thinking that justice took much of the joy out of life.

The one thrill of the dreary journey came to us on the night when we reached the border of what had once been the ancient kingdom of Bohemia and which was now the boundary-line of the free Republic of Czechoslovakia. For an hour the whole train had hummed to a vast excitement, for among the legionaries were many men who had gone into exile as youths, and others who had been fighting for four years, out of touch entirely with their homes and people. No sooner had we stopped at the little station across the border than every legionary was off the train, kissing the sacred soil that had been won at last from the Austrian. Officers and men embraced with tears running down their cheeks, then the entire thousand grouped reverently and, lifting their faces to the hills and the stars, sang the national hymn of Bohemia—a song in a minor key for the most part, like the songs of all oppressed peoples—but rising at the end to a tremendous challenge that rang like a trumpet. And after that a great cheering for America, "the hope of the world."

We reached Prague Monday noon, January 13th, and a second thrill came to us as its patriot citizens received the heroes who had helped to make independence possible. A wonderful old city and a still more wonderful people. As we came to see them and hear them it was easy to understand how they had held to their national aspirations through five centuries of oppression, rising at last in unity and strength. Not even Americans are more in love with freedom than these Czechoslovaks, and, what is finest, their patriotism did not disintegrate with victory. They massed behind the beloved Masaryk as a unit, putting country above party and political feuds, and in the Cabinet that worked as a team there were Socialists, Agrarians, and even a jolly old Catholic priest as director-general of railroads. Of all the countries in Europe, Czechoslovakia had courage, purpose, and high resolve.

We saw President Masaryk almost immediately, were quickly put in touch with other officials, and in twenty-four hours work was under way. One group went at the task of "tuning up" the government wireless station to a point where it could receive our service from Paris, and the rest of us grappled with the questions of paper and printing.

The five pamphlets intended for distribution were these: *How the War Came to America, German War Practices in Conquered Territory, German Intrigue in the United States, America's War Aims and Peace Terms,* and *The German - Bolshevik Conspiracy.* For each of these we had the translations in Czech, Polish, Magyar, Croatian, German, and Ukrainian. This circulation was of vital importance, in the opinion of President Masaryk and his associates, for out of the fifteen million inhabitants of Czechslovakia full three million were Germans and there were also large numbers of Hungarians. The selected pamphlets were meant to do three things: first, to drive home the meanings and purposes of America; second, to show the guilt, the cruelty, and the monstrous plans of Germany; third, to expose the German direction of the Bolshevik revolution. Mr. Haberman, head of the Department of Education, put his machinery at our disposal and assumed entire responsibility for the distribution of the pamphlets to schools, churches, the papers, and the leaders of thought in every community.

421

Leaving Captain Voska to follow through the printing arrangements, Mr. Sisson, Mr. Byoir, and I left on Friday for Cracow, for Poland, also had a very grave German problem in Galicia. In a stay of two days we managed to put the government wireless station in touch with Paris, but the paper and printing situation forced us to reach the decision that Prague would have to take care of our Polish publications. Telegrams from Paderewski urged me to come to Warsaw, and a special train was put at our disposal, but as such a trip was without values other than social and sightseeing, we were compelled to refuse.

Leaving Cracow, with committees still beseeching us to go to Warsaw, we returned to Prague by way of Slovakia. We had interpreters with us, but it was amazing always in Czechoslovakia to see how many spoke English. As a result of conferences usually held on the train, complete arrangements were made for the pamphlet distribution in Slovakia and Moravia.

Reaching Prague at noon on Thursday we found that Captain Voska had the wireless arrangements well under way and that the printing program was going through without a hitch. That very afternoon I left for Budapest, taking one interpreter with me. Captain Voska was to stay in Prague until he had finished the work and Mr. Sisson and Mr. Byoir were to leave on Friday for Vienna to look after the Austrian end of the machinery. It was agreed that we should meet in Trieste on Monday morning, an arrangement that meant hard traveling.

We were lucky enough to get a compartment on the night train to Vienna, and Czabulk, my interpreter, and I had visions of an uncrowded night. At the last moment, however, we picked up Lester Perrin, a young Detroit boy who had wandered into Prague after his release from the German prison-camps in Poland. The poor youngster was without money, and the certainty of his delay in getting in touch with the American military authorities in Paris made me decide to take him with me. In Vienna we left Perrin to wait for Sisson and Byoir and hurried on without halt. Where once fifteen express-trains ran daily between Vienna and Budapest there was now but one a day, a wretched collection of battered third-class cars. The very highest official influence was necessary to get us a compartment on this train and it took a guard of soldiers to force us into it through the jam of passengers. Once in, we locked the door and gave ourselves over to happy contemplation of the two long seats that would permit us to have a regular "lie-down" sleep. The corridor, however, was jammed with people and I found it utterly impossible to shut out the consciousness that the women among them were facing a long, bitter night on their feet. For a full half an hour my selfishness fought with my shame, but at last I told Czabulk to open the door and announce that the first women to reach the four seats could have them. We drew a Turk, two Hungarians, and an Austrian, and while the ample Turkish lady took far more than her fair share of room, she contributed a genial radiation that added materially to the comfort of the night. We stopped two hours at the Austrian frontier while the entire train was searched for food-smuggling, and there were other stops of every kind, so that we did not reach Budapest until ten the next morning.

The Hungarian situation was deplorable to the last degree. Count Karolyi was in the president's chair, but it was plain to be seen that he could not last more than a couple of weeks unless the Allies decided upon some helpful action in his behalf. It was Karolyi who had agreed to the Franchet d'Esperey armistice, and it was the provisions of this armistice that were now being violated daily. On three sides the Czechs, the Jugoslavs, and the Serbs were making steady encroachments, while on the fourth side the Rumanians were sweeping forward in utter disregard of what should have been sacred agreements. The food situation was also reaching a crisis and Bela Kun, plentifully supplied with Bolshevik money, was preaching the gospel of a new revolt.

The whole thing was tragic in the extreme. There was little or nothing that could be done, however. The only Americans on the ground were two representatives of the Food Commission, while I myself had neither the power nor the desire to interfere in the political matters that were the sole province of the State Department. All that I could do was to send an instant report to Paris, outlining the situation, and it was this report that brought a declaration from the Peace Conference to the effect that the boundary-lines laid down by Franchet d'Esperey must be respected. This helped tremendously for the moment, but as nothing was done to give force to the declaration, things became worse than before and in the course of a few weeks Karolyi was deposed and Bela Kun rose to power.

I made arrangements for the government wireless to take our Paris service, but the first survey of the field made me realize that it was hopeless to attempt printing or distribution of any kind in Budapest. As a consequence, I sent instructions to Prague to have all the Magyar editions printed there.

Getting out of Budapest was even worse than getting in. At five o'clock on Sunday morning Czabulk and I climbed drearily into the usual cold, damp compartment of a third-class train, and at eight o'clock that evening reached Praegerhof, where we were supposed to change to a through train to Trieste. Instead of that we were transferred to a local and rode until one o'clock in a car that had pine boards in place of windows. At Leibach, under Jugoslav control, we had another passport battle and changed again to the worst train of the trip. Not only was it without windows, but every inch of upholstering had been taken out. One explanation was that the soldiers used the plush for clothing, but, although I looked hopefully for some such gleam of color, I failed to discover that any such use had been made of the material. At four o'clock in the morning we were thrown out at the town of Loich and found it in the hands of Italians, at that time busily engaged in pushing forward their "historical boundaries." Only some petty officers were in charge and the fact that we came from Budapest made us the object of instant suspicion. For three mortal hours Czabulk argued in every tongue at his command, but without the slightest avail as far as I could see. The train for Trieste came along at seven and I told Czabulk to convey the information that we were going on board whether they liked it or not, since death itself was far preferable to another hour in such a hole. The officers followed us to the very steps, debating furiously, but in the end let us go our way in peace. Again we found ourselves in a car without windows or upholstery and all night a blizzard blew that bit through blankets and overcoats and froze our very bones. We reached Trieste at noon, and late that night the rest of the party came in from Vienna. At eight the next morning we were on a boat to Venice, from Venice we sped to Turin, and from Turin to Paris, reaching there the morning of January 31st.

A hard, driving trip, but without a single neglect or one unspared effort to mar the achievement. In Prague we were printing the five pamphlets in Czech, Polish, Magyar, Croatian, German, and Ukrainian, with arrangements fully made for distribution to the schools, press, organizations, and leaders of thought in Czechoslovakia, Galicia, Saxony, Austria, Hungary, and certain parts of Jugoslavia. The wireless stations at Cracow, Prague, and Budapest were in touch with Paris. As far as humanly possible, we had carried the message of America to Mittel Europa!

One other thing we did! Immediately upon arrival in Paris we laid a detailed report before the high authorities of the Food Commission, and it was this special pleading that won quick and effective relief for Czechoslovakia and Poland.

With this satisfactory completion of the Middle-Europe task, and with every office closing with the exception of the cable and wireless service, the seat of settlement was now Washington.

III

IT is doubtful if in all the annals of business, public and private, there is record of anything more utterly uncomprehensible than the action of Congress in destroying the Committee on Public Information in the very midst of its orderly liquidation. On June 30, 1919, every dollar of our appropriation, every dollar of our earnings, was swept back into the Treasury, and the Committee itself wiped out of existence, leaving no one with authority to sign a check, transfer a bank balance, employ a clerk, rent a building, or with any power whatsoever to proceed with the business of settlement. The action was so utterly mad that it could not have been anticipated, and yet had we been able to see into the future there was nothing that we could have done about it.

When I returned to the United States in March, accompanied by Mr. Sisson and Mr. Byoir, it was to find that Mr. O'Higgins, the associate chairman left in charge, had carried out the demobilization orders successfully, and that each of the domestic divisions had either ended its audit or else was completing it. The work of settlement in the Washington office was proceeding slowly, owing to the resignations of purely clerical employees, but as this was a matter that concerned the business management only, I gave release to all executives upon the turning in of their accounts. I discharged myself on April 1st, but as a private citizen continued to assume full responsibility for the settlement, journeying to Washington week after week at my own expense, directing the liquidation personally. It seemed at the time, as indeed it was, a very simple proposition of checking up, paying bills, collecting moneys due, and handing balances over to the Treasury. Mr. Sisson, Mr. Byoir, and Mr. Lee lived in New York and were at all times available for reference, and all other division heads stood ready to answer any call.

The question of adequate clerical help became more and more a problem, however. The report spread that Congress was planning to "put the Committee out of business" entirely on June 30th, and while I protested that an auditing force would be retained, I could not give any definite pledge. As a consequence, the business office personnel dwindled daily as men and women accepted permanent positions elsewhere. All through May and June we pleaded with Congress for a small appropriation that would permit the Committee to wind up its affairs. The Paris and New York offices were not to be closed until June 15th; there were many foreign commissioners yet to report; and in various banks reposed large balances waiting for audit and acceptance. Nor was it the case that the Committee begged with empty hands. We had already turned more than two million dollars into the Treasury, and yet we still had sufficient funds on hand to settle every bill and meet every liquidation expense. What we asked, in effect, was the right to use a small portion of our own *earnings* for proper purposes of settlement. At the last moment Congress refused flatly, and on June 30th the Committee on Public Information ceased to be.

Acting entirely without authority, I persuaded E. H. Hobbs, an accountant, and Miss Gertrude Gocheler to stay on in charge of the books, and hired a night-watchman at my own risk. Then began a dreary round of the various

428

departments in search of some one willing and able to take over the Committee's liquidation. Under the Overman Act the President had the power to assign this duty, but the trouble was that no department in Washington had money enough even for its own purposes and all strenuously resisted the effort to foist a new expense upon them. Once the President went so far as to sign an executive order turning the Committee's affairs over to the Treasury Department, but Secretary Glass entered such vigorous protest that the order had to be withdrawn.

Of the Committee's three buildings, only one was being retained, and on June 30th notice of dispossession was given by the owners. Army trucks were borrowed, and the accumulated records of two years were packed and sent down to the old Fuel Administration building, where several small rooms were assigned to us. The whole proceeding was a nightmare. I had full responsibility without the slightest shadow of authority. Only Mr. Hobbs and Miss Gocheler were on hand to superintend the moving, and the forced nature of our departure, together with the absence of clerks familiar with the records, made confusion unavoidable. Files and books and papers were piled miscellaneously by the truck men and the one effort for weeks was to straighten out the tangle. Additional auditors could not be employed, and as Hobbs himself was under a heavy bond, the situation commenced to get on his nerves.

There was no secret as to my plight, but the correspondents, in the story sent out, seemed to regard it as a joke more than anything else and were of the opinion that "Congress had the laugh on Creel." Not until August 21st did the mangled remains of the Committee find a resting-place. On this day the President signed an order that constituted the Council of National Defense our liquidating agency. As a consequence, the books and papers of the Committee were dumped into trucks *for the second time* and moved to the Council's own building. Whatever resemblance of orderly arrangement remained was entirely smashed by this last transfer.

I went immediately to Secretary Baker, head of the Council, and to Mr. Clarkson, its director, and put myself, every executive, and every division head at their disposal. Particularly did I urge the employment of a competent accounting force in order that there might be speedy untanglement of the surface confusion caused by two months of inaction and the cartage of the Committee's records from place to place. As carefully as might be, I explained to the new force the nature of all unfinished business, and asked to be kept in constant touch with the liquidation. I heard nothing for weeks and on various occasions thereafter I went to Washington in an attempt to find out the causes of delay. I was so absolutely at the mercy of the Council, however, that I could not run the risk of arousing irritation by complaint or what might be conceived to be undue insistence. The records were mine and the responsibility was mine, but I was utterly without power or authority in the settlement.

On October 30th, out of a clear sky, *The New York World* printed a long despatch from its Washington correspondent purporting to recite the contents of a report filed with Congress by the Council of National Defense. The positive statement was made that this report charged me with "gross neglect," and there were equally positive statements that the Committee had cost $6,600,000, that all of the executives of the Committee had deserted on the very day of the armistice, that checks and important papers littered the floors, and that it was virtually an impossibility to find out where the money had gone because of the utter confusion of my accounts. This story was copied almost word for word by the other New York dailies on the following morning, and the Associated Press made haste to distribute it from coast to coast. Not one single paper or press association made the slightest effort to see me before printing the story in order to ascertain its truth or to permit me defense or explanation. Before the whole country I and my associates were held up to public shame as incompetents who had spent "a few delightful months wallowing in public money and then went away and left the whole mess to be cleaned up by others." Many papers were not content with printing these glaring charges, but followed the story up with editorial comment containing speculation as to how much money had "stuck to my fingers."

I made instant answer, portions of which were printed by the more decent dailies, and then proceeded to Washington at once. Upon arrival I learned that the Council of National Defense had filed no report with Congress and that it had made no charges of "gross neglect" against me, or charges of any kind whatsoever. What had happened was this: The Council had been compelled to ask an auditing appropriation, and Senator Warren, chairman of the Senate Committee on Appropriations, had requested the Council to file a memorandum setting forth the uses to which the money would be put. This memorandum, in the form of a letter to Senator Warren, merely detailed the confusion of the Committee's records as the Council found them. Some member of the Committee, more concerned with newspaper favor than with his sense of honor, sneaked this letter out secretly to the correspondent of *The New York World.*

I read the letter to Warren over very carefully, and while it was true that no charges of any kind were made against me, it was equally true that the letter was an invitation to misconstruction in many important particulars. For instance, the statement that checks and important papers were "on the floor" might well have been accompanied by the explanation that they were because Congress itself had dumped them there. It would have been more generous and much more true had the Council pointed out the dispossession of the Committee on July 20th, the forced dismissal of the working force, our forced removal to the old Fuel Administration building, and the second removal to the building of the Council of National Defense, the last under the supervision of the Council's own employees.

There was also a statement that the Committee had issued expense allowances "far in excess of the $1,000 maximum limit fixed by Congress." I pointed out that these expenditures were from the President's fund, to which the Congressional limitation did not apply. As a matter of course, when men were sent to Russia, to China, and to other far places, it was absolutely necessary that they be given a lump sum for disbursement, although vouchers were required showing the expenditure of every dollar. The auditor confessed that he had not been aware of this ruling with respect to the President's fund and admitted the mistake.

The statement to which I took most bitter exception, however, was this:

It appears that immediately after the signing of the armistice practically all of the officials of the Committee on Public Information threw up their jobs and returned to private life, leaving but a few of the minor officials in charge of the affairs of the Committee.

The auditor's answer was that he thought that he was quoting *me*. What I had told him, however, was that the purely clerical employees of the Committee began accepting other positions as soon as the armistice was signed and when they saw that the Committee offered no hope of permanent employment. As I pointed out to him, he had the books before him that proved conclusively that *no* executive left until April 1st and that he knew by my own assurance, and by their own offers, that every man of them had been and *was* at his disposal.

There was no disagreement on the statement of facts, but when I asked that these corrections should be embodied in an open letter there was instant demur. "*They*" knew and "*they*" understood and "*they*" regretted, and the "best thing to do" was to consider the incident closed. Any attempt at correction would only result in new publicity, and owing to the malicious attitude of many of the papers the situation might be made worse instead of better. Also was it not the case that I "exaggerated" the importance of the happening? While it was true that I and my associates, after two years of thankless drudgery, were being shamed as incompetents, deserters, and thieves, this was merely "part of the political game," and I should not "permit it to worry me."

What was there to do but wait for the vindication of results! The Council agreed to push the work at top speed and also acquiesced in my demand that no bill of any kind whatsoever should be paid without reference to me and to the proper division head. It was admitted that the domestic accounts were in very good shape and that the chief trouble was with respect to the foreign work, particularly the wireless and cable service that continued until June 15th, just two weeks before Congress wiped the Committee out of existence. Mr. Rogers and Mr. Bullard were in Washington and came down to give further aid in the foreign accounts. Mr. C. D. Lee, the Committee's business manager throughout its existence, also left his affairs in New York for a Washington stay, and Mr. Sisson and Mr. Byoir were constantly in conference with me in the matter of accounts. The records were straightened out eventually, and as I had known from the first, the seeming confusion was found to be nothing more than the displacements of moving. Every dollar was found to have its proper voucher, and in addition, care and competence stood proved in the expenditure of every single cent.

APPENDIX

I

THE AMERICAN NEWSPAPER PUBLISHERS' ASSOCIATION

I T can be stated as an indisputable fact that not once
in its existence was the Committee on Public Information attacked by any one with the slightest first-hand
knowledge of its activities. In no case was denunciation
ever preceded by the least attempt at investigation.
Speaking advisedly and after careful checking, I say that
every single public charge against the Committee was
made by a person or persons who were in absolute ignorance
of what we were doing, who made no effort to find out,
and who even after the attack could not be induced to
pay a visit of inspection.

Perhaps the most illustrative incident of the kind was
the case of one Hopewell Rogers, who, in the closing hours
of the convention of the American Newspaper Publishers'
Association, made a speech in which he scored the Committee as useless, branded me as "incompetent and disloyal." It was a cruel and cowardly attack, for he timed
it in such a manner that I was given no chance to appear
in reply, and what gave it added bitterness was that
Rogers, while slandering the sacrifices of hundreds of devoted men and women, was himself holding his peace-
time job and enjoying his peace-time profits. Putting
personal anger to one side, however, I addressed myself
to the task of turning the attack to account by using it
as a means of *forcing* an investigation that would once

29   437

and for all establish the Committee's competency or incompetency. How the effort failed is set forth in the following correspondence:

April 29, 1918.

MR. FRANK P. GLASS,
The Birmingham News, Birmingham, Alabama.

MY DEAR MR. GLASS:

The following telegram was sent by me on the evening of April 25th:

HOPEWELL ROGERS,
American Newspaper Publishers' Association,
Waldorf-Astoria Hotel, New York City.

Have just read report of your speech criticizing publicity policy of government. I assume your absolute sincerity, but feel that no criticism can be constructive when based only upon hearsay and personal opinion. In the interest of larger effectiveness I respectfully urge you to come to Washington, either with a committee or your entire membership, for a full and frank discussion of these mutual problems. I pledge full information as to every activity of the Committee on Public Information, and will welcome advice, suggestion, and co-operation. In view of your criticism given publicly as the head of a great organization, I feel strongly that your acceptance is compelled by fairness as well as the national interests.

It does not appear that this telegram was communicated either to the directors of the Association or to the delegates, nor have I had any reply from Mr. Rogers himself. I am writing to you as the newly elected president of the American Newspaper Publishers' Association, for the matters involved are of too great importance to be dismissed as a mere convention incident.

When Mr. Rogers accuses me of disloyalty, I am not greatly disturbed, for I feel that the devotions of a lifetime will weigh against any single reckless, unsupported statement made in prejudice and partizanship. When Mr. Rogers attacks my competency, however, the personal element disappears, for not only does he assail the entire educational work that the Committee on Public Information is doing in the United States, and in every other country in the world, but he impugns the motives and merits of thousands of patriotic men and women who have given themselves wholeheartedly and unselfishly to this branch of the national service.

Three thousand historians are at our call in the preparation of pamphlet matter; virtually every writer of prominence is giving time to the work of the Committee; the Division of Advertising enlists the energies of every great advertising expert in the United States; there are close to fifty thousand speakers in the Four Minute Men; the war conferences of the states are under our supervision; men and women of all nationalities go from coast to coast at our bidding; the famous artists of the United States are banded together for the production of our posters; the motion-picture industry has been mobilized and is giving us ungrudging support without thought of financial return; and in every capital in the world there are men and women serving with courage and intelligence.

I can readily understand how the Germans might insist that our effort was worthless, and that these thousands were laboring vainly and even disloyally, but it is amazing indeed that one who calls himself an American should level such a charge, especially when he has never taken the trouble to call upon me and knows absolutely nothing of the work of this Committee, its aims, and its plans.

I insist that the American Newspaper Publishers' Association is compelled by every dictate of patriotism to prove or disprove the charges that Mr. Rogers made as its president. As stated in my telegram, I shall be glad to receive any committee, no matter what its size, welcoming the fullest possible investigation —and so confident am I that I permit you, and even urge you, to compose it of men who have the idea that my work could be done more effectively.

I have long felt the need of an advisory committee made up of those truly representative of the press of the United States, but I think you will agree with me that such a selection is attended with many difficulties. The American Newspaper Publishers' Association is the one great body in the field, and yet even this does not express the views and desires of the editorial room, with which the government is concerned, but represents the business control. That body of the press which deals with the news itself is without national organization, and any attempt to select from its vast personnel would involve an unfair discrimination at the very outset.

I beg you to believe it is not only an injustice that I am seeking to have remedied. It is a great and necessary work that I am trying to protect. If the American Newspaper Publishers' Association can help me in any manner, or point out to me what larger efficiency can be secured, it is its duty. I shall be glad to receive this committee at any time.

Sincerely,

GEORGE CREEL,
Chairman.

May 4, 1918.

MR. GEORGE CREEL, Chairman,
Committee on Public Information, City.

MY DEAR MR. CREEL:

Since the conference with you at the Cosmos Club on the part of Mr. McAneny and myself, we have been much engrossed with another matter of urgent interest to our Association. Nevertheless, we have given your complaint and suggestions serious consideration.

As the successor of Mr. Rogers in the presidency of the American Newspaper Publishers' Association I do not think I have any function in replying to your strictures upon his recent criticism. I do not believe that Mr. Rogers could have had any wish to imply that his utterances were to be accepted as the opinion of the American Newspaper Publishers' Association rather than as his own personal views. I may assure you, however, that I do not entertain, myself, the view that you have been disloyal to our country in any of your utterances or work.

Nevertheless, I am impressed with an important lesson of the incident, and that there should be a more thorough knowledge on the part of the public of your Committee's function and work. I am convinced that such a knowledge would be most beneficial to the country and especially to the newspapers. It is also probable that thereby your Committee's power for good would be strengthened.

In line with this view and with your own urgent request I

440

shall, therefore, appoint a committee of representative newspaper men connected with the membership of our Association, to come to Washington and to give the proper time to a careful inquiry into the work your Committee is doing, with the belief that it will find many excellent things to commend, and with the hope that it may develop suggestions that will prove valuable both to you and to the various official sources of information which you are trying to co-ordinate.

You have been unselfish enough to suggest that this committee be made up of some of your severest critics, but it seems the better way to appoint a thoroughly representative judicial body of men, who would not be tempted to sustain destructive criticism and who may be constructive in their report.

Unquestionably such a committee as yours can be of even greater service to our beloved country at this vital juncture, in giving the departments of the government a thoroughly acceptable publicity and at the same time of a type to which the newspapers will respond with the fullest sympathy. As soon as this committee is made up, I will take pleasure in giving you its personnel, in order that an agreement may be made as to the time for its work. Trusting this may be satisfactory, I am,

Sincerely yours,

FRANK P. GLASS.

May 4, 1918.

MR. FRANK P. GLASS,
The Raleigh Hotel, Washington, D. C.

MY DEAR MR. GLASS:

I am very happy to learn of your decision, and I agree with your point of view entirely. Virtually every paper in the country took the view that Mr. Rogers was speaking for the American Newspaper Publishers' Association, and nearly all of the headlines made the flat statement that it was "the publishers" who denounced me. The whole thing was so cruel and unfair that it was impossible for me at the time to keep out all feeling.

Will you be kind enough to let me see you before you announce a committee, for I think the appointments should be accompanied by a letter defining its attitude and its functions in line with the views expressed in your letter of May 4th. This accompanying statement can be framed so as to lift the whole thing out of the personal and up to the higher level of the co-operative.

Sincerely,

GEORGE CREEL,
Chairman.

It will be seen by these letters that I agreed to the elimination of the "Rogers incident," instead of insisting that he be forced on the witness-stand, and yet even after this concession I was not able to force the investigation that was due the Committee as a matter of common decency. Mr. Glass and Mr. McAneny gave good and honest effort to bring it about, but all the king's horses could not have dragged one of my enemies to Washington for the purpose of surveying the work of the Committee and reporting upon it. They preferred their prejudices to facts, their lies to truth.

II

ONE of the chief bitternesses against the Committee on Public Information was that it did not preach a gospel of hate. It is significant indeed that the attack never proceeded from the fighting force itself, or from men and women actually and actively engaged in war-work, but came invariably from "leagues" and "societies" operating in the name of "patriotism." It was not that these groups were bloodthirsty, or that they did not want to be helpful, but simply that chauvinism was forced upon them by the necessities of their organization. Being dependent for existence upon cash donations, it was essential that they "make a showing" in order that contributions might continue to be attracted. As they were outside the regular war-machinery, and especially as they were not organized for fixed service, it was inevitable that these "societies" and "leagues" should turn to the emotions as a field of activity, and try for an effect of value by noise, attack, and hysteria.

In the first days the Committee tried faithfully to establish working relations with such organizations, but it soon developed that they did not want to put their emotionalism in harness, but preferred to keep it free for exhibition purposes. For a time they filled the air with all sorts of sensational charges with regard to "spies" and "intrigue," but after one high official was called before a New York grand jury and forced to admit sheer recklessness of statement, they confined themselves to general thundering. The following correspondence is submitted as an illustration of method:

March 27, 1918.

GEORGE CREEL, ESQ.,
Committee on Public Information, Washington, D. C.

DEAR MR. CREEL:

As patriotic citizens endeavoring to support the Administration and to help win the war, we now feel compelled to bring to your attention a feature of the activities of the Committee on Public Information which we believe to be harmful. We protest that the attitude of that Committee is so pacific that now some of its work amounts to giving comfort to the enemy.

As an exhibit, we cite herewith the letter of the United States Commissioner of Education, Dr. P. P. Claxton, to Dr. R. L. Slagle, president of the University of South Dakota, published by the Creel Committee on Public Information on March 19th, in an *Official Bulletin*, from which we quote the following astounding statement: "Germany may even yet become one of the leading nations for the preservation of the peace of the world." We are greatly surprised that Mr. Creel should publish this pro-German letter in the *Official Bulletin*.

We respectfully point out that on the side of our enemies the present war has no parallel in any of the previous wars in which our country ever engaged. The rapacity, the ferocity, and the unspeakably vile methods of the military millions of Germany constitute a factor never before met with in warfare between civilized peoples. Our present enemies are in a class by themselves, and the conditions they have created must be met on our part by new alignments of thought and action. We can fight Christian enemies who fight honorably and fairly, and with humane regard for the weak and the defenseless, and easily become friends with them after the conflict. This is possible because fair-fighting enemies do not forfeit respect.

With Germany, however, we are confronted by a totally different case. On account of innumerable brutal and debasing acts, the whole German nation has forfeited our respect; and aside from a very small minority, the acts and the character of Germany

444

and the German people will not be forgotten by the American people in any less than one hundred years. Every true history of the war will be a history of the crimes of Germany.

Although the crimes of Germany in Europe have been committed by men in uniform, so far as we know, no eye-witness observer of the so-called "German people" ever has published one statement that the civilians of Germany were opposed to the war, or that they deplored the ruthless methods of the German military monsters of cruelty and destruction. On the contrary, we know from eye-witness testimony that "the German people" have universally taken great delight in the destruction of the unarmed people of London by air-craft bombs, the destruction of the passengers of the *Lusitania* and hundreds of other merchant ships by submarines, and they have silently acquiesced in the murder of eight hundred thousand Armenian Christians by the brutal Turks.

It is our conviction that the great majority of the American people now regard the army, the navy, and the people of Germany with horror and aversion. We are quite sure that the German language now is a hated language, and long will remain so. We believe that all efforts to condone its use in our schools will be resented by the American people, as we ourselves resent them. We regard the letter of Commissioner Claxton as an error of judgment, and decidedly calculated to give "comfort to the enemy."

Furthermore, we believe that the Creel Committee on Public Information has signally failed to put into the hands of our American soldiers and sailors any publication adequately telling them in plain language what they are fighting for, and why they should hate the enemy they are expected to meet and kill. We say this because we are informed that to-day many soldiers are asking their officers why America is in the war, and we are told that those officers need the information in order to give it out. In speaking of captured American soldiers now in Germany, the *Vossische Zeitung* newspaper says:

"They don't seem to entertain any deep-rooted hatred of Germany. If you ask them why they are making war on Germany you will always get the same answer: 'Because Wilson says it is necessary!'"

It is common knowledge that about three months ago out of about one hundred American soldiers in France who were asked one by one, "Why are you in the war?" the great majority of the answers showed an astounding lack of information regarding Germany, of appreciation of the crimes of her troops, and of the real reasons why we are in the war.

Very truly yours,

THE AMERICAN DEFENSE SOCIETY.

R. M. HURD,

Chairman, Board of Trustees.

H. D. CRAIG,　　　　　　HENRY C. QUIMBY,
Secretary.　　　　　*Chairman, Executive Committee.*

April 2, 1918.

MR. R. M. HURD,

American Defense Society, New York, N. Y.

DEAR SIR:

Your circular letter, sent to various officials of the government, as well as to myself, deals principally with the Claxton letter which appeared in the *Official Bulletin* of March 19th. I admit to you that I am absolutely opposed to many of the points made by Doctor Claxton, and had I seen the letter prior to its publication I would not have consented to its appearance. It came over from the Department of the Interior, however, and the editor of the *Bulletin* felt that it was official matter duly authorized, so did not take it up with me as is usually the case with articles involving policies. I have not made the matter the subject of any public dissent, for I feel that these mistakes of judgment should be remedied through personal approach, and not in the columns of the press.

Your flat statement that the Committee on Public Information has signally failed in its duty to acquaint the people in the fighting forces of the United States with the causes of war, and the true nature of the foe, proves only that you have not taken the trouble to examine the matter sent out by this Committee. As to why we fight, I am sending you, under separate cover, a copy of *How the War Came to America*, *The War Message and Facts Behind It*, *The President's Flag Day Speech with Evidence of Germany's Plans*, together with various other pamphlets bearing upon the same subject.

As evidence of the cruel and inhuman character of the war

446

methods of the foe, I send you also a copy of *German War Practices, Conquest and Kultur*, and other pamphlets of similar nature.

Your quotation from the *Vossische Zeitung* strikes me as a trifle naïve, for it is the point of view that a German paper would naturally take, and is in support of the lies with which they have been filling their people from the beginning. To have the American Defense Society swallow their propaganda whole is indeed a victory for the German campaign.

Your insistence that the great majority of soldiers in France show "an astounding lack of information regarding Germany," and "of appreciation of the crimes of her troops," is somewhat amazing to me. For three years the daily papers of the United States have been filled with the horrors of Belgium, the shame of the Serbian campaign, the ravishment of northern France, and the brutalities of the U-boat campaign, and what you ask us to assume is that the youth of America have never read these papers, and are waiting for some government pamphlet to tell them about the *Lusitania* and other crimes of the Imperial German government.

It is true that this Committee has never preached any doctrine of hate, for it is not our duty to deal in emotional appeals, but to give the people the facts from which conclusions may be drawn. And nothing is more untrue than to say that we have failed in this regard. Proof of this can be found in inspection of literature we have issued, the articles we have sent out for publication in the press, the speeches of Four Minute Men, and all the other varied activities of the Committee.

I dispute flatly your assertion that after three years of German warfare the people of the United States are still ignorant of German savagery, just as I dispute flatly your assumption that the speeches of the President of the United States, defining the causes of war, have not been read by any one. The people of the United States *do* understand, and the proof of it lies in the fact that the mothers of the country have given their sons to the Selective Service Law without question, that every Liberty Loan has been oversubscribed, and that no request of government has ever lacked complete response. Perhaps it is that this very indomitableness of resolve, this iron determination, leaves no room for the manifestations of surface passion.

Very truly,

GEORGE CREEL, *Chairman.*

HOW WE ADVERTISED AMERICA

The National Security League

September 12, 1918.

National Security League,
    31 Pine Street, New York, N. Y.

Dear Sir:

Certain New York papers, under date of September 12th, carry articles to the effect that the National Security League has forced the suppression of a book, entitled *2,000 Questions and Answers About the War*, with the foreword by me, the plain inference being drawn that this "Masterpiece of Hun Propaganda," as your organization styles it, was being freely circulated without criticism of any kind until your own investigators took patriotic action.

I cannot forgo a public protest against the singular dishonesty and even indecency of this publicity. The book, instead of being without responsible authorship, bore the imprint of *The Review of Reviews*, and so far back as June 26th I wrote the following letter to Dr. Albert Shaw:

June 26, 1918.

Dr. Albert Shaw,
    Review of Reviews, New York City, N. Y.

My dear Doctor Shaw:

While it is true that I glanced through the proofs of *2,000 Questions and Answers About the War*, before I wrote my foreword, it is equally true that I relied less upon my hasty reading than upon my absolute faith in you.

The last week or so I have made a more careful study of the book, and I must confess to a very definite disturbance of mind. The whole tone of the book strikes me as being 50-50, for nowhere in it can I find the fundamental truth that Germany was entirely responsible for this war, and that it is a war of self-defense upon the part of the liberal nations of the world. In connection with atrocities, deportations, hostages, use of gas, I am also unable to find anything that is in the nature of a straight-out condemnation of the Germans.

I feel sure that you yourself could not have had much to do with the book, or else the articles would have had a more intense Americanism and less of the evasive, straddling note. If there is a second edition, I do wish that you would take the whole

APPENDIX

matter up with me, so that this very valuable contribution to
war can be given greater effectiveness.
Sincerely,

GEORGE CREEL
Chairman.

This letter was followed at once by seven single-spaced type-
written pages, pointing out specific objections. Doctor Shaw
replied at once, promising instant correction and fullest revision.
He also stated that the book was based upon the accumulation
of material secured in advance sheets from the well-known
British journalist, the son of the late William T. Stead, and because of its source the editors had not given it the necessary
searching scrutiny.

I then took up the matter with Mr. George H. Doran, the
publisher, who, with his usual eager patriotism, agreed that the
sale of the book should be stopped until its contents were satisfactory to me. Because there was not the slightest evidence
of any premeditated pro-Germanism in the matter, because the
good faith and true Americanism of all the parties in the controversy were so obvious, and because the book itself had been
stopped and a new edition under way, I avoided all publicity
in the matter out of my desire to work no injustice to any one.

All these facts were laid before Professor van Tyne of your
organization. By his careful suppression of them in the story
that he gave to the press, I am led to believe that his sense of
honor is somewhat subordinated to his weakness for a little
cheap notoriety.
Very truly,

GEORGE CREEL,
Chairman.

September 20, 1918.
MR. CHARLES E. LYDECKER,
President, National Security League, New York City, N. Y.
DEAR SIR:

Your letter of the 13th instant, for some reason or other,
ignores entirely the fundamental questions in controversy.
Over his own signature, Dr. Claude H. van Tyne, speaking for
the National Security League, made this explicit statement:

HOW WE ADVERTISED AMERICA

"No author's name is given, so that no one else is responsible but the writer of the introduction.

"If Mr. Creel indorses ideas like these, as it seems he must, since he heartily recommends this book in his introduction, is he a safe man to occupy the position he does, so potent for the good or ill of our cause?"

At the time when he made this statement he was fully informed that the book, *2,000 Questions and Answers About the War*, had been prepared by *The Review of Reviews*, and that Dr. Albert Shaw was responsible for its issuance.

Also, at every point in the publicity of Doctor van Tyne, he gave the inference, and permitted the deduction, that I had done nothing whatsoever in the matter of suppressing the book, but that his task of suppression was undertaken by others more vigilant and more patriotic than myself.

At the time that he gave this unfair and misleading impression to the public he had been informed that at my own request, made two months before, the first limited edition of the book had been withdrawn from sale; that the new edition had been held up, and that every force in my power had been devoted to preventing the circulation of matter against which I myself had been the first to protest.

It was because of these two things, and these two alone, that I branded the publicity of the National Security League as "indecent and dishonest," and by this statement I stand unalterably.

The New York Times, in its issue of September 13th, after considering the whole controversy, concluded with this paragraph:

"The National Security League, through its publicity agent, E. L. Harvey, said, when asked why the explanation of *The Review of Reviews* had not appeared at the same time with the attack on the book, that it was not the business of the League to defend the magazine or its publishers. If they had any defense, he added, they could make it themselves."

I say to you very deliberately that this point of view, whether that of any employee or of the organization itself, is in itself as singularly dishonest and indecent as the original offense.

This whole matter is worthy to be dealt with in some detail, since it establishes quite clearly the fundamental differences between the Committee on Public Information and the National Security League.

APPENDIX

When Dr. Albert Shaw first approached me with regard to a foreword, I glanced hastily through the proofs in order to ascertain its nature. The purpose impressed me as important and my failure to give the book any closer reading was due to these facts: my faith in Doctor Shaw; knowledge that the material came from British sources exclusively, and that every line of it had passed through the British censorship. This may not be an excuse, but it is an honest explanation.

The book was issued on June 20th in an edition of five thousand. On June 26th, certain disturbing points having been called to my attention by my associates, I wrote Doctor Shaw, protesting specifically against the 50-50 tone of the book and its failure to make a straight-out condemnation of the Germans. I followed this up immediately by a personal interview with Doctor Shaw, in which he gave his assurance that no single other copy of the book would be issued until it had been changed to meet my own ideas and the ideas of the French and the British. In confirmation of this, Mr. George H. Doran, the publisher, returned every unsold book to *The Review of Reviews.*

I had then two courses of action open to me, either to make public announcement of my position or else to rest satisfied with the instant and eager acquiescence of the publishers in the work of suppression and correction.

To take the first course was to save myself from attack at the expense of the men in whose honesty and patriotism I had every faith. Like myself, Doctor Shaw had accepted the source as authoritative; Mr. George H. Doran, the publisher, is a one-hundred-per-cent. American, and at no point was there the slightest evidence of premeditated pro-Germanism. To-day the whole matter is being rewritten by British and French official authorities and by the highest sources of American public opinion.

It is also true that my relations with the publishers of the country are very intimate and very important. Without force of law, and with no larger authority than an appeal to their patriotism, I have procured the suppression of scores of books that, while not pro-German in any degree, have at the same time given false and misleading impressions of America's war aims. All this work has been done without blare of trumpets. It has been done without discredit to honest publishers, and so it was that I resolved to adhere to this fixed policy and rested content with the virtual suppression of the book.

It is with this policy that the National Security League seems to be in fundamental disagreement. Your emphasis is on the destructive rather than on the constructive; more on your own identity and less on justice and unity.

Very truly,

GEORGE CREEL,
Chairman.

WHEN I "THANKED GOD"

WASHINGTON, *April 10, 1918.*

SENATOR OLLIE JAMES,

The Senate Office Building, City.

MY DEAR SENATOR JAMES:

I have just received your note asking for the facts in connection with the charge that I "thanked God" that we were not prepared when America entered the war. I am only too glad to give them, but trust that you will not let your generous feeling in the matter lead you into any open discussion on the Senate floor.

These hues and cries are best handled by being permitted to die of their own violence. Lies are only fanned to new flame by thrashing at them. My enemies—newspapers and partizan malignants—do not mean to be fair, and I have found that this very unfairness comes in time to be my best defense. It is also the case that I am driven night and day by the demands of my work, and I have not the time, even if I had the inclination, to engage in long, tedious debates or correspondence whenever a reporter or a member of Congress tortures some act or word of mine into a crime.

The speech in question was made before the lecturers of the Lyceum and Chautauqua Association, men and women who go from coast to coast in the course of the year, talking intimately to thousands. The meeting, in fact, was held in Washington at my request, for I wanted these people to gain the inspiration bred by hearing Cabinet members, high executives, ambassadors, and all others concerned with the direction of the war. As part of my regular work I secured their speakers, and no more important list was ever compiled.

In opening the session I told them that they should regard

452

themselves as soldiers called to the colors in the fight for public opinion, and that wherever they went, wherever they spoke, it was their duty to drive home the justice of America's cause. In the sane sense of the word, these men and women were pacifists, meaning that they hated war. And Chautauqua audiences, for the most part, are rural in their character, sharing little in the mob excitements of cities, peace-loving to the last degree, and holding deeply to the traditional prejudice against "entangling alliances."

What I tried to do in my speech was to prove conclusively that the war was a war of self-defense, and that our free institutions were as much attacked, and in as great danger, as if the foot of the German was on our very soil. And because the question of our "preparedness" was, in its essence, the moral ground upon which we rested our justification before the world, I went into it from the very beginning.

In my remarks, I tried to point out what seemed to me the state of mind of the American people during the first years of the European War. It was not immediately, by any means, that the full horror of Germany's crimes and purposes penetrated the national consciousness. Not at the time of the German invasion, or for months afterward, was the question of a protest by the United States even suggested in Congress or advocated in the press. The visit of the Belgian deputation in September, 1914, moved our sympathies, but not our resolution.

As the war progressed, it became increasingly apparent that the neutrality approved by the nation and enforced by President Wilson was menaced at many points by the refusal of the Imperial German government to abide by international law. As our protest was against the use of force as a means of solving international disputes, our first logical and consistent course could have been no other than an honest appeal to the law that we were insisting should be respected.

President Wilson, following in the footsteps of Washington, Adams, Jefferson, Lincoln, and Grant, all of whom were Presidents during periods in which belligerents violated American rights of neutrality, held to orderly procedure, refusing to resort to force until every peaceful means of adjusting differences had been exhausted.

The notes to Germany were more than diplomatic exchanges designed to redress certain definite wrongs. They were affidavits attesting our passion for peace and the utter selflessness of our purposes; they were the foundation stones for our present justification; and because of these notes it is the case to-day that the citizen confesses disloyalty and treason who dares to say that war was not forced upon America and that it is not a war of self-defense in behalf of free institutions and human liberty.

Even in Germany to-day they admit the justice of our cause when they debate the wisdom of their policy in driving us into the war. At home, this historic and just policy laid the foundations for unexampled national unity on the part of our people in support of measures against a power whose hideous purposes stood self-confessed. It created a national morale which will not only weather every storm, but stand unshaken when the deeps of our national and domestic life are stirred by sacrifice and suffering.

I stand absolutely on the sense of my words when I say that it is the glory of America, as it is of Belgium and of England and France, that is asking and expecting these sacrifices to the uttermost; we can say honestly to every man in the trenches and every home in sorrow that we strove to keep the peace, and that these supremest offerings may be given to a nation that never betrayed itself or its people by striving for peace as a blind for preparing for war.

What I thanked God for was that America could stand before the world with conscience clear of blood-guilt; that to the future we could hold clear hands; that while we pleaded for peace we did not tug secretly at the sword; that not until pleading became dishonor did we put down the pen and turn to the business of war.

I shall always thank God for this fact. I would rather be an American, killed in the unpreparedness that proved devotion to declared principles, than a German living as the result of years of lying, sneaking, treacherous preparation for a wolf's spring at the throat of an unsuspecting world. And it is this deep conviction of honor and faith that will *win* for us.

I can only add in conclusion that the men and women who heard me united in an unanimous vote of thanks for my "most patriotic speech."

Believe me, sir,

Very gratefully yours,

GEORGE CREEL.

APPENDIX

PUBLICATIONS OF THE COMMITTEE ON PUBLIC INFORMATION
IN THE UNITED STATES

RED, WHITE, AND BLUE SERIES

1. *How the War Came to America*................ 5,428,048
   Swedish edition......................... 67,487
   Polish   "   82,658
   German   "   292,610
   Italian   "   129,860
   Spanish   "   96,816
   Bohemian   "   121,058
   Portuguese   "   9,375
2. *National Service Handbook*.................... 454,699
3. *The Battle-line of Democracy*................. 94,848
4. *The President's Flag Day Address, with Evidence
   of Germany's Plans*....................... 6,813,340
5. *Conquest and Kultur.* Edited by WALLACE NOTE-
   STEIN and ELMER E. STOLL (University of Minnesota)................................... 1,203,607
6. *German War Practices.* Part I. "Treatment of
   Civilians." Edited by DANA C. MUNRO (Princeton University), GEORGE C. SELLERY (University of Wisconsin), and AUGUST C. KREY (University of Minnesota)..................... 1,592,801
7. *War Cyclopedia. A Handbook for Ready Reference on the Great War.* Edited by FREDERIC L.
   PAXSON (University of Wisconsin), EDWARD S.
   CORWIN (Princeton University), and SAMUEL
   B. HARDING (Indiana University)........... 195,231
8. *German Treatment of Conquered Territory.* (Part
   II of *German War Practices.*) Edited by DANA
   C. MUNRO (Princeton University), GEORGE C.
   SELLERY (University of Wisconsin), and AU-
   GUST C. KREY (University of Minnesota)..... 720,848
9. *War, Labor, and Peace: Some Recent Addresses
   and Writings of the President*.............. 584,027
10. *German Plots and Intrigues.* Edited by E. E.
    SPERRY of Syracuse University and W. M.
    WEST, formerly of Minnesota.............. 127,153

WAR INFORMATION SERIES

1. *The War Message and the Facts Behind It.* Edited by WILLIAM STERNS DAVIS (University of Minnesota).......................... 2,499,903
2. *The Nation in Arms.* Two addresses by Secretaries LANE and BAKER................... 1,666,231
3. *The Government of Germany.* By CHARLES D. HAZEN (Columbia University)............. 1,798,155
   German edition....................... 20,500
4. *The Great War: From Spectator to Participant.* By ANDREW C. McLAUGHLIN (University of Chicago)............................... 1,581,903
5. *A War of Self-defense.* Addresses by Secretary LANSING and LOUIS F. POST, Assistant Secretary of Labor........................... 721,944
6. *American Loyalty.* By American Citizens of German Descent........................ 702,598
7. *Amerikanische Bürgertreue.* A German translation of Number 6........................ 564,787
8. *American Interest in Popular Government Abroad.* By E. B. GREENE (University of Illinois)..... 596,533
9. *Home Reading Course for Citizen Soldiers.* Prepared by the War Department............. 361,000
10. *First Session of the War Congress.* By CHARLES MERZ.................................. 608,950
11. *The German War Code.* By G. W. SCOTT (Columbia University) and J. W. GARNER (University of Illinois)............................... 514,452
12. *American and Allied Ideals.* By STUART P. SHERMAN (University of Illinois)................. 228,986
13. *German Militarism and Its German Critics.* By CHARLES ALTSCHUL...................... 303,600
    German edition...................... 103,300
14. *The War for Peace.* By ARTHUR D. COLL, Secretary of the American Peace Society.......... 302,370
15. *Why America Fights Germany.* By JOHN P. TATLOCK (Stanford University)............. 725,345
16. *The Study of the Great War.* By SAMUEL B. HARDING (Indiana University)............. 678,929

APPENDIX

17. *The Activities of the Committee on Public Information*.................................. 23,800
18. *Regimental History of the U. S. Regular Army* (for war correspondents only)................... 1,000
19. *Lieber and Schurz: Two Loyal Americans of German Birth.* By E. B. GREENE (University of Illinois)................................ 26,360
20. *The German-Bolshevik Conspiracy.* Documents and report by EDGAR SISSON............... 137,375
21. *America's War Aims and Peace Terms.* By CARL BECKER (Cornell University)............... 719,315

LOYALTY LEAFLETS

A series of leaflets of ordinary envelope size

1. *Friendly Words to the Foreign Born.* By HON. JOSEPH BUFFINGTON, senior United States Circuit Judge of the Third Circuit. (Translations into the principal foreign languages.) 570,543
2. *The Prussian System.* By FREDERIC C. WALCOTT, of the United States Food Administration 571,036
3. *Labor and the War.* President Wilson's address to the American Federation of Labor, November 12. 1917............................ 509,550
4. *A War Message to the Farmer.* By PRESIDENT WILSON................................. 546,911
5. *Plain Issues of the War.* By ELIHU ROOT, ex-Secretary of State....................... 112,492
6. *Ways to Serve the Nation.* A proclamation by the President, April 16, 1917............... 568,907
7. *What Really Matters.* By a well-known newspaper writer............................. 574,502

PUBLICATIONS FOR "THE FRIENDS OF GERMAN DEMOCRACY" (In German)

My London Mission (Prince Lichnowsky).......... 661,300
The Meaning of America........................ 10,421
The Democratic Rising of the German People in '48... 20,320

On Loyalty, Liberty, and Democracy	19,070
American Friends of German Democracy	61,500
Democracy, the Heritage of All	30,000
The Root of the Evil	30,000
No Qualified Americanism	30,100
German Militarism and Its German Critics	1,500

PUBLICATIONS FOR DIVISION OF AMERICAN ALLIANCE FOR
LABOR AND DEMOCRACY

Why Workingmen Support the War	313,535
Who Is Paying for This War	313,082
German Socialists and the War	316,005
To the Workers of Free America	323,605
What Can Your Local Branch Do?	15,000
Labor's Red, White, and Blue Book	99,385

PUBLICATIONS FOR FOREIGN SECTION

The Freedom of the World (Spanish)	102,967
The German Plan (Spanish)	95,798
American Loyalty (Spanish)	124,229
The Meaning of the War	125,100
The Lichnowsky Revelation (Spanish)	46,850
Labor and the War (Spanish)	48,611
A Call to My Fatherland (German)	60,500
German Plots and Intrigues (Spanish)	49,750
German Plots and Intrigues (Portuguese)	15,000
America's War Aims (Spanish)	98,000

MISCELLANEOUS

National School Service	4,251,570
The Kaiserite in America. By HARVEY J. O'HIGGINS	5,550,521
Germany's Confession	324,935
The German Whisper. By HARVEY J. O'HIGGINS	437,484
Farmers' Bulletin	8,000
Purpose and Scope of the Speaking Division	25,000
Issues of the War at a Glance	25,000
For Freedom (Serbian National Defense)	5,000
War Savings Campaign Appeals	6,000

APPENDIX

War Publications Bulletin	**13,126,006**
Division of Films Bulletin	121,119
Selective Service Registration Bulletin	756,700
Advertising Bulletin (for Registration Day)	112,000
"Register" (Four Minute Men)	1,606,350
Poster. "Why Germany Wants Peace"	31,000
Posters. "Capitol Building"	26,100
Posters. "Independence Hall"	26,100
Posters for War Cyclopedia	2,050
Posters. "America Gave You All"	7,500
Map. "The Pan-German Plan"	122,000
Newspaper, United States Department of Labor	80,000
Streamers, Four Minute Men	25,000
Nine lectures to accompany slides	45,000
War Work of Women in Colleges	50,000
Post-cards	1,687,408
Official Bulletin	2,154,809
46 Bulletins for Four Minute Men	4,974,000
26 Bulletins for Bureau of Cartoons	25,000
America in War and Peace (Ukrainian)	40,000
A Message to American Hungarians (Magyar)	40,000
Abraham Lincoln (Russian)	40,000
	75,099,023

INDEX

A

Ackerman, Lieut. F. E.,   67, 365.
Adams, Herbert, 134.
Adams, Samuel Hopkins, 88, 225.
Altrocchi, Dr. Rudolph, 300.
Altschul, Charles, 107.
Anderson, Louis M., 186.
Andreen, Gustav, 185.
Andrews, Mary Shipman, 262.
Antonsen, Carl, 185.
Arnold, Perry, 234, 251, 254.
Atherton, Gertrude, 261.

B

Bagley, W. C., 112.
Bagues, Mme. Edith, 292, 293.
Bakeman, George, 380.
Baker, Ray Stannard, 413.
Banning, Kendall, 118.
Barnes, H. Y., 279, 380.
Barr, Gertrude, 300.
Baruch, Bernard, 52.
Beach, Rex, 225.
Becker, Prof. Carl, 103, 106.
Beeman, Marcus A., 122.
Bennington, Arthur, 300.
Bergquist, J. C., 185.
Bernays, Edward 266.
Bernstein, Herman, 278
Berton, Claude, 293.
Bestor, Arthur E., 149, 150, 154, 155.
Bjorkman, Edwin, 184, 185, 230, 265.
Blair, William McCormick, 66. 88, 93.
Blaisdell, L. S., 370.
Blankenburg, Rudolph, 188.
Blashfield, E. H., 134.
Bohn, Dr. Frank, 153, 191.
Bohn, Dr. William H., 153, 188.
Bonaschi, Dr. Albert, 186, 199.

Bonnifield, R., 231.
Bothwell, George, 380, 392.
Bowles, George, 121.
Boyle, Virginia Frazer, 225.
Brace, A., 293.
Bricker, William R., 189.
Broun, Heywood, 81.
Brown, Prof. G. S., 371.
Brown, L. Ames, 80, 226.
Brown, P. P., 231.
Brown, William Adams, 380, 383, 396.
Brown, Major W. L., 152.
Bruère, Martha Bensley, 225.
Brulatour, Jules E., 274.
Bullard, Arthur, 19, 70, 100, 102, 248,
   278, 279, 288, 375, 379, 380, 383,
   385, 394, 395, 433.
Bullen, P. S., 231.
Bullock, W. F., 231.
Butler, Ellis Parker, 225, 261
Butman, Carl H., 82.
Butz, Otto C., 188.
Byoir, Carl, 66, 248, 275, 404, 419, 427,
   433.

C

Call, Arthur D., 106.
Carnes, William, 380.
Carpio, Señor Manuel, 227.
Casey, F. De Sales, 134.
Cassuto, Aldo, 230.
Catt, Mrs. Carrie Chapman, 212.
Ceglinsky, Nicholas, 199.
Chadbourne, Waldmar, 346.
Chilberg, J. E., 185.
Child, Richard Washburn, 225.
Christensen, John C., 185.
Clark, Miss Eleanor, 219.
Clark, S. H., 88.
Clark, S. J., 231.
Clark, Victor, 111

HOW WE ADVERTISED AMERICA

Clarkin, Franklin, 380.
Clarkson, Ralph, 134.
Clausen, W. B., 253.
Collins, James H., 225.
Collins, John, 253, 372.
Collins, Sewall, 346.
Collins, Seward B., 343.
Commons, Prof. John R., 106.
Connell, Catherine, 219.
Connor, Professor, 111.
Converse, Miss Antonio Thornton Jenkins, 219.
Cook, Sir Theodore, 255.
Coolidge, Prof. A. C., 111.
Cooper, F. G., 134.
Copeland, C. W., 371.
Cordner, E. Q., 300.
Corwin, Professor, 108.
Coss, Dr. J. J., 108.
Cotillo, Senator Salvatore, 300.
Craig, H. D., 446.
Crawford, Arthur, 82.
Crocker, Frederico, 368.
Crossley, Captain, 346.
Crow, Carl, 249, 254, 361.
Crowder, General E. H., 195.
Culbertson, Henry C., 152.
Cusack, Thomas, 158.
Czabulk, Gustave, 422.

D

D'Arcy, W. C., 144, 158.
Davenport, Prof. Eugene, 225.
Davies, W. W., 231.
Davis, Jerome, 377.
Davis, Malcolm, 380, 383, 393.
Davis, M. W., 394, 395.
Davis, Prof. S. W., 102.
Dawson, William, 368.
Dayton, F. E., 134.
de Bryas, Countess Madeleine, 151.
Decker, Capt. Benton C., 339, 345, 346.
de Courtivron, Marquise Crequi de Montfort, 153.
Deeds, Col. Edward A., 45, 46, 52.
Delavaud, Henri Collins, 231.
De Lima, Arthur, 309.
Delmas, H., 231.
De Mora, Señor I., 346.

Dever, Lem A., 380.
Dilnot, Frank, 231.
Dodd, Professor, 111.
Dodge, Philip L., 88.
Doran, George H., 451.
Doskow, I., 134.
Dowling, Loretta, 220.
Durant, Kenneth, 83, 300.

E

Eaton, Walter Prichard, 262.
Eberlin, Viggo C., 199.
Edwards, Paul L., 332.
Egan, Martin, 291.
Erskine, Prof. John, 225.
Espinosa, Dr. M. K., 313.
Evans, Sid., 380.

F

Falls, Charles B., 134.
Ferber, Edna, 262.
Ferrera, Dr. F., 231.
Ferretti, Andrea, 231.
Fife, George B., 321.
Fish, Professor, 111.
Forbes, Helen, 219–220.
Ford, Guy Stanton, 66, 86, 101.
Fordney, Representative, 54.
Forster, Dr. William, 189.
Foster, Maximilian, 257, 291.
Franck, Harry A., 284.
Fraser, Sir John Foster, 231.
Frisbie, J. B., 316.
Frost, Wesley, 153.

G

Gallatin, Albert E., 134.
Gardner, Frank S., 254.
Garner, Prof. J. W., 107.
Garrett, John Work, 328, 334.
Gay, Señor José M., 346.
Gibbons, Herbert Adams, 296, 297.
Gibson, Charles Dana, 134 139. 244.
Gilbert, Cass, 134.
Glaman, Otto J., 380, 393, 396.
Glass, Frank P., 438.
Gleason, Arthur, 262.

INDEX

Gocheler, Gertrude, 428.
Goldman, Emma, 241.
Gorton, Miss Elizabeth, 216, 217.
Grahame, Leopold, 231.
Greeling, Doctor, 191.
Greene, Prof. Evarts B., 106–111.
Greenleaf, Ray, 134.
Griffis, C. V., 248, 280, 368.
Grinndal, H. Gude, 198.
Groszmann, Doctor, 264
Grover, Oliver D., 134.
Gundlach, E. T., 86.
Gutmann, James, 108.

H

Hackett, F. E., 224.
Haggerty, Dennis J., 380.
Hahn, Kurt, 331.
Hall, E. W. M., 231.
Hall, Henry N., 231.
Handley, Mrs., 280.
Hangan, Hauman G., 186.
Hanse, Jens C., 185.
Hansen, Sundby, 198.
Harding, J. W., 231.
Harding, Prof. Samuel, 108–111.
Harn, O. C., 156, 158.
Harrell, David, 346.
Harris, Gerrard, 83.
Hart, Charles S., 120–144, 244, 275.
Hart, Wilbur H., 279.
Harvey, Ellen, 217.
Haskins, Frederick, 110.
Hatada, Y., 231.
Hatrick, Edgar B., 293, 294.
Hazen, Prof. Charles D., 107–111.
Hearley, John, 299, 419.
Hecht, George J., 226.
Hecht, Harold E., 129.
Hellrung, Axel, 185.
Helwig, Capt. A. L., 190.
Henius, Max, 185.
Henschen, Henry S., 185.
Herman, W. J., 231.
Herrick, Robert, 261.
Hertz, Henry L., 185.
Hillier, Frank, 231.
Hinkovic, Doctor, 187.
Hirsimaki, Charles H., 199.

Hirt, Dr. William H., 268.
Hitchcock, E. H., 83.
Hittinger, Capt. Joseph H., 142.
Hoagland, H. C., 277, 301.
Hobbs, E. H., 428.
Hoffman, Dr. Frederick L., 188.
Hoffman, Miss Malvina, 134.
Hogue, Miss Helen M., 218.
Houston, Herbert S., 156–158.
Hovgaard, William, 185.
Howells, Wm. Dean, 262.
Howland, John P., 185.
Hull, Professor, 111.
Hurd, R. M., 446.
Hurst, Fannie, 262.
Hyde, James Hazen, 293.

I

Ingersoll, William H., 88–93.
Inman, Harry P., 279.
Irwin, Wallace, 82, 225, 262.
Irwin, Will, 200, 202, 247.
Ivanowski, Sigismund, 136.

J

Jacobi, Dr. Abraham, 188.
Jacobsen, Halvor, 185.
James, Major A. L., Jr., 287, 293.
James, Senator Ollie, 452.
Jameson, Prof. J. Franklin, 111.
Jasberg, J. H., 186.
Jenison, Miss Marguerite, 219.
Jenkins, John Wilbur, 81.
Johns, Wm. H., 158.
Johnson, Professor, 111.
Jones, Francis, 134.
Jones, Lewis B., 158.
Jury, Sir William, 299.

K

Kaupas, Julius, 199.
Keeley, James, 284.
Kellogg, Dr. Vernon, 152.
Kelly, E. W., 231.
Kennaday, Paul, 261.

HOW WE ADVERTISED AMERICA

Kerney, James F., 245, 248, 251, 284, 290-297.
Kinkaid, Mrs. Mary H., 212.
Kitchen, Miss Dorothy Lewis, 214.
Klein, Arthur, 224.
Knecht, Marcel, 231.
Knopf, Dr. S. Adolphus, 188
Knutson, Representative, 55.
Koenig, Prof. A. E., 153.
Koettgen, Julius, 188, 189, 199
Konta, Alex., 187.
Kranz, Carl, 392.
Krey, Prof. A. C., 106.
Kuhn, L., 314.

L

Langquist, Andrew, 185.
Larson, O. J., 186.
Lauzanne, S., 232.
Lawson, S. Levy, 232.
Lee, C. D., 433.
Leicht, Miss Gretchen, 226.
Leland, Professor, 111.
Levy, Leon, 232.
Lewis, Read, 279, 380.
Lewis, Wilmot A., 293.
Lichnowsky, Prince, 189-312.
Lieber, Richard, 189.
Lindsey, Judge Ben B., 300.
Lingelbach, Professor, 111.
Livingston, Prof. Arthur, 263.
Lodge, Senator H. C., 59.
Loewy, Captain S., 232.
Low, A. Maurice, 232.
Lund, Harry A., 185.

Mc.

McAneny, George, 440.
McClure, Frank W., 155.
McConaghy, W. J., 80.
McCormack, John, 204, 207.
McCormick, Vance, 275.
McGoodwin, Preston, 372.
McGowan, Miss Constance Marguerite, 216.
McIntyre, Gen. Frank, 75.
McLaughlin, Andrew C., 106.
McReynolds, Prof. F. W., 223, 224.

M

MacCallum, N., 232.
MacFarlane, Arthur, 226.
Mack, Louis B., 119.
Mansfield, Frank M., 293.
Marion, Frank J., 248, 337, 338, 347.
Markus, Alfred, 199.
Marriott, Crittenden, 225.
Martin, "Mac," 88.
Masaryk, Dr. Thos. G., 186.
Mason, Warren, 232.
Mathie, Dr. Karl, 153, 188
Matson, Norman, 270.
Matthews, Arthur F., 134.
Mattingly, Archibald, 83.
Meek, Thos. J., 89.
Meeker, Geo., 124.
Mellet, J. C., 82.
Merriam, Prof. Charles E., 244, 248, 299, 300.
Merwin, Samuel, 225, 262.
Miller, Mrs. Laura, 217.
Mladineo, Peter, 199.
Montenegro, Ernest, 232.
Mooney, Hon. Daniel, 368.
Moran, Prof. Thos. F., 155.
Morgan, Edwin V., 248, 372.
Morgenstern, B., 377.
Morris, Ira Nelson, 354.
Morris, Miss Mildred, 214.
Morris, Ambassador Roland, 249, 363.
Morrison, Martin A., 224.
Moses, Kingsley, 300.
Moses, Miss Margaret, 214.
Mundell, Mrs. William A., 214.
Munroe, Prof. Dana C., 106-111.
Murray, Robert H., 227, 228, 245, 248, 303, 308, 309.
Myhrman, Othelia, 185.

N

Navarro, Prof. M. Romero, 341, 346.
Neal, Jesse H., 158.
Neble, Sophus F., 185.
Nelson, Bertram G., 88.
Nestor, Byron M., 300, 301.
Newdick, Edwin, 82.
Nicholson, Curtis, 88.

INDEX

Nicholson, Meredith, 225, 262.
Niebuhr, Walter, 119.
Nielsen, Truels P., 185.
Nolan, Gen. Dennis E., 287, 293.
Normile, Mrs. Florence, 216.
Norton, Charles Philip, 279.
Norton, Eric, 185.
Norton, Phil, 380.
Notestein, Prof. Wallace, 106–111.

O

O'Higgins, Harvey, 225, 427.
Olander, Victor, 185.
Olsen, Harry, 185.
O'Reilly, Lieut. P. S., 228, 254.
Osland, Berger, 185.
Owens, Hamilton, 263.

P

Paderewski, 186.
Paine, Ralph D., 225.
Palavacini, Señor Felix, 227.
Palmer, Eric, 248, 354.
Paxon, Professor, 108.
Payne, Will, 262.
Peccorini, Lieut. Albert, 300.
Peebles, Miss Catherine H., 219.
Pennell, Joseph, 134, 342.
Penrose, Senator Boise, 36–58.
Pergler, Charles, 186.
Perigord, Capt. Paul, 151.
Pernis, James J. Van, 199.
Perrin, Lester, 422.
Perry, Paul, 248, 298.
Peterson, Charles A., 185.
Pettijohn, Prof. J. J., 155.
Pew, Marlen, 82.
Plottier, A., 232.
Plowes, Señor Zamora, 227.
Poindexter, Senator Miles, 58.
Polignac, Marquis de, 154–293.
Polonsky, Joseph, 199.
Poole, Ernest, 70–103, 243, 244, 261, 353.
Post, Louis F., 107.
Potter, C. J., 160.
Pou, Representative E. W., 61.
Pousette-Dart, N., 134.

Powell, J. B., 362.
Pratt, Llewellyn, 144.
Preciado, A. A., 248, 372.

Q

Quick, Herbert, 225.
Quimby, Henry C., 446.

R

Raine, Wm. MacLeod, 226.
Randall, Helen, 214.
Rankin, W. H., 146, 156, 157.
Rascovar, E., 232.
Reilly, Leigh, 80.
Reilly, R. R., 254.
Reinsch, Dr. Paul, 249–361.
Renault, Louis, 296.
Reuterdahl, Henry N., 134.
Richards, Livy, 82.
Rickey, Harry N., 247, 248, 298.
Riesenberg, Henry, 153, 189.
Riis, George Edward, 248, 349.
Riis, Jacob, 248.
Rinehart, Mary Roberts, 77, 225.
Roche, Josephine, 191, 202.
Rochester, E. S., 208.
Rochon, R. J., 254.
Rogers, Hopewell, 437.
Rogers, W. A., 134.
Rogers, Walter S., 231, 250, 254, 258, 260, 414, 417, 433.
Rohe, Alice, 300.
Ronconi, Romeo, 232.
Root, Elihu, 106.
Rose, Miss Anna Maria Perrott, 220.
Rosenmeyer, Doctor, 191.
Rosenwald, Julius, 52.
Rosett, Dr. Joshua, 380, 394.
Rothapfel, L. S., 122.
Rothman, A., 232.
Rubel, Lawrence E., 118, 129.
Russell, Charles Edward, 153, 154, 248, 293, 298.
Russell, Prof. William, 380, 394, 395.
Ryan, John D., 52, 298.
Ryerson, Donald, 84, 88, 93.
Rygg, A. M., 186.

S

Saperston, Alfred M., 226.
Schafer, Professor, 111.
Schauer, George, 189.
Schlegel, Charles J., 188.
Schoolfield, Miss Sue, 219.
Schoonmaker, Edwin, 380.
Scott, Prof. G. W., 107.
Scott, John Reed, 225.
Searson, J. W., 112.
Sellery, Prof. G. C., 106.
Sevier, H. H., 248, 281, 365.
Sharp, Ambassador, 291.
Shaw, Dr. Albert, 448.
Shaw, Dr. Anna Howard, 212.
Shepard, William, 261.
Sheridan, Jack, 134.
Sherman, Prof. Stuart, 106.
Shick, Miss Marie, 224.
Shinn, Anne O'Hagan, 262, 270.
Shotwell, Prof. James J., 103–111.
Sigel, Franz, 187.
Sihler, Dr. Christian, 188.
Sihler, Miss K. Elizabeth, 188.
Sisson, Edgar G., 19, 70–80, 103, 107,
    247, 248, 277, 278, 287, 288, 353,
    374, 404, 411, 419, 427, 433.
Sleicher, William, 188.
Smith, Guy Croswell, 248, 277, 355.
Smith, Preston Morris, 346.
Smulski, John, 186.
Snow, Dr. Francis, 263.
Solari, Pietro, 230.
Spargo, John, 225.
Sperry, Prof. E. C., 106.
Spilman, Miss Emily A., 224.
Starr, E. L., 280.
Steele, Rufus, 127.
Stella, Dr. Antonio, 186.
Steward, George F., 332.
Stoica, Captain, 186.
Stone, Melville E., 32.
Stoll, Prof. E., 106.
Stryckmans, Felix J., 205.
Stuart, Wilmer, 232.
Stub, Rev. J. A., 186.
Sullivan, Denis, 124.
Suter, Herman, 254, 417.
Suydam, Henry, 248, 276, 327.

Sweeney, Charles P., 83.
Swensen, Lauritz S., 185.
Swensen, Magnius, 185.
Swettenham, Sir Frederick, 299.
Szlupas, Doctor, 187.

T

Tarbell, Ida, 212, 262.
Tarkington, Booth, 225, 261, 262, 353.
Tatlock, Prof. John P., 107, 131.
Taylor, Mrs. Clara Sears, 212, 217, 220.
Taylor, Graham, Jr., 375, 393.
Thomas, Llewellyn R., 277, 333.
Thorne, Van Buren, 232.
Tobenkin, Elias, 263.
Todd, Capt. David W., 251.
Torrisen, Oscar M., 186.
Tozzi, Capt. Piero, 300.
Train, H. Scott, 134.
Treadway, Representative, 54, 61.
Tuerk, Lieut. John, 275, 281, 282.
Turner, Prof. F. J., 111.
Tuttle, Frank, 265.
Tvrzicka, Mrs. Anna, 199.

U

Usher, Roland G., 225.

V

Vail, William L., 305.
Van Noppen, Lieut. Leonard, 332.
Verner, S. P., 248, 372.
Vezey, H. Curtis, 388.
Voska, Capt. Emanuel, 418.

W

Walberg, Carl, 159, 164
Walcott, Fred C., 107.
Walker, Mrs. Susan Hunter, 216.
Wallen, Theodore, 254.
Walling, Wm. English, 225.
Wanger, Lieut. Walter, 299, 301.
Warren, Waldo, P., 86.
Watson, Capt. Mark, 287.
Webster, Henry Kitchell, 261.
Webster, H. T., 134.

Rogerson, Sidney. **Propaganda in the Next War.** 1938

Summers, Robert E., editor. **America's Weapons of Psychological Warfare.** 1951

Terrou, Fernand and Lucien Solal. **Legislation for Press, Film and Radio:** Comparative Study of the Main Types of Regulations Governing the Information Media. 1951

Thomson, Charles A. H. **Overseas Information Service of the United States Government.** 1948

Tribolet, Leslie Bennett. **The International Aspects of Electrical Communications in the Pacific Area.** 1929

Unesco. **Press Film Radio,** Volumes I-V *including* Supplements. 1947-1951. 3 volumes.

Unesco. **Television:** A World Survey *including* Supplement. 1953/1955

White, Llewellyn and Robert D. Leigh. **Peoples Speaking to Peoples:** A Report on International Mass Communication from The Commission on Freedom of the Press. 1946

Williams, Francis. **Transmitting World News.** 1953

Wright, Quincy, editor. **Public Opinion and World-Politics.** 1933

INTERNATIONAL PROPAGANDA AND COMMUNICATIONS

An Arno Press Collection

Bruntz, George G. **Allied Propaganda and the Collapse of the German Empire in 1918.** 1938

Childs, Harwood Lawrence, editor. **Propaganda and Dictatorship:** A Collection of Papers. 1936

Childs, Harwood L[awrence] and John B[oardman] Whitton, editors. **Propaganda By Short Wave** *including* C[harles] A. Rigby's **The War on the Short Waves.** 1942/1944

Codding, George Arthur, Jr. **The International Telecommunication Union:** An Experiment in International Cooperation. 1952

Creel, George. **How We Advertised America.** 1920

Desmond, Robert W. **The Press and World Affairs.** 1937

Farago, Ladislas, editor. **German Psychological Warfare.** 1942

Hadamovsky, Eugen. **Propaganda and National Power.** 1954

Huth, Arno. **La Radiodiffusion Puissance Mondiale.** 1937

International Propaganda/Communications: Selections from *The Public Opinion Quarterly,* 1943/1952/1956. 1972

International Press Institute Surveys, Nos. 1-6. 1952-1962

International Press Institute. **The Flow of News.** 1953

Lavine, Harold and James Wechsler. **War Propaganda and the United States.** 1940

Lerner, Daniel, editor. **Propaganda in War and Crisis.** 1951

Linebarger, Paul M. A. **Psychological Warfare.** 1954

Lockhart, Sir R[obert] H. Bruce. **Comes the Reckoning.** 1947

Macmahon, Arthur W. **Memorandum on the Postwar International Information Program of the United States.** 1945

de Mendelssohn, Peter. **Japan's Political Warfare.** 1944

Nafziger, Ralph O., compiler. **International News and the Press:** An Annotated Bibliography. 1940

Read, James Morgan. **Atrocity Propaganda, 1914-1919.** 1941

Riegel, O[scar] W. **Mobilizing for Chaos:** The Story of the New Propaganda. 1934

INDEX

Wedda, John, 186.
Weeks, George F., 311.
Wells, Capt. Chester, 346.
Welsh, H. Devitt, 134.
West, W. M., 106.
Wheeler, Miss Gertrude R., 219–220.
White, J. Andrew, 231.
White, William Allen, 262.
Whitehead, Walter, 134.
Whitehouse, Mrs. Norman de R., 229, 248, 276, 317–326.
Whitehouse, Mr. Norman de R., 230.
Whitlock, Brand, 312.
Wile, Fred H., 412.
Wiley, John C., 332.
Williams, T. Walter, 232.
Willing, J. Thompson, 134.
Willoughby, Charles, 83.
Wilson, Admiral, 291.

Wilson, E. F., 254.
Wilson, P. W., 232.
Winters, Robert, 380.
Wister, Owen, 261.
Wojcieszak, Miss Wanda, 199.
Woods, Arthur, 247.
Wooley, Edward Mott, 225.
Woolley, Clarence, 52.
Wright, Mrs. Helen S., 220.

Y

Youngman, Elmer, 270.

Z

Zethelius, Olaf P., 198.
Zook, Prof. George F., 132.
Zorn, Prof. Otto Manthey, 189.

THE END